In Search of the Gracious One

In Search of the Gracious One

An Account in His own Words of
The Spiritual Search and Discipleship
of
Sant Ajaib Singh

compiled by Michael Mayo-Smith

Sant Bani Ashram
Sanbornton, New Hampshire
September 2007

Printed by Keystone Press, Manchester, NH
First printing: September 2007, 2000 copies

ISBN: 978-0-89142-051-4
Library of Congress Control Number: 2007929269

TABLE OF CONTENTS

Editor's Preface vii

1. Childhood 3
2. The Search Begins 37
3. Coming to the Feet of Baba Bishan Das 53
4. Into the Army 75
5. Further Experiences in the Army:
   Baba Bishan Das Makes the Foundation of My Life 97
6. At the Feet of Baba Sawan Singh 121
7. In the Bushes of Rajasthan: Cultivating the Two Words 181
8. The Meeting with Kirpal 227
9. At the Feet of Kirpal 253
10. Kirpal the Gracious One 301
11. Into the Underground Room:
    My Soul Mingles with Kirpal 345
12. Separation from Kirpal 379

Appendix: The Finding of Ajaib 399

Epilogue: The Mission of Sant Ajaib Singh 429

References 431

Glossary 441

Mujhe apna bana lo Kirpal,
Dyal tujhe sab kahete

O Kirpal, make me Your own
Everyone calls You the Gracious One

— *Sant Ajaib Singh*

The word "kirpal" means gracious. In Punjabi, often it is said that God Almighty is "Kirpal," He is the Gracious One, He is the Ocean of Grace.

Editor's Preface

Those of us who sat at the feet of Sant Ajaib Singh observed that He told many stories from His own life to illustrate points in His talks. As years passed it seemed like a wonderful book could be created if these stories were collected in chronological order, making in essence a life story in His own words. I asked Sant Ji about this in 1990, and He told me that such a book would be very inspiring to the dear ones. However, He did not give a clear indication at that time whether to proceed or not. Therefore, in December 1996, in what turned out to be my last interview with Sant Ji, I asked about this again. The transcription of His response is as follows:

"Welcome. You are welcome. I am pleased to see you. Your thinking is very good and if you will go ahead and get this project done, it will prove to be a very good thing, a very helpful thing to the people who will be coming in the future. In fact it will serve like a lighthouse to the coming generations. This is because in it there will not be anyone's criticism; there will not be comment on any particular religion or belief. Whatever you collect or whatever I have said, or whatever you write about me, it will be related to, or it is connected only to Spirituality.

"When I talk about the past historians, when I say that they have written a lot about the worldly kings and they haven't written much about the Saints, that is absolutely true. The life stories of the ten Sikh Gurus and also the life story of Kabir Sahib were not written at the time by any of their disciples. The information was collected by some people who were not the initiates of those Masters, and they had gotten the information from the initiates or other people, and then they wrote the life sketches. There are many books that we get to read about those past Masters in which neither their date of birth is written correctly, nor is the place where they lived written correctly. They don't agree with each other because everyone has written according to his own understanding.

"What I have pondered upon and what I have understood, and what Master Kirpal and what Baba Sawan Singh have understood and what They have taught is nothing but Spirituality. The teachings of the past Masters were not adulterated. They were not polluted. They were preserved as they were written and we have understood the real teachings, the real *Banis* of the perfect Masters and that is what we talk about. The writings of the Masters talk only about Spirituality and nothing else.

"Baba Bishan Das himself was a unique example of a researcher. He also researched a lot and he used to say that it is very unfortunate that none of the initiates of the past Masters wrote about the reality, about the real life and teachings of the past Masters. So if you do this book understanding it as *seva,* and in doing this work if you will take the support of any other wise person, any other learned person, it will be very good, not only for the people of the present time but also for the people who will come later on. They will also be benefitted. The book that serves as a lighthouse and serves as a guiding light to the people who come later on in the world, the book that serves that purpose is always considered as the very good book.

"There are very few *bhajans* of Mira Bai which are available but still people read them, and sing them, with much love and affection. In the same way, very few bhajans, very few verses written by the other women Saints like Sehjo Bai and Daya Bai are available. There is not much literature available by Them but still, whatever is available, people respect it and they read it and they enjoy it.

"Well it is very good. I think that Master Kirpal Himself is encouraging you, He is inspiring you, and if you have the time, you have a very good opportunity. You should do this book."

A few words may be in order on the process by which the stories were collected and collated. I went through the volumes of *Sant Bani Magazine* and photocopied stories Sant Ji told of His life. This source was supplemented by some stories transcribed from unpublished talks available on tapes from Sant Ji's tours or from the group programs when disciples had gone to India to be with Him. Often several versions of the same incident existed, each of which contained different details. In such cases I collected the different versions and merged them into a single version in a way that read as smoothly as possible and accurately captured the story. In the reference section (see pg. 431) the sources for each story are cited. As the stories are presented in the first person, as Sant Ji's words, I adhered to the principle of using only primary sources — talks by Sant Ji Himself. An exception to this principle was the inclusion of details of some incidents from Mr. Oberoi's book *Support for the Shaken Sangat.* These details are based on Mr. Oberoi's interviews with Sant Ji, and as Sant Ji Himself on many occasions referred to this book and noted that whatever is in that book is completely true, I felt comfortable including them. Similarly a couple of details are included from Russell Perkins' account: *A Brief Life Sketch of Sant Ajaib Singh,* published during Sant Ji's lifetime and based on Russell's interviews with Sant Ji.

Gradually the sequence of the stories fell into place, and the various chapters were created. In many cases the exact timing of events that Sant Ji is talking about in His life is quite clear, although in others it is not. In particular, the exact chronological order of several events towards the end of Sant Ji's discipleship is hard to sort out. When it was not clear, I prayed for guidance and did the best I could. It is worth noting that Sant Ji on many occasions stated He had no head for dates and could not always remember exactly when things happened in His life. Fortunately the exact timing of many of the stories is of little or no consequence to their spiritual significance or to an appreciation of their role in Sant Ji's life.

The one point I did wish to clarify was the duration of time Sant Ji lived in the Kunichuk Ashram [Khuni Chak in Singhpura] after being initiated by Kirpal and the point at which He left to go into full time meditation in the underground room in the village of 16 PS. In hearing the various stories that Sant Ji tells, this point is sometimes unclear. At my request Mr. Oberoi interviewed several disciples in Rajasthan who knew Sant Ji from even before the time He met Kirpal and who remained associated with Him throughout His time at the feet of Kirpal. They were also uncertain as to specifically when Sant Ji left to go to 16 PS, but confirmed that Sant Ji remained at Kunichuk for a number of years after His Initiation and that Kirpal visited Him there on several occasions when on tour in Rajasthan. This is consistent with the many references Sant Ji makes to events occurring when Kirpal was visiting Him in Kunichuk and the stories of Sant Ji's years with Kirpal are organized to reflect this.

* * *

Included throughout the book are English translations of bhajans or spiritual verses. These are identified by their Hindi or Punjabi titles as they appear in the book *Songs of the Masters.* All bhajans were written by Sant Ji unless otherwise noted.

There are many spiritual terms, Punjabi/Hindi words, and references to historical figures used in Sant Ji's stories. Some are explained in the text. For others a brief explanation is given in the Glossary (see pg. 441). For a deeper understanding of the spiritual terms used here, please refer to any of the books about Sant Mat. We have included a section, For Further Reading (see pg. 448) at the end of this book.

Acknowledgments

In closing I would like to thank Russell Perkins, for being one of the "wise and learned persons" whose help and support I sought per Sant Ji's suggestion, and for his positive comments on early drafts that were most reassuring. Thanks also go to Mr. A.S. Oberoi, another "wise and learned person," for the encouragement and help he offered, and for interviewing Pathi Ji about his role in the finding of Ajaib. Jan Classen and Jane Jorgenson devotedly transcribed material from unpublished talks. Charlie Boynton and Jonas Gerard provided the front and back cover photographs. Other photos used throughout the book were drawn from the Sant Bani Archives; thanks to the many photographers who contributed to that resource. Raaj Kumar Bagga ("Pappu") translated Sant Ji's talks at the time they were given. Roberta Wiggins and Cab Vinton proofread the pages. Richard and Susan Shannon made valuable suggestions during the course of the project and contributed many hours to the editing and layout of the book for publication. I appreciate the help of all these people.

My greatest thanks go to both Master Kirpal Singh and Sant Ji for allowing me to contribute to the publication of this work. It is said that grace comes not because of who we are, but in spite of who we are. The opportunity to perform seva like this is a special grace, and I cannot express the depth of my appreciation for this opportunity.

Michael Mayo-Smith
September 2007

In Search of the Gracious One

Sant Ajaib Singh (1926 – 1997)

ONE

Childhood

The Yearning of My Heart

It seems that the longing for realizing God and the yearning to see Him filled my heart before my heart was made. You know that the age of five years old is a very young age, but when I was five years old, I had the yearning for God. I still remember the thoughts that were within me. I used to weep and think, "Where have I come from? Where am I going? How can I face the problems of this world? Is there anyone who can bring me relief from all this pain?" Always I used to have this thought — "Is there anyone upon whom I can look as a protector?"

The Stories of the Sikh Gurus

When I was very young, maybe five or six years old, before I was old enough to understand the things that were taught there, I used to go to the *Gurdwara*, the holy temple of the Sikhs, with my parents, because I was born in a Sikh family. There I would hear the glory and praises of the ten Sikh Gurus, and the desire of doing the devotion of the Lord would come into my mind. Even at a very young age, I loved to read the *Gurbani*, the writings of the Sikh Gurus, and to read the *banis*, the verses, of all the Saints or beloveds of God.

Whenever I heard the stories of the great Masters and Their disciples, a question would arise in my within. I would wonder if I would be so fortunate to have such a Master in my lifetime. I used to wonder what it was like for those disciples who had the Masters like the Sikh Gurus: Guru Nanak, Guru Angad, Guru Ramdas, or

Guru Arjan. How did they feel when they were sitting in front of their Master? Will there be someone in my life at whose feet I will sit? Will I also get a Master such as Guru Nanak or Kabir? Will I come across some Master who will cool down my heated heart? Many times I wondered about those disciples who were fortunate enough to sit at the feet of the great Masters. I always used to wish that the day would come when I would be able to sit at the feet of such a perfect Being. I always had this yearning: "May I meet an emperor who is the treasurer of *Naam** and made by God Himself."

Also, whenever I heard stories of disciples who got Initiation from a perfect Master and then later, obeying their mind, left their Master I would feel pity for them. I wondered, "How could those people do that when they had a perfect Master? How could they not believe in their Master and not believe in the commandments of their Master?" At that time I had in my mind that if by grace I would come across a perfect Master and get Initiation from Him I would do what He told me to do. I would think, "If I were ever fortunate enough to get such a Master in my lifetime, then I would never obey the mind. Whatever my Master should tell me, that I would do." These were my feelings when I was very young.

The Prayer of My Childhood

Just as children play with dolls, I used to make some doll-like thing, imitating the people worshiping the idols in the temple, thinking, "This is my God." In those days there weren't anything like plastic dolls in India, so I made a doll or idol from leftover pieces of cloth. I would put sweets and other things in front of him and request him, "O God, first you eat this and then I will eat." But nobody came to eat there, and when people found out about that they laughed at what I was doing.

This was the request and the prayer which I made in my childhood: I requested that unseen Power, that God, to come to my door. I told Him, "Whether You know me or whether I know You or not, please come to me. I will sacrifice everything — my whole being — for You, if You will come to me."

The Example of My Parents

My real parents who gave me birth — my real mother and father — left the body as soon as I was born. However, there was another husband

---

*Naam is the same as Word (as used in the Bible), the God-into-Expression Power. Please see glossary for explanation of non-English terms.

and wife who adopted and raised me and they brought me up as their own son. I understood them as my mother and father and in them I had a very good family. These parents were very loving, very affectionate towards each other, and they always set a very good example for me. I never got any bad impressions from them. They always showed by their conduct that the relationship between husband and wife is that of love and is not a relationship where you fight and abuse or criticize each other. My mother was very devoted and she used to serve my father very much. Because she had inherited the quality of serving others, she was always serving my father. I have seen that many times when my father would get sick and be in pain, my mother would go on giving massages to him all night long.

My father was a very religious-minded person and he always used to involve himself in the Sikh religion in which his family had raised him. Whatever rites and rituals the Sikh people perform, he used to do that. He was a great devotee of the Sikh Holy Scripture, the *Guru Granth Sahib*, and he was a very great lover of the Gurdwara, the Sikh temple. Once every six months in our home he would perform *Akhand Panth*, a ceremony where the Sikh scriptures are recited non-stop, day and night. My parents were vegetarians and my father was so strict in the matter of diet that he did not even like to sit near a person who had the habit of drinking alcohol or eating meat. He never allowed any of us to go near a person who was eating non-vegetarian food or who was drinking. Because of his strictness I was also a vegetarian since birth.

My mother was a very devoted lady and it was only because of her that I got the inspiration to do the devotion of God. She filled me with the desire to do the devotion of God. My mother had a Master, and while I don't know whether he was a perfect Master or not, she was very sincere, very honest and she would do the practices given by her Master. She used to do a lot of meditation. She was a very good soul, she took very good care of me and she brought me up in a very good way, even though she had not given birth to me. She used to tell me many stories from her life and she used to tell me very good things about doing the devotion. She would tell me that one should do the meditation, one should do the devotion, "because that is the only thing which will go with us. Otherwise nothing else from this world will go with us." As I grew up, I understood more about my responsibility and about the importance of the human birth. The mother has a very great effect on the life of the child, and the inspiration which I got to do the devotion of God Almighty came to me from my mother. It was only because of her devotion for her Master that I got the inclination to do the devotion of God.

The good deeds of the parents have a very great effect and impact on the character of the children. In history we can find many examples and incidents from which we learn how the goodness of the parents had a good effect on the children. These stories show us that because the parents were good and did not do any bad things in front of their children, the children also became good like them. If the parents understand how much responsibility they have for making the lives of the children, they can easily do this. If the mother is a meditator herself, then easily she can not only discipline the child herself, but she can also make the child obtain the status of a Saint.

A very famous story about the Sufi Saint Farid tells of his childhood. His mother was a good meditator: she used to go within, and she was interested in teaching the way of devotion to her son. She wanted her son to start doing the devotion of God from his early childhood and to become a devotee. So she started telling him right from a very young age, "Son, you should do the devotion of God."

You know that the children are always interested in eating sweets, so he said, "Will God give me some sugar to eat?" His mother replied, "Yes, if you will do the devotion of God, He is very sweet and He will give you some sweets and sugar candy." In the beginning she had to work hard and she had to teach him how to do the meditation. She would spread the prayer mat for him and she would give him her attention and he would sit in meditation. After a while she would put some sugar candies in a bowl and put it in front of him and tell him, "Okay, now you leave off. God has given you the sweets."

She had to work hard only for a few days, but later on when he started doing the devotion, when he started enjoying the intoxication of the Naam which he was getting from within, he did not crave the sugar or the sweets outside. When He became a perfect Master He wrote, "No doubt sugar, sweets, honey, and milk are very sweet but, O Mother, the sweetness of Naam cannot be compared to any of these."

My mother also used to tell me the story of a man whose mother was responsible for his misfortune. In this story there was a boy who got into the bad habit of stealing from others. When he would bring anything home, his mother would not rebuke him, but instead she would inspire him to go and do more. She was always very pleased that her son was bringing things from outside, that he was stealing. She went on inspiring him and finally one day he became a great *dacoit*. Once he went to commit robbery and someone was murdered. As a result he was caught by the police and he was sentenced to death. Before they took him to the gallows they asked him if he would like to see anyone or if he had any final desire. He said, "I don't have any desire, I don't want to see anyone except my mother. If you would bring my mother I would be very happy."

So when his mother was called she was very happy. Since she was still interested in wealth, she thought, "Maybe my son is going to tell me some secret, maybe he is going to tell me about some hidden treasure."

So when she went to see her son, he said, "Mother, bring your ear close to me, I want to tell you something very secret." His mother became very happy and she brought her ear close to the bars and he at once bit her ear off. He rebuked her, saying, "It is because of you that I am going to climb the gallows. If you had stopped me from stealing things, I would not have become a dacoit. This is only because you went on inspiring me to steal from other people that I have become a dacoit."

The Attitude of My Mother

In my family I had an aunt who had a very bad temper. She would always rebuke her children. Every day she would go on saying that she had worked so hard in taking care of her children; she would try to make her children feel that she had done a lot for them. Even though she did not bring them up in a good way, she would say things like: "I have worked so hard taking care of you children, even now there is dirt under my fingernails." When she would say that, her son would say, "Mother, get me the scissors, and I will cut not only your nails, but also your fingers," because he knew what kind of care she had given to him.

My mother, however, was a very good lady. One day I asked her, "Mother, you have done so much for me, how can I pay you back for all that you have done for me?" She said, "No, dear son, I have not done anything for you. It was all due to the grace of God Almighty that I got the opportunity to take care of you, and I have just done my responsibility. I have not done any favor to you; I am very fortunate that I became your mother." My mother would never try to make me think that she had done anything for me. It was only because of the good quality of my mother that I got the desire to do the devotion of the Lord.

So you can see the difference between my mother and my aunt. If we also have an attitude of service toward our children, like my mother had, then our children will also become good. Usually if some mother does anything for her children, she always goes on saying, "I have done this for you... I have done that for you." When relatives or friends come, she goes on complaining about the child, saying, "He does not go to school, he does not obey me...," and things like that. They make their children feel like they are nothing, and that they are always doing the wrong things. That creates an inferiority complex within them, and that makes them depressed. Instead of that, if one would always praise and encourage the children, and not criticize them in front of others, that would have a very good effect on them. Even if they may not be what one is telling them they are, still if one encourages them and doesn't criticize them in front of other people, they will try to become like that. That will have a very good effect on them.

Troubled by the Mystery of Death

Right from my childhood I felt that I had lost something. I always felt this lacking, in the days and in the nights. When I was seven years old, there was an old man who used to sit under a tree near our house, and whenever I would go out with my mother I would always see that old man sitting under that tree. He was very old at that time and he was always sitting leaning forward. So I asked my mother, "Why is that old man leaning forward?" My mother replied, "This stage comes in everybody's life. Everybody has to become old some day." That affected me very much. I thought, "Why is man always changing? Why is man not remaining permanently in one position?" Then I felt sorry for my own body also, for when we cannot maintain our body for a long time, then what is the use of being attached to this body?

I saw that old man sitting in that way for one year, and one day when I went out with my mother I didn't see him sitting under the tree. I was very surprised and I asked my mother where the old man had gone. She told me that he had died. I had not seen anyone dying before that, so I asked her, "That old man is now dead; where did he go after dying? Will he be able to come back into this world?" My mother replied, "I don't know where a man goes after dying but no one can come back into this world after death. At the time of death they leave this world completely." In that state of innocence, I questioned myself, "When a man does not know where he goes after death, and when a man does not know whether he is coming back into this world or not, then why does a man like to be attached to this world?"

Later, when I was still very young, a friend left the body and I was very curious to know what had happened to him. Because many people were weeping and mourning over his dead body, I thought maybe he would listen to all the weeping and sooner or later he would get up. But, to my surprise, he didn't get up, and when I saw four people carrying his dead body to the cremation ground, I asked my mother, "Mother, where has he gone?" She replied, "He has left this world and his body has been burnt so that he cannot come back." I understood that even my parents didn't know where a man goes after death. So I thought, "Those who don't even know where a man goes after death, how can they ever help me with this problem of death?" At that time I was told that whoever takes birth in this world, one day his end will come, and he will have to leave this world. Because of that I was worried about my end time. So that is why day and night I would weep to find some solution to the pain of that problem. At that time, even though I was very young, still I was weeping. This was only because my soul was separated from God, and being separated from God I was crying.

This mystery of death troubled me always, day and night. I used to wonder, "Why does death come? What happens when one dies? Who is there who comes to help at the time of death?" Because I was troubled by this mystery of death, I was always sleeping alone, so that I could think over this problem very deeply. I was thinking about this question so much that I lost my sleep. My mother used to have a soft bed for me, but I would never sleep on it. I had found a gunnysack from somewhere and in the nighttime, when she would go back to her room, I would sleep on it on the floor. But because I was a child, my mother used to come into my room, early in the morning — two o'clock, three o'clock — and check on me. Sometimes, before she would come into my room, I would hear her footsteps and wake up and get back into bed.

Nevertheless many times she would come and catch me sleeping on the floor. She would get upset at me and ask, "Why are you not sleeping on the bed? Why have we made all these comforts? If you don't use them, for whom are we collecting all this wealth? You are still very young to do the devotion." But I had been thinking that when fires burn, the smallest sticks caught on fire very soon, and the bigger ones later. So I told her, "I understand that maybe I am going to die before you," and I was afraid that I might die without solving this problem of the mystery of death.

My parents were afraid and worried about what was happening to me, that I would try to sleep but was unable to, for I was very young. My parents thought that maybe something had gone wrong with me and that maybe some ghost had control of me. They used many amulets and other things to remove the fear of that ghost or spirit. However, there was nothing like a ghost or spirit bothering me. When I was trying to sleep, sleep would not come, because I went on thinking, "What is that thing which is lost from me?" Right from that very young age the desire was within me to realize that God Who was separated from me for ages and ages. I did not know Who He was or where He was living, but still that desire for realizing that hidden Power was going on within me. Nothing looked good to me and I always felt some loss, because that unseen Power would not come before me. He sent restlessness within, because I was not one with Him and I had not realized Him.

I could not describe my condition even to my mother. I would only tell her, "I cannot tell you what I am missing because I don't know. I haven't seen the thing that I am missing."

The Heaps of Sand

When I was very young, I always had faith in my parents. I thought they were my only protectors and that they would protect me in every field of life. I had full faith in them because I did not know then that parents are going to die one day, and that in reality God is the only protector. But on another occasion I saw someone's parents dying and the thought came into my mind, "When this boy's parents are dying that means that my parents will also die, so how can I think that they are my protectors, because they will die before me." Even though my real parents had already died, this thought did not come to me earlier, because I was not conscious of them. But when I saw somebody else's parents dying, I thought, "My parents, the parents who are bringing me up, are also unreal because they are going to die, and I can't count on them as my real protectors."

At that time I was playing with some other children and I don't know where the thought came from, of doing something very special, which transformed my life. I remember this like a dream. I started making heaps of sand, small house-like things, while I was playing with the children. I made ten or twelve, each representing a brother or sister or relative, one for each member of the family. After making these house-like things, I asked a question to each one of them, "Will you help me? Will you protect me at the time of death?" Then I would get the answer from my own within, "No, because when we are involved in the births and deaths, when we don't know how to protect our own selves, how can we say that we will protect you?" I would become disappointed and when I didn't get a positive answer, I would demolish that house. I asked that question for every brother or sister, for all the worldly relations I had, and I went on demolishing them, one by one, saying, "This is my sister and she is going to die; this is another sister, she will also die; this is my brother, this is my father, this is my mother; they are all going to die."

In that way, going through all the heaps I smashed all the heaps. In the end only one heap was left and I thought that represented the Hidden Power for whom my soul was searching. I had not seen that Power but I knew there was some Power in this world Who would protect me. So when I had made that heap, and I had asked that question, I got the answer from within, "Yes, I am the One Who will protect you. I will surely come and help you at that time." I thought that this is that Almighty God and I bowed down to that heap and thought, "He is my only Protector."

Normally parents do not pay attention to what their children are doing when playing, but if they watch them and the child is playing a game which the parents do not know about, they become curious and want to know what the child is doing. My father was watching me doing all that and he came to me and asked me what I was playing. He asked, "Why did you make all these sand heaps, and after that smash them all except one? What were you doing in front of that leftover heap?" I told him, "I was counting on you as my protector, but when I saw the other boy's parents dying, I understood that you will also die, and in that way you cannot be my protector. I thought deeply about my sisters and brothers, all the relatives, all our community, and all the people in the world, that they will also die one day, as you will. All these small houses I made, one was for each of my brothers and sisters and all my worldly relations." I told my father that I was asking that question to them and I did not get any positive answer, so that is why I demolished them. "This one which is left, signifies God Almighty, because I know — I have not seen Him — but I got the answer from my within that He is the One Who will help me. You know that God is never going to die. He is my Protector, and He will save me from death."

Hearing all those things my father was very surprised because he did not realize that my thinking was very deep and very high. He became upset and told me, "We take such good care of you. We feed you very well and we give you all sorts of good things and still you say that we will not protect you?" He was thinking from his level: he was thinking according to his narrow mind and he did not know what I was talking about. He became very sad and said, "Dear son, you are very young to think about things like this. You see that I have made this beautiful house for you, and all this property that I have collected, that is only for you. Don't worry; I will give you everything you will need. I will even arrange your marriage and you will have a very beautiful wife."

I spat on the ground and I said, "Father, I am asking you about the Inner World. Will you be able to come with me within; will you be able to help at the time when no one from this world can help me? All these worldly properties, all these worldly possessions, are nothing more than this spit for me: they do not have any value for me." I asked him, "Father, tell me, will that wife not die, or is she going to live forever? Can she save me from death?" He said, "No, she is also going to die; how could she save you from death?" So I said, "I don't want to marry and now I know that only God can save me from death." My father felt it very much, but what I told him was the reality.

When you have the thoughts like this, when you call for Almighty God, when you give up all other support and have only the one support of Almighty God, then God cannot resist. He also comes down and helps you. As Kabir Sahib says, "When I looked around, I found that nobody was going to help me. No family, no relations, no power, no wealth, no property of this world was going to help me at the time of death. When I looked around and found that Master is the only One

Who will help me from this suffering world, I stretched out both my arms and I called for Almighty God. He could not resist and He pulled me by my hands and He took me up." So right from that day I never had any attachment for the worldly possessions, wealth and properties, and at that time the renunciation and yearning for God Almighty came within me.

When we have thoughts like this, we realize that in this world nobody can help us, we realize that we only have the support of Almighty God. When we start relying on Him, then He selects us and He sends us to someone who can teach us how to do the devotion of the Lord.

O Writer of Fortunes

O Writer of Fortunes,
Graciously write on my heart, love for the Master.

In my hands, write the service of the Guru,
Write the sacrifice of my body and mind for the Guru.

On my tongue, write the name of the Guru,
For my ears, write the voice of the Sound Current.

On my forehead, write the Light of the Guru,
For my eyes, write the darshan of my Guru.

Don't write one thing: separation from the Guru.
It doesn't matter if separation from the whole world is
*   written.*
— Likhan Valya Tu Hoke

My mother used to tell me that there is some hidden power that writes the fate or fortune of the person on his forehead, and according to what is written there the person enjoys or suffers that fate. From my very childhood I got the inspiration to write *bhajans*, spiritual verses, and in the yearning for God Almighty, in His remembrance, I wrote many bhajans even as a child. So in my childhood, long before I met the Master, I wrote this particular bhajan, and since my childhood I have been singing this bhajan to God Almighty Who is Omnipotent, Who is present everywhere.

Even though I had not seen Him, still in my heart I used to feel as if I had lost something that my soul was looking for. I used to wonder how fortunate those souls would be, how beautiful those souls would be, who had the privilege of getting the Living Master in their lifetime. That is why I wrote, "O Writer of Fortunes, write love for the Master on my heart."

This was my prayer, "Graciously write the service of the Master in my hands. Write the sacrifice of my body and mind for the Guru." Right from my childhood I had this habit of closing my eyes and sitting on the ground on a mat-like thing. When I started sitting like this and when I started sleeping on the floor, my father worried very much about me. He called a pundit and with a pen of gold the pundit wrote "OM" on my tongue. So my father said, "I have done all this for you and now you don't talk to me?" That is why I said in the bhajan that I don't want the "OM" written on my tongue, I want to have the name of my Master written on my tongue.

I had the experiences of the Inner Sound Current and the Inner Light right from my childhood; that is why I wrote, "O Lord, write the Sound of Almighty God in my ears and write the Light of the Master on my forehead." Even though the holy souls are able to hear the Sound Current in their childhood and even though they are able to see that Light, still that Light and Sound cannot guide those souls up. Unless they meet a perfect Master, and unless they meditate with the guidance and instructions of a perfect Master, that Light and Sound cannot pull the soul up. So I wrote, "For my eyes, write the *darshan* of my Guru."

At that time I also used to think, "How can the people who have the Master live if the Master goes away?" So at the end of the bhajan, I prayed to the Fortune Writer, "You may write anything you want in my fortune, but don't write on my forehead, in my fate, that I may be separated from the Master, no matter if I have to leave this world."

My Mother's Brother-in-Faith

My mother had a brother-in-faith and he had Initiation into the first Two Words. I was very young and I did not know about the Words and I did not know that he had Initiation, but I knew he was doing some sort of devotion. My mother would give him very good food, a good place to stay, and everything he needed because he was very devoted. She always used to love those people who were involved in doing the devotion.

He used to live in our house and every night he would stay up all night and do meditation. Whenever we would wake up, we would go and look in his room and we would always find him awake and doing his devotion. But during the meditation we heard him say many different things. Sometimes we would hear him say, "Yes, have you come now? So now all of you have come together? All right, all of you sit down." He was a cobbler, and he used to have shoe-making instruments like needles with him. Sometimes he would say, "Okay, all of you have come now to bother me? I'll kill all of you with this needle, this weapon that I have. I will break all of your teeth," and things like that. He said things that gave us the sense that many people were coming to visit him, and he did not like them, and he was trying to chase them away, but we did not know what was happening. We were surprised to hear him saying all these things because he used to sleep alone and nobody was going into his room, so we could not figure out what he was talking about. Sometimes we would think that he had gone mad, or that some spirits were coming to him in the nighttime and he was talking with them. We did not know with whom he was talking or what he meant by the things he was saying.

In the morning when I used to go to him with some tea, because I was very young at the time, I would play with him and climb on his shoulders. I would laugh and joke with him, saying "Okay Uncle, should I also take your teeth out? Will you kill us? Will you beat us? I have come to you." I would laugh at him, not knowing what he was doing. Then he would say, "Son, now you are playing jokes with me, but you may come to know about all these things when you grow up. If, fortunately, you get involved in doing the devotion, then you will know what I was talking about. When and if you are given the meditation practices that I have been given, then I will ask you — how will you struggle in doing this meditation? It is possible that you may make a bigger needle than I have when you will have to struggle with the mind."

I did not know at that time what he was talking about, but when I grew up, and when I started doing the devotion, I realized that no spirit was coming to that uncle, and there was nothing bothering him except the thoughts. I realized how he was having a hard time with the mind, how the thoughts were bothering him. Whenever any thought would come, he would say, "Okay, you have come; I will kill you," or whenever he would have the streams or flow of thoughts, then he would say, "Okay, now all of you have come? I will deal with you." So he was replying to the thoughts and in order to remove those thoughts he was sitting up all night doing his practices. When one starts doing the devotion, then he has to start dealing with the thoughts, because thoughts are very potent. When they come and attack the devotee, then he has to deal with all these things. I did not come to realize this until I myself started doing the devotion.

Taking Care of the *Guru Granth Sahib*

As a child, together with some other boys of the village, I used to do *seva* in the gurdwara of the village. There we had the holy book of the Sikhs, the *Guru Granth Sahib*. We were told to believe in the *Guru Granth Sahib* as the Master, as God, and so we used to take very good care of that holy book. In the winter we would even cover the book with a heavy quilt so that it would not feel the cold, for we had this in our minds that we should take care of it like it was one of us.

Once a Sikh man came into the gurdwara and he wanted to spend the night there. It was very cold so he asked for some blankets to keep himself warm. Unfortunately we didn't have anything except for the quilt that was covering the *Guru Granth Sahib*, so we told him we didn't have anything for him. We told him that if he wanted to just lie down there without any blanket he could do that; otherwise he should leave. When he lay down he saw the quilt covering the holy book, and he asked us, "Why don't you give me that blanket?" We felt very bad and told him that it was for the *Guru Granth Sahib*, for the Master. He said, "But that book, that *Guru Granth Sahib* is not feeling the cold, so why don't you give it to me?" Instead of understanding his point, we threw him out. We told him to go out and as we were chasing him out, he said, "Tell me one thing: In the winter you provide a quilt to the *Guru Granth Sahib*, but what do you do in the summer when he feels hot? Do you take him to the bathroom and make him take a shower?" We didn't have any answer for that.

At that time I believed in that holy book as God, as the Master. I did not understand that it is of no use if we just go on worshipping the holy scriptures without molding our lives according to what is written there. In the *Guru Granth Sahib*, the writings of Guru Nanak, the first Guru of the Sikhs, are included. Before He came in

India, people used to worship the four *Vedas*. Guru Nanak worked very hard, and He told the people that it was not useful only to worship the *Vedas*, to burn incense in front of them and do those sorts of rites and rituals; the *Vedas* are meant to be read and understood, and people should live up to what they say. Guru Nanak worked very hard and removed the illusion from many people, but in the end His own teachings were worshipped in the same way that He did not want and that He taught against.

The Village Sadhu and an Important Lesson

There was a *sadhu* of the *Udasi* sect who used to live in the gurdwara of our village. He was disliked by many people, especially by my father, because he used to drink wine and smoke tobacco. However I liked him, because I thought, "This man has left his home and everything, he is wearing the colored clothes, and he is sitting here in remembrance of God." I thought that meant that he had realized God, so I had respect for him. Even though he was not liked by the other people, I thought he was a good *mahatma* and I used to go and spend time with him. Whenever I had a chance to get some money from home, I would bring it and give it to that *baba*. He would buy intoxicants with it. My father was very strict and I couldn't ask money from him, but my mother was very soft and whenever I would ask her to give me money, she always would. I thought that maybe this baba would give me something of God and maybe he would help me.

Although he used to drink wine and smoke cigarettes and do all sorts of bad things like that, I did not know how bad they were, because I was a young child of only nine years old at the time. My father knew about that sadhu and he told the sadhu that he should not allow me to come and sit near him, but the sadhu did not do anything about my father's request. My father also tried to explain to me that I should not go there, but I did not listen to him because I thought that man was a good sadhu. Even though my father would rebuke me, still I had faith that someday maybe that baba would teach me about God, and I was not afraid of the rebukes of my father.

Finally my parents thought of a plan to intimidate me and stop me from going to that sadhu. One night I had gone to see him; he was sitting on a bed and I was sitting cross-legged on the floor. At that time he was smoking a cigarette and he was taking snuff because he was addicted to that also. I was sitting there when suddenly my father came from behind and kicked me on my neck with his foot, and hit me very terribly. He started beating me in front of all the people in the village. I started weeping and I started running because I was afraid that he would hit me again. It was very quiet in the village, since it happened at night, and as he was chasing me he made more noise and beat me less. Finally I came to my mother and requested her to save me from the beating of my father. But she said, "No, I cannot do anything today."

Even though my father gave me a very severe beating I was not upset with him for the rebuke and the beating. At that time I was very happy that at least I was getting a beating for the sake of God! My mother told me to apologize to my father and he would make me free, but I said, "No, I won't ask for forgiveness." The other people who were there also told me, "You should be ashamed that you are not apologizing to your father even though you have made a mistake." But I replied, "No, I have not made a mistake and I don't feel any shame in going to a sadhu because I think that it is a good thing." Anyway I continued to plead with my mother and finally she saved me from the beating.

While I did not apologize to my father at that time, nonetheless that experience made such an impression on me that afterwards I stopped going to that sadhu. My father had said to me, "Why do you go there? Do you want to learn smoking and other things which that sadhu is doing?" Until I got that beating I did not understand, but after my father gave me that beating I understood and I stopped going to that sadhu. At that time I did not understand why it was important for my father to give that kind of punishment, but later on the result became very clear to me. I came to realize what would have happened in my life if I had continued going to that sadhu; if I had started learning smoking and the other things that he was doing I would have ruined my life.

So after that I stopped going to that sadhu. And later on, just remembering that experience, that beating which my father gave me, I never went to anyone who would smoke and do other things like that. I have been to many communities and religions, where I met with people who were involved in smoking tobacco, drinking wine, doing drugs and things like that. However, because of the effect of my parents' goodness, I did not drink wine, I did not smoke tobacco, and I did not get attracted to any of the bad things in which those people were involved. Even though I went to all those people and I saw them involved in all those things, still I did not have any bad feelings for them. I remained strong only because of the influence of my parents.

The Element of Kindness

The real kindness comes within us only if we are the fortunate ones. Since my childhood this element of kindness and forgiveness has been present within me and I think this is a gift of God.

Once, when I was very young, a husband and wife were passing through my village on their way to their own village. On the way the buffalo which they were leading delivered a baby calf. They did not have anybody else to help them with the delivery and they wanted to take the calf with them to their home. I was present there and they asked me if I could find anyone who could help them to take the calf to their village, which was about one and a half miles away. I said, "Well, you cannot find anyone else better than me. I am ready to help you." They did not know me. They did not know whose son I was and because they wanted someone to help them they did not even care to know who I was. So they allowed me to carry their calf which was heavy and dirty also. But I did not mind and I took the calf to their home. When they wanted to give me money for that I told them, "No, I won't accept any money because I did not do this work for money. I was sent by God to help you."

My father was very rich and was well known in that area, and when they learned that I was Lal Singh's son they were very afraid and they brought some other people with them to my father to apologize. They said, "We did not know that he was your son otherwise we would not have allowed him to do this work." I did not say anything and they apologized a lot until I told them, "There is no need to worry. I did not do this work for money or anything like that. I did it only because I had mercy and kindness for the calf."

Drinking the Water of the Muslims

In the time of my childhood the issue of caste and untouchability was a big problem in India. The people of the higher castes did not like to even see people of a low caste or of the untouchable caste. What to speak of touching each other, if even a drop of water would touch the body of the untouchables and then get on the body of the higher caste person, they would get upset. If such a thing happened, they would then take the water of the holy river Ganges and, sprinkling some of that water on their body, they would feel purified. At the places where people used to get their drinking water, they had different pipes for the different castes: one pipe for the Muslims, one pipe for the untouchables, and one pipe for the Hindus and Sikhs (for in our community the Sikhs were considered higher caste like the Hindus). The higher caste people did not like to touch the water used by the lower castes, even though all the water was the same.

There was a Muslim man who used to work as our servant; his name was Mohamadi. Once after he had finished his work in the field he covered his pitcher of water and told us not to drink that water and not even to touch that water. I was curious to know why he had said that because in the village I saw that there was only one well from which everybody got their water. The bullocks used to take the water out from that well using only one container. The water would come out in the same container and, after it was out of the well, then it would get divided into different sections. One section was for the Hindus and Sikhs to take water and one section was for the Muslims, who were the low caste people in our village. As a child, I was always curious to know why this was done and why they were dividing it. Why did they say that this water was for the Hindus and that water was for the Muslims, when the same water was coming out from the same well in the same container? How did it become different when it was put into the different sections of the well? But whenever I would ask my parents or the other adults they would not have any solid answer to that, and they could never satisfy me on that question.

So when Mohamadi, that Muslim servant of ours, told us that we should not drink that water, I was curious and I asked him "What is the difference? Is this water heavier than the water that we Sikhs and Hindus drink, or will this water get stuck in my throat? What is the difference between your water and our water?" He replied, "You are Sikhs and I am Muslim, and the Sikhs do not drink the water which is touched by the Muslims." In those days in India the problem of untouchability, the belief in caste and creed, was at its peak and most of the high caste people used to believe in this kind of thing. So after he had left I thought, "Let me drink the water from his pitcher and see how it tastes. Let me see whether it is heavier or if it gets stuck or what pain it will give to me." So I drank that water and I found no difference in it.

When Mohamadi came to know that I had drunk the water from his pitcher he became upset and afraid. He went to my father and told him, "Your son drank water from my pitcher and now you should do something to purify him. Whatever you want to do, you may do, but he drank the water from my pitcher." When I came back home my father got upset at me and he called a *pundit* to purify me. He told the pundit that I was contaminated by drinking the water of the Muslims and now he needed to do something to purify me. In those days people used to bring water from the holy river Ganges at the city of Hardwar and they used to use that water for special purposes such as purifying people. In our home we also used to have some water like that from the holy river Ganges. So when the pundit was called he said, "I will do the repetition of some mantras and will give him this pure water of the Ganges and in that way he will become pure." So he did some repetitions of the mantras and afterwards he made me drink the water of the river Ganges and then he said that I was purified. For doing these things, that pundit got a lot of things from my father. My father gave him one cow and then he gave him some clothes, some grain and a lot of money, just for doing these things to purify me.

At that time my father told me, "You see I had to spend so much money just to purify you because you made that mistake. You should never do that again." I asked my father lovingly, "Father, tell me what was the reason that you did all that? I didn't find any difference between the water of the Muslims and the water we use, so in what way did I become contaminated? Moreover, the water which you gave me just now, the water from the river Ganges, that also was not different than the water from the pitcher of our Muslim servant." He could not give any answer to me and then I thought that this type of thing was occurring only because of the narrow-mindedness of the people. It was just hypocrisy that people believed in high and low caste because, when everybody is born in the same way and everybody lives on the same earth, how is it possible that one person is higher than the other? It is only because of narrow-mindedness that people believe in such things or consider that one person is untouchable or of low caste.

On another occasion I was traveling with my mother on a train, and in those days whenever a train would arrive at a train station, at the station they would sell water to the travelers. Those selling the water would shout out, "Water for Hindus! Water for Muslims!" and would give certain water to the Hindus and different water to the Muslims. At that time we came to a train station and the people selling the water were calling out like that. I called the person who was giving the water for the Muslims and was going to take the water that was for the Muslims. However, my mother came to know that I had called him and she got upset. She said, "No, take this water away because my son is Hindu." But to me, that made no difference.

She had some doubts that, even though I had not drunk that water, but still, since I had the thought of drinking that water, it meant that I had become a little bit impure. She told my father, and since my father was easily upset, he went to the pundit again. In those days, they didn't have jeeps or good means of transportation like that, so he carried the pundit back on his shoulders. When he was brought to our house, he was fed *kheer*, which is rice cooked in milk, and it is a very delicious food for a pundit. After all the rites and rituals to purify me were done, my father forgot to give money to the pundit, so that pundit became upset and he vomited that kheer up. My father then thought there was something wrong in what he had done to purify me; maybe my mother had not bathed before making the kheer, or maybe the people attending were not having pure thoughts. So he told my mother to bathe and then make the kheer again. After the kheer was made, my father told us to bathe also. We all bathed in cold water, and we all were told to sit in front of the pundit with our both hands folded in front of him while he was eating the kheer. We were all repeating the chant *Wahe Guru* from the Sikh scriptures. We were all requesting God that this time the kheer should definitely stay in the stomach of the pundit and not come up. After the pundit ate the kheer, my father thought, "I forgot to give him money the first time, so let me give even more than I was planning to give the first time." He gave the pundit five *rupees,* instead of one and a quarter, and the pundit became pleased and the kheer remained in his stomach.

From the very beginning I didn't have any thoughts of untouchability, and I didn't have any discrimination between the people of low or high castes. Because of this, many times I was a problem for my family members.

The Question of Food

My father was very fond of eating very good foods. Just as the great royal people eat many foods, in the same way daily he would eat many types of vegetables and other dishes, and on the table there would be many types of foods. But all his life he remained a vegetarian and he never ate meat nor drank wine.

In India at that time there was no restriction on marriage and a man could marry as many women as he wanted. My father married four times, and all the four wives were alive. The last marriage he did when he was very old, and he did that marriage only because that wife was a very good cook. Because he was fond of very good food, that is why he married that young woman.

He tried to give me that habit, with all his tricks. However, right from my childhood I never paid any attention to the food I was eating. I never filled up my stomach and I never had any problem with my stomach. I ate whatever I got, never paying any attention to the food, because I was always attentive to and thinking about the main work for which I had been sent into this world.

Once when I was about eight years old, my mother made some *halvah*, which is a very delicious type of Indian sweet. She made many types of halvah, but I was not interested in sweets, so I didn't eat that. My grandmother who was very old at the time saw this and became upset that I was not eating the delicious dish my mother had made. She came to me carrying a stick and said, "Why are you not eating this halvah? You should eat it!" and she told me that if I did not eat the halvah she would give me a beating with the stick. But I said, "No, I don't want to eat that." When she was pushing me very much to eat that, I told her lovingly, "You just look at my patience also. There are three types of halvah lying there, but still I don't want to eat that. The other people when they look at just one type of halvah, the water comes in their mouth and they want to eat that. Just look at how patient I am." Hearing that, she understood and she became very pleased, and she loved me very much.

If I had the love of the tastes of the tongue, it never would have been possible for me to come to the Path of God-realization.

Performing the Seva

Once in Muktsar, a place in Punjab, the Sikh people were making a pond near a gurdwara that was located there. Many Sikh people from different parts of the country went there to help with that project and to do the seva, and my parents were among them. At that time I was very young and I didn't have any idea of what the value of seva was or why one should do the seva. Still, because my parents were doing that, I also was attracted to it. At that time I didn't have any knowledge about the spiritual Path or about God. I had the desire to do seva because my parents were doing it and I was trained by their example. I would take foodstuff from my home to the *langar,* the free kitchen, there. I would take tea and sugar, and whatever money I could afford, and take that as donations to the langar.

In the countryside of India the people go into the fields and use them as latrines. They don't have bathrooms or toilets there. When I was at that place, I saw that after the people would go to the bathroom in the fields, many flies would come and sit on that area and then the same flies would sit on the foodstuff in the langar. In order to prevent that from happening, all day long I would go and put sand on that waste to prevent the flies from going and sitting on the food. Nobody told me to do that seva, because nobody liked doing that job, since it is a very low type of seva to put sand on the latrine waste. Nobody told me to do that, but the desire to do that came from my within, for at that time I wanted to do whatever seva I could. I thought, "This is a good opportunity; I could serve the people in this way." So I did that.

The Sign of the Star and My First Meeting with Baba Bishan Das

When I was about ten years old many blisters and sores erupted on my body. They were all over my body: there was not even one part of my body that was without those boils and blisters. They were so bad that pus was coming out from them and whenever I would wear any clothes they would get stuck to the wounds. It was very difficult for me to bear that and even though that happened in my childhood, I still remember those painful moments. It was very painful, and my father also used to cry looking at my condition because I was his child. Nobody else would love me because I had those boils: nobody would allow me to come near them. My parents and family members used to love me only because I was their child.

In those days people in India didn't believe much in medical treatment. They used to believe that if you take a sick person on pilgrimage and bathe in holy waters their sickness would go away. So they took me to all the holy people and to all the holy places, but I could not get rid of the sores. In those days it was good for me to go to all the places of pilgrimage, but when I realized that nobody liked me, that they didn't want to stand near me, it became very difficult for me to bear that.

After that failed my father took me to a mahatma named Baba Bishan Das. That was the first time that I met Baba Bishan Das. When my father brought me to Baba Bishan Das, my father wept in front of him and told him, "God has given me only one child and I don't know how many bad *karmas* he has done in his past life that he has these boils and blisters and he is suffering so much. I cannot bear to see him suffering. Either God should take him back or he should be cured." Baba Bishan Das laughed and said, "God never takes anyone back: everyone has to suffer on account of their own karma, or someone who becomes responsible for the karma of that person can pay it. Otherwise that person who is suffering has to suffer." Then Baba Bishan Das asked my father, "Are you ready to pay the account of the karmas of this boy?" My father could not say anything, because you know that it is very difficult for anyone to agree that he will suffer for someone else. We may say outwardly, "I am ready to suffer." The parents love their children very much, but when you ask them, "Are you ready to suffer for your children?" nobody will be ready — because who wants to suffer for others? We can hardly suffer for our own selves: how can we think of suffering the pains of another soul? When my father did not agree, Baba Bishan Das said, "Okay, I will take him to a place of pilgrimage in Punjab and over there he will become all right. But I will have to put some signs on his body: this is the Will of God and his body should have some signs."

Baba Bishan Das took me to a sacred place named Taktupara, the place where Guru Nanak Sahib had done the meditation for some time, sitting underground. There Baba Bishan Das told me, "Nature wants there to be some signs on your body. Your body should not be stainless. So you will have to get three stains — or three signs — on your body and then you will be able to get rid of all these sores." So this tattoo on my hand, and also two other signs which I have, were given to me at that time when Baba Bishan Das took me to that place of pilgrimage. He also wanted to put a sign on my forehead, but my father again wept and requested him not to put a sign there because it would look very bad. My father asked Baba Bishan Das to put signs on my body in such a way that they would not look bad.

The person who was putting those signs on my body was not pleased about it because I had so many sores that he was afraid that when he used his machine on my body, it would be painful for me. But Baba Bishan Das told him not to worry about that, because I was going to get better after I had the three signs. You know that Saints have Their own way of curing things. It is Their grace which cures the diseases, but They have to do certain things outwardly also. So there they put those signs on my body. When I left that place I walked about one hour to a village about four miles away, and without using any medicine, without doing any kind of other treatment all the boils and blisters went away, and my body became as clear as it is now. People may say that it was because I was taken to the place of pilgrimage that all the boils and the disease were cured, but that is not true. It was only because of the grace of Baba Bishan Das that this body is sitting in front of you without any other stain or sign. Baba Bishan Das was very gracious and I don't know how many karmas I had, how many bad karmas I had done, and how much Baba Bishan Das suffered in order to remove the boils of my body. It is possible that a lot more complications were going to follow because of those boils, but graciously Baba Bishan Das removed all the problems; he took all the complications and suffering on his own body.

So this is the grace of the Master. When we request the Master to heal us, to make us all right, then we are not ready to pay the karmas which we are suffering. We are, in a way, requesting the Master to take those karmas on His body, which He lovingly does, and that is why He suffers for us. His body suffers when we don't meditate, because when we meditate we get the inner strength to bear the karmas, but when we are not strong enough to suffer the karma, then someone has to suffer, and who else can suffer our karma except our Master?

My parents had given me the name Sadara Singh and it was on that day when I was cured of those boils that Baba Bishan Das gave me the name Ajaib Singh. He said, "The name Sadara Singh does not have any meaning; it is a useless name. 'Ajaib' means wonderful and 'Singh' means lion. Today he has become a beautiful Singh: he has become beautiful." So that is why he gave the name Ajaib Singh to me that day.

Our Domineering Dog

We had a dog in our home who was very domineering. He had a very strong body and he always used to frighten the children. He would never sit on the floor; he would always find some way to get on the comfortable bed. He would sit there and he would look at us with anger whenever we tried to say anything to him about that. He would not eat any bad food but would always want to be given very good food. He would never eat dry *chapatis* but would only eat buttered chapatis. Everybody was very troubled by him. Moreover he also used to fast one day a week, every Tuesday. Nobody told him it was Tuesday, and he had not read it in any newspaper, but he knew from within that the day was Tuesday and on that day he would take his food, leave it outside and not eat it.

My parents had a lot of faith in Baba Bishan Das; however, he only came to our home one time. When he came to visit us, my father asked him, "What is the reason that this dog is so dominating and why does he behave like this? He is like a commander to all of us." The mahatmas are all-conscious and they know everything of the soul, the past and the future of the soul. Whenever they look at a soul, they look to the depth of the soul and that is why they know everything about the soul. So when my father asked Baba Bishan Das about the dog, he smiled and asked my father, "Lal Singh, don't you recognize this dog?" My father replied, "How can I recognize him? He is an animal and I am a human being." Then Baba Bishan Das graciously told my father, "He is your father. Because of his attachment to you, he has come back into your home. Now, since he was elder to you and he was your father, that is why he still has the same quality of ordering you around and that is why he is like that." Then my father realized that indeed the dog was his father because his father also used to fast once a week on Tuesday. He had the same kind of habits as my grandfather. After my father came to know this, he always respected that dog and took very good care of him and served him very much. After that dog left the body, he was cremated with full honor, in the same way as the physical father of my father would have been, and my father even requested Baba Bishan Das to give a place to that dog at his feet.

Once somebody went to Guru Arjan Dev and asked Him, "Master, what is this world and how do families come together, how do we form the relations in this world and how should we live in this world?" Guru Arjan Dev lovingly explained that this world was not created by itself. Some Power has created this world and everything is pre-planned; everything is happening at the appropriate time. He said, "Just as in the evening birds from all different directions come to a tree and they stay there all night, and during the night some birds indulge with each other, some fight with each other, some eat and some do other things. But the next morning they all fly out to their own destinations. Nobody waits for anyone." Lovingly He said that, in the same way, in the family someone comes as a father, someone comes as a mother, someone is born as a son and so on. According to our karmas with each other, we either love each other or we hate each other. But when our time is finished, when our time comes to leave that family, to leave the world, then nobody consults another person about his departure. Nobody can tell us from where he has come and where he is going.

The Masters say that a soul is born in the place where she had give and take or where she had dealings in her last lifetime. They say that a person does not go very far, but comes back to the family or relatives. Not even a bird will come into your home if it does not have some connection with you from the past: but you don't know what connection you had with him. Who was he to you in your past lifetime and who are you to him in this lifetime? Mahatmas who have been able to reach only up to Brahm can tell us about our past lives. But real Saints, the perfect Saints, tell us not to perform such miracles and not to waste your meditation, after working hard for it, to learn about your past.

My Father and the *Jap Ji Sahib*

As I have written, I was born into a Sikh family and in the Sikh religion it is considered that those who read the *Jap Ji Sahib* early in the morning are doing a good deed. So my father, because he was a Sikh, read the *Jap Ji Sahib* in the early morning. Once he met a mahatma who didn't have any knowledge of going within and who did not know the secret of the inner worlds, but he was a good mahatma and he gave my father a rosary to move. He told my father, "If you will move the rosary along with the reading of the *Jap Ji Sahib* then all your difficulties will go away." So my father used to read *Jap Ji Sahib* in the morning along with moving the rosary. My father had this habit of criticizing and shouting at his servants every morning whenever they would work. So on one side he would be reading *Jap Ji Sahib* and moving the rosary and along with doing that, at the same time he would be calling names at the servants and abusing them, and he would be rebuking everyone in the family.

Both my mother and I would ask him to tell us what he thought God would accept — "Will He accept your reading of *Jap Ji Sahib*, your moving the rosary, or your calling your servants names?"

So when my father went to Baba Bishan Das, Baba Bishan Das told him, "Instead of moving the rosary and reading *Jap Ji Sahib* and doing everything at the same time, you should sit at one place quietly, read *Jap Ji Sahib* and move the rosary. Then all your difficulties will go away and the people who will see you doing that may get impressed that you are not fighting with anyone, that you are not rebuking anyone, and in that way they will see that you have improved your life."

A Pure Heart

Once when I was about thirteen or fourteen years old, I was walking along a canal and an old man who was a lawyer by profession passed me on his bicycle. When he saw me, he stopped and said, "Dear Son, if you don't mind I would like to ask you a question." I said, "It is all right, you can ask me anything, and I will try my best to reply to that."

He said that he had read in a book that whatever a person has in his heart that shows on his face; if there is someone who can read the face he can easily know what the person has in his mind and, "As far as I can see on your face, you are a devotee. You are doing some kind of devotion of God." I replied, "No, up until now I have not started doing any meditation, but it is true that I am looking for the Path of devotion. I am searching for the practices, but I don't know yet how to do the devotion."

If there is anyone who can read the faces, he will easily tell you what is in your heart. An experienced man can easily look at the faces of those driven by lust and tell that they are suffering from the disease of lust, even if outwardly their faces look bright and they look very healthy.

Nowadays neither the men are taught about the importance of chastity nor are women given the knowledge of how important it is to maintain chastity. Since the parents do not maintain chastity themselves, they are not a good example for their children. That is why even before the children reach their youth, as soon as they start producing the vital fluid in their bodies, they start losing it by many unnatural ways. Since they have lost a lot of their vital fluid before their bodies are fully developed, they do not have good health and they are not physically fit because they have lost a lot of vital energy from their body. When we lose the vital fluid in a great amount, it affects our body, it affects our mind and it affects our thoughts.

When children are given the knowledge of lust and dirty things right from their childhood how can they keep their thoughts pure? When their thoughts are not pure, how can they keep their minds pure? If their mind is not pure, how can they get any strength of the soul to concentrate at the Eye Center? How can they collect their soul at the Eye Center and go beyond that? This is my personal experience that in the villages we used to play together up until the age of twenty years old. The boys and girls used to play together even at nighttime, but nobody had any thought of lust or anything like that. However, nowadays you will find that a young boy, a young child of even two years old, would know about lust. Why is it so? In the past times parents would not even sit together in the same bed in front of the child, and there was no question of kissing or hugging in front of the child. That is why the children did not know anything about that. But nowadays we go on kissing and hugging each other in front of our children, and whatever we do our children copy us and they do the same thing.

Death Does Not Spare Anyone

There was one very wealthy person in our village, and when I was about fifteen years old he passed away. When he was about to die, when he started feeling the pain of death, he cried out and said, "You know I am very wealthy. I have so many homes and so many possessions. You go to that person," and he named a certain person who was very poor. He said, "Well, why don't you go and take him?" He thought that just because he had a lot of wealth he would be spared, that death was only for the poor people. That is why he was mentioning the name of that poor person and he was asking the Lord of Death to go and take that poor person instead of him.

That incident showed me that death does not spare anyone. Kabir Sahib says that even those great people whose words became law, who were so powerful that they could break mountains and they could drink the water of the oceans, even those great people were not left alone. They also had to leave; they also had to face death. Now we kick their graves and the time will come when people will kick our graves. Now the dust of those great people is coming in our eyes and the time will come when the dust of our graves will go and bother other people's eyes. So again I saw that in this world no one lives forever; one day everyone has to leave.

The Enticements of My Parents

In the beginning, when we first start following the Path and doing the meditation, our parents don't like that. They taunt us and say we have become renunciates and now we don't like being in the world. In order to distract our attention they even say, "You are too young to do the devotion of God. This is our time because we are old." They don't want us to meditate or do the devotion of God, they want to distract our attention from that, and that is why they try their best to take our mind away from the Path of devotion. Then the relatives come and they say that this person does not obey his parents; he has become a renunciate and is doing meditation. When we first start doing devotion, all the world becomes our enemy. All the four ages bear this testimony, that the world has never liked the devotees of God.

In order to trap me in the worldly work, my parents left no stone unturned. God had blessed my parents with limitless amounts of wealth and all the things of the world and I was their only child. My father did not hesitate in giving me any worldly comfort, any luxury. Whatever he thought would be good for me, he gave me that. He tried everything a father could do in order to take me away from the Path of devotion. He provided all the facilities and worldly things for me to enjoy and he even built me a beautiful house and garden. He did so much, wishing that I would find my heart in my home and that I would remain attached there.

Nowadays the means of transportation have changed a lot and you can find jeeps, cars, buses, etc., everywhere. But when I was a child, in the area I grew up there were not so many means of transportation. People used horses a lot to go from one place to another and I also used to ride horses a great deal. In Punjab there is a place of pilgrimage called Muktsar, and once a year many people get together there and they have a horse race. Riders from all over the country go there and participate in that race. Once my father took me to attend that fair and my father liked the horse that had won the race. He went to the owner, whose name was Inder Singh, and asked him how much was the cost of that beautiful gray horse. Since that was the best horse, Inder Singh said, "Why are you asking me? Are you ready to buy it?" My father said, "Yes, I want to buy it; that is why I am asking you." So my father gave him whatever he asked, and bought the horse. It cost five thousand rupees, and in those days the value of the rupee was very much and it was very difficult for an ordinary man to collect that much money. My father thought that when I would ride on that horse I would look very good. He said to me, "Take this horse and ride on him. What do you have to take from all this devotion? You should do worldly things." Many times he would make me sit on that horse and ride it and he would become happy.

However, even after having so many things, I still felt a lacking in my heart. I was missing something. I always felt that one part of my heart was yearning for something, and unless I got that, I would not be satisfied. I told my father "I am not your man. I have not come into this world for you. I have something else to do." There were so many conveniences in the home of my father and my father was a very good person who made sure that I could easily get whatever I wanted. Still when someone once asked me if I had ever seen hell, I said, "Yes, our home is like hell."

Once my father paid 1,000 rupees to one so-called sadhu and told him, "My son doesn't stay in the house. He wanders here and there to sadhus and saints. Do something so that he will remain in the house and do worldly things." That sadhu said, "All right, I know what you mean. I will control him." He stayed one night with me and gave me some amulets and recited some mantras at me, but it didn't have any effect.

When we start doing the devotion of God, not even our parents like that and they always oppose us. First of all they use the instrument of love to distract our attention and then, if we don't obey them, sometimes they will even punish us because they don't want us to meditate.

As long as I lived with my parents, I did all that a son should do for his parents. Even though I was not born from the parents who were taking care of me, still, I performed whatever duties I had as a son. However, when they tried to stop me from doing the devotion, then I didn't obey them.

The Question of Marriage

In India, unlike the Western countries, children are not free to choose their own partners. The parents arrange their marriages, and in many cases the boy may not have seen the girl, or the girl the boy, but still they cannot refuse their parents. The time when I was young was such that no son could dare to say no to his parents about marriage. From my youth my parents urged me to get married, but I had no intention of getting married, because right from my childhood I was aware of that power, the mind, residing within me which was creating all my problems and confusions. I thought, "If I cannot control this thing within me, and I get married to someone and I have to deal with the power which is residing within that person also, how am I going to do that? Until I can control the power within me, how can I deal with the power within someone else?"

When my parents told me about marriage I told them, "No, I don't want to get married to any woman." I used to say that the person with whom I have to get married would come to me by Himself. They said, "No, how is that possible? How can you get married to a male? You have to marry some woman!" I used to tell them that Guru Nanak Sahib said, "In this world there is only one Male, and we are all His wives." I used to tell them that we are not males, we are trying to become male, because He who protects the honor of others, He who comes to rescue us from this world, is the Male: the rest of us are all His wives. I was the only son of my parents, and because they wanted to see some happiness, they wanted to see my wedding. They pressured me very much to get married and they even said if I would not get married they would jump in a well and finish their lives. But I told them, "No, it is not for me. I won't marry any woman." Because I did not want to hurt their feelings, I had to explain to them that I could not get married. I wept in front of them and somehow I convinced them that it was not for me.

The Merchant from Shergarh

There was a merchant in the town of Shergarh who had lost his son when he was very young, and he went mad because he was his only son. Day and night, he was always calling his son's name, and he was always weeping. My father came to know about that man, and because I was very much detached from the family, because I wanted to do the devotion, and because I had told my father "I am not your man," he wanted to show me what that pain looks like — the pain of a father when his son is not with him. He wanted to show me so that I would change and become attached to him. He brought me to that person and told me, "You see, his son left the body twenty years ago, but he is still remembering him and he is suffering so much that he is calling his name day and night and waiting for him to come. Do you see how much pain a father experiences when he has lost his son?" He did this only to teach me that he also had this pain. I told him lovingly, "Father, there is something more precious than a son which a man has to realize and which is separated from him for ages and ages, and that is Almighty God." When my father heard this reply, he didn't have anything to say; he understood what I meant.

In that way, although I had not seen that Power, and I knew nothing about that Power, still I was waiting for that Power to come. I did not even know whether or not that Power was manifesting in this world or not, but still I was waiting for Him to come. Always, day and night, this request was going on before Him: "Whether You know me or not, whether I know You or not, still please come to my door and quench my thirst."

Baba Bishan Das' Blessing

Once my father took me to Baba Bishan Das because he thought that maybe I was in the control of some spirit or ghost, and that was why I was always searching for Saints or Beloveds of God. My father did not like the fact that I did not show any interest in doing the worldly things, and he wanted Baba Bishan Das to treat me, because my father thought I was sick. He took me to Baba Bishan Das and told him, "Look at him very carefully, because he remains sad, and won't do any worldly things." Baba Bishan Das looked at me and he told my father, "Oh, old man, this man is of no use to you." At that time I was very skinny and I thought maybe it was because of my thin body that this baba was saying that I was of no use. But now I realize what he meant: he meant that I was of no use to the family.

Then my father told Baba Bishan Das, "Do something to my son." So Baba Bishan Das laughed and said, "All right, I will do something for him, but still he won't be of any use to you." And this is true, that Baba Bishan Das did a great thing for me — he put his gracious hand on my head, so that after that I never took any interest in the worldly work.

TWO

The Search Begins

Leaving My Parents' Home

Those who have the divine love, who are in love with Almighty God, right from their childhood they have the real yearning for God Almighty. Even though they have not seen Almighty God, still within themselves they always feel as if they have lost something. They always remain sad: they are waiting for Him. If someone like that is asked, "Why are you sad? Have you lost anything?" outwardly he may say, "I am all right," but he always feels that he has lost someone or something. Deep within he feels that sadness because he has not seen his Beloved God Almighty. All the Saints have had this sadness. Guru Nanak had this sadness and because of it people used to say that he had lost his senses — "He does not have that power of intellect, he does not have that power of thinking," or "Some ghost has taken him over." In the lives of many Saints such things have happened when They went through this period of deep sadness. People always talk about such things, but only the Saints, who have felt this sadness, know what it is like.

Such dear ones, right from their childhood, always get the messages of love in their soul. If they are born in a rich family they throw away that richness and do their devotion. If they are born in a poor family they do not crave to become rich and they do not go on collecting the material wealth of the world. Their effort, their desire is only to find that thing which they have lost, and they always crave for the Beloved. Right from their childhood, they have this desire and they always wish they had met with the Almighty Lord.

I was thinking about the mystery of death so much, and I asked my mother's brother-in-faith, the one who lived in our home, about this mystery. He told me to contact any Saint or Mahatma, because only They could solve that mystery. To solve this mystery I left my home and started off in search of Saints and Mahatmas and in search for God. At that time I very much wanted to open my inner vision: I was wishing that my inner vision should be opened and that I should manifest the Master within. My life had been that of a renunciate right from the beginning. I left my parents' family because my thoughts and theirs were different. They wanted to involve me in the worldly life, but I did not want that because I was longing for God and I was looking for someone who could teach me how to do the devotion of God.

My Promises to My Mother

When I started my search and left my home, my mother came with me for three miles. She told me, "Dear Son, just get married and then I will not tell you not to do the devotion." I said, "Mother, then you will not have to tell me not to do the devotion, because the one who will tell me will already be with me when I get married. You will not need to tell me." I told her that if I was supposed to get married then that person would marry me. If it is written in my fate that I must get married, the person who is going to marry me will come to me by himself.

At that time my mother made me promise a couple of things. She told me, "Dear Son, if you want to get married, you should come home and get married. We should not hear from other people that our son is having a relationship with a woman or is wandering here and there." I promised her that if I could not control my mind, if I could not control myself, then I would definitely get married. "Since I drank your milk, I will not defame your milk: I will never commit adultery."

I received a great amount of love from my mother. The way she took care of me and the way she gave me love, not even hundreds of mothers together could give such love to their children. I am sorry that I could not fulfill the worldly desire that my mother had. She wanted me to get married but I could not do that. It was my mother's desire, not mine.

The other promise was this: she told me, "You should always wear clothes that you have bought yourself and you should not accept anybody's clothes. If anybody is bringing things for you, if anyone is bringing clothes for you, you should first pay him for that and only then you should wear those clothes."

Even up to this day, I am keeping those promises.

Giving up My Inheritance

My father had the problem of his wealth, and he was worried about what was going to happen to it. He wanted me to inherit it, but I did not want to. So I had asked him, "Father, what do you want of me? What do you want me to do?" He replied, "Find some solution for this wealth — someone to inherit it." I then thought of one boy from our village who was a bastard boy. In India at that time children who were born to women who were not married were considered outcasts. They were treated without respect and had a very difficult time. So I thought of that boy and I had all the wealth transferred into his name.

Early Encounters with Different Mahatmas

In India there are many monasteries, many religious communities and many institutions established in the name of spirituality. I went to many of them and in those days there were not many means of transportation and I had to walk a lot. I went in many directions and I went to many people. I went in the forests and I went in the mountains. I didn't wander here and there to see the sights, but as soon as I came to know that there was some mahatma, some devotee of God living anywhere, or whenever I came to know that there was even someone who was talking about God, I would go there to see him. I went to many saints and mahatmas, to all the Sikh so-called "mahatmas" and many different types of sadhus. I did all the rites and rituals which people used to do in India in those days. I performed austerities, I did the practices of water and I moved the rosary. I went to different temples, mosques and holy places.

At that time in India people used to believe so much in different castes and religions and they used to place a great deal of consideration on such things. However, for me all the religious places were the same: I did not hate anyone, I did not criticize anyone, and I did not comment on anyone's practice or their path. I went with all my faith and love and I did not feel any difference between those holy places because I was searching for God Almighty.

Many times I did not get enough food to eat; I would have some chick-peas with me and I would just eat a few of them and drink some water. On other days I did not eat food at all and remained thirsty. Many times I would not have any place to sleep but would sleep on the floors. When people used to see my condition, they used to taunt me. Many people said to me, "Why have you left the life of comforts and are wandering here and there? Are you all right mentally or not?" However, I had the desire to know God and so even when I was walking or sleeping or doing any other thing, I was longing for God. I was always wondering, whether I was asleep or awake, whether or not some day would come when I would see God.

As I was born in a Sikh family, I had the idea that if you visit the holy places where the Great Masters had been, you can get liberation and peace of mind. So I visited every place where the Great Masters had gone – all the Sikh holy places, all the great temples – but I didn't get any peace. At that time I also understood that God was residing only in the Golden Temple of the Sikhs, which is a very costly building. The priest of that building was very much respected by many people who were going there, so I thought that he would have met God or known God. But I was not satisfied with him; I was very much disappointed.

After that I visited one place called Sarwali in the Punjab, and I heard about one mahatma, one so-called sadhu there, who was very popular because he was using many supernatural powers. I heard that he was a so-called good sadhu and that he could transform his body into the body of a lion or tiger or any animal and he could fly also after transforming his body. He was very famous and people used to praise him a lot because he used to show people how he could change his body. I spent six months with him and I served him daily with my whole heart and being. When he was pleased with me, because of my seva, he wanted to teach me his skill. Without my asking he said, "I am pleased with you and now I can give you what I know. I can teach you how to convert your body into a snake, how to convert your body into the body of a tiger and the animals like that." However, I knew his real state, so I told him, "Baba, I am very sorry to know this, because I came here and served you, and had your darshan because I want to go beyond this human body. I want to rise above the human body; I don't want to change my body into the bodies of animals. But you are telling me you only know how to convert the manbody into the body of a snake and other animals. I can also get those bodies by myself without serving you, because if I do bad karmas in this lifetime, then definitely I will get those lower bodies. So what is the use of serving you here? I can get that by myself."

But he told me, "I have only this thing with me. If you want, you can have it; otherwise not." I didn't like that skill of transforming the body and I didn't learn it.

That sadhu also gave me a book in which some of the signs of a true Master were given. When I read that book, I didn't find any signs of the true Guru in that sadhu and so I left him.

At that time in India one could find many great yogis and sadhus who used to do the repetition of God's name outwardly, very sincerely, and I met many of them. I made a rosary and people told me to repeat some name, some mantra, for 24,000 times a day. But in the love and pain of separation from God, I did double the amount; I did 48,000 repetitions, and moving the beads I got blisters on my hands. However, this did not give me peace, as I found that by repeating the name of God outwardly, one can get many supernatural powers, but they involve us in the name and fame of the world. After that I went to see another sadhu in Lahore who was also working miracles. Whoever went to him, he would tell what was in that person's heart. But there also I was not satisfied, because I thought, "What is the use of doing the practice from which the soul gets no peace?" I was longing for the knowledge of Naam, as Guru Nanak had written, and I was not interested in miracles. That sadhu took an interest in me however, and gave me the mantra, *"Hai Ram, Hai Gobind,"* which I repeated for many years.

Obtaining the Degree of Gyani

Since I was born in a Sikh family I believed in the gurdwaras (the Sikh temples), and the other elements of the Sikh religion. When I was searching, I joined one sect of the Sikhs called *Nehungs*. This particular sect had come into existence after Guru Gobind Singh. They were the soldiers of Guru Gobind Singh, and were even called by Guru Gobind Singh as the "Beloved Army." They put a lot of emphasis on reading the Sikh scriptures, so when I joined them I did all the types of chanting and the other traditional Sikh practices that they were doing. In order that my mind and soul might find peace I even became a *bhai* or priest of the gurdwara. I went to class, to the State High School of Sangroor in Punjab, and obtained the degree of *gyani,* which means the knowledgeable one. I used to believe that if one obtained that knowledge and passed those examinations, if one got the degree of gyani, then one got peace of mind.

I will not say there is anything wrong with doing those practices, but it was my own experience that I did all those things but I didn't get any peace of mind. Even after reading all the books and obtaining the degree of gyani I did not get any contentment. There were twenty-five people in my class and out of those twenty-five, only five people used to abstain from meat, wine and those kinds of things, and the rest of the people were the "gyanis" who used to drink and eat meat and do things like that. I have seen so many people who have passed the examination of being a gyani, so many learned people, but they drank wine and did so many other bad things, they were full of ego and they did not have any peace in their within.

In the language of the Saints, he is not called the gyani who has got the degree of gyani or who has read many books or attended many lectures. Guru Nanak Sahib has said, "The real knowledge, the real understanding, is the one which knows about the Limitless and Unsung Melody." In the language of the Saints, he is the gyani who goes and merges into the Divine Melody, into that Limitless Melody. As Guru Arjan said, "He is the true gyani whose light of the soul has gone and become one in the Light of the Oversoul."

Doing the Sevas

When I was searching I went to many places where they were building temples, gurdwaras or other buildings like that. When I came across such activity I always used to do the seva there, working physically to help. I also did many lowly things, like cleaning the latrines and washing the clothes of the little babies. However, at such times, after doing these sevas I would never think, "I am doing the seva," but instead would always be thankful that I was doing something for the holy cause. The Masters say that *sevadars,* those doing the seva, who do it only for show, and after doing it, who go about saying to people, "I have done this seva," and "I have done that seva," they are like those who prepare some delicious food and afterwards put sand on it, spoiling it. So I always used to think that one should try to do seva, but never think, "I am doing something."

This was also my practice, that if I found anybody naked, without clothes, I would remove my own shirt, my own clothes and let him have my clothes. In the town, in the market, people would then taunt me for wearing only underpants: "What is he doing? What is he doing here without more clothes?" This was my habit in life, and up until the age of forty I would do this.

The Udasi Sadhus

In India there is an order of monks called Udasis. They grow their hair very long and keep it all tied up in a big bundle on their head, believing that by keeping their hair in this way they can get liberation. They paste their bodies with ashes, wear colored robes and move the rosaries. Whenever people come to visit them, they close their eyes, although when no one is there they keep their eyes open.

I went to such people also. Before I went there I used to think that those who have the big rosaries and who wear the colored clothes are the ones who have met with God Almighty. Whenever I would meet with anyone who had a rosary around his neck and who was wearing colored clothes, I would always bow down in front of him, thinking that he had become one with God. So, because the Udasis also wore colored clothes and they also had rosaries around their necks, I went there. However, when I went to them I saw that many were smoking tobacco and drinking wine and doing other things like that. They encouraged me to do the same thing. They told me if I wanted to become one of them, if I wanted to follow them, I would have to do that: I would have to drink wine, smoke tobacco, and not only that, I would have to bring all those things for them. So I just folded my hands to them and said, "If you have only this to offer me, then it is better for me to leave you, because I have come here to do the devotion of the Lord, not to get involved in all these kinds of things."

I was able to do that only because of the good effect my parents had on me. I know how pure my parents had kept their home — they did not allow those things in their home — and why it is so important for us to maintain purity. Because my parents' goodness had such an effect on me, I did not drink wine, I did not smoke tobacco, and I did not get attracted to any of the bad things in which those people were involved. Even though I went to all those people and I saw them involved in all those things, I did not have any bad feelings toward them, and I remained strong. This was only because of the impact I had from my parents, and only because of this I was able to resist and not follow the path of the Udasis.

In the Punjab there was an Udasi master and his disciple in a village called Vala. I served them, both master and disciple, for one or two months. They first gave me the job of collecting milk from everybody's house for them. In India people are very happy in giving donations to so-called sadhus or godly people, so when I would go and collect from door to door a lot of milk would be collected. I would bring it to them and they would drink that and eat butter. After that, in order to digest that food, which they were eating so much of, they would just go on doing exercises right from the morning. That master would tell me to climb on his body and then he would go on sitting down and standing up, sitting down and standing up, and doing practices like that. Once when I was on his body and he was doing that practice, I started laughing, because looking at his condition, I couldn't help myself! He got upset with me and called me names and said, "Why are you laughing?" I said, "You should have eaten less. Why do you eat too much and then do this exercise to digest that food?" Then he said, "Have you come to learn something from us? Or have you come to teach us?"

After eating food and doing their physical exercise they would bathe, and then they would put ashes on their bodies and sit with closed eyes as if they were meditating. He told me to tell people who were coming to him, "Now Baba Ji is in deep meditation, his attention is inside, so don't bother him. Whatever you have brought for him just leave it with me and go away. Come after one hour and he will get up." People were told that they should never come empty-handed to see that baba, they should always bring something. So people would bring butter and milk and food, and I would tell them, "Baba is in deep meditation. You go and come back after one hour, and whatever you have brought, just leave it with me." So they would give it to me and after one hour they would come back, again carrying more food, because they were told not to come empty-handed. And in that way a lot of food was collected daily which the master and his disciple would eat. I did that for several months, and after that I asked him, "Give me some knowledge of *Shabd* Naam*." He said, "Don't you ever come here. We only have this 'Shabd Naam' — of standing up, sitting down, standing up and sitting down."

Once Guru Nanak went to a place called Kurukhshetra where there was a fake sadhu who was famous because he told people that he could see whatever was happening in all the three worlds. He would always close his eyes and sit with a cup in front of him. People were coming to worship him and they would put some money in that cup and he would just keep his eyes closed. After some time, he would open his eyes a little bit and see how much money had been collected in that cup so that he could transfer it to another bag that he had behind his back. So Guru Nanak went there, and in order to teach him a lesson, Guru Nanak took that cup which was in front of him and he put that cup behind him. Then Guru Nanak sat in front of him, folding both his hands. When that so-called sadhu opened his eyes to see how much money was collected, he didn't see that cup there. So he opened both his eyes, and he asked Guru Nanak, "Where is my cup? Where is it? Who took it?" Guru Nanak said, "I am sitting here. I didn't take it." The sadhu got upset and angry and he said, "Then who else has taken it?" Then Guru Nanak said, "You say you have the knowledge of the three worlds. You can see what is happening there, but you can't even see the cup which is behind you."

Rotinand, the Sadhu with Faith in God

I also met one Udasi sadhu named Rotinand. As is the custom in the Udasi sect, he used to accept chapatis from people, but this sadhu would only take as much as he could hold in his hand, and he would eat them while continuing his walk. He would not keep anything in stock, in his home or anywhere. He used to live like that, by getting as much food from people as he could hold in his hand.

Once it so happened that he became sick, and he did not have anything to eat and he could not go out to get food from the people.

---

* Another term for Sound Current or Naam.

One day somebody gave him four *annas* (one sixteenth of a rupee), which at that time would buy three or four kilos of wheat flour, on which you could live for many days. However, he did not buy wheat flour, or chapatis, or anything else that he could save. Instead he bought sweets with that money, which was very little, and he ate some of them and he shared the rest with two people who were sitting with him. He had so much confidence in God Almighty that he used to say, "God Who has given me food today will give to me tomorrow also," and he used to say, "He who eats dry food and remains content in the Will of God — he who eats half of the food he has and shares half with others — he is the dear one of God." I was impressed with him and remember him and he became my friend. Such mahatmas are always confident and have faith that God Almighty Who has given them food today will give them food tomorrow also.

In the langar of Guru Amardas, the third Guru of the Sikhs, He used to tell the sevadars to cook and serve all the food they had on hand each day. After serving it all, they would clean the vessels and say, "God Who has given us food today will fill our vessels tomorrow."

Blowing the Conch

Once a sadhu told me that by blowing the conch you could get a lot of intoxication and it was a very good thing because whoever heard your conch would say, "Wahe Guru" or "Ram." They would remember God Almighty and you would get the benefit of that. Well, love is after all love, and yearning is after all yearning. In my search for God Almighty, whatever I was told by anyone to do, I did that, and so I started blowing the conch.

Even a parrot, if taught, will repeat the word "Ram" or "Lord." When I would blow the conch, there were a couple of dogs in the neighborhood that would imitate me. When I blew the conch they would also go on making a noise like "oouh" — like the sound they heard from the conch. So one woman who was in the neighborhood heard me blowing the conch and heard the dogs accompanying me by making a similar sound. She came to me and she said, "If nobody else is giving you food, I'll bring food for you, but don't go on doing that." After that, I stopped blowing the conch.

Wear and Tear Money

In India, the householders invite those people who leave their homes and go into the wilderness and become so-called sadhus to have food and visit with them. By doing so they think that they are doing a good deed and will get the blessings of God. In the olden days, when these sadhus would go to people's houses to eat food, the householders would make very delicious food for them because they wanted to please God. After eating the food, the sadhus would ask for money to cover the wear and tear of their teeth. They would say, "We ate your food using our teeth, and you should pay us for that," and the householders would also give them money.

When I was searching for God, once I was in the company of a man named Lundu Baba, a so-called sadhu, and we were going from one place to another in search of God. Once when we were in Punjab, we came to a farmer's home and he prepared very delicious food for us. After eating the food, that baba asked for wear and tear money. The farmer gave one rupee to me and another rupee to the baba. I did not want the money and I gave it to the baba, but the farmer felt very bad. He said, "If this is going to happen, my religious deed will not be completed. Unless you accept the money, I won't get any benefit." I told him lovingly, "Listen, I am not after money. I am the son of a farmer. I have even more wealth than you have. And I can eat any food; I don't have to eat all this good food. But I am search of God, and that is why I am accompanying this baba. I don't accept any money because I have a lot of my own, so I am giving this money to him." That baba took the money quietly and put it in his pocket without saying anything. I told that farmer, "Up until now I have eaten many types of different food, very hard food and very soft food also, but I have never found that my teeth suffered from any wear and tear. I still have good teeth."

Once there was a yogi who used to oppose and criticize Guru Amardas very much. Because the Masters are always gracious and forgive their critics, Guru Amardas invited him to eat with him. But the yogi was so much against Guru Amardas Ji that he wouldn't accept the invitation. He said, "What is the use of going to such a person?"

Later on Guru Amardas Ji announced that anyone who ate in the langar, would not only be fed free, but they would be given a lot of wealth. When this was announced, many people came to eat the food, including that ascetic — but he didn't dare to come all the way in and eat the food with the other dear ones. He was interested though, so he started walking here and there outside the langar, thinking that maybe Guru Amardas would come out and invite him again, and this time he would accept. But Guru Amardas didn't come out. He had invited him already, but he hadn't come, so what was the use of inviting him again? Guru Amardas knew that he was waiting outside, but he paid no attention to him. Nobody came to invite him, and he didn't dare come in, but he was attracted by the wealth, so he thought of sending his son. So he sent his son in his place to eat and collect the promised wealth. When the satsangis and others who knew the story saw his son, they laughed at him and said, "Look at that yogi! How greedy he is! He was criticizing Guru Amardas on the grounds that he was greedy for name and fame and wealth, but now he cannot control his greed, and he sends his son to take the wealth!" Greed is such a funny thing.

The so-called sadhus go to people's houses and eat food, and even then, because they are so greedy, they ask for the "wear and tear" money. They find some excuse for getting money from the householders. Greed is a very dangerous passion and one must become free from this bad habit if one wants to realize God.

The Angry Muni

There is one sect or path of the *Munis*, in which the followers take a vow of silence and they keep quiet all the time. Even now one can find some people who are practicing that here and there in India. I heard about one mahatma of that path, that he had not spoken a word for twelve years and that he was a good mahatma, so I went to see him.

At the time when I went to see him, it had happened that he had asked some rich man to make a house for him, and the rich man was doing that. However, the builders had made some mistake and something was not right. It had not been done according to what the mahatma had wanted, and he was very upset. Now, he was a Muni and he could not speak because he had taken the vow of silence, but still he was very angry. If he were to express his anger through words, through his mouth, then his vow would get broken. So, instead of letting his anger come out through his mouth, he was letting his anger come out through his nose. That rich businessman who was building the house for him said, "Baba, don't you worry. I will get another made for you and we will repair this." But even though he was not able to speak, still he was not able to contain his anger.

When I saw him in that condition, I just wanted to leave. He looked at me and through another person he asked me why I had come. Such people do not ask anything through the words, but whatever they want to ask from the people, they ask in writing. I told him, "Baba, I came to have your darshan and I have had your darshan, and now I am going."

Guru Nanak used to talk about such people. He said that one is sitting as a Muni, sitting as if he is detached from the world, but within his heart he is moving the rosary of the worldly materials. When Kabir was asked a question about such Munis, He said, "If just by keeping the silence, if just by keeping quiet, one could get God Almighty, then all these four-legged animals — who do not speak — and even the dumb people, those who cannot speak — they all would have realized God."

O Sadhu, There is Nothing in Hypocrisy

O Sadhu, there is nothing in hypocrisy.
The hypocrite goes in the cycle of 84 lakhs. That is why I say that you should search in your within for God.

O my swan, even if you fly without wings or beak, even if I don't see you flying, even if you bring me news from far away, but still I won't believe in you, as there is nothing in hypocrisy.

Even if you sit in the cave and I cannot see you, even if you change your body and delude the people, but still I won't believe that you are the real one, as there is nothing in hypocrisy.

Even if you burn the fire and sit in it and I cannot see you, even if you change your body into a tiger and come and frighten me, even then I won't believe in you, as there is nothing in hypocrisy.

If you become a monk by growing your hair and sitting in deep meditation, even if you fly in the air and carry your cushion without any support, then also I won't believe in you.

By loving the crows you will not become a swan. Kabir says, "When you become one with the Shabd, only then will you become a swan."

— Hymn of Kabir Sahib
Pakhand Me Kuch Nahi Sadho

Once when I was searching, I went to a very famous organization that had a very big *ashram,* or spiritual center. The mahatma there had a very large following: millions of people went to him. They asked me to sing something from the *Gurbani.* So I started singing this bhajan written by Kabir Sahib, which says, "O Sadhu, there is nothing in hypocrisy." At all these places, those that preach to others, they don't have any peace themselves. The peace is millions of miles away from them. So when I started singing that bhajan over there, they did not like it and they threw me out. They only allowed me to sing two lines of that bhajan before they threw me out. If I had not left when they asked me to leave, it is possible that they would have given me a beating. I told them, "You said that I should sing from the *Gurbani.* This is a bhajan written by Kabir Sahib; it is the bani of the Masters." They said, "Could you not find any other shabd or hymn from the *Gurbani?*"

So what happened was that, since they were the hypocrites, they could not stand what I was telling them, what I was singing in the bhajan. Since I do not do any hypocrisy, no matter how many times you may sing that bhajan in front of me, it will not bother me. However, if someone is a hypocrite and you go and sing a bhajan about hypocrites in front of him, he will not like it.

Instead of becoming preachers to the world, first we have to become preachers to our own selves. First we have to make our mind understand, first we have to rise above the passions and pleasures, and first we have to make our soul free from the clutches of the mind. After taking our mind to *Brahm,* the third inner spiritual plane, only after that can we think about preaching to others and making other people understand. But what is our condition? We have not become preachers to our own selves, instead we have become preachers to others. We worry about others and we have become responsible for them, but we have not taken care of ourselves. First we have to improve ourselves, and only then can we think about talking to other people about their improvement.

Nowadays it is the time of preaching; everywhere there are preachers, people preaching to others. They advertise so much in the newspapers and on television to attract people. They say, "Come to us and we will bring peace to you." You will find so many preachers all over, and they all put so much effort into attracting people. But what do those people have with them? They have not preached to themselves, they have not improved themselves, but they are inviting other people to come and improve.

So I had the opportunity to meet many mahatmas and many masters whose institutions and missions were very popular and who were very well-known in India. When I asked them about their meditation, they had excuses. They either said that they had done the meditation in their previous lives, or that they had done sacrifices in their previous lives. Some mahatmas said that their ancestors had given them this job and had given them this power.

Before going to the feet of, or taking refuge with any Master, we need to find out about him. Has he done any meditation and has he done any sacrifice? We need to know his history and we need to know what he has done in the Path of Spirituality to become the Master, because in order to become anything, hard work is required.

The Practice of Jaldhara

At the time I started my search, people used to perform the austerities and religious practices that were common in India. In my early days I got the opportunity to do many different types of outer rites and rituals and I used to perform the austerities and do the *jaldhara*. Jaldhara is an austerity that is done in the cold winter months of December or January. A rectangular tank is constructed which has a little hole in it. The tank is filled with water that is very cold and through that small hole a very small stream of water flows on the head of whoever is doing that practice. Some people have about one hundred pots of water flow on their head and some have more than that. The person who is doing that practice sits there, under the flow of cold water that falls on the center of his head for hours at a time, and repeats some kind of mantra of the name of the Lord. It is a very difficult thing to do, but I did that many times. Because the water is very cold, many people become so cold that they fall down before they finish their practice. Then they are put on very hot ashes so that their bodies warm up again.

Some hypocrites, who want to attract and impress people, don't let the water fall on their heads. Instead they do something that does not allow the water to fall on their head: it goes to some other place. They make it appear to the people that water is falling on their head but they have the water fall on their hand. They also use a lot of marijuana and a lot of other drugs to impress people that they are intoxicated. But the loving dear ones do not do that. They do it correctly. They let the water fall on their heads and they do not mind even if they become cold.

When I was doing the austerities I also came across many sadhus or holy men who would stay up day and night struggling with their minds and sense organs so that their thoughts would not become impure. They would work very hard, because they did not want to have any impure or bad thoughts. Why do people do so many difficult practices? People don't understand that just by saying the word "difficult" it is not a big thing. But doing the austerities is a very big thing, for the austerities which I did were very difficult practices. I did many difficult austerities and many other people were also doing them. Why did we do that? Why did we suffer so much and do so many difficult practices? Only because we were searching for God. We wanted to have peace and that is why we did all those difficult practices.

In my childhood and also in my youth I was very beautiful; I had a very attractive face. Not only the women, but also the old men were attracted to me and they would come to see me. They would praise my eyes and my face. When I used to perform the austerities, sometimes women would watch. They would say that they couldn't understand how my mother allowed me to leave home and do what I was doing. They used to ask me about the pain and why I was causing my body so much suffering. They wanted to know why I was doing that. I was doing all that only because of the love of God. I was doing all that only because I was searching for Him.

THREE

Coming to the Feet of Baba Bishan Das

I Ask Baba Bishan Das to Show Me God

I went in many directions and I went to many people. I did the rites and rituals and performed the austerities, I did so many things, but I did not get any satisfaction, I did not get any contentment and I did not get any peace of mind. Everywhere they would only explain the theory and they would only talk about God and that is all. Nobody gave me any practical experience. What to talk about getting peace and satisfaction from doing all this, instead of getting satisfaction, my thirst increased!

Because I did not find anything, I went to Baba Bishan Das. If I had found anything from performing the austerities, I would not have gone to Baba Bishan Das. The path for me was started by him. When I went to other people, I would not get any satisfaction, and until I went to Baba Bishan Das and bowed at his feet, I did not get any peace.

The first time I went to Baba Bishan Das, I asked him to show me God. He took my head and made me look at the sun. He said, "Go on looking at the sun constantly and tell me how long you can go on looking at it." I could not look at the sun for more than a moment, and I felt embarrassed. I said, "I cannot look at it any longer because it is too bright." So he told me, "You have to see thousands of suns like this. God is Light and God is even thousands of times brighter than this." We cannot even look at this outer sun — just one outer sun — constantly for a long time. How then can we see the radiance of God, which is much more than the radiance of this outer sun, within? If we have not developed eyes that can see the brilliance of God, how can we ask the Master to show us God?

Baba Bishan Das told me, "All these outer practices do not have any connection with our soul. If by sitting under the water one could get liberation, then why are the fishes and frogs and other creatures that live in the water not liberated? One cannot achieve liberation by sitting in the fire, as there is already a lot of fire within. There are the fires of lust, greed, attachment and egoism. What is the use of having more fire outside?"

Obeying the Instructions of Baba Bishan Das

When I first went to Baba Bishan Das, two other dear ones went with me. After we met him, he gave us some farming work to do. The other two dear ones were farmers, but I had not done the work of farming before that. However, whatever Baba Bishan Das told me to do, I did that, even though I was not very skilled in doing farming. The other two dear ones did not do that farm work, even though they were excellent farmers. They had done that kind of work before, so they thought, "We have done this work many times, so what is the use of doing it?" They thought that maybe Baba Bishan Das was testing them to find out if they were capable of doing farm work, and because they knew they were, they didn't obey the orders of the Master.

In the evening when Baba Bishan Das came there to see what we had done, I was doing all the work that he had told me to do, even though I was not doing it perfectly. I requested Baba Bishan Das to forgive me because I had not done that kind of work before. I told him, "I have not done this work at my home, but by coming to your feet and with your grace I have been able to do this work. Please forgive me if there is any fault in it." On the other hand, the other two dear ones told him to give them some other type of work. They told him they had been doing that kind of farm work since their birth and that is why they didn't have any interest in doing that. Baba Bishan Das was not pleased with them and he didn't give them any grace. He became gracious only on this poor one who obeyed his instructions when I went to his feet.

The Spiritual Heritage of Baba Bishan Das

Baba Bishan Das was a very strict mahatma. He was born in the royal family of the state of Nabha in Punjab, and from his birth he had all the amenities and conveniences. I have seen with my own eyes the property, the wealth, and the palaces, which he owned. In those days the kings used to rule over India and King Hira Singh of Nabha wanted to make Baba Bishan Das his successor. For that reason Baba Bishan Das became very well educated on the worldly level and had read many scriptures. In those times, it was very difficult to get any kind of education in India, but he was sent to England to study and get the highest degrees; he even got a Ph.D. from London. This was a very big thing at that time in India, and if anyone had studied in England, people would give him a lot of respect. However Baba Bishan Das used to say the learned do not take anything with them and in the Path of Spirituality it makes no difference whether one is educated or not.

Baba Bishan Das could have lived a very comfortable life, but he preferred to live a very hard life. He also did all sorts of austerities and did all sorts of things in search of God. Then he went to Baba Amolak Das, who was not a very learned scholar like Baba Bishan Das; he was illiterate. He could not even sign his name in the Punjabi language. However, Baba Bishan Das did not ask him any questions or mention any books. He simply folded his hands to Baba Amolak Das and said, "Master, please liberate me from this hell."

Baba Amolak Das then ordered him to bring thorny bushes from the wilderness and make a fence in an area which did not belong to Amolak Das and which did not have any crop or anything which needed any protection. Still Baba Amolak Das ordered Baba Bishan Das to do that job. For a month and a half Baba Bishan Das went into the jungle, brought thorny bushes, and made a fence. Only after Baba Bishan Das had obeyed and followed that order did Baba Amolak Das give him the Initiation into the first Two Words and teach him to meditate.

Baba Bishan Das and Baba Amolak Das were in the line of Masters that started from Sri Chand, one of Guru Nanak's sons. Guru Nanak had two sons, Sri Chand and Lakhmi Das. Even though Guru Nanak was God Himself Who came into this world to give knowledge to the people and many people took advantage of His coming into this world, neither of His sons took Initiation into the Five Words from Him. Lakhmi Das was not initiated and he used to eat meat and do all the bad things. Sri Chand went to Abinashi Muni, who had Initiation of Two Words and belonged to the Udasi sect, and got Initiation into the path of the first Two Words from him. Abinashi Muni taught him to perform austerities on the banks of rivers and to keep his body naked except for a loincloth and do outer rites and rituals. Sri Chand used to give Initiation into the first Two Words only, and the Udasis follow the path of Sri Chand. This is a very famous path in India and the Udasi people believe that Sri Chand was the incarnation of the great Indian sage Shankar.

When Guru Nanak met Bhai Lehna, He gave him Initiation and Lehna became so successful in his meditation that Guru Nanak made him His Successor, after which He was known as Guru Angad. Perfect Masters know everything that is going to happen, and Guru Nanak knew that, after He would leave, Bhai Lehna would not be appreciated and respected by His sons, His family, and the people around Him. Bhai Lehna lived as a servant in Guru Nanak's home, but before Guru Nanak left the body He told Bhai Lehna that he should go away from Him, because His sons would bother him. So six months before Guru Nanak left the body, Bhai Lehna went to his own village, started doing meditation in a closed room and connected himself within with Guru Nanak.

When Guru Nanak completed His journey on this earth and left the body, His sons did not come near and did not participate in the funeral rites. They were upset with Guru Nanak since He had not given the successorship to them. Sri Chand and Lakhmi Das said, "Bhai Lehna is the servant of our home so how can we accept him as the Master?" Even though Bhai Lehna had become the Successor of Guru Nanak, the sons of Guru Nanak did not take Him as the real Master, and Sri Chand started a path parallel to the path of Guru Nanak. But since he had the knowledge of only the first Two Words, he used to give out only those.

It is not a new thing that some people go to the Successors of the perfect Masters and others don't. This has been going on for ages and ages. There are some fortunate souls who will not find any peace unless they go and find the Successor of the perfect Master. However, there are many who don't want to go, or those who don't have the desire to seek the Successor, and it is all according to their own fate, their destiny. Those in whose forehead it is written that they will go to the Successor of the perfect Master, only they are brought to His feet. The rest of the people, the other dear ones, who do not have this written in their fate, they just wander here and there.

Sri Chand lived a very long life, and so when he met Guru Ramdas, the fourth guru of the Sikhs, he noticed that Guru Ramdas' beard was very long. So he asked Him, "Why have You grown Your beard so long?" Guru Ramdas answered, "Only to wipe off the shoes of great souls like you." When He said this so humbly, Sri Chand started weeping and said, "Only because of Your humility we did not get the successorship. Only because of Your humility there is nothing left with us; You have taken everything from us."

Sri Chand lived a very long life and Baba Amolak Das also lived a very long life. Baba Amolak Das lived for about one hundred and forty years and Baba Bishan Das received Initiation from him. Baba Amolak Das initiated only two people, Baba Bishan Das and King Bhupinder Singh of Patiala. Baba Amolak Das was still alive when I went to the feet of Baba Bishan Das and I had the opportunity to meet him and serve him some milk. He was a very good sadhu, a very good mahatma. The path of Sri Chand is very famous in India, and I know many true stories about that sect. These are not things which I learned from the books, but which I have seen myself and which I heard from Baba Amolak Das and Baba Bishan Das.

Baba Amolak Das Gives a Boon to Hira Singh

Baba Amolak Das used to live in the state of Nabha, halfway between the city of Nabha and a village called Baroukhai. There he had made a place for himself and he used to stay there. Many people would come to him but he would not give Initiation to anyone. However, there was one very poor person whose name was Hira Singh, who used to have a camel cart on which he delivered goods from the village of Baroukhai to the town of Nabha. He was so devoted that every time he went by Baba Amolak Das' place he would always stop. He would go and bow down to Baba Amolak Das and then he went on to Nabha. On the way back also he would not miss going to Baba Amolak Das and seeing him. Sometimes he would bring things for Baba Amolak Das; he was very devoted to him.

This went on for a long time. One day he had come there and Baba Amolak Das was sitting with many other people. Baba Amolak Das told him, "Hira Singh, ask for anything and you will be given it." He replied, "No, Master, I have everything. I don't want anything because you have given me a lot. With your grace, I have everything." But Baba Amolak Das said, "No, you should ask for something and it will be given to you." Again, Hira Singh said the same thing. Three times this went on, with Hira Singh saying that he was very content with whatever he had. However, such is the Will of the Saints that when it comes in Their Will that They want to give something to the disciple, They will give it. So Baba Amolak Das insisted and said, "Today whatever you will ask for, I will give you that. If you want I can make you the King of Nabha."

That seemed a very unlikely thing because Hira Singh was illiterate and was very poor, so how could he become the king? The other people who were sitting with Baba Amolak Das also thought, "Hira Singh comes to see Baba Amolak Das very often and brings fruit and other things and, in order to please him, Baba Amolak Das is saying this, but this statement has no meaning." However, when the Saints say anything, that always has some meaning, whether we believe in Their words or not. Whatever They say, that always carries some meaning and it always becomes true.

So Hira Singh replied, "Master, I don't want anything, whatever you have given me I am content with that. I am pleased with that." Still Baba Amolak Das said, "Okay, but from now on you have been made the King of Nabha." The people around him still didn't want to believe, and in order to make a joke they said, "Okay Master, you have made him the king, so why don't you make the person who comes with Hira Singh the minister, because he needs some minister." So Baba Amolak Das replied, very seriously, "My job was to make him the king and I have made him the king; now it is his job. If he wants to make his friend the minister, it is up to him." After that all Hira Singh's friends started making fun of him. In the marketplace they would always say, "Okay, let us go and put our load on the camel cart of the King of Nabha."

After some time, it so happened that the King Bhagwan Singh of Nabha died and since he did not have any heir, it was very difficult for the people to find the person who would be the king after him. There were two other kingdoms nearby, the kingdoms of Jind and Patiala. They were very strong kingdoms and they wanted to take over the state of Nabha. But at that time the British were ruling there and they did not want that to happen. Furthermore the British were very just rulers, and if a king died and there was no successor, they would try to find the person who was the closest relative to make that person king. So the British wanted to know who were the far and near relatives of King Bhagwan Singh so the closest one could be made the successor. In India, when anyone is cremated, they take the leftover bones (which they call the "flowers") and ashes to the holy waters at the city of Hardwar. There they pour them into the holy waters of the Ganges and that is the last funeral rite. When anyone takes the ashes there, there are pundits who keep the names and addresses of the family members. So if anybody wants to know the names and addresses of the family members, even if that family member died hundreds of years ago, you will find their name in the city of Hardwar. There they have the family pundits who keep those accounts.

So the British went there and they met the pundit who used to keep the account of the family of King Bhagwan Singh of Nabha. To their surprise they found that Hira Singh, that person who used to go to Baba Amolak Das, was the only living relative of King Bhagwan Singh of Nabha, and so he was made king. But when he was made the king, since he was illiterate, he wanted someone to help him. So he made his friend, who used to go with him to see Baba Amolak Das, his minister. After that he ruled the state of Nabha in such a just and religious way that he was given very noble titles by the British people and he became the leader of all the kings of the states of India. He always appreciated the Saints and he always respected the sadhus, because he was given that position with the grace of the sadhu.

When the Saints come into this world, They always give us one or the other boon, and whatever They say always comes true. But we people do not believe in Their words because we are controlled by our mind and that is why we say that whatever the Saints are saying has no meaning. But later on it is always found that whatever the Master has spoken always carries some meaning and always comes true.

The Efforts of Baba Bishan Das

Baba Bishan Das was a very strict mahatma, but he was also very loving. He knew all the tricks of the mind and he had struggled very hard because the early practices of the Path are very difficult. In the lower planes of Creation you have to struggle very hard, although later on, when you have become competent in going within, you get satisfaction and happiness, and it is easier to progress in the higher planes.

Baba Bishan Das had the knowledge of only the first two inner planes and had perfected himself only up to those two planes. Still to achieve the perfection up to the first two inner planes is also worthy. It is worth sacrificing for such a person who has perfected himself that far. God had given all the conveniences and comforts to Baba Bishan Das, but once he got Initiation from Baba Amolak Das, he never tasted any salt, sugar or pickle. He suffered a lot of hunger and thirst, and for twelve years drank only the juice of vegetables. Moreover I have seen Baba Bishan Das meditating: He had one wooden bench in which he had nails fixed, and whenever he would feel sleepy he would sit on those nails and meditate.

Baba Bishan Das was also against lust. He came to this Path at age thirty and lived to be ninety years old, and while he was married, he had only one child. He had only one child because he went only once to his wife and even then, because of that, he would say, "I have committed one mistake in my life."

Baba Bishan Das would never allow people to take his photo although many people would try to do that. He was a Sikh, but he was not bound by the rituals. He did not wear a turban, but would leave his long hair loose. He was an independent thinker.

Baba Bishan Das and His Mind

Once Baba Bishan Das was struggling with his mind, and when the mind started giving him a lot of trouble, he threw it out, and as a symbol of that he bought a pig and tied it to his door. There were many Muslim people around the place where Baba Bishan Das' ashram was located because there was only one street between his ashram and their mosque. The morning after he did this, when the Muslims came to worship in the mosque, they saw that there was a pig and the Muslims don't like to see pigs. They take that as an inauspicious thing. So when they saw that, everybody got upset at Baba Bishan Das. They got together and started saying, "What has Baba Bishan Das done? He is an atheist!" and they started talking against him.

Baba Bishan Das came out and said, "Well, you have a lot of anger in you and that is why you are getting angry at me. But first listen to me, talk to me, and then if you think that I am guilty you can give me any punishment that you want." There were some people there who were wise so they said, "Well, what is wrong in talking with Baba Bishan Das?" and they came forward and talked with him. Baba Bishan Das said, "First of all tell me what is meant by 'pig' in your holy book — who is called 'pig' and who is the one whom you don't like to see?" They were wise people and knew about the sacred teachings, so they said, "In our book it is written that the unruly mind is like a pig and we should not have anything to do with that unruly mind and that is why we don't like to see the pig, which is the symbol of the unruly mind." Baba Bishan Das said, "I have tied this pig to my door only to show that my mind has become like a pig; he has become very unruly and I have thrown him out. I am showing that I have thrown out my mind and he is in the form of the pig. You people have that mind within you and I have got him outside. What wrong have I done?" So hearing that, they were all satisfied and stopped fighting with him.

Baba Bishan Das also used to call his mind a dog, and he used to say, "This dog barks unnecessarily, and he always creates a disturbance." Sometimes when I would see him sitting very quiet and peaceful, I would ask him, "Baba Ji, today you are looking very peaceful and quiet. What is the reason?" Then he would say, "Yes, today I have tied up my dog, and he is not barking anymore." Sometimes I would ask him to eat some food, and he would say, "No, I do not want to eat food. Today I have tied my dog and he is not barking and I don't want to feed him." He used to say, "When you will understand your mind like this, then your mind will stop barking unnecessarily, and he will come under your control."

When we get Initiation and come to the Path of the Masters, our struggle with a very obstinate enemy — our mind — starts, and in this battle we do not have any weapon except the weapon of the Naam. In the battle of the world, we may have to fight for one or two hours, or for a couple of days, but this battle with our mind goes on throughout our entire life. And just like if we win a battle in the world we get honors, in the same way, if we win this battle with our mind, we also get the prize and the honor, and it is the real honor. God gives us a place in His Real Home, and He gives us such an honor which is our real property, our real wealth, and the Negative Power cannot take that away from us.

The Religion Does Not Matter

Baba Bishan Das was born in a Sikh family and there was also one Muslim Fakir called Fati who lived very close to him. They had their *deras*, their ashrams, very close to each other; there was only one road separating those two deras. Baba Bishan Das had the Initiation of Two Words and Fati also had knowledge up to that level. Even though one was Sikh and one was Muslim, they both used to say that it doesn't matter if one goes to the ashram of one or to the ashram of the other, the main thing, the main purpose, is to remember God.

Like all the Masters, Baba Bishan Das understood that people are stuck in so many superstitions. People think that if, after going to a church, they repeat the name of Ram, the Hindu name for God, then Ram will get upset, because that is not the right place for a person to go and remember Ram. If someone goes to a mosque and repeats the name of God, the Christian name for God, he may think that God will get upset, that He will not be pleased because he is not remembering Him in a church, he is remembering Him in a mosque. Similarly, if a person goes to a temple, and remembers God in the name of Allah, then he thinks that maybe Allah will not be pleased, that He will get upset. People are stuck in so many superstitions like this, even though in the temples, in the mosques, and also in the churches the same God is talked about.

The True Remembrance

Usually a person follows the tradition of the family in which he or she is born and does the same type of practices that the other family members are doing. My family were very devout Sikhs and my father and my grandfather were great devotees of the holy *Guru Granth Sahib*. The people who are devotees of the *Guru Granth Sahib* have five different banis, five different writings, from the *Guru Granth Sahib* that they learn by heart. They make it a point to sing them every day. These banis are the *Jap Ji Sahib*, the *Jap Sahib*, *Chaupai*, *Rahiras*, and the *Anand Sahib,* and my father would recite these writings every day. However, I was so devoted that, in addition to those banis, I learned by heart and did the reading of *Sri Asa Ji Di Vars*, another bani called *Dakni Onkar* and also the *Sukhmani Sahib*. Very lovingly and faithfully I used to read these eight banis every day. I would get up at one o'clock in the morning and for eight hours continuously I would go on reading those Holy Scriptures. However, when I would recite those banis, only in the very beginning, for the first five or six minutes, would I be aware that I was doing that. Then at the very end when I would be reading the last line of *Sukhmani Sahib*, I would again become aware of what I was doing. But for the rest of the time in between, the seven or eight hours that I was spending every day in repeating those banis, my attention would never remain there. For that time, my mind would take me outside and I would think about the world. During that time, I would be going here and there mentally, visiting my family members and talking to almost everyone in this world. I would never remain aware that I was doing that kind of devotion, but still I used to think that I was sitting for devotion for eight hours.

So when I met Baba Bishan Das, I told him that I was doing that kind of devotion, he asked me, "Dear One, have you ever seen any light within yourself? Has your mind become quiet by reading all these writings? Have you ever received any peace or happiness?" I told him, "No, I have not seen the light within by reading those banis and I have not gotten any peace by reading those banis." He made me realize that I was not doing the devotion: instead I was sitting there and thinking about the world and I was not doing the repetition for the whole time. Only then did I realize how we have to struggle with the mind and how powerful the mind is.

Because we are involved in this kind of practice, when the Masters say such true things, it tastes very bitter. However, if you are a true devotee, then whenever a wise person tells you anything, instead of getting upset you start thinking and you realize that what you are doing is not good and that you are not getting anything.

At that time I was influenced by my father and my family who were very devoted to the Sikh religion. My father used to visit the gurdwaras and understood the priests of the gurdwaras to be the ministers of God. He thought that by going to the gurdwaras and doing the devotion of God there he would get liberation. Because of this influence I also believed in Guru Gobind Singh, the tenth Guru of the Sikhs, and all the past Masters and I was also thinking that whatever other people were doing was the right thing to do. But when I went to Baba Bishan Das, Baba Bishan Das would rebuke me and ask me, "Did you ever see Guru Gobind Singh? Will you be able to go and see Guru Gobind Singh? How can you be sure that He will take care of you and will liberate you?" I had no answers to all his questions and I didn't know what to say. I would get upset, but later when I would think about it, I would find that whatever he said was true. So I would go to him again, hoping that he would tell me something more about Guru Gobind Singh, or would give me some more knowledge. But he would do the same thing, which would again make me upset. But later on, again I would realize that what he was saying was true.

Because of my family, I also had the idea that if you visit the holy places where the great Sikh Masters have been, you can get liberation and peace of mind. So I also visited every place where the great Masters had gone — all the holy places, all the great temples — I left no place out, but I didn't get any peace. When I came to Baba Bishan Das, he also told me that unless we go within, unless we visit the most holy place that is the human body, we cannot realize God. He told me that unless we go within, we cannot get rid of greed and the other passions. He told me that the waves of greed, lust, anger, all come from within and that nothing comes from outside. Outside we just act according to the feelings or thoughts that come into our mind. Since the disease comes from within, then the medicine for removing the disease is also within.

Baba Bishan Das Explains the *Guru Granth Sahib*

Because my parents believed in the Sikh holy book, the *Guru Granth Sahib*, I also used to think that there was no use in following any Master other than *Guru Granth Sahib*. I was taught that there is nobody else whom we can call Master except the ten Sikh Gurus. In the beginning, when I used to go to Baba Bishan Das and he would praise his Master, I would feel very confused and I would argue with him. I would tell him, "Nobody is the Master after Guru Gobind Singh; it is written in the book." I told Baba Bishan Das about the things which I thought were written in the *Guru Granth Sahib:* that there would be no Master after Guru Gobind Singh, the last Master of the Sikhs, and that the book should be taken as the Master. That is what most Sikh people believe: that it is written in the book that Guru Gobind Singh said, "After me there will be no Master, there will be no prophet. I am the last Master, and after me this book will be your Master." However, Baba Bishan Das denied that these things were written in the book. He said I could read the book patiently and lovingly and I wouldn't find these lines in the book.

At that time I was very confused, and I thought, "How is that possible? I have been reading this book since my childhood, and I believe that it is written there, because everybody says so. Why is it that Baba Bishan Das is denying that?" I was not satisfied. I went to Amritsar and bought three copies of *Guru Granth Sahib*. I had two other friends who were with me and for six months continuously, we three people read that book many times. We studied it and we worked very hard in order to find those lines that would say that there can be no Master after Guru Gobind Singh. However, we did not find those lines and we realized that the statements which we believed in were not there. We came back to Baba Bishan Das and surrendered to him. We said, "Baba Bishan Das, you are the true one. The words which we thought were in the book *are not* there. What you have said is true."

Baba Bishan Das told us that those lines were written by other people *after* Guru Gobind Singh left. People say that that couplet was written by Guru Gobind Singh, but in fact it was not. It was written by someone else and is not included in the *Guru Granth Sahib*.

When Baba Bishan Das told us that the lines which we thought were in the *Guru Granth Sahib* were not there, he also said, "Let us suppose for some time that it is in the book. I will explain to you what that means. Even though it is not the writing of the Master, and someone else has written that, still if we explain that in its real sense, in its real meaning, then also you will find that it is inspiring you and guiding you towards the living Master. That couplet says, "When the timeless Lord ordered me, then I came into this world and started this Path. Now it is the order of God to all the disciples, all the Sikhs, that they should take the *Guru Granth* as their Master. They should take *Guru Granth* as their Master and they should manifest the body of the Master. Those who have truth in their heart will definitely get the company of the Master."

Baba Bishan Das told us that it was the Master saying, "When God ordered me, I came into this world and started this Path. Now whatever is written in this book, you should take the teachings of this book as your Master." Baba Bishan Das explained to us, "When we take anybody as the Master or when we take a book as the Master, we have to obey what the book or the Master tells us. *Every single line of Guru Granth Sahib is inspiring us to go to the living Master.* Reading the teachings of this book, you should search for the living Master, you should search for the Master in the body. Those who have truth in their heart, they will definitely go in the company of the Masters. When you go to the living Master — if you have truth in your heart — you will get the company of the Master. And when you go in the company of the Master, He will explain to you what all these things mean."

I respect *Guru Granth Sahib* very much and have much love for it. I have been reading it since my childhood, and I have found that it talks about the importance of Satsang, it sings the glory of Naam, and it talks about the perfect Master. In *Guru Granth Sahib* nobody is criticized and all the Truth is presented as Truth. However, from reading the Bani, singing the hymns and even doing the *Akhand Panth,* the non-stop recitation of the *Guru Granth Sahib,* many times, I did not get any spiritual peace. But longing was created; *Gurbani* created the pangs of separation. It was helpful to me because *Gurbani* inspired me to go to some perfect Saint. My life started with *Gurbani* and *Gurbani* inspired me and told me that there is another Bani that will give peace to the soul, and there is some Bani, other than what can be spoken or read, which will liberate me.

All the hymns of the *Guru Granth Sahib* are praising "Guru, Guru." It respectfully appreciates Gurus, Saints and Sadhus, but we are not taking advantage of the Bani or following its advice. Guru Gobind Singh, Who read as well as composed hymns in praise of the Saints, could have written, "After me there will be no more Saints," but He did not. I have also studied the Muslim tradition and read the *Koran* very carefully and have found written nowhere that Mohammed Sahib said, "After me there will be no *Nabi,* there will be no Prophet." Nonetheless the orthodox Muslims have made this rule: that there is no Prophet, no Master, except Mohammed Sahib. However, Prophet Mohammed Himself wrote in the *Koran,* "O Man, go to the Masters, so that they can break the seal of your ears and you can hear the divine music of God which is resounding within you. Because I have got a Master I am able to hear that and you should also go to Him."

Whatever things the past Masters said we should not do, people are doing only those things. Guru Nanak Sahib has written a lot against reading the Holy Scriptures thinking that they will bring liberation. He has written that no matter with how much love and affection you read tons of books, you will not get benefit from it because the liberation is in Naam and you can get Naam only if you go to the living Satguru. People think that they will get liberation only through reading scriptures constantly, or reading certain parts of scriptures or reading them in certain ways. They don't go beyond that and that's why they don't appreciate the living Masters. Living Masters have always emphasized the need of having a living Master, and They always say that you should practice the teachings.

> *Listen my friends! I am requesting you:*
> *This is the time to go in the company of the Saints.*
>
> *Take advantage (of the presence of the Saints) here,*
> *So that you may dwell happily there (after)*
> *Life is decreasing day and night.*
> *O mind, meet the Master and complete the work.*
>
> *All this world is in the useless delusion.*
> *Only the Brahma Gyani crosses over.*
> *The one who is awakened and given the drink of nectar by Him,*
> *Only he knows this unwritten story.*
>
> *If you want that thing,*
> *Make your mind dwell on Satguru.*
> *Happily and easily you'll get your own home.*
> *You will not have to come back again.*
>
> *O All-Conscious Lord, Who fulfills all the desires of the mind —*
> *Nanak the servant asks for this boon: Make me the dust of the Saints.*

— Guru Arjan Dev
Karo Benanti Suno Meri Mita

The Two Pundits

Even though in India at that time it was very rare to find such people, Baba Bishan Das had a Ph.D. He was a very learned person, but he was still above the learning. He was very fortunate in that he practiced what he had learned. He knew that learning or reading is not all, and he would tell this story about the two pundits.

Once two pundits came to an innocent farmer's home and that farmer became very happy. Thinking that the learned people had come to his home, he felt very fortunate. He welcomed both of them with much love and respect and he prepared very good food. Before the pundits were served that food, one of them went outside for something. The farmer told the other pundit, "I am a very fortunate one that you learned people have come to my home. You seem very learned and the other pundit who has gone out, he also must be a very learned person." You know that the learned people very seldom appreciate the other learned people. So the pundit who was there in the house replied, "Well, what learning has he done? He is not more than a buffalo. He has not learned anything." So the farmer kept quiet.

When the other pundit came back and this first pundit went out he repeated the same thing to the other pundit. He said, "Well, I am a very fortunate one that today two learned people have come into my home. You seem like you are a very learned person, and the other pundit also seems like he is a very learned person. Maybe he is more learned than you are?" The pundit replied, "Well, what does he know about the learning? He has not learned anything. He is not more than a donkey."

Again, that innocent farmer just kept quiet. But when the time for the meal came, instead of serving all the good food that he had made for them, he brought them hay and grass and other things which are fed to the buffaloes and donkeys. When those pundits saw that kind of food offered to them, they got upset and said, "Well, are you making fun of us? Are you fooling with us, are you insulting us, or are you going to give us food to eat?"

He replied, "I am not doing anything wrong. You said that he was a donkey, and you said that he was a buffalo. This is what the donkeys and buffaloes eat and that is why I have given this food to you." When they got such a reply from that innocent farmer, they didn't have anything to say. They felt very embarrassed and left without eating.

Now if those pundits had been doing the meditation, if they had been going within, and if they had any contact with God, they would have appreciated and praised each other. Furthermore, if that had been the case, their host, that innocent farmer, would have gained something from them.

Baba Bishan Das Teaches Me about Criticism

Baba Bishan Das taught me that the perfect Mahatmas, the Beloveds of God, neither criticize anyone themselves, nor do they allow their disciples to get involved in criticism. Criticism cuts the root of Spirituality. He used to quote the Greek writer Aesop, who said, "Every person carries two bags, one in front of him and one behind. In the bag in front of him, he carries the qualities of others, and in the bag behind, he carries his own. That is why he does not hesitate to describe the bad qualities of others because they are right in front of him. However, he doesn't sweep under his own bed or look into his own self to see what qualities, good or bad, he has." Swami Ji Maharaj has said, "People look at other people's faults and laugh and smile but they do not see their own faults which have no beginning or end."

The Story of Sheik Chili

Baba Bishan Das also used to call the mind, "Sheik Chili." Sheik Chili was a great daydreamer. Once it so happened that a soldier told him to carry a tin full of *ghee* (clarified butter) to his house and promised him two annas as pay. So he was carrying that tin on his head and he started daydreaming: "From the two annas which I will get from the soldier, I will buy a couple of eggs, and from those eggs hens will come out and then when they are grown they will lay more eggs and I will then sell those hens and eggs and I will buy a goat, and that goat will also have children, and I will sell all of them, and then I will buy a cow, and she will bear many calves, and for them I will collect so much money and then I will get married. Then I will have many children, and I will take care of them. When they fight I will teach them not to, and if they continue fighting after they grow up, then I will kick them with my leg." At this point in his fantasy, he actually kicked with his leg as if he were kicking his children, so that suddenly that tin of ghee that was on his head fell off and all the ghee was gone. The soldier got upset and said, "You have lost all this ghee!" but Sheik Chili replied, "You are worried about your ghee, which is worth only a few rupees, but I have lost all my family!"

So Baba Bishan Das used to say, "Our mind is just like Sheik Chili. There is nothing material there, but still he is thinking about this and that, and he goes on indulging in fantasies." Mahatmas lovingly tell us, "There is no one in this world who has finished or fulfilled all his desires." He may have finished or fulfilled some of his desires, but not all. You may even find someone who has finished most of his desires, but there will still be a couple which are not fulfilled.

The False Attachment

One of my cousins had a hard time getting married, so my aunt told me that she would believe in my Master Baba Bishan Das and would go to see him every month if he somehow would get her son married. She told me to request this of Baba Bishan Das when I saw him next. Therefore, when I saw Baba Bishan Das I told him of my aunt's request. Baba Bishan Das asked my aunt, "Do you promise that you will come to have darshan every month if your son gets married?" She said, "Yes, if he gets married, I will definitely come to see you every month." Baba Bishan Das replied, "Okay, we will see. Your son will get married and you will have a daughter-in-law in your home. Let us see whether you come to have darshan every month or if you chase me to beat me."

The boy did get married. But my aunt had a very bad temper; she always used to find fault with the daughter-in-law, and they suffered a lot because of that. Once, when I was going to have the darshan of Baba Bishan Das, I told my aunt that I was going there, and asked if she wanted to go with me. She was so upset with her daughter-in-law that she said, "I will believe in your Master only when both my son and daughter-in-law die."

Baba Bishan Das would say about the relatives, "O Careless One, talking in very sweet words your aunt and other relatives have deluded you. Just as the barber shears off your hair, in the same way, they have shaved you. They have taken all that you have." He would explain that our relatives, our brothers and sisters, love us as long as we are in this body. In the beginning they are very excited and love us very much, but there comes a time when no one is interested in us and no one pays attention to us. It is a surprising thing that although we know that they are not going to help us at the time of death, still we are attached to them. As Guru Nanak said, "Give up the attachment of these worldly people and sing the glory of God."

Baba Bishan Das used to lovingly tell this story about a young man who was very devoted to one Saint and he used to go to Him every day. The boy would not miss even a day. He would always go there, do the seva of the Master and then he would go to his home and have his meal. He was so devoted and so punctual that the Master was very pleased and very happy with him. One day the boy went to his Master and, according to the tradition of this world that when young people grow up they get married, he told his Master, "Master, I am engaged today." The Master said, "Well, from now onwards you are of no use to your friends and your near and dear ones."

After some time he started arriving a little late to do the seva of the Master. Then the wedding day came and he got married, so he went to the Master and said, "Master, I am married today." The Master replied, "Now you are of no use to your family members." The boy could not understand that comment either and he went away.

Before he was engaged and married, he used to go to the Master every day without missing. He was very punctual and he would have his meal only after doing the seva of the Master, but now it all changed. First he started coming a little late and then, after he got married, for many days he did not come. When he returned after some days the Master asked him, "Dear One, why have you been coming so late and why didn't you come for many days?" He said, "Master, you know now I am married and I have a wife and she loves me very much. She loves me so much that she doesn't eat until I go back home. She says she will die if she doesn't see me. That is why I didn't come here, because she loves me and I also love her very much, and she will do anything for me."

The Master just kept quiet and he said, "Okay, let me give you something. I will give you this medicine. Take this medicine and go back to your home and we will see what happens."

As the Master had told him, he took that medicine which made him unconscious and made him appear to be dead. His family members were very worried and they called the doctors. The doctors came and said, "Well, now we cannot do anything; he is no more, he is dead." The family thought that maybe they should go to the boy's Master and maybe He could do something, maybe He would bring him back to life. They went to the Master and said, "Your disciple, your dear one has left the body and you should come and help."

The Master became very happy and He said, "Okay, I will come." He went there and He said, "I will bless this water, I will do some mantra on the water, but the condition is that someone has to drink this water and then this boy can live again. The person who drinks the water will have to die. So whoever loves this boy the most should drink the water." First He offered the water to the boy's mother, the same mother who used to say, "O Son, what would I do without you? You are the light of my eyes and you are my life. I would have no life without you." The same mother said, "No, I do not want to drink the water, I don't want to die." Then the water was offered to the other family members, to the father, to the brothers and sisters, to the relatives, but everyone just refused. No one wanted to die in his place. Then the wife, about whom the boy was very proud and appreciative because she loved him so much that she would do anything for him, was offered the water. The Master said, "You know that it is the question of your husband; if you will drink the water he will live."

She said, "Well, what do I have to do with the husband? If I am going to die, what is the use of having a husband?" Therefore, she also refused to drink the water.

Baba Bishan Das would explain that our story is the same. All the love stories that we have with our family members, with our worldly attachments, are like this. No one wants to die in our place; no wants to do anything for us. We are just attached to them and we say that we love them, or that they love us very much, but when the end time comes, no one comes to help us, and no one comes to our rescue. We all have these experiences in our life, but still we are attached to them.

Baba Bishan Das Gives Me Knowledge of My Past Lives

You know that Baba Bishan Das had Initiation into the first Two Words and he was practically successful in meditation on them. At that time I didn't believe in reincarnation, so he made me understand what my previous birth was — where I was born and who my parents were. He graciously told me about all the rites and rituals and all the austerities, including the fire practice, that I had performed in my past life. He showed me the very place where I had done the austerities, and the smoke was still coming from that place. He even showed me the spot of my cremation in my last life and made me dig the land there and he then showed me the bones from my previous birth. At that time he told me, "Your parents of your past life are still alive and if you want I can make you meet them." I touched my ears, a gesture of repentance, because I was convinced, and folding my hands to him I said, "No, Master, don't make me see them, because I am already bothered by my present parents. I am not able to become detached from them. If you make me meet my past parents, it will become difficult for me and I do not want to meet them."

Only with his grace was I able to know my give and take with my present parents, the parents who brought me up and took care of me. Only because of his grace was I able to tell my parents how long I was going to be with them. Many years before I left my home for the final time I told them that I would be leaving my home at that time. He made me realize my give and take with other people as well, and I was able to finish my give and take with them also. It was all the grace of Baba Bishan Das that I was able to know all that.

When a mahatma who had the knowledge of only Two Words could tell so many things and know so much, imagine how much more knowledge one can have if he is on the complete Path. One can imagine how much realization and awareness one can achieve, if one had the knowledge of all Five Words, and one practiced that Path.

Sant Ji during His army service, circa 1940

FOUR

Into the Army

I Volunteer to Join the Army

During the Second World War, Hitler was advancing and his army was not being stopped by anyone. At that time the British were taking people from India into the army, but nobody wanted to join because everybody was being sent to fight against Hitler. People were sure that those who would go to fight Hitler would never come back home, as death would be certain for them. They were taking people by force and making them join the army, but many people were so afraid of going to the war that they preferred to go to prison for twenty years or more rather than fight. They thought that joining the army was like committing suicide.

I met a mahatma who told me that if a man dies in the army, he goes to the heavens. That is why, even though I was not ordered to do so, even though it was not my turn and no one was forcing me, I gladly accepted the offer to go into battle — because I very much wanted to see the heavens. I was the only person in my village at that time who was happy to go into the army. I was very happy in giving my name to the people in charge: I told them I wanted to fight on the battlefield. At that time I was very young, I was not even eighteen years old. When I appeared in front of the commander and other officers they looked me over and were wondering how such a young boy had joined the army. They were very surprised, looking at my courage, and said, "Look at that young boy. He is so young but still he wants to go fight and he is ready to sacrifice himself." At that time I had so much enthusiasm, I was not afraid of death. I was prepared to face any challenge, anything.

Just a month after we joined and when we were about to go to the front they called all of us and we were sent for a medical check-up. The doctor who examined us told us all to take off our shirts so that he could see who was weak and who needed milk. When he asked the commander who should be given the milk and who should not, the commander felt very sorry for all of us and said, weeping, "They are all the goats of sacrifice and they all will be sacrificed. They are all going to die, so it is better if they all can have milk in their last days."

That was such a time when nobody wanted to go into the army because death was sure for everyone. Nevertheless, I was very willing to do. I felt much courage and I think that this was only because of the vegetarian diet on which I was raised right from birth. I was not worried about death because I knew that death would come in whatever way it is destined for you, no matter where you are. I did not feel any fear and I did not have any regrets about joining the army.

Baba Bishan Das Explains the Value of the Heavens

When I again came to Baba Bishan Das and explained to him about joining the army, he asked me, "What is there in the heavens?" He told me clearly that in the heavens, birth and death are there, fighting and enmity and love are there — everything is also there in the heavens.

Baba Bishan Das told me the story of Lord Indra, who is the leading god in the heavens. He told me that just as here on earth we have physical bodies and we have physical pleasures, in the same way, in the heavens we have astral bodies and there are astral pleasures. Where there are pleasures, there is no contentment. There is no happiness or peace in the pleasures, whether they are physical or astral. Wherever there are pleasures, wherever there is a body, there is always suffering.

Where there is the body, the mind is also attached to it, and where there is a mind, there is no peace or contentment. Lord Indra was the king of the heavens and when lust bothered him, he did not get any satisfaction from the astral women who were there in the heavens. He fell for the wife of one *rishi,* who used to do the devotion of God Almighty, and in order to satisfy his lust Lord Indra assumed a human form, came into this world, and raped the rishi's wife, and in that way Lord Indra lost his peace.

Lord Indra was cursed by that rishi, and as a result of that curse he had to go into exile. So if this was the condition of the king of the heavens, what would be the condition of the other people who live in the heavens?

So Baba Bishan Das told this story to me and he concluded by saying that people in this world perform the *yajnas,* the religious ceremonies, and do so many good deeds. They perform the austerities and all the other things in order to get to the heavens. However, what is the condition of the people who are living in the heavens? One does not have any peace or satisfaction indulging physically, and when one goes to the heavens, all the indulgences and pleasures are in the astral form. Those who indulge in the passions in the astral form also do not get any peace or satisfaction. So, what is the use of going to the heavens?

The Valuable Lesson of Obedience

I learned so many things from serving in the army. What a person learns from serving all depends upon his experience and understanding. The most important thing I learned was the habit of obeying the commandments and remaining in the discipline. In the army it is a principle that first you carry out the work that you have been given, first you obey the orders, and later on if you have any doubts or questions you can ask them. When they would give the orders, you were supposed to obey without making any excuses. If they told you to go and cook the food, you could not say that the fireplace is not good, or you do not have any wood or any excuses like that. You were expected to go and do it. So in the army I developed this habit of obeying, because if you would make excuses, the officer would get upset at you and he would say, "First go and do it, then come and give me the report." Many times when people would not obey, they would be punished. So when I was in the army, I obeyed the orders of my officers wholeheartedly and they became very pleased with me. Just by obeying their commandments I earned a lot of their pleasure.

It is the same in *Sant Mat*, the Path of the Masters; first obey the commandment and remain in the discipline. What is the meaning of remaining in the discipline? In *Satsang* and at the time of Initiation many instructions are given, and to remain within the limits of those instructions is called remaining in the discipline. In Sant Mat we also have to be brave like a soldier. We attend to our worldly duties and our government duties even if we are having pain. In the same way, we should always be afraid of the *Satguru* and we should obey His commandments.

As I said, this habit of obeying the orders and keeping discipline without making any excuses was the most important thing I learned in the army and it helped me a great deal later in my life when I met my Master. Whatever He told me to do, I lovingly did that and it was only because of this habit that I was able to obey Him.

Learning to Shoot

I learned another valuable lesson in the army when they were teaching us how to shoot our rifles at a target. They taught us that first of all you should keep your body, the gun, and the target all in one line, steady and fixed, and your attention should be on the center of the target. Then you were to look through the two portions of the rifle, the back sight and the front sight, and keep the crosshairs of the two sights in one line and it should be in line with the target. You should hold your breath, you should not look here or there, and very slowly, very smoothly, you should pull the trigger. Those who shot according to the training, keeping everything in one line and doing it very gently and smoothly, would always become successful. But some people did not keep their body, the gun, and the target in one line, or they would move, or they would not hold their breath. Those who did not do it correctly never became successful.

The same thing also applies in the practice of meditation. When we sit for meditation it is like we are trying to hit the center of the target, but in this case the Eye Center, the area between and above the two eyebrows, is our target. In this meditation we have to keep our body as still as in the army when we are using a rifle. If our body is still, our mind is still, and if we are concentrating correctly at the Eye Center, we can progress a lot after only a few sittings in meditation. If our body is not still, if we do not take up a posture in which we are relaxed and comfortable without any tension in the body, then we have to change our posture again and again, and that will break our attention and we will not be able to hit the target.

Those who used to change their aim at the target again and again would not become successful. This was my personal experience that we had to shoot five bullets, placing them in an area of one inch. I did that only by keeping one target all the time, only by trying to hit the same place again and again. The same thing helped me a lot in Sant Mat, because the Master teaches us, "Dear Ones, if you go on changing your contemplation, if you go on changing the place where you concentrate, you will not become successful. You have to go on looking at the same place if you want to become successful."

Maintaining a Pure Life

In the military there are various types of people. Some of them only know how to use obscene words, drink wine, and go to prostitutes; they are not very spiritual or religious. However, I was never affected by them and I was never worried about them. I remember that in the beginning, in the evening some people used to drink wine and come to my bed, dancing and using very bad words. They would dance on my bed and they wanted me to join them, but I used to sleep with my sheet over my head and I never paid any attention to them. Sometimes they would pull the sheet from my body, but I never allowed them to take it from my eyes. They did that for the first few days and later on, when they came to know that I was not like them, that I was doing my devotion, they didn't disturb me. We were all living in one big barracks, but still after a few days, when they realized that I was doing devotion, they were so impressed that nobody dared drink wine in that barracks. They would go out of the room to drink wine.

If we are sitting doing our *Simran* (remembrance of God) and there are people sitting next to us talking, if we pay attention to their talking and become nasty towards them in our heart, we are not doing the devotion, and we are no better than the people who are talking. They are talking, using their tongue, and we are talking, using our mind. But if we do not pay any attention to them when doing Simran, since God is sitting within them also, after some time they will realize they are making a mistake. If our Simran is strong and constant, and if we are true to our own Self, then no matter how many people are talking in the room, God will make them quiet, and by themselves they will leave the room. If we are strong in our

Simran, then God will find some way to make things easier for us so that we can do more Simran.

If I had told those people who were disturbing me that they should keep quiet or be silent while I did my practices, would they have done that? If I had told them to keep quiet, they would have made more noise and disturbed me even more. Therefore, I did not pay any attention to the disturbance that they were causing. I just kept on doing my work without paying any attention to them, and in that way I was able to avoid them.

Even when I was in the army I was not in the habit of socializing with people. I don't even know how to play cards or games like chess, and I never did that. I did not go to places where crowds might be. I did not go to the marketplaces or into the cities. If I was in need of soap, or any clothing, or anything like that, I would not go to the city and buy it for myself. I would tell my friends to buy it for me. I would just go out, do my work and come back to my barracks. People used to taunt me and laugh at me and say, "Why have you come into this world when you don't know anything about it?"

I never went to see any movie in my whole life. In the military once a week on Sunday they would show us a movie free of charge and people tried to persuade me to see them. Everybody praised the movies, and they would tell me, "It is very good entertainment, and you don't have to pay anything. Why don't you go and see it? It is very beautiful." Even the officers would ask me why I was not going to see the movies. However, when people would ask me this, and try to inspire me to go to the movies, I would inspire them in return to go within and see the inner movie. I would tell them, "Poison, even if it is given out free of charge, will still work. It will have a bad effect. That is why I don't want to see the movies." I would tell them, "I don't want to make the world my own. I don't say that the world is bad, but I don't want to make it my own. All these modern conveniences make men extroverted, and I am trying to become introverted. I know that by watching movies the waves of the world come into the mind more, and the mind gets spread out in the world more. If I watched the movies, then when I sit for meditation, instead of doing the work that I am supposed to do in meditation, I would start seeing all the things that are shown in the movies and I would think about them. If you want to get real peace, if you want to see the real beauty, you should sit at one place and you should try to look within and see what is happening. I know there are many beautiful things in the within. One will get tired enjoying the outer entertainment after two or three hours. However, the inner entertainment is such that one will never get tired of looking there. So I am trying to go in the within; I am trying to see that living movie which is going on in my within. That is why I do not want to see these movies."

People go to the cinemas, and although nothing on the screen is real, they spend so much precious time just sitting watching the movies. They do not pay any attention to the inner things, but waste so much time on the unreal things. How can we have a good effect by seeing the bad movies? It spreads our thoughts more, so how can we concentrate our thoughts? How can we collect our thoughts?

I requested my commanding officer to give me any duty rather than tell me to go see the movies. Therefore, my officer never forced me to go and see them. He used to tell me, "Okay, if you are not interested in this, go and rest." The other people used to go to the movies, but I always sat and repeated the names "Hai Ram, Hai Gobind."

Although I did not have Initiation into Shabd Naam when I was in the army, still I was not very much in the outer world. Whenever I would close my eyes in meditation and look in the within, I would see many beautiful things over there. When one's inner experience is full of all these beautiful things, if one goes within even a little bit and sees even a glimpse of what is within, then one would not go to see any outward movies. What to talk about going to see any movie, one would not even go into the cinema house to use its toilet, because the inner thing is so beautiful.

While I had these beautiful inner experiences, still I didn't know where to go and where not to go in the inner worlds. I came to know that the within is full of many fantastic things, but its key was with the perfect Master. Unless I met some perfect Satguru, I would not be able to know where to go and where not to go.

So, when one joins the army, of course the people already there want to increase the number of people who share their way of thinking. The people who ate meat were always praising eating meat. The drunkards were always telling me the advantages of drinking wine. However, if one was strong and did not want to eat meat or drink wine, nobody forced him to do that. It was my personal experience that where there is a will there is a way. I found that avoiding those things was not too difficult.

Serving the Officers

In the army, in order to please our officers, we would sometimes have to stand outside the house where the officers went to drink wine. They would enjoy while we waited outside, because we were in their service and we did not know at what time they would call us and ask for something. At these times I felt very sorry for myself because right from my childhood I had been desirous of realizing God. I repented within myself that if I had spent that precious night in the remembrance of God I would have gotten something, but just to please the worldly officers I had to stay awake all night. After the night passed and when in the early morning the time for devotion came, the devoted people would start doing their devotion and chanting in the gurdwara. Even after staying awake the whole night I would go and join them. However, the others would go to sleep and they would abuse the people of the gurdwara for doing all the chanting. When the time of devotion would come they would go to their beds, abusing the devotees.

Mahatma Charan Das has said, "What is the use of staying awake for filling up the hookah? What is the use of staying awake for other people? What is the use even of staying awake to enjoy with the women? If you are doing that and you are not staying awake for your own Self, for doing meditation and the devotion of God, you cannot cross the ocean of life."

The Man Dancing Dressed as a Woman

When I was eighteen some people came to entertain the soldiers at Lahore. That was the first chance I had had to see dancing and I was curious to see what it was like. Among those people was a man who was wearing the clothes of a woman, and he was dancing in front of all the men and making people happy. In those days it was very difficult for a woman to come and dance among the men. After the dance was over everybody gave that person one rupee. I also thought, "She is very brave and I should also give her something," because the other people were giving. But when I asked one man, "How is it that she is so brave that she is dancing here among the men?" The people laughed at me and said, "Oh no, she is not a woman. It is a man and he is just wearing the clothes of a woman and is dancing here to collect money. It is not a girl."

I was very surprised, and I was very pleased, because I had learned a very great lesson from him. I thought, "This man has changed his clothes and has become a woman only for the sake of money." In this world, what will people not do for the sake of money! This man, in order to get one rupee, sacrificed his own being: he became ready to change his sex. I compared that with our search for God. What is the value of God? God is such that there is no other thing in this world as valuable as He is and in order to realize Him we need to sacrifice a lot. We should be willing to change ourselves and sacrifice everything to realize God.

I was so pleased with that man, because I learned a lesson from him, that I gave him ten rupees instead of one. I thanked him because he had taught me that lesson.

Missing the Train

Once I came home on two days leave with four friends who also lived in the same area. We all had to go back on the same train that came to the station of our village at exactly twelve noon. However, we didn't leave our homes until one-thirty, and by the time we got to the station the train had already left. As a result we got back late to our unit. When we got there late we were told that we would be questioned because we had not come back on time.

The next day we were summoned by the officer and he asked all of us, "Why were you late? Why didn't you inform us? Why didn't you send a cable?" This was the first time we had made a mistake and usually for the first mistake the soldiers are forgiven and just given a warning, so we were not very worried. Still, when the officer started questioning us, we became very confused and did not know what to do. He started asking each one of us why we did not come on time. All the other four friends said that the train was delayed, but when that officer came to me I felt that I should tell him the truth. I told him, "Dear Sir, the train did come on time but we left our home late. That is why we missed the train. Now it is up to you; whatever punishment you want to give us you can give us." Because I had told him the truth and I had surrendered to him he became very pleased and he forgave us.

At that time I learned this lesson: that if we had left our home at eleven o'clock, an hour earlier than the train, we would have gotten to our duty on time and nobody would have questioned us. Nobody would be scared of any punishment and there would be no reason for us to be confused and perturbed and there would be no reason for anyone to speak a lie. It was only because we wanted to rest one more hour in our homes that we had to go through all this difficulty. And then I thought, "As we were afraid of that officer and we were confused and the other people were not even able to speak the truth, are we ever afraid of our Master like this? Do we ever take our meditation so seriously?" What about those people who don't do their meditation or remember the Simran? When the Master summons them and asks them questions, what will they say? Will they be strong enough to tell Him the truth? We don't care for the Master as much as we care for a worldly officer.

Keeping the Schedule

Another thing I learned in the military was the benefit of keeping a schedule. All the things of government happen on an exact schedule; the trains move on time and the flights operate on time. If they do not maintain those schedules and they are not timely that causes problems for many people.

Many times people take this very lightly and we do not take the time seriously. I came to understand that God has given us this measure — time. God has made a schedule for the seasons to happen and He has made a schedule for the suns, moons and stars. You see how the sun always rises at the exact time and the moon also rises at the exact time. Because the schedule of God is perfect and every natural thing is happening according to a perfect schedule, God made the people of this world understand how they have to make the schedules. God has also made a perfect schedule of how much time we have to live in this world and how many breaths we have to take, and there will be no addition or subtraction to that. Whatever schedule God has made He will stick to that and that is why we should learn to appreciate the time. We should never miss our schedule and we should always make the best use of our time, because God has given us a limited time in this world and we must do our work in that limited time. So, I came to understand we should definitely make a schedule for our day-to-day life and we should not miss any part of the schedule that we have made. If one makes a habit of doing everything on time, on a schedule, and remaining in the discipline, then one can make a schedule of one's day-to-day life in which one can go to bed on time, one can get up and go to work on time and one can meditate on time. If one follows that schedule strictly then not only in one's spiritual life but also in one's worldly life one can become successful and in that way we may easily progress to God.

My Work as a Signal Man

In the beginning I used to do the work of a signalman. Before the wireless (radio) systems came into existence the army used to send signals using sunlight by flashing with mirrors or at nighttime through the use of the light of a lamp. In both cases the lights were coming straight into the eyes. We had to fix our gaze constantly without averting our gaze even for a minute, and sometimes the message lasted for twenty or thirty minutes. If we blinked our eyes even once we could miss a lot of the message.

During the day the signals were very radiant and bright but when I used to do the work of the signaler my eyes were so good that I could tolerate the radiance of the sunlight and could read the signals very well. Most people's eyes would start to water when they would read those signals and many people wore sunglasses when doing that but I didn't need to. Similarly at night my eyes would not water and I would receive those signals very clearly.

Later I was trained to become a wireless operator and was sent to school to take the course on that. There was a lot of reading and writing involved in that, but every night I would go to bed only after finishing the work that I was given to do. I never would think that I would do the work later. Whatever work was given to me by my teachers I would finish that and only then would I go to bed. So studying hard in this way, I passed many difficult tests on this subject in the army, even the test which they gave in the place called Poona, which was the most difficult test at that time. The instructors we had there were very strict. They would say, "Either you come to the school after studying your lesson, or you should be prepared to leave this place. If you do not do well then we will mark an 'F' on your examination and we'll send you back from here." They would also say, "We don't believe in those gods and goddesses to whom you have prayed before coming here. We only believe in the hard work which you have done in preparing yourself for the examination."

Even though that examination was very tough I was never afraid or worried whether I would pass the examination or not; I would just do my job. Since I was confident and I had worked hard, I knew that whatever question I had answered was correct and that I would definitely pass the examination. After writing my answers in the examinations, I would write next to the questions "R" which means "Right." When I took that examination my teacher was also there. He was just taking a walk around the exam room and when he saw that I was doing my paper well and that all my answers were right, he was happy. When it was announced by the English officer that I had secured the full score and that they were going to give me a salary of two levels higher as a bonus, my teacher became very happy and he lifted me up and expressed his happiness. The English officer said, "Even though this person was so confident about his answers that he wrote 'R' — which he did not have the right to do — still I am very happy that he has secured the full score."

If a wrestler goes into the ring thinking that he is going to be defeated, he will definitely be defeated. If a wrestler goes there with confidence that he will defeat the other person, only then can he defeat him. This attitude of confidence is also important for the disciple. The disciple should never lose his confidence. He should always have faith and love in the Master and confidence in his own self that he will definitely pass the test and become successful in his struggle.

Later on I had to work as a radio operator in the war. I found that in the war the enemy also has radio operators, whose job it is to create disturbances in the radio messages between the people of the other country. If two people on one side were communicating, there would be an enemy soldier with a set whose work would be to cause a disturbance so that the first two cannot communicate well. But radio operators know that this disturbance is from the enemy, so they change the frequency of their set and pay no attention to the disturbance. In this way they can go on communicating with each other.

Sometimes in the war the radio operators of the enemy will also speak friendly words and will try to talk with the people of the other side. They will ask, "What is happening? What do you need?" In that way they will try to find out the situation on the other side. If the operator on this side is not wise and doesn't recognize the voice as that of an enemy, then his side will suffer defeat because he will tell where they are marching and things like that. When the enemy side learns those things they can attack.

I found that the efforts of the enemy radio operators were very much like the efforts of the mind. The mind's work is always to cause disturbance. He doesn't have to take any message and he doesn't have to give any message; his work is just to cause a disturbance when we are communicating with God. When the mind is causing disturbance he will also often come as a friend, using very sweet words, and tell us, "do this" or "do that" or "get up from meditation." We feel that he is our friend and we do not even think that what he is telling us to do will lead to a negative thing.

But the wise meditator pays no attention to the disturbance the mind is causing but always keeps himself in the Simran. The wise meditator, like the wise radio operator, knows how to differentiate between friends and enemies. He is able to recognize whether the thought is coming from the Master or from the mind.

The Religion of the Teacher Doesn't Matter

In the schools the teachers are from different religions. There are Christians, there are Sikhs, and there are Hindus. They may be from different countries, but when we are going to the school to learn something, we never have any objection about the religion they belong to. This is because we go to the school only to get the knowledge from them; we don't go there to make any relationship with the teachers.

When I was at the signal operator's school in Poona, we had some teachers who were Christian. My teacher was Lali Khan, a Muslim, and there were some Hindu teachers also. Nobody minded that and even now I have great respect and appreciation for those teachers in my heart.

In the same way, in the Path of Spirituality, all the Saints have said that one doesn't have to look at the caste, creed, or religion of the Saint. One should not even pay attention to which country He belongs, for we are going to Him only to get the knowledge of Spirituality. Just as we get the worldly knowledge from the teachers regardless of their religion, in the same way, we get the knowledge of Spirituality from the Saints regardless of Their religion. Kabir Sahib has said, "Don't ask about the caste of the Master; ask for the knowledge He has. Value the sword; don't pay attention to the case." The body is the case and the Power of Spirituality, the Naam manifested within the body of that Mahatma is the sword; we have to obtain that from Him.

Doing the Work that the Teacher Gives Us

If, as students, we wholeheartedly study what we are being taught, and if we make our life pure, that will help us very much in our future. We can get the qualities of our teachers if we respect and obey them, because if a student is obeying and respecting his teacher, the teacher gives that student much of his attention; he helps him and he loves him very much. Whatever the teachers are teaching us, that is for our own good. We are studying for making our own success; we are not doing any favor to our teachers. So if our teachers start telling us to do anything, we should do one extra thing for them. If they are telling us to solve one question, we should solve one more question, because whatever we are doing, that is for our own good. We should always respect our teachers and obey whatever they tell us to do.

When I was in the army, I had many teachers who were teaching me the job of wireless operator. The job of a wireless operator is complicated because it involves many things and I would never have been able to do that job if not for my teachers. I always respected my teachers. That is why they gave me a lot of extra attention and in that way they made me an excellent signaler. Even in their private time they would teach me about that job. If we have respect for the one who gives us any good qualities or good teachings, we are honored in this world.

In my childhood in India there were not very good arrangements for school and education, but regardless, three of us in my village were sent to school. One was the son of a weaver and two of us were farmers' sons. When we went to school, our teacher gave us some lessons to learn and then he went away for some other work. Two of us started learning that lesson, and we both learned that lesson by heart. However the third boy, the son of the weaver, did not want to study, so instead of learning that lesson he went and sat on the wall of the school, and enjoyed the cool breeze that was blowing there.

When the teacher came back, he asked the two of us who had

been studying whether we had learned our lesson or not. We both had learned that, so he was very much pleased with us. He saw that the weaver's son was sitting on the wall, so he asked him, "Have you learned your lesson? Why are you sitting on the wall? Why aren't you studying?" The boy replied, "Well, why do you bother? I was enjoying the cool breeze while sitting here. If I want to learn the lesson, I will learn it by my own self. Why are you worried about me?" The teacher got upset and he said, "Well, come here and catch hold of your ears," which in India is a sign of repentance. However, when the teacher told him that, instead of catching his own ears he came to the teacher and caught the ears of the teacher. So that poor teacher became even more upset and he slapped him, because in those days in India the children were given a very good beating if they did not obey the teacher. That boy became upset and at last the teacher told him to leave the school and in that way he was thrown out of the school. He left the school right then and after that he never came back to the school.

After I went into the army, when I used to come back home from the army, that boy, who was grown up by then, would come to me and ask for clothes because he was living a very poor life. He would ask for clothes and he would claim to be our classmate. Even though he had only been to school with us for one day, still he would say that he was our classmate. If he had also studied like we did, he would also have made his life good. He would have made his life good and he would have lived comfortably, but he did not go to school and that is why he didn't make his life. He worked all his life as a laborer and he suffered a lot. Later on in his life he realized that by not obeying the teacher he had not gained anything and he repented that he hadn't obeyed his teacher. Finally he died like that, still in a difficult condition, without living a decent life.

So, whatever work one is given, whether we are studying in school or studying Spirituality from the Master, it is much better to do the work which the teacher or Master has asked us to do while the teacher is still in front of us. If the student finishes the job that he has been given by the teacher, right in front of the teacher, will it not be better? It is possible that he may have some difficulty in doing that work, and if he is doing it in front of the teacher, the teacher can help him also.

In the same way, when the Angel of Death comes to the soul, will He give her more time? Will He say, "Okay, you go and complete the things you want to do, and then I will come and take you?" He will not give us any more time, and that is why whatever work we are supposed to do, we should do it right away. So, with love, we should study wholeheartedly. We should respect our teachers, because whatever they are teaching us is for our own good. If we obey them, it will make our future bright.

A Brush with Death

One time we were at a camp in the city of Sangroor and we were getting training in how to use guns. When we were using the rifles we found that one of them was not working, so we put that gun aside and we used another. At the end of the day all the guns and all the bullets were counted. In the army people were very strict about counting all the arms and ammunition, but nobody paid any attention to the round that had not fired.

After we were done with the shooting practice we would stand in a line, while the major would go to the higher officer and say that everything was fine. Only after that would we be released. We were three signalers and we all were standing in a row, and another person was told to get that gun which had not fired and stand behind me. As soon as he came there with the gun, as he laid that gun on the ground, suddenly it fired without anyone pulling the trigger or doing anything to shoot it. When that bullet was shot from that gun, first of all it went between my legs, because we were standing in the standard "at-ease" position. That bullet burned my underwear, then it went through the space between the arm and body of the person standing in front of me, and finally the bullet struck the head of the person third in line in front of me, and he died on the spot.

In the army people are very strict about counting the guns and ammunition. However, because the Negative Power has determined the time and cause of death for every individual, when that time approached all the wisdom and planning just didn't work, because that death was supposed to happen. There is no way one can put off or avoid one's death, because it is all predetermined and it has to happen.

When they counted all the bullets, they should have found that one bullet was unfired in that defective gun and they should have taken that bullet out of that gun, but they didn't do that. When that man came and stood behind me and that bullet shot out from the gun, I should have died first, since I was standing right in front of that gun, but I didn't die. After I had escaped, the second person in line, who was standing right in front of me, should have died. He also did not die because it was not written in his fate to die in that way. However the person who never expected the bullet died on the spot.

In whatever way you have to die, that is written in your fate. No matter if one tries to run from that situation and avoid those circumstances, still one will die in that way, because it is all predetermined.

Winning the Race

In the border area in the city named Nowshera, there was a cantonment and once they had a sports meet there. Sportsmen from all the different battalions of the army were invited to take part. Our battalion was invited and a battalion of Pathans also came from across the border. The Pathans were very tall and sturdy and healthy-looking. They were also very well known for their athletic abilities.

In my regiment I was the person who always defeated everyone in running. I was fond of running and when I was running I used to feel as if I had springs in my body, as if I were jumping. At that time I used to do the simran of "Hai Ram, Hai Gobind" and whenever I was running I was doing my simran also. I would not even know whether I was running or just riding on my simran. So whenever I would run, I never allowed any of my competitors to finish ahead of me. I always used to be the first one to finish the race, so many people knew about me. One Pathan who was a well-known champion in his battalion came there also. Somebody told him that there was one boy named Ajaib Singh who was very good at running, who would be running that day also, and that maybe I would defeat him. That Pathan was proud of his running so he came to me and asked if I was Ajaib Singh. I replied that I was. Looking at my skinny body, he was surprised. He asked how much meat I ate and I replied that I had never eaten meat. So he laughed at me and said, "After the race starts, I will carry you in my arms and I will run like that. I won't even give you a chance to run with me." I told him, "Okay, time will tell who will carry whom. I am not that proud of my self, but I can say that if God is willing, I will just leave you right where you are standing. I will just run away." They made a joke of us vegetarians. They used to say, "The vegetarians eat the cereals with the cereals, they do not eat any flesh and that is why they will never get a sturdy body." The Pathans boasted, "A vegetarian can never defeat us because our flesh is made of flesh," but I was very sure of myself also.

We had to run for one mile; there were four rounds of 440 yards each. I used to run normally for the first three rounds but in the last round I would run very fast. Even if a mare was chasing me, she could not catch me because I used to run so fast in the last stretch. So for the first three rounds when that man was ahead of me, the people of his battalion were encouraging him to keep ahead of me. When they saw that I was in the back, they started teasing me, saying, "You were saying that you will defeat him, but now you are way back!" The other Pathan soldiers were praising their man who was running with me, and he said, "Okay, don't worry. I am ahead of him and I will definitely win this race." When I came near the people of my battalion, they asked, "Why are you so far back? Just go ahead and win this," and they were encouraging me. However, my colonel knew how I used to run the races, so he said, "Whatever you are doing, that is fine."

Hearing the encouragement of the people of my battalion, I got so much enthusiasm in me that I started running very fast when the last round came. I passed that Pathan and when he saw me running he thought that it was as if some bullet had been shot out of a gun. He became so disappointed that he forgot that he was running and he just stood there and his friends also stopped cheering him when I passed him and came in first. What I had said earlier, that I would leave him standing right there, that came true. In the beginning he was running ahead of everybody, but when the race ended, he was the last one to finish.

Those people used to laugh at me because I was a vegetarian, but when the time came for competition, then they came to know how much energy I got from the vegetarian food. They were very tall and sturdy looking, and when that man was standing next to me I looked one-fourth his size, but nobody noticed that when I passed and defeated him.

In the army the meat-eaters always praised the eating of meat. They would tell me that much strength was obtained from doing that. So whenever they said that, I would tell them, "If you are proud of your strength, come and run with me." Nobody could beat me. I was very good at running and won many prizes in running competitions. This is just an excuse of the mind, that by eating meat we get strength. Now that God has blessed us with so many vegetarian foods, there is no need for anyone to eat meat.

In the same way, those who drink encourage others to drink wine. In 1942, I went to England to participate in some games and we had to go by ship. Some people said that when you go by ship and you go up on the upper deck to do the physical training exercises and see only water all around you, you would feel like you are losing your heart and at that time you need to drink wine. However, when we went on that journey I did not have to drink wine. I did not lose heart and I was very strong. I was much stronger than the people who used to drink wine. In fact, those who are vegetarians and who don't drink wine are stronger than those who are not vegetarian and who do drink wine. Even the animals that are vegetarians have more stamina to fight and can fight longer than the animals that eat meat. You know the tiger eats meat but he does not have much energy to go on fighting for a long time. But the elephant that is vegetarian can fight for a very long time.

Throughout my youth, and throughout my life, up until sixty years of age, I always enjoyed good health. I never used any vitamins and I never went to any doctor. I did those things that are necessary for maintaining good health. I always felt like there was some kind of spring in my body and I was always inspired to go running.

The Wrestlers in the Ring

In the army once they had a wrestling match. There were two people wrestling and one of them ended up on top. The other person who was underneath started saying, "Let me get on top and then I will show you!" At that time the person who was on top, even though he was a strong young man of 21 or 22 years old and even though he had already almost won the match, started getting very worried. He began to worry, "What will happen if this guy will get on top of me?" So our commander said, "Why are you worried? Just don't let him get on top and you have won the wrestling match."

Our officer used to say, "We should not let them come and dominate us. They will bother us only when we let them bother us." So from this I learned a very important lesson. I found that we should have confidence, because a coward can never achieve any success. Only a strong-hearted person can achieve success. In the way of Spirituality also, a coward cannot achieve success. One has to have a heart made of iron; one has to be a strong-hearted person. One should have faith in the Master and one should have confidence in himself that he will easily go and fight and defeat all the forces that are in the way.

Whatever I experienced in the army, the stories and incidents of army life, I found that they are in accordance with the teachings of Sant Mat. If a general asks, "Why does my opponent have so many forces? Why do they have so many weapons and armor? How am I going to fight them and defeat them?" If he asks all these questions, he can never win the battle. Instead of asking all those questions, he should have confidence. He should know about his army, the route he has to take and the difficulties in the way and he should be confident in his army. He should have the determination to fight and win the battle, and only then can he do that.

Regularity in the Devotion

In my army days, I still used to perform the rites and rituals of the Sikh religion. I had a miniature folding gurdwara constructed especially for me and I always kept it with me, even when I was in the battlefield. Whether I would travel in a train or in a truck, when I had to go to the battlefront, or even when I crossed the sea on a ship, I always used to do the rites and rituals at the fixed time. Whenever the time for these practices would come, I would know by myself that the time had come. Just as an addict does not find any peace if he does not take his drug, in the same way, one who is regular in his practices will not find any peace unless he has done his practices.

I have seen the Muslim people doing their *Namaz*, offering their prayers, even in the moving trains. Many times I have seen them offering their prayers in the airplanes also. Even at the place where the bombs were dropping, the Muslim people, at their scheduled time, would offer their prayers and do their Namaz.

So, I found that if one does his meditation regularly, if one has made a routine of meditating every day, one will find it very easy to sit, and when doing the devotion one will not even remain aware of how the time passes.

My Experiences in Combat

During my military service, I had many experiences. I flew in airplanes many times and even jumped out of airplanes using parachutes. During the Second World War, I got the opportunities to go to many European countries. London, as you see it now, was not like that during the war. It was ruined by all the bombardments. In the same way, Paris is not as you see Paris today. I went to Italy, to Java, to Burma and many other places during the war.

During that war, I had many opportunities to witness death. I saw many British, Muslims, Sikhs, and many great officers, generals and colonels, who used to control a large number of soldiers, I saw them killed by the bombs. I got the opportunity to do their final rites — to take care of their cremation or their burial.

Once I was carrying a wireless set and a bullet went through my wireless set. Although it went through the set, still our communications did not break. I was near the bombs and other dangerous events. We say that we are not the ones who are going to die, that it is someone else who is going to die. Mahatmas tell us that this life is not going to be here forever; it is very short. Furthermore, nothing of this world — no family, no power, no wealth, no knowledge, no skill of this world — will go with us. We are born with a closed fist but when we leave this world we go with our fists stretched open. We do not realize that all the wealth that our forefathers possessed did not go with them, but we think that we will be able to take all those things with us. We are very attached to all these things and we always go on counting how much we have.

All this is egoism. Unless we withdraw our mind from all these things we cannot go within, because all the Masters have said that the inner path is very small: it is much smaller than the size of a hair. In order to go within we need to become very small, but because of all these things that we count as our very own, our mind has become as big as an elephant, and that is why we cannot go inside.

During the war I saw how many people were being killed. I saw how Hitler was so full of egoism because he was defeating and killing everyone. He was so determined to take over the whole world that whenever he would decide to have a cup of tea at a certain place he would advance to that place and he would fulfill his desire of having tea at that place. All that was nothing but egoism. Do you think God will open His door to such people who are so filled with egoism? Do you think that Hitler would ever have thought, at that time, that he would even make his own country the slave of other countries?

If you have a human heart and if you witness that this is how death comes, that this is what happens, will you not get the encouragement to become small and humble? The experiences that I had in the army were an inspiration to become small and humble.

FIVE

Further Experiences in the Army:
Baba Bishan Das Makes the Foundation of My Life

"Hai Ram, Hai Gobind"

While in the army, I was still repeating the mantra, "Hai Ram, Hai Gobind," so much so that the repetition had become automatic. While on parade duty we were supposed to be saying, "Left, right; left, right" as we marched, but this mantra had become so much a part of me that I would say, "Hai Ram, Hai Gobind" instead. One time a Punjabi-speaking native officer heard me and became very displeased with me for doing that. He singled me out and made me repeat the mantra in front of everyone, which I did, repeating "Hai Ram, Hai Gobind" exactly as before. However, a British officer of higher rank was also present. He interceded on my behalf and then excused me from parade duty. From that time on I had a great deal of freedom to pursue my spiritual practices. That officer became very friendly with me and told me that even though I was younger than he, he felt like I was a father to him.

Baba Bishan Das Teaches Me About Sleep

Whenever I would tell Baba Bishan Das that it was hard to get up in the morning to do the meditation and that I had to struggle very hard, he would tell me a long story about what had happened in India. In the early days when the Mogul emperors came from outside and invaded India many times, they were not lazy and they were always prepared to fight with their enemies. In those days the natives of India were lazy and were not equipped with arms and weapons, so they were not able to fight back and eventually the Mogul emperors conquered all of India and set up their own empire. But later on, when the Moguls had no enemy to fight, they became lazy and started torturing the Hindus and the other people in the country. They tortured devotees, demolished their temples, and forced their religion on the Hindu people. They were very hard on those who did not accept their form of devotion and their religion. They became fond of enjoying the worldly pleasures. They even used to kidnap the daughters of the Hindus and in that way they used to torture them. All these things happened only because they became lazy and fond of worldly pleasures.

When Guru Gobind Singh came, He could not bear to see this torture. He formed an army and told His soldiers to stay awake all night long. He told His people that they should get up at three o'clock and do the meditation of Naam, but along with that they should always remain alert to fight the enemy. Because the torture of the Mogul emperors was too much to bear, Guru Gobind Singh fought with them, and He shook the roots of the Mogul empire. After Him, no Mogul emperor was able to establish his empire in India; either they were killed or they lost their empire. What was the trick behind that? The alertness of the army of Guru Gobind Singh was the only reason for the defeat of the Moguls. The Mogul army would go on fighting all day long, but in the night they would sleep and enjoy.

Baba Bishan Das told me that the fact that the Mogul army was lazy and did not remain alert was the only reason for the downfall of the Mogul empire. The Sikh people were able to defeat them only because they were getting up at three o'clock and they were not at all lazy or fond of the worldly pleasures.

One can become successful in any work, worldly or spiritual, only if one is alert and one stays awake at night and spends the nights in devotion or work. One cannot become successful in any work, spiritual or worldly, if one does not sacrifice one's nights and one's sleep.

Once I came from the army to visit Baba Bishan Das. When I came to see him, my mind played a trick on me. Baba Bishan Das used to wake me up at one o'clock because he used to get up then to meditate, so whenever he got up he would wake me. One day my mind made me think, "What is the use of coming here to the ashram of the Master if you still have to get up at one o'clock to meditate?" I was thinking of the ashram as a resort for me because I was spending my holidays and my leave there. So when Baba Bishan Das woke me up at one o'clock I said, "Master, why do I have to get up when you are already up and you are sitting for meditation?" At once Baba Bishan Das knew that this was a trick of the mind, that I was being fooled by the mind. He said, "Well, if you don't want to meditate, don't, but at least get up and come here. I want to tell you something; come with me." I didn't know what Baba Bishan Das had in his mind, what he was going to do to me.

Near the dera there was a pond and the water was very cold as this was in the month of December and it was one o'clock in the morning. He started talking with me and suddenly he took me near the pond. He held my hand and was just about to push me into the pond, but I said, "Well, Master, if you want me to go there, I will, but let me take off my clothes." He said, "No, because I know that if I give you that much time, your mind will fool you again and you will run away." So he pushed me into the pond, and when I came out my condition was like that of a mouse which has been thrown into water; when it comes out it is shivering with the cold.

That was the last day when I thought about sleeping later than one o'clock. After that I never in my whole life slept after one o'clock. That is why I always say, "It is not in my heritage to sleep in the early hours of the morning." What Baba Bishan Das did was the best thing for me. That was his way to teach me that we should never obey our mind. Mind is always with us and it is our enemy. If we obey our mind once, if we postpone our meditation once, in obedience to our mind, then the next day he will play the same trick as he is still within us. So in the morning the mind says, "Sleep now, tonight you have plenty of time and you will meditate later on; sleep now." Later he will advise you to meditate tomorrow and in that way he will never let you meditate.

On this subject Baba Bishan Das also used to tell another very short story from the Sikh history. He used to say, "Once Guru Nanak Sahib met with Laziness. Laziness was sewing a small blanket that had many holes in it. So Guru Nanak asked, 'Who are you, and what are you doing?' He replied, 'I am Laziness and every morning I put this blanket on people so they won't get up and do the devotion of God. However, it is a pity that those people who get Initiation from You, they tear my blanket and make so many holes. I have to sew this blanket every day, because they don't accept me and they throw my blanket away.' "

The Diamond Light of Chastity

Baba Bishan Das would talk about the light within, and at that time I was seeing light — like a diamond light — in my brain. I was intoxicated with that light and I was very happy to see that light because I thought that I was seeing the same light that he was talking about. I had read in all the books about the Light and Sound, and I always thought that this light was the same Light that I was reading about. I had read what Guru Nanak has written: that seeing the Inner Light and hearing the Inner Sound means that you are in contact with God. So I thought that I had contacted that Light, but I was waiting for connection with the Inner Sound Current.

When I went to Baba Bishan Das and told him about seeing that light he told me, "Dear Son, you are in an illusion. This is an illusion created by the Negative Power, and the light that you are seeing is of the lower *chakras*. When you sit for meditation, the light you see is the light of your own body, of the *ojas,* the power from continence. It is not the True Light, the Light that is coming from the Home of God. That Light is different." He explained that light was of the brain, and was present because of chastity, because of the storage of the semen, the vital fluid. It is said it takes one hundred pieces of food to produce one drop of blood, and one hundred drops of blood to produce one drop of vital fluid, and one hundred drops of vital fluid to produce one drop of ojas, and that resides in the brain. If chastity is maintained and all the semen is stored in the body, that gives such light that one feels much bliss and happiness enjoying that light. But Baba Bishan Das explained to me that this light, the light of ojas, is not the True Light, the Light that becomes the means of our liberation.

Baba Bishan Das always emphasized living a chaste life. He never allowed me to eat much and he never allowed me to sleep deeply. He used to put wooden sticks on the bed in a position like a "V", so I would not have deep sleep and lose control over sexual desire. He would tell me that if you look at a body of a man or a woman, you will find that the bodies are not more than dirt, because dirt is coming out from the eyes, from the nose, from the mouth and from all parts of the body. He gave me this instruction and he gave me this boon that I did not find any attraction in looking at the body of a woman because I understood that the physical woman is just a bag of dirt.

Up until that time, and in fact through my entire life, I have never known *kam,* sexual desire, even in the dreams and never lost the vital fluid. If I had experienced kam, sexual desire, even once, I would have married, but this thing never entered my mind. Since my childhood my only desire has been for the knowledge of God.

Those who have maintained their body right from childhood, those who have preserved their vital fluid from their very beginning, naturally they have light within them. For such people it is very easy to get the Light of Naam. It is just like bringing a flame in contact with gas or petrol; it explodes. Similarly when such people who have kept themselves pure are given Initiation, they go right up.

A Great Incident in My Life

When I was twenty years old, one great incident of my life happened. I came across one woman who was older than I was and she wanted to make me enjoy lust with her, but I didn't want to do that. She even offered me a great amount of wealth, but I was very strong at that time. I told her, "No, I won't do this bad thing. You should be ashamed to ask such a thing from me because you are much older than me. I am like your son and you are like my mother and you should not insist on me doing that." However, she said, "I love you and that is why I am telling you to do this." I told her, "If you love me, you can love me considering me as your son, so you should not think like that." So I did not do that thing, and as it happened, thirty years later that same lady realized her mistake and she came to me and asked for forgiveness.

I was able to do this only because of Baba Bishan Das. When I met Baba Bishan Das, he held his beard in his hands and he told me, "Respect my beard and just for my sake, please be ashamed if any bad thing comes across your path and don't do any bad thing." Baba Bishan Das was the man who made my life. He stopped me from the bad things and the bad habits by strictness with love, and for this reason still I have much appreciation and respect for him in my heart.

The Boy with No Self-Control

In the army there was a boy from the Punjab, whose name was Guru Dev Singh, and he had this habit of masturbating. He became very weak. He was not able to function properly, he was not able to run with us and he was not able to do any work because of his weak body. However, he did not stop doing this bad habit. Once our officer asked, "What is wrong with Guru Dev Singh? Why is he becoming so weak?" Since I knew about his habit, I told the officer that he had that bad habit, that he was masturbating. So that officer told me to watch him and make sure that he did not do that again. Well, how can one guard someone who is involved in this bad habit? I tried to guard him, but whenever he would go to bed, in his bed he would do that. So I told the officer that I could not guard him because he finds one way or another to masturbate. Gradually he became so weak that he was not able to move properly and the government had to fire him and he lost his job.

Masturbation is a very bad habit and it is very difficult to get rid of it. One should be very careful and never form such a habit. When a man and woman indulge, they may lose a little vital fluid, but if they are masturbating they lose a lot more vital fluid. In addition the veins in which the vital fluid is made and through which it flows out, they are also damaged if people are masturbating. This habit also eventually leads to many diseases in old age. It is like throwing the vital fluid in the fire, and the vital fluid is considered the main element in the creation of this world. That is why in the *Shastras,* one of the Hindu scriptures, it is written that those who masturbate, those who waste their vital fluid with their hands or by artificial means, are doing a great sin.

Everyone should abstain from lust, but the Saints say that it is worse to masturbate.

Kabir Sahib said, "Listen, O men and women, to the true words of the Master. In this world there are many poisonous fruits. Don't taste them. Don't say, 'Let us taste it once and then we will not eat it.' Don't do it, because once you taste this poisonous fruit, once you get the bad smell of this unchaste deed in your brain, it will bother you over and over again, and you will never be able to get rid of it." If you put more wood on a burning fire, the flame will increase. It will never be extinguished; you can never satisfy the fire. In the same way, obeying your mind, if you will indulge more, your mind will not get any satisfaction. He will ask for more and more and the desire will become more and more, and it will create a lot of heat in your body. Following that, every now and then your mind will make you indulge again. He is like a competent lawyer sitting within you, and he may tell you, "Well, do it now and don't do it later on." However, later on he will make you do the same thing. Whenever he gets the opportunity, whether it is in the morning, the afternoon, or at night, he will always make you indulge in this and he will make you his slave.

Just as the men have vital fluid in their bodies, in the same way women also have the vital fluid within them. Women need to preserve the vital fluid as much as men need to. As men experience a loss by losing their vital fluid, in the same way, women also lose the same power. The teachings of Sant Mat are the same for both men and women.

Earlier I told about my experiences running. When I was running I used to feel as if I had springs in my body, as if I were jumping. Anyone who preserves the vital fluid can have the same type of jolliness in their body and they can be very happy to do any type of work. Those who preserve the vital fluid remain happy from their within. The most important element of my life has been the maintenance of chastity and abstaining from lust. We people give much attention to diet and things like that, but the most important thing which we are doing, losing our vital fluid, we don't give any attention to preserving it. In my life I didn't drink much water, I didn't eat much butter, I didn't drink much milk or other nourishing foods, but still whatever work I was doing I never felt tired doing that.

Content in the Will of God

Once while I was in the army, at a wedding, I met a colonel who was my relative, although he did not know me personally. At that time I was only an ordinary soldier, of very low rank. When he recognized that I was his relative he asked me, "Why don't you come to me and I will help you in getting a big post?" I told him no, that was all right. I told him that Guru Nanak said that we should not ask for anything from anybody because whatever is in our fate, our destiny, we are going to get that. Poverty or wealth, sickness or health, happiness or sadness, this is all written in our fate and we have to enjoy that. Therefore, there is no need to complain about all these worldly things. Guru Nanak has also written that we should ask God only that we should be united with Him again. For ages and ages we have been separated from Him. We have been given many forms, and in each body we are always getting and getting from Him but we are not giving anything to Him. Therefore, now we want to give Him something and that is meditation. We should pray only that we should meditate and become One with Him.

On another occasion when I was in the army I suffered some injury and was losing blood. The doctor could not help me, but he knew that I was a disciple of Baba Bishan Das. He told me, "Well, you have a guru, so you can tell the guru to stop the loss of blood. You should go and tell him, and you should pray for this thing." Lovingly I told that doctor that my guru knows everything, but this injury is because of my past karmas and I have to suffer that.

After I was treated and felt better I went to Baba Bishan Das. However, I was still thin and pale, so Baba Bishan Das asked me what had happened. I told him, "You are all-conscious, you know everything about me, so why are you asking me?" Then he asked me, "Have you written some letter, telegrammed or cabled me about your condition?" I replied, "You know everything about me, so why are you asking me?" He wanted to test me like that, but I never complained. I never appealed to him, "I am having this suffering, please help me."

Requesting Leave to See Baba Bishan Das

Once I went to my commanding officer and asked for leave because I wanted to see Baba Bishan Das. He granted me leave but said that when I went to my Master, I should also remember him over there. I said, "No, that would not be the true thing. I don't want to remember you over there. I don't even want to take a message from you to my Master. Because this is a very sacred time for me, over there I only want to remember my Master and God."

A Punishment for Not Playing Cards

Once I had to go from the town of Nabha to Dehra Dun because we were going to be posted over there. I was going in a truck, and as I was the wireless operator, I was going with my signal officer and my second operator, along with our wireless set. On the way, when we were about to reach the town of Saharanpur, something went wrong with the truck and we got stuck there. Suddenly it started raining and the weather got very bad, so it was very difficult to go out and find someone to fix the truck. We had to stay there for about three or four hours, and since it was raining very heavily there was no way out.

That signal officer was very fond of playing cards, and he decided that he wanted to play cards to pass the time. There were only two other people in the truck and I was the fourth one, and while both of the others knew how to play cards, I was not in the habit of doing that. The officer told me, "You come on and join us and play cards with us." I told him, "No, I have not played cards in my life and I don't want to touch them. I don't want to play." So he said, "You just come and sit with us and I will teach you how to play." Without a fourth person they could not have a good game and that is why they were telling me to play with them. However, I told them, "I don't know how to play cards and I don't want to learn to play cards." I said that it is a sin even to learn something that is not good; I understood playing cards was like gambling and I didn't want to get involved in that kind of bad deed.

The officer got upset; he told me to get out of the truck. He told me to stand outside in the open and to stand guard for the whole night, even though it was very cold at that time and I was not supposed to do that work. However, after I got out, he told me to come back in because it was raining so hard outside. But then he told me to still keep on standing while they were playing cards. I preferred to take that punishment of standing for four hours, but I didn't want to spoil myself by learning that game, by learning how to play cards. I preferred to have that punishment.

These bad habits which we do not see as very bad things or as major things, they do affect our thoughts. If we give up all these minor worldly things, these small bad habits, by themselves the thoughts will become pure and we will gain concentration. Then you will not find it difficult to take a courageous step in making your life better.

My life in the army was very pure. Whenever we would get surrounded by the enemy, we did not know when the enemy would go and we would be able to come out. At such times the officers, even though they were older and more experienced than I was, would ask me how long we would have to stay in that position. They were afraid, because they had families and small children. They would ask whether we would survive and would ask me to tell them what was going to happen next. This was only because of the purity of my life that they would ask me those things; they would say that since I did the devotion, I might know what was going to happen next. When you lead a pure life, you can know what is going to happen next; you can know many things.

The Encounter with the Dacoits

During this time I was doing the simran of "Hai Ram, Hai Gobind" and I was doing that constantly. I was convinced that the strength or power that one can get from the devotion of God, one could not get from any food that exists in this world. I realized that heavy people do not have any strength in them. If one keeps one's body light, if one preserves one's body and takes good care of one's body, one will always remain strong. With this strength and this lightness in my body I used to play tricks on people. Many people were afraid to shake hands with me because I used to play a trick on them when they did. Whenever anybody was bringing his hand to shake hands with me, I would put my hand on the back of his neck and jump over him. So people were afraid to shake hands with me. Nevertheless, even though I did these kinds of tricks, I was very fond of spiritual knowledge also.

Once when I was in the army I was travelling by myself on the train. In those days in the Punjab the law was not very well maintained and people would rob train stations and other government places. On that occasion I got down from the train at a train station called Phusmundi, and it was nighttime. The village was two miles from the train station, and I had heard that people were robbed there at nighttime because there were many dacoits in that area. At that time I was absorbed in doing the simran of "Hai Ram, Hai Gobind" and when I got off the train I did not even notice that dacoits were sitting there, drinking wine and waiting for someone to come. When one of them approached me to take my things, I was doing simran and when I saw him I just jumped over him and started running. The dacoit was not expecting such a thing from an ordinary man and when he saw that something had jumped over him he got upset. He thought that maybe some ghost had jumped over him. So he called one of his companions, saying, "Something has jumped over me; I don't know if it was a man or a ghost, and you should catch him!" The dacoits had been planning to rob someone who got off the train, and they had a very well planned out scheme. Some members of their team were stationed ahead of where the first man was, and that first man called out to those others who were ahead of him. However, the next man was also unable to catch me, so they blocked the bridge at the canal. I just swam across the canal and then ran fast until I came to the village. There I saw a fire and there was the hut of a sadhu, so I went there.

The dacoits came searching for me and they also came to the hut of the sadhu. They told the sadhu, "Something jumped over our friend and after that he came in this direction but we don't know where he has gone. We don't even know whether he was a man or a ghost." Then they looked at me and when they saw me they thought that maybe I was the man they had encountered earlier, for my clothes were wet and in very bad condition. However, I was not afraid at all for now I was with that sadhu and they wouldn't do anything to me. Moreover because my clothes were wet, it was easy for them to know that I was the man. So I told them, "Yes, I am that man."

I was doing simran when I jumped over that man and when I was running. That is why I didn't have any fear. I was so absorbed in simran that I didn't feel any fear and only because of the simran I was doing I was able to get rid of that dacoit. Such strength comes through simran that one becomes fearless and can face any danger that comes. If one is chased by some thief or dacoit, because of the fear, one won't feel strong enough to run, but if he is doing simran, he won't feel any fear and he can face any danger. Even though the simran that I had was not given by any perfect Saint, still it had so much strength that I was able to do miraculous things like this. Moreover, if one gets the Simran from a perfect Saint, behind that Simran the charging of the great Saint is working. If you also do that Simran there is nothing in this world that you cannot do. The people do not know how much strength the Simran has. They do not know the value of Simran and they do not know what is the reality of Simran.

The English Magician and the Power of Constant Repetition

Our colonel was very interested in the various yoga practices and in Spirituality. In India at that time many sadhus would dig a hole in the ground, would sit in it and then would have the people cover it up while they were still in it. They would remain in the ground for a certain amount of time, such as one week or one month. At the end of that time the people would open up that underground area and the sadhus would come out still alive. Because our colonel was very interested in such things, once a Westerner came to our regiment and he showed us this. He dug out a ditch in the ground and after that he cemented it, he sat in it and then had it covered up. After one week it was uncovered and he came out alive. However, he told us that this was his job. He was not doing that for the sake of meeting God, it was only to earn his livelihood.

On another occasion a retired English Army major came and he was a magician. Before coming to our group he had performed many shows in front of other troops. People were very impressed, and said he could even put life into a dead bird. When he came he said, "Okay, I will show you a very great thing." He held a bird in his hand and invited someone to come and cut off its head. Someone did that. People saw the blood dropping down on the earth and that the bird was dead. After some time, he just joined the two different parts of the body of the bird and he made that bird fly. Everyone was very impressed. Then he said, "Okay, you bring some sawdust and I will turn that into sugar. I will make tea with that sugar in it and give it to you." There were many high officers there who wanted to see this trick also. Some sawdust was brought, he turned that into sugar. Tea was made and the officers were given that tea to drink. When they took the first sip, he asked them, "Is it sweet?" They replied, "Yes, it's like regular tea." But then, when they took a second sip, they found that there was no sugar there — it was all sawdust!

He showed many tricks and afterwards he showed us a flute and said, "I do all these things only because of my flute. All my power is in this flute." He wanted to play that flute, but at that time I also had some concentration of mind, and I had a habit of just harassing such people, so when he started playing his flute, I used my concentration and he was not able to play. He was very surprised, because nobody up until then had done that. No matter how he tried, he was not able to play the flute, and he was not able to do the rest of his show either. So he was worried and he said to my commander, "There is somebody in your troop who has some power and he has stopped my flute. I request of him, I beg of him, to please release his power so that I can do my work." So that was released.

Then he said, "You should not understand that this is real

magic. You should not think that I could really put life into a dead body. If I could, the people from England never would have allowed me to come here. The King or Queen would have kept me in his or her service, because nobody wants to die. I do this only to impress people and I can do it only because I have concentration of mind. Because my mind is concentrated, I can make people's minds believe in me, and I can impress you." He meant to say that whatever he was doing was only because of concentration of mind.

I had concentration because I was also doing meditation at that time. Of course, I did not have the charged words, but still I was doing repetition and I was doing it constantly. That is why I had concentration of mind. People have no idea of the value and the power which simran or repetition has. If we are strong in doing our simran, and if we gain the concentration of the mind, we can have many powers, just by doing it. Regarding simran, Baba Bishan Das used to say, "By doing simran we can get many powers — we can read the hearts of people." He also used to perform many miracles like this, and he was able to do it only because of simran. Many supernatural powers come within us, and if the one who has perfected his simran wants, he can stop a moving train. If he puts his attention toward the moving train, just in a moment the train will get stuck there and it will not be able to move an inch. One can do many surprising things if one starts concentrating his mind. When one does simran and has control over the mind and its many forces, one will realize its value and will not give the simran up, but will always want to do it.

When I was doing the simran of "Hai Ram, Hai Gobind" I had many supernatural powers and I would show miracles to people. At that time I even got the power of flying. Many people were praising me, saying, "This sadhu is very good, he knows everything." But still I was afraid in my within that I was not doing well. At that time Baba Bishan Das warned me, and gave me the example of a turtle. When that animal sees a man, he withdraws within himself, so in the same way the sadhus have to beware of this. Swami Ji Maharaj said, "If the Master is showering some grace on you then don't tell the world, don't show the world." The Masters always instruct their disciples not to misuse the supernatural powers, because this is misusing the meditation. Instead one should always preserve the meditation.

The Stolen Guns

Once in the army there was a theft and many guns were stolen. They said it was because of the carelessness of the guards, and the commander was very upset. Because they did not know who had stolen them, they were going to punish many people, including many innocent people, as they did not know how to find out the truth of who had really stolen the guns. In the army they often used to call me "Bhai Ji" or "Gyani Ji" and they knew I was a very sincere, truth-speaking person. They respected me a lot. So our commander told everyone in our group in the army to come and touch the body of this man, "Gyani Ji" and say that they were sincere and didn't know anything about this theft. Out of fifteen hundred people, there were only four people involved in that theft. Only they were not able to touch my body and say truthfully that they did not know anything about it. I did not tell them that I was pure, and I did not threaten them or do anything. It was only because of my purity that they could not dare to touch me and lie. The others who came were sincere and had no problem — they came and touched me and said, "I don't know anything about it." But when the real thieves came near me they started trembling.

When you are living a pure life, when you are pure within, your purity is such a great thing that it will be spread everywhere and even the bad people will not dare to stand in front of you and lie. Do you think that when you live a pure life, your friends and neighbors will not be aware of it? They will definitely be aware of it, because purity spreads like a fragrance. In the army it was a very unusual thing for a person not to eat meat or drink wine, but I was one of those people who did not. People knew that I did not eat meat or drink wine. I was very religious-minded, I spent my time in the religious places, and lived a pure life. Only because of that purity I was known everywhere and people even used to swear in my name.

My Experiences Sight-seeing in Delhi

When India was going to become independent in 1947, our battalion, the First Patiala Battalion, was given the honor of going to salute the first Prime Minister. As this function was going to happen in Delhi, we were sent to Delhi and for two months we were allowed to stay in the Red Fort, which is a famous fort built by the Mogul

Emperors. One day our commander told us that since we had been there for such a long time, we should go out into Delhi and see all the good things over there, the things worth sight-seeing; we should go out and see those things.

First a guide took us around and showed us all the different things and different places in the Red Fort, where we were staying. He took us to the place where the king used to hold court for the public and also the place where he would meet his very personal courtiers. He took us to the place where the famous Peacock Throne used to be kept, and told how that place used to be studded with precious stones like diamonds and rubies, which by then had all been taken by the government. Afterwards the guide took us to the place where the king used to bathe, where there were two tanks, one for hot water and one for cold water. He also showed us that beautiful place where the king used to change his clothes and he went on telling us about all of those places.

After telling us all about those places, he also told us about the emperor, Shah Jahan, who had made that Red Fort, and what had happened to him. Even though he lived such a luxurious life, still towards the end of his life he was put into prison in Agra by his own son Aurangzeb. There he was not allowed to eat or drink enough and he died a very torturous death. Aurangzeb was a very strict orthodox Muslim, and he tortured and killed many Hindus in India. It is said that once Shah Jahan wrote a letter to Aurangzeb saying, "You are killing the Hindus even though the Hindus are such good people that they even give donations in the name of their departed parents. And here you are, my son, and you are not even giving me enough water to drink, so you should order the person who is taking care of me to give me enough water." The reply from Aurangzeb to that letter was, "Whenever you feel thirsty you should suck the words which you have written with this ink and in that way you should satisfy yourself. You will not get any more water to drink."

I heard all this, about how Shah Jahan used to live such a luxurious life in the beginning but when the end of his life came he had to suffer all those things and die like that. All at once, when I heard all that, I became very sick. I became feverish, thinking what was the use of all the luxuries in the king's early life, when he was going to suffer like that towards his end. No matter how much happiness one has, still, one day, he will have to face unhappiness.

There were many other army men along that tour with me and they were all enjoying their day and were very happy listening to all those things about the king. They had their perspective and I had my own perspective.

The next day my officer told me kindly that I should not go to worldly places such as the Red Fort. I should go to the holy places, like temples. So he sent me to one of the very good temples in Delhi. When I went there, the first thing I saw was that the pundit there would put a garland around the neck of those who gave him a rupee. To those who gave him less than a rupee or those who did not give him anything, he would not even put a *tilak* mark on their forehead, and there was no question of putting a garland around their neck. While I was watching all that, a group of foreigners came there; one of the women went and offered a rupee to that pundit and he put a garland around her neck. She became very happy and she called her husband also, saying, "Come here, he will put a garland around your neck." That person just put his neck in front of the pundit, but the man did not give the pundit a rupee, so the pundit did not put a garland around his neck. Then that woman remembered to give the money, and her husband got the garland. Seeing all this, how the pundit was doing that just for the sake of money, I felt very bad.

Then I started to climb the stairs to go into the temple, and at that temple just a little way up the stairs there was a picture of Kabir Sahib. When I saw that I was so surprised, and I felt so bad, that I thought, "Well, what is the use of going any further? I should leave here." Kabir Sahib was a famous Mahatma who struggled all His life and suffered so many hardships because He condemned idol worship. However, what had the people done there? They had made a picture of Kabir Sahib and they were worshipping Him in the form of an idol. So I thought, "What is the use of going any further?" and I returned from there.

Death is Predetermined

In 1947, when India became independent of the British, the separate countries of India and Pakistan were formed and there was a war between them. It was not my turn to go to the front during the war with Kashmir, but there was a man who requested that if I would go in his place, he would appreciate that. He had little children and he didn't want to go, because he was afraid of death. I told him, "Okay, I am ready to go." Since the commanders were not doing that type of substitution, that dear one asked me to ask the commander. So I told my commander that we had switched, and the commander said that I should not do that. However I said, "You see, I am not afraid of death, so why are you stopping me? You want one person, and I am ready to go there in his place. I am not afraid of death, because, even if you are afraid of death, you cannot avoid it. Death will come at its own time, and we do not know from what cause our death will come. What can we do to stop it? So let me go and do a good thing for this man."

So I went to war and I was not hurt even a little bit in that war. Even though the bullets came close to me, I was not hurt. I was not afraid of what was happening, and I continued doing my work. However, the person who had been afraid of death and who had asked me to go to the war in his place, when he returned to his home, he got cholera and after a few days he died.

It has come in my understanding that if we think about death in this way, if we think about trying to avoid death, it shows the weakness of our mind. Instead of thinking about death, we should keep our mind in Simran. Simran makes our mind strong, and if we have strength in our mind, then no matter what happens to us or no matter in what way death comes to us, we will be very happy to face it. The time and cause of death for everyone is predetermined, and a person will leave the body in those circumstances. People die even when they are living safely and happily in their homes and villages, whereas others die in car and train accidents. The time and cause of death is predetermined. So even though I fought in two wars, because my death was not written in those wars, although I was involved with bombs and all those things, I didn't die then. In whatever way you have to die, that is written in your fate, and no matter how much you run from that situation, still you will die in that way because it is all predetermined.

The Austerity of the Five Fires

In the war between India and Pakistan my unit was involved in fighting on the borders of Kashmir. We were in the mountains where it was very cold and snowy. Because we had spent a lot of time in the cold, the doctors recommended to the government that we should be kept in some hill station for one year, so that we could maintain our good health. They thought that if we went suddenly into the hot parts of the country there would be danger of sickness.

So we were given orders to stay for one year in the hill station of Simla, and also, because we had been successful in the war, the government gave us six months leave. But the desire for God was still within me, and someone told me about one mahatma. I went to him and requested him to tell me something about God. He didn't want to tell me anything, he just wanted to get rid of me, so he told me, "You can realize God only by performing austerities. Until you perform the austerity of the five fires, you cannot realize God. By doing this austerity you will get complete peace." That is the hardest of all practices and he thought I would not do it; he said that just to get rid of me.

On one hand the government had told us not to go in the hot parts of India because there was a danger of getting sick, and they had given us many conveniences and comforts to maintain our good health. But on the other hand, the fire which was burning within me — the desire for God — was so consuming that I did not find any comfort in that hill station, and I went to that mahatma who taught me to do that austerity.

In that austerity you sit in the middle and there are four fires burning all around you very close to your body. The fifth fire is the heat of the sun overhead, for you do this austerity in June, which is the hottest month in India. You don't wear anything, but just to protect your eyes you cover your eyes with a blind-fold. He told me to perform that austerity for four hours a day, starting at twelve noon and he told me to repeat the name "Ram" 24,000 times each day and to do that for forty days continuously.

He told me to do the simran, the repetition of that name 24,000 times, but I was doing it 48,000 times, and instead of sitting for four hours, I was sitting for eight hours between those fires. Instead of going to Simla and enjoying a vacation like the other people did, I chose to come down to the plains and I performed this austerity in the month of June. I did not perform the austerities to collect money from people. I performed the austerities only with the wish that maybe by performing them and by burning my body in the fires, I would realize my Beloved One. If I could do that, I thought that still it would be a very cheap bargain.

I knew that one cannot realize God by performing the austerities. I knew that by remaining hungry and thirsty one cannot realize God Almighty. I knew that God cannot be realized this way, but still I performed all those practices only because I didn't want the mind to make this body make me lose my way in the pleasures of the world. That is why I gave all the difficulties and hardships to my body and to the mind that was in this body.

I did that austerity, but I got nothing from it except the burning of the body. My mind didn't get any peace or happiness from that; my soul didn't get any peace or happiness from that. I only got ego in my mind, saying that I have also performed an austerity and that I am also something. No doubt people were giving me respect, saying that I was a good mahatma because I had performed that austerity. But I was feeling ashamed within, because people were calling me "mahatma" but I didn't have any qualities of a mahatma. After doing that austerity the desire for God that was inside me started burning in its full force again, and again I was disappointed. I was disappointed because I didn't get anything from that mahatma regarding God.

After working very hard at one or another type of practice I would go back to Baba Bishan Das and tell him what I had done. I would always go back to him, like the needle of the compass always points to the north. But he would always find some fault in the practice that I had done. He would always ask me if I had achieved anything from that, he would taunt me for doing that, and he would make me realize that what I was doing was of no use. So after I performed this austerity, when I went to Baba Bishan Das, I was feeling that now he would accept me and appreciate what I had done, because I thought that it was a very good deed that I had done. When I went to him and I told him about the austerity, he told me, "Dear One, you already have five different types of fires which are burning within you, which are consuming your within. The fires of lust, anger, greed, attachment, and egotism, are burning the body. When we have so many fires burning within us, then what is the use of burning the fires outside and sitting near them? You have burnt your body, but you have not removed any of the fires which are burning within you."

My Strict Treatment from Baba Bishan Das

While we were posted in Simla, one night I felt a great longing to see Baba Bishan Das and I started out at midnight to see him. At that time I was feeling that I was doing the work of bravery for Baba

Bishan Das. In the village in which he lived there were many relatives of mine living also. In order to get to his ashram, I had to go through that village after getting off the train. In the military they have orders that you have to fix your beard and mustache very well, using some fixer. Because I was a military man and because I was a Sikh gentleman, I was well dressed and I had fixed my beard and mustache; I was looking just like a gentleman.

When I was going to see Baba Bishan Das, the villagers were very curious, because they knew how Baba Bishan Das was going to treat me. They started talking with each other, saying, "Look at this man! Now he is well suited and well booted and when he goes to Baba Bishan Das, let us see how he will treat him." When I went to see him, I bowed right down to him, but he pulled my beard and mustache down and he removed all that fixer. My relatives who lived right there felt very sad and they rebuked me. But my heart was not affected by any public shame. I felt, "I am lacking in karmas. My karmas are not good and that is why this mahatma is not gracious to me."

Baba Bishan Das was very great. He was very loving but he was very strict also. Whenever I used to go to him, he would always treat me very strictly. He never allowed me to drink a cup of tea or eat food from his ashram. Many times I would go to Baba Bishan Das with all my income — whatever income I got from my property as well as whatever I got as pay from the army — as a donation. He would take it and from that he would allow me to have only five rupees from all those earnings. Even after that he would say, "Since you are working for the army, you are getting a uniform from the army and all your needs are taken care of by the army, you don't even need these five rupees." Then, and this is true, whenever I would take money to him, he would give me a beating, he would slap me. This happened to me many times in front of many people. Instead of thanking me for the donation, he would give me a beating. He never told me he was pleased with me or that I was very good for bringing that much money to him. Furthermore, whenever I would take him more than usual he would slap me more than usual. It is very easy to go and offer money to the Master if He just takes it and then thanks you for it. However, just imagine if you give Him the money and instead of thanking you, He slaps you on the face, He beats you — how would you feel?

Still at that time, I would never get upset at Baba Bishan Das and I would never feel bad about this treatment. I used to think, "There is something lacking in me. Maybe I have some faults in me or there is something wrong with my karmas. That is why the Master is not pleased with me, and he is rebuking me and scolding me." As I have said, I used to read the banis of the Sikh Gurus, and I used to read in the writings of Guru Nanak, "The Master becomes pleased with you only if you are the most fortunate one." So whenever I would get the rebukes and scoldings from him I used to think that maybe my karmas were not good and that was why I was not pleasing the Master and he was rebuking me. And many times, after those occasions when he did not treat me well, I would come out of his room feeling sad, and I would see one old man sitting outside. That old man would sing a verse about the diamond hidden within each one of us and he would always tell me, "Maybe one day he will shower grace on you."

One day I asked Baba Bishan Das, "Why do you beat me and not love me? As far as I know, I don't come to you after committing any sins, I just go on loving you. Why do you beat me and not love me?" Instead of replying to that question, he gave me one more kick. So I was disappointed and then I went to Baba Amolak Das, the Master of Baba Bishan Das, who was still alive at that time. I went to him and asked him, "Baba, can you tell me why Baba Bishan Das is always beating me and why he doesn't love me? As far as I know I have never done any bad thing for which he might be giving me the punishment and I always try to remain free of any bad things. So why is he giving me the beatings?"

Baba Amolak Das told me, "The reality is that if the Saints want to give you something, then They will not praise you, They will not love you outwardly, but instead They will always go on rebuking you and will always go on insulting you in front of all the people. This is because They know about everybody's inner desire; They know what is the desire of the person in front of them. Those who are desirous of name and fame, the praise of this world, those who are desirous of the outer things, They praise them in front of all the people. They always insult those dear ones who have the desire for Spirituality, who are fond of Spirituality and the inner things, so that their vessel may get ready. The Master does that so that they may get the strength of enduring and bearing the criticisms and insults of all the people. He does that so that the disciple may get ready for the inner things that He is going to give. Master

Saints always come to give in this world. Whatever feeling one has, or whatever desire one has, he gets from the Master according to his desire. If the person is desirous of name and fame, the Saint gives the name and fame. However, those who want the spiritual things, the inner things, they never get any praise from the Master, but they always get kicked. They always get rebukes and insults from the Master."

Baba Bishan Das was doing all this because he wanted to make my life. He made me go through so many things only because he wanted to make me the strong one. Just like when you cut the soap, you make the soap go through a very sharp wire, in the same way, it was as if he made me go through that sharp wire. It was very torturous and difficult, but he was the one who made my life.

It is very difficult to reduce the amount of food that you eat. Those who have done that know how difficult it is. Sufi Saint Farid Sahib has written, "O Farid, hunger is worse than death. One eats at night, but the next morning once again he feels hungry and he feels like eating." So Baba Bishan Das first made me reduce my intake of food. After that he made me eat only vegetables and then he kept me on a very, very simple diet. When the hunger started bothering me, many times I would cry out and I would become very perturbed. I would cry out and I would say, "Baba Ji, I feel like I am going to die." He would say, "No, you are not going to lose anything, you are not going to die. In fact, now you are going to live."

In the beginning, the practices of Sant Mat are very difficult to do. It is very difficult to reach and go through the lower planes, but afterwards it becomes very easy. One gets the confidence and then it gets very easy to go in the higher planes.

Even now I am very grateful to Baba Bishan Das for all that he did for me. In fact, he made my life by doing all the things he did. I have very much respect for Baba Bishan Das in my heart, and whenever I remember him or whenever I talk about him I feel like weeping. I know now that if he had praised me in my young age when I used to go to see him, there are many chances that I would have gone bad. If he had not been so strict with me, I would not have maintained the discipline and I would not have improved my life. I stepped into the Path of Spirituality in my young age and it is possible that if he had not been strict with me, if he had not rebuked me as he did, I would have taken my thoughts to some other place. If he had not showered grace on me, it is possible that this poor soul might have developed many faults in him, because you know it is very difficult to live your life, especially when you are not married. He prepared me and he taught me a lot. It is only because he made me do the sacrifice, the hard meditation, that later when I met my Master I was able to do what He asked me to do. Because Baba Bishan Das made my foundation strong, only because of that, later, when I met my Master, I was able to understand and appreciate His love.

Baba Sawan Singh (1858 - 1948)

SIX

At the Feet of Baba Sawan Singh

My Fortune Awakens; I Meet Baba Sawan Singh

Great are You, my Sawan. Great are You my Giver. You are the support of the miserable ones. You dwell within all but are different from all.

You can make a beggar rule over a kingdom, and You can turn a king into a beggar.
You can make an ignorant one into a scholar, and You can turn a scholar into a fool.
Sometimes You spread Your jholi for alms, and sometimes You become a Giver.

You can change the water into earth; You can change the earth into a well, and over that well You can create a mountain.
You can make the sky cover the earth; You can make the risen sky fall.
You Yourself become the support of him who has no protector in this world.

There is no one without You. You dwell within all, whether he is king or pauper.

Master Sawan Singh

*Your Light is within everyone; Your plays are unique.
You make Your presence felt everywhere.*

*You have liberated demons like Kode and Vali Khandari.
You have even liberated sinners like Ganaka the prostitute; Your plays are unique.*

Sometimes You become a trader and open a shop; sometimes You do farming.

As the sons are dear to the mother, the devotees are dear to You.
Being controlled by the devotees, You do everything for them.
Ajaib's fortune has awakened; He met You, the Beloved Sawan.

— Vah Mere Sawan

Once I was posted in the cantonment of Nowshera, which is on the frontier near the border of Pakistan and Afghanistan. Some Pathans, tribal people of that area, used to come in our cantonment to sell *neem* sticks to the army. People use branches of the neem tree to clean their teeth. It so happened that Master Sawan Singh was on tour in the areas near the border and one place where Master Sawan Singh went was Peshawar, which was not very far, only about two or three hours by train, from our cantonment. Two of the Pathans had come from Peshawar and they were initiates of Baba Sawan Singh. They were talking between themselves about the radiance and glory and beauty of Master Sawan Singh and I overheard them talking. They were saying, "We don't know how far Master Sawan Singh has gone within or how great the Master is. We don't know anything about His inner condition, but outwardly He is the most beautiful One. He has a beautiful white beard, His face is very radiant and He is a God-like man. It is possible He may be Guru Nanak. If He is not Guru Nanak, we would say He is not less than Guru Nanak."

I was very interested and curious and I wanted to know more about Master Sawan Singh. The commander of our army at that cantonment was very fond of visiting Saints and Mahatmas. He would always be very happy whenever he could see a sadhu or Mahatma and wherever our army was stationed he would always find some way to visit a nearby sadhu or Mahatma. So I told him about Baba Sawan Singh, saying, "I have heard about a Mahatma who is in Peshawar now, and if you are interested we can go and see Him." He said we should go, so we collected more information from those Pathans, and about twenty or twenty-five people, including the commander, all went to Peshawar to see Him.

Baba Sawan Singh holding Satsang at Peshawar

Since Baba Sawan Singh Himself had served in the army, He knew how difficult it was for the army people to get time off from their jobs. Whenever anyone serving in the army used to go to see Him, He would always make time for them, so when we went to see Him, He came out to see us.

You know that I used to believe in the Sikh Gurus and I was very devoted to Guru Gobind Singh, the tenth Guru of the Sikhs. Even though I had not had the opportunity of having the darshan of Guru Gobind Singh, still I knew from looking at pictures what Guru Gobind Singh looked like. I knew that He wore a special type of turban, carried a bow and arrows, and had various other distinctive features and I had that picture of Him in my mind. You know the mind is very tricky and never lets any opportunity go by without utilizing it. So when we were going to see Baba Sawan Singh, my mind told me, "I will believe in this Mahatma only if He appears to me as Guru Gobind Singh." When we arrived and saw Baba Sawan Singh I thought at once of Guru Gobind Singh, and after some time I saw Baba Sawan Singh turn into the form of Guru Gobind Singh. Even though Baba Sawan Singh was not wearing that type of turban or those other things, still I saw His form turn into Guru Gobind Singh, and He appeared wearing all those things that I had in my mind about Guru Gobind Singh.

At a later time I asked Him why I had seen Guru Gobind Singh in Him on that occasion. He replied, "One sees the form of God according to the feelings he has for the Mahatma in his mind." He explained that if you are remembering a True Master, with full love and devotion and have the form of that Master in your mind, then if you look at some other Mahatma sitting in front of you, if the same Power is working in that other Mahatma, you will see the Form of your own Master in that Mahatma.

The attractive, impressive form of Baba Sawan Singh was so beautiful, so enchanting, that I could not take my eyes away from Him. I was so fascinated by the beautiful form of the Master that I could not forget Him. I did not know anything about His inner condition, but I felt for sure outwardly that He was a perfect Mahatma.

Later at that meeting I went, with several of my fellow soldiers, to Baba Sawan Singh to request Initiation. He was very happy. He was in a very jolly mood and He was very gracious. We had brought some donations for the langar that we wished to give Him. The donations of the others were accepted, but my offering was returned. I was dejected and later went to see Him in private to make a similar request again, asking if my contribution could perhaps be increased. Very lovingly He again refused to accept it, telling me that I need not bother. He told me, "The time will come when you will have to do a lot of seva and will contribute a lot, both financially and physically." A large number of my fellow soldiers obtained Initiation, but He told me I would have to wait. He told me, "This is not the time for you to get Initiation. Everybody's time is predetermined and you will get the Naam at the appropriate time. He who is supposed to give you the Naam Initiation will come to your home by Himself."

That was the time when the yearning was created in my within and I started wondering about the Mahatma whom Baba Sawan Singh said would come to my home and give me the Naam Himself. I said, "Master, how will I be convinced that He is the same Mahatma about whom You have said that He will come to my home by Himself? How will I know that He is that Master whom You mean? How will I have faith in Him?" Master Sawan Singh said, "He who is going to come to you by Himself will also give you the faith. He is within you and He will come to you by Himself. I have to make you do a lot of seva."

Then I told Baba Sawan Singh about my Master, Baba Bishan Das. Baba Sawan Singh told me the location of His dera at Beas and He told me to bring Baba Bishan Das there.

I Take Baba Bishan Das to Meet Master Sawan Singh

The darshan of Baba Sawan Singh made me so happy that I couldn't keep it to myself. I went back to the Punjab and told Baba Bishan Das about Him. The great thing about Baba Bishan Das was that although he was initiated into the first Two Words and was successful in his meditation up through the first two planes, he knew there was something more than that. He believed in the planes above the planes that he had attained. He was not a narrow-minded person, he was not like a frog in the well who does not believe in anything beyond what he can see; he had a very big heart. When he had explained to me about the first Two Words and the first two planes, he had also told me, "There is something beyond this. If you ever come across a Master who is capable of giving you more, then you should take me to have the darshan of such a Master. If I come across someone who knows more than what I know, then I will also take you there." So when I told him about Master Sawan Singh at once he got ready to go, saying, "We should not delay in going to see Him, because who knows when we have to leave this world? We should go at once to have His darshan."

Earlier I have told you about the Muslim Fakir named Fati, who had his ashram just across the road from Baba Bishan Das. Like Baba Bishan Das, Fati had Initiation into the first Two Words, and he was practically successful in that and in his meditation went through the first two planes. Since he loved Fati a lot, Baba Bishan Das invited him to go meet Baba Sawan Singh also and Fati came along with us to the dera of Sawan Singh at Beas.

When they met, Baba Sawan Singh was very pleased to see Baba Bishan Das and spoke with him in a very loving way. Baba Bishan Das was also very happy and asked Baba Sawan Singh for Initiation. But at that time Baba Bishan Das was very old and his body was very weak, and so Baba Sawan Singh told him that this was not the time for him to get Initiation and meditate. Baba Sawan Singh said, "Now you do not have much time, but this is my promise: that I will take care of your soul in the within." Baba

Sawan Singh promised to liberate him, to take him up at the time of death and make him meditate in the inner planes.

At that meeting we were sitting with Master Sawan Singh with a small group of people. At that time Fati, the Muslim Fakir, told Master Sawan Singh, "Master, before You came into this body, in Your previous birth You were born as the King of Faridkot." At that time Faridkot was an independent state in the area, although now it is part of the state of Punjab. Baba Sawan Singh laughed and He said, "Yes, I remember that once I was born as the King of Faridkot. I was going to get birth again in the same place, but because of certain reasons I was born in Ludhiana." Then in a very serious mood He said, "I also know that in many of my past births I was born in very poor families. I suffered a lot of hunger and poverty. Do you think that if I were to go back now to those palaces which I owned in my past lifetime and claimed to be the owner of those palaces, that they would recognize me and let me in?"

The perfect Masters have the knowledge of Their past births. They know everything of Their own past and They know about Their future. They also know about the past and future of all Their disciples. They are omniscient and they are all-conscious. Only the Saints of Their own degree can understand and appreciate the glory and grace of the Masters. How can we, the worldly people, know the grace of the Master?

At that time Baba Bishan Das was very pleased with me. He said, "I have made a very good disciple, because he has told me about this very great man. Because of him, I have come into contact with this great Mahatma."

At that first meeting Baba Bishan Das told Baba Sawan Singh about me, about how I had performed the austerities and done so many different kinds of practices in search of God Almighty. Baba Sawan Singh Ji said, "Yes, this man has performed many austerities and he has done many other things, but still he has not got the real thing. I have one devotee here who also has done a lot of searching for God and who also used to perform the same kind of austerities before he came to see me. He even had long hair which he cut off only after coming to Beas." Then Baba Sawan Singh called Baba Somanath and we were introduced. That was my only meeting with Baba Somanath, there in the presence of Baba Sawan Singh.

Baba Somanath Ji was a disciple who worked very hard and made very great sacrifices in His life. He had done all the different kinds of rites and rituals and performed many austerities. However, because He was very sincere and true in His heart, in His devotion, God Almighty Himself showered grace upon him and brought him to the feet of Baba Sawan Singh. There His search was completed and He got the knowledge of God. It is very easy to criticize any Mahatma, but to work as hard as He did and live a life like that Mahatma is very difficult. Later Baba Sawan Singh gave Baba Somanath Ji the duty of spreading the teachings of Sant Mat in the southern part of India. He told Baba Somanath Ji, "You should awaken the souls in South India. Connect them with God Almighty and make them do the meditation of Naam."

The Beauty of Master Sawan Singh

The eyes saw millions of faces, but no one dwells in my sight.
He who does the meditation fills up the jholi. He who is shy goes empty.

Your glance is very intoxicating and is the giver of life.
O Sawan, my merciful to the poor ones, by uttering Your Naam the boat remains upright.

Those who have had Your darshan are liberated from both the worlds.
O forgiving Lord, forgive us. Here we find no success.

We are the sinners — forgive us! We have come to Your door — give us the darshan.
O Giver, show us the radiant glimpse as our soul has not awakened for many ages.

The soul will become tired from wandering to door after door, and she is bored in the cycle of birth and death.
If True Sawan makes us have the darshan, the soul of Ajaib will not get stuck in the swamp.

— Lakha Shakala Takiya

After my meeting with Master Sawan Singh my troop moved and we were stationed at Beas, very near the dera of the Master, so I had many opportunities to see Master Sawan Singh. Furthermore, my commanding officer, Lieutenant General Bikram Singh, became a very devoted

initiate of Master Sawan Singh and was very fond of going to see Him. Because he was in the army and was a general, he got the opportunity to go and see Master Sawan Singh whenever he wanted. I was the wireless operator for my general, and as the radio operator always goes along with his general, wherever he went I had to accompany him. Because of that advantage I got even more opportunities to see Master Sawan Singh. I had many meetings with Baba Sawan Singh, and I had the very good fortune of having many opportunities to sit at His feet and listen to His Satsangs.

I was a very fortunate one that I got the darshan of Master Sawan Singh when I was a young man. It was a very pleasant time as His form was so beautiful, so attractive, that even though I saw millions of other people's faces in the world, no other face, no other form attracted my attention, and no other form dwelled in my mind like His did. For this reason I wrote in this bhajan, "I have seen millions of faces, but no face has attracted me as much as Your form."

His innocent and holy face was full of love and I cannot forget how He used to smile. His face enchanted and attracted me so much that not even for a moment could I take that form away from my vision. That form of Baba Sawan Singh had a deep effect on my life and the darshan of that form became the food of my life. Even though I tried my best, still I could never forget the form of the Master. That divine form caught hold of my soul and it always remained within my eyes. Even now I am not able to forget that beautiful form of Master Sawan Singh.

Only the jeweler knows the value of the jewels. Those people who recognized Master Sawan Singh were seeing two flames of light always going on in His forehead. His face was such that those who were having a little bit of control over their soul and who were maintaining even a little bit of concentration would always feel a pull whenever they saw Him. Those whose souls were not as pure would not feel that pull, but the pure souls would feel a great pull when they looked at Him. This pull would come through His face. People who were not initiates of Master Sawan Singh would also praise His beautiful face. They would say, "We don't know what His inner beauty is, what miracles He performs on the inside, but outwardly He is so radiant, so beautiful, that from every single hair of His beard the light comes out. His face is so beautiful that we have never before seen another like it." Physically He was so beautiful that I have never seen another person as beautiful. He came into this world in such a form that I have never seen any other person like Him anywhere that I have traveled.

Sawan came and showered the rain. He made the souls reach Sach Khand.

His sweet words are beautiful. The drops of nectar are showering.
The Sangat is yearning to see His beautiful, enchanting face.

After coming from Sach Khand, Sawan decorated this beautiful garden.
Planting the plants of True Naam, He watered them with the water of Satsang.

He is far from us in body only. The True Shabd is not separated from us.
He is living within all, but we have not the eye to see.

Oh my Beloved Emperor Sawan, I cannot write about Your favors.
Ajaib is grateful millions of times. You have liberated our heated hearts.
— Aaya Sawan Jhadiya La Gya

Baba Sawan Singh was so beautiful, so handsome. He had a white beard, He had a broad face, and He was the true gentleman Guru. He had a gold chain fitted to His watch and He was such a gentleman that He would not let anything stain His white clothes. Just as His clothes were always very white, very pure, in the same way, He was very pure and holy in His within also.

Always in the Satsang He would come and say, "Do not understand me as someone else's and do not understand me as a stranger; I am your very own." The loving way in which He would say this would touch the hearts of the dear ones. He had so much sympathy for everyone and people would wonder how it was possible that He had so much sympathy for everyone alike. Just as His words were full of sympathy, in His within He also had sympathy for everyone.

Sawan's Love for His Guru, Baba Jaimal Singh

The love that Baba Sawan Singh had for His Master, Baba Jaimal Singh, was so deep and so great that it cannot be described. It cannot be talked about, it cannot be written in any book. It was very deep, and whenever that Ocean of Love would come in Sawan Singh, when it would come in its full force, then it would break all the barriers and

Master Sawan Singh would see Baba Jaimal Singh everywhere.

Baba Jaimal Singh always told Baba Sawan Singh that when the disciple gets the Naam Initiation from the Master, after that, not even in the state of dreams, not even in the state of forgetfulness, should he think that the Master is a human being; he should always understand the Master as the One who has come into this prison to release us, the prisoners.

I heard Baba Sawan Singh talking about his search for God. He had searched for a Master for 22 years. Now you can imagine how if someone has searched for God Almighty, for the Master, for 22 years of his life, isn't that human pole where the Master Power is manifested aware of such a disciple, such a devotee? Will He not Himself go and find him? Master Sawan Singh did not go in the refuge of Baba Jaimal Singh by himself, even though he had searched for so many years. But when the time came, Baba Jaimal Singh Himself, traveling five hundred kilometers, went to the place where Baba Sawan Singh used to live and He Himself found him.

Just imagine how much yearning, how much pain of separation, Baba Sawan Singh, who searched for 22 years, had. When such a person gets to the perfect Master after searching for so long, and after having so much yearning, he sacrifices everything for the Master. Baba Sawan Singh had so much love for His Master and He was so fond of His Master that such an example is very hard to find. I have seen the canopy under which He used to sit and hold Satsang, and everywhere on the canopy it was written, "Baba Jaimal Singh Ji, have mercy on me; Baba Jaimal Singh Ji shower grace on us." Whenever He would talk about the form of the Master in Satsang, His voice would choke and the tears would start rolling down from His eyes. He often used to say, "If Baba Jaimal Singh were to come and give me the darshan of His physical form, I am willing to give up everything that I have."

The Hard Work of Master Sawan Singh

Those who lived in His company knew about the life of Baba Sawan Singh and how hard He worked. After taking Initiation He used to meditate full-time, and He would come out of His room only to attend the call of nature or to do other important work; otherwise He would remain in meditation. He would eat and sleep very little and sometimes He did not come out of His room for many days. He had a

Sawan Singh at the entrance to His house. The lettering above the door reads "Dera Baba Jaimal Singh Ji Maharaj."

wooden stand, shaped like the letter "T," called a *beragan,* on which you can rest your elbows. When He would get tired, He would stand up, and using that beragan, meditate during the night.

Bhai Banta Singh was the driver for Master Sawan Singh and he also used to cook food for Him. I met him many times and he used to tell me how Master Sawan Singh would go into the room to do the meditation and He would not come out for many, many days. Master Sawan Singh would leave the instruction, "You cook the food and leave it there; whenever I want, I'll come out and eat it."

Once in the Satsang Baba Sawan Singh said, "I did not do anything. It is all the grace of Baba Jaimal Singh Ji." Bhai Banta Singh was there and he said, "Master, then what were You doing bearing the hunger and thirst for so many days? When You would not come out from Your room, You would just stay there and meditate, what was that?" Sometimes the lovers of the Masters say such things. Guru Nanak had bedding which was made of stones and pebbles and sitting on that He meditated for eleven years. Kabir Sahib also lived His life very simply. Such Mahatmas are examples of hard work, sacrifice and meditation.

Master Sawan Singh Explains the *Guru Granth Sahib*

Once my army troop had the non-stop reading of the *Guru Granth Sahib* and when we were about to complete that we invited Baba Sawan Singh to attend. When we invited Him, He became very pleased, and He came to the Beas railway station where we were doing that ceremony. He used to love the army men very much because He Himself had been in the army. He said, "I am very glad that even though you are in the army, still you have so much love for *Guru Granth Sahib*. This bani is of the great Masters and this belongs to everyone. Guru Arjan Dev Ji Maharaj also said, 'This is the bani of the great beings and this belongs to everyone.'"

Very lovingly Baba Sawan Singh would explain the principles of the Path using the *Guru Granth Sahib*. Like me, Master Sawan Singh was born in a Sikh family, and He also used to recite or read the five banis that devout Sikhs usually recite every day, the *Jap Ji Sahib*, the *Jap Sahib*, *Chaupai*, *Rahiras*, and the *Anand Sahib*. Very lovingly He would say, "This bani of *Guru Granth Sahib* talks about some other bani also, which cannot be written and which cannot be read. In the hands of the Saints is the key to unlock that Bani."

Baba Sawan Singh was born in a time when people had given up the path of Naam. They had forgotten the teachings of the great Saints and Mahatmas. They had forgotten God so much so that they started searching for that conscious being, Almighty God, in stones, idols, and water. They forgot where God is and how we can meet Him.

Baba Sawan Singh was born in the month of *Sawan* which is the month of the Indian calendar near June and July and that is why He was given the name "Sawan." That month is when rain comes in abundance and it is very important to the people who live in areas where there is little rain and where there are no good means of irrigation. Rain is their only source of water and so that month is very important to them. At the time Master Sawan Singh was born there was a very severe drought in India, and when He was born it rained so heavily that the drought was ended. It rained so heavily that the people who were hungry and did not have enough food to eat, all those people's hunger was satisfied. For those souls who were thirsty for God Almighty, Sawan came into this world just as that rain comes in the month of Sawan to quench the thirst of the earth. God Almighty assumed the body of Baba Sawan Singh for those thirsty souls who were yearning to meet Him. Just as in the month of Sawan it rains, in the same way, Master Sawan showered the rain of Naam and He reminded the people who had forgotten the teachings of the past Masters of those teachings. He connected them with the Naam and took them back to the Real Home — not only in India, but all over the world.

After coming into this world, Baba Sawan Singh showed the Real Path to those who had forgotten the path of devotion. He embraced those who, after worshipping the stones and idols, had become like stone and He showed them the Real Path. He told them the truth that we cannot realize God from anywhere outside. God is within us; God is hungry for our love. Also He lovingly explained to them that God Almighty is for all, He is not the personal property of any one religion or community or country. He is for everyone. God is for all those who remember Him and do His devotion and everyone has an equal right to meet Him.

Master Sawan Singh would explain that in the holy *Guru Granth Sahib* the writings of many great devotees are included, regardless of whether They were Sikh, Hindu or Muslim and regardless of what caste They belonged to. Guru Arjan Dev, the fifth Guru of the Sikhs, compiled the *Guru Granth Sahib.* He had a very great heart and when collecting the writings of the different Mahatmas and deciding on which writings to include, He only took into consideration the spiritual attainment of the Mahatmas. All Those Who preached and practiced the Five Shabds, the Five Names, and Those Who used to go to *Sach Khand,* Their banis were included in the *Guru Granth Sahib.* Guru Arjan Dev did not ignore any Mahatma on the basis of caste or religion. Many Mahatmas came into this world long before Guru Arjan Dev came. From wherever He could get the bani of the true Masters, from far or near, He collected all those writings with much love and with much effort and He got them printed.

In the *Guru Granth Sahib* Guru Arjan Dev did not criticize anyone. He did not criticize any community or any religion. He understood all the communities and all the religions as His very own. In fact, in the holy *Guru Granth Sahib* He even said, "Giving up the duality, all of you, all the brothers, should get together and sit together. All together you should sing the praises of God. Together you should connect yourselves with the Naam of God."

Master Sawan Singh would say that when *Guru Granth Sahib* was written, at that time the people who were very strong in their religious beliefs opposed Guru Arjan Dev and criticized Him in front of the Mogul Emperor Jahangir. They would say, "In the *Guru Granth Sahib* there is criticism of every religion, every community and it talks against Islam," which was their religion. So four times the *Guru Granth Sahib* was taken to the court of Jahangir to find out if there was any criticism of Islam. But they did not find anything because in this holy book no religion is criticized. There is nothing against Islam. In the *Guru Granth Sahib* only the love of God is talked about and all the creatures, all the beings are termed as children of the same Light.

I have seen this with my own eyes that when Master Sawan Singh would explain the *Guru Granth Sahib,* then many Sikh people, those who had not been initiated, who only used to read the bani, would start weeping. When they listened to Master Sawan Singh commenting on the bani they would realize the meaning of the bani, and they would repent. They would feel very sorry for wasting their time. They would say that they had been reading the bani for a long time but up until then they had not understood what the bani was really saying. They would say, "Oh, so great and so pure and so holy are the teachings in this holy book, but what have we been doing with them? Just as if we had put some water in our mouths and spit it out without swallowing it, in the same way, we have just been reading the bani and throwing it out without understanding what the bani is teaching."

The Humorous Nature of Baba Sawan Singh

Master Sawan Singh was very jolly and His nature was very humorous. Whenever He would laugh it would seem as if His whole being was laughing and as if flowers were pouring down from His mouth. When He laughed like that He was so beautiful, so handsome.

Sawan Singh during Satsang at Beas

Just like a mother explains to her child, giving so many different examples, in the same way, He used to give examples to make us understand things. He knew many idioms, many sayings, many examples, which we use in our routine life. He would use them to explain the teachings of this Path in a very humorous way. Using the examples of the world, and telling things in the form of jokes, He explained the teachings of the Path to us.

Master Sawan Singh would often need cloth for mats for the langar. In those days in India there were not many looms to weave cloth, so most of the time the women used to make thread using a spinning wheel and then they would weave the cloth by hand. Many women would take the seva of working on the spinning wheel to make the thread and then weave the mats. When quite a number of women got together to do that seva Master Sawan Singh would go there and He would sit among the women on a chair. He would talk with the women in the same way that the women talk with each other and it was so humorous that people used to laugh a lot. The way He used to talk with the women was so humorous that nobody could control their laughter.

The Masters have their own way of showering grace upon the people, and I don't think that those men or women who were present and who witnessed those scenes could ever forget the grace of the Master which they received at that time. Those who have had the good fortune of seeing Master Sawan Singh smile, they have not been able to forget His beautiful form.

The Value of Darshan

Master Sawan Singh used to say in His Satsangs that when we come to the Satsang and sit in front of the Master, then right from the moment the Master comes into the Satsang and is seated in front of us, we should look constantly at the forehead of the Master. We should not pay any attention to the sounds or noises that come from the right or the left or from any other side. Our attention should be constantly towards the forehead of the Master. He used to say that we should get so absorbed in the darshan of the Master that we should not even remain aware who is the *pathi*, the one singing the verses, or what the pathi is wearing. We should not pay any attention to anything except the forehead of the Master.

Master Sawan Singh would say that in the Satsang we should try and sit in such a place from where we can have the darshan of the Master. We should not try to sit way in the back or on the side or at a place from where we cannot have the darshan of the Master. The people who come first should go and sit in the front and the people who come later should not try and go and sit in the front; they should sit at some other place. But wherever you sit in the Satsang, you

Satsang with Master Sawan Singh at Beas

should always be sure that you are able to have the darshan of the Master.

He also used to say that it would be much better, after attending the Satsang, to remain seated in meditation for some time and remain absorbed in the darshan which we have had during the Satsang. If we go on talking after the Satsang, our heart, which has become full with the darshan of the Master during the Satsang, starts to become empty. The more we talk after the Satsang, the more empty we become, and eventually we become exactly like we were in the beginning when we came to the Satsang. He would also say that before sitting in the Satsang, if we could do a little bit of meditation, that would also become very successful.

140   IN SEARCH OF THE GRACIOUS ONE

Daily Satsang at Beas

With my own eyes I saw the dear ones doing this and I myself practiced this. In order to sit in the front and have the darshan of Master Sawan Singh we would come and sit there at least five or six hours before the Satsang, so that we would not be pushed back. If we came later, we would not get a good seat. When Master Sawan Singh would give Satsang, the dear ones would have such fixed attention that even if there was a noise or disturbance in the back they would never look back and they would never pay any attention to that disturbance. Their attention would always be on Master Sawan Singh. They were so attentive to Master Sawan Singh that they were not even aware of which pathi was doing the singing. Even if Master Sawan Singh would talk to someone their attention would always be on Master Sawan Singh and they would not pay any attention to the person to whom He was talking. Usually after the Satsang the dear ones would not talk to each other. They would quietly leave for their homes or they would sit there and do more Simran or try to practice their remembrance of the beautiful form of the Master.

This advice would even apply to when one was not in Satsang. I remember one time the commander of my army unit, who had a lot of love and affection for Master Sawan Singh, asked Him about the darshan of the Master when He was sitting in His room and talking to people. Master Sawan Singh replied, "I will say, regarding the darshan of the Master, that you should continue looking at the Master even when He is talking to other people. You should not pay any attention to the person with whom the Master is talking. Your attention should always be toward the Master because if you are paying attention to the person with whom your Master is talking it means you are becoming disrespectful to the Master Who is Almighty, the Owner of the Creation, and Who has come into this world and taken up this body full of dirt and sufferings only for your sake. If you remove your attention from the Master even for a moment it is as though you are being disrespectful to Him and do not appreciate Him."

Many times Master Sawan Singh would shower His grace on His disciples by handing out the chapatis to the dear ones. I have seen many dear ones who would take the chapatis in their hands, but all the time they were receiving the chapati their attention would always be at the forehead of the Master.

It is the Indian custom to touch the feet of a person who you respect. So people would come to Master Sawan Singh and bow down and try to touch His feet. He would say, "What is there in my feet? Everything lies in the eyes. If you want to take any advantage or benefit from me, you should look into my eyes." He would explain that whatever the Master has, it is all in His eyes. Guru Nanak expressed the same thing saying, "O Nanak, one blessed glance from the Master makes us prosperous." It means that if the Master looks at you graciously once, He gives you everything.

In order to explain the value and the importance of the darshan of the True Master, very often in Satsang Master Sawan Singh would tell this story about a merchant who went to a village to reclaim the loan that he had given to a farmer. That farmer was very poor and he had nothing to give to him, so the merchant took all the farmer's belongings and made him homeless. The farmer was so upset that he told the merchant that he would not help him take his things to the nearby town from where that merchant had come. Looking at his condition the other farmers also thought that there was no need to help that merchant, as he was a very cruel man. "Today he has mistreated our brother, tomorrow he can do the same thing with us, so we should boycott him and not help him," they all thought.

That merchant needed someone to take his luggage to the town, so he was looking for someone but no one came to help him. There was a Mahatma there who saw all that, and He felt very gracious on that merchant. He said, "I will help you take the luggage to the town, but there is one condition: either you tell a story to me and I will nod — I will say, 'yes, yes' — or I will tell you a story and you should listen to it very carefully." The merchant thought there could not be any cheaper bargain than this, so he said, "Okay, Mahatma Ji, you carry the luggage and tell me a story, and I will listen to it."

That Mahatma was very gracious — Masters are always very gracious. They tell us stories, but They are telling us stories not because They want to entertain us, but rather so that we may listen to the stories and understand what faults we have. That Mahatma told him many stories and through His stories He told him what faults he had. So gradually, as He was going on telling him stories, the merchant realized his faults.

When they came near the town the Mahatma told him, "Okay, now take your luggage and go. But let me tell you one thing: You have realized that in your whole life you haven't done a single good thing. You have no good karmas, and you will not get the fruit of any good karma. You have done only one good deed — you have spent this hour with me, and you will get the benefit of it. Very soon you are going to die, and when you die you will go the Lord of Judgment. When you go there, He will ask you if you want to enjoy the fruit of this good karma before going to hell, or if you want to enjoy it later. You should tell Him that you want to come to me before going to hell, and when you come to me then you will realize how very important it was for you to be in my company."

When that merchant died, he went to the Lord of Judgment. The Lord of Judgment looked at his account and told him, "Well, you don't have any good karmas in your account except for one thing: you spent one hour with a Mahatma. Because of that, you will be allowed to go and see Him once again, but only for a few moments. Do you want to do that before going to hell, or do you want to save that until later?"

The merchant remembered what the Mahatma had told him, so he said, "Who knows when I will come out of hell? Let me go see that Mahatma and express my gratitude to Him before going to hell." So

Baba Sawan Singh giving chapatis

the Lord of Judgment sent the angels of death with him and told him that he could go the plane where the Mahatma was living. He told him that since the angels of death were not allowed to go to that plane, he should go there alone, but after a couple of moments the angels of death would signal to him that his time was up, and at that point he should come back.

When the merchant came to that Mahatma, the Mahatma said, "Dear One, so you have come." He said, "Yes, Mahatma Ji, I have come, but I'm afraid that I will have to leave very soon because the angels of death are waiting for me. They have told me to come back after two moments. So what should I do? I am very afraid." So the Mahatma said, "Don't worry. Keep quiet and sit down here. Don't worry about them, don't pay any attention to them, because they cannot enter this place."

Then that merchant realized how very important it was for him to be in the company of the Master. After he had gone in the company of the Master, he was allowed to see Him once again for a couple of moments, but because that Mahatma was very gracious and loving towards him, He forgave all his sins and paid off all his karmas and liberated him from the sufferings of hell.

By telling this story Baba Sawan Singh would explain that when the Masters give us Their loving, gracious darshan, at that time They are showering a lot of grace on us. He was showing how the company of the Master is always valuable, but we don't realize how much we are getting by coming in contact with the Masters, we realize it only when we go into the Court of the Lord.

> *In which things is Sawan pleased; how can I know the secret of Sawan?*
>
> *When Sawan came all the flowers bloomed, the doors of Kal Power were closed.*
> *He won the game of Sat Naam.*
>
> *By giving Satsang, He explained the Path. He wants to take the souls to Sach Khand.*
> *Meditate on Naam — don't become the disobedient one.*
>
> *Becoming Sawan Shah, He came into this world and glorified the name of Jaimal Singh.*
> *He cured those who were diseased with ego.*
>
> *O Sawan, come and give us Your darshan.*
> *Remove the disease of birth after birth so that Ajaib the suffering one may become well.*
>
> — Sawan Kehria Ranga Vich Razi

Sawan Singh and His Critics

In the time of Master Sawan Singh many foreigners and people from different parts of India came and took advantage of His presence and His work. But Master Sawan Singh also had to face a lot of opposition from many different religions and from many people who lived near his ashram. The *Akalis*, an orthodox sect of the Sikhs, even built a gurdwara right across the road from His dera and they used to go on criticizing Him there from morning to evening. They even wrote a book against Him and opposed Him in that way.

Master Sawan was told by people that He should respond to their criticism, but He replied that there was no need to do that, as Saints are unique examples and the critics would learn something. He was so gracious that He did not mind the criticism. Master Sawan Singh never answered the criticism, in the same tone, as the Masters always forgive and never take revenge. Instead Master Sawan Singh, Who was an abode of forgiveness, used to say, "Brothers, the langar over here in this dera is of the Master. You may be hungry and needing food as you are doing this work from morning to night. Since you don't have any means to eat food over at your place, you are welcome to have food here." He was always graciously inviting them — His opponents, His critics — to come and have food in His langar. Just see how much humility He had. Such humility can only be had by the great Masters.

Many times those Akalis would invite other Akalis to come and discuss how to work more effectively against Master Sawan Singh. But when the new people would come there and see the dera right behind the gurdwara they would attend the Master's Satsang in the evening. After hearing the Satsang they would become so impressed with Him that instead of criticizing Him, they would take Initiation, and leave the company of the critics. As the Akalis saw that many people were becoming impressed by Master Sawan Singh, and were even becoming initiates, they decided to move away. They turned that gurdwara into a school, which still exists.

We know that we satsangis do not have much capacity for patience, but the Masters, the Saints, have a lot of patience in Them. That is why whenever Master Sawan Singh Ji used to invite His opponents to come and have food in the langar, the satsangis around Him would get upset and say, "But they are criticizing us." Master Sawan Singh Ji used to say, "No, they are not doing anything wrong to us, in fact they are doing our work. You see that you do not have to do any publicity and you do not have to tell people about the Path. They are the ones who are telling people about the Path, so in fact they are doing your work, and we should feed them, we should help them."

Reading history we become ashamed when we understand that the Saints came into this world to liberate us for our own benefit, but instead of taking advantage of Their coming into this world, we people gave them a very hard time. We know how Christ was crucified, and how Guru Arjan Dev was tortured. Swami Ji Maharaj was also bothered very much and many other Saints who came into this world for the sake of the souls were given a very hard time. Reading all this history we feel very embarrassed: the Mahatmas come into the world for our sake, and what do we do in return?

When Master Sawan Singh was opposed very much like this by different religious people, He used to say, "It is only because of the

British rule that I am able to do Satsang freely. If it were not for the democratic rule, we would have also been judged like the past Masters." He would say that if it were like the past, if one particular religion was governing the country, He would have been troubled and opposed, as had happened to the Saints in the past. Only because of democracy and the British people, He was able to hold Satsang freely and He was able to convey His thoughts to the people.

However, Saints know who are the people who criticize others. They know that only those who have weakness within themselves criticize others, and that they criticize and comment on other people's ability only to hide their own weakness. It is my personal experience that perfect Masters never criticize anyone. They themselves never criticize anyone nor do They teach Their disciples to criticize others. They neither criticize anyone in the Satsang nor in Their private time, and They never allow Their dear ones to criticize others. Master Sawan Singh used to say that from every sense organ there is some pleasure or some taste. But criticism does not have any taste; it is neither sweet nor sour. But it is such a thing, that once one gets attached to it, it does not leave that person alone. However, Saints have big hearts and that is why They even have love for Their critics; They always forgive them. Master Sawan used to give the example of the Muslim Saint, Mansur. He said that when Mansur was being killed, He told God Almighty, "O Lord, forgive them because they do not know what they are doing. They do not recognize me. But I have so much sympathy, so much pain, for them in my heart."

Advice on Marriage

Master Sawan Singh used to say, "When people come to me and ask, 'Master, should I get married,' I tell them, 'Well, if you can carry the burden, then you may get married. If you can maintain the married life, then you may get married.' And when people ask me, 'Master, should I not get married? Is it all right if I live without getting married?' I advise them, 'Well, if you can maintain chastity without getting married, if you can abstain from committing adultery, then you may remain unmarried.' "

As you know, I got many opportunities to sit at the feet of beloved Master Sawan Singh, and I heard many of His talks, and still these words of that great Master are sounding in my ears. He used to say this very often in the Satsang, that if you cannot maintain chastity, if you cannot remain celibate while being single, then you should get married. He used to say that in the Path of the Masters, it is not a bad thing to get married. However, from outside people pretend they are good meditators, that they are celibate, and so they do not get married, but inside they are always thinking about women and thinking about lust. He would say that if you don't have thoughts of lust, even in your dreams, then you can say you have maintained chastity, and then it is all right if you don't get married. But if lust is bothering you, even in your dreams, even in your thoughts, then there is no harm in getting married and one should, without any hesitation, get married. That would help a lot in one's spiritual upliftment.

Master Sawan also used to say that once we get married it is very important for us to maintain that marriage. No Master has ever inspired people to divorce; They have never inspired people to commit adultery. He used to say that the woman who has many husbands, how is she going to please them all and how is she going to care for them all? In the same way, the man who has many wives, many companions, how is he going to please them all? Just as it is very difficult to develop love for one Master, even if we go on working for it throughout our lifetime, in the same way, it is very difficult to develop the love for one husband or one wife in our lifetime.

Master Sawan Singh was married and He lived a householder's life. Many Saints lived a householder's life and many Saints were renunciates. Neither the householder Saints said that renunciation is bad, nor have the renunciate Saints said that the householders are bad. They all said that it makes no difference whether you live a householder's life or the life of a renunciate, but the thing that counts is the strength with which you maintain your way of life. If the Saints were renunciates, They were completely renunciate, and if they were householders, They always maintained the religion of the household.

On the Vegetarian Diet

Master Sawan Singh used to say, "As we have the right to live on this earth, in the same way all other living creatures have the right to live on this earth. If you want to eat flesh, eat your own flesh. Why don't you cut some flesh from your body and eat that? Because when you kill some creature to eat its flesh, do you think it will be giving you its best wishes? As we would not like our body to be cut up, in the same way no living creature would like the same treatment from us."

One time my troop was stationed near Beas station and one soldier was slaughtering innocent sheep for food. When he was killing them, by accident he cut his own leg. I saw this with my own eyes, and I saw that when his leg got cut, he started crying and weeping, and he was taken to the hospital. Not only was he suffering and weeping, but the other people who saw him suffering, they also started weeping.

When we are killing animals to eat them, even they cry, even they weep, but who listens to them and who pays any attention to their crying and weeping? The innocent, speechless animals are being killed every day; millions of them, and men put spices on them and eat them. It is possible that those who have become goats and animals at this time might have been wealthy people or good human beings in their past, but because they did not take advantage of that birth, as a result of their mistakes they have come back into this world in the lower bodies. If we do not do the devotion of God and if we do not do the good deeds, what will happen to us if we come back into the bodies of the animals? How will we feel if, when we are in their place, they cut our throat? How will we feel if they put spices on us and they eat us?

For this reason we should always try to protect all living beings because we are all created by God and we all have an equal right to live on this earth. Master Sawan Singh also used to say that we have to teach all these things to the children. We should tell them about the benefits of the vegetarian diet and about how eating meat and eggs and other animal products increases our burden of karma. It is our duty to lovingly explain to our children, so that they become free of this burden of karmas, and so that they do not eat such things that create the load of karmas for them.

The Sevadars' Fighting

Once there were some sevadars of Master Sawan Singh who were doing seva when they started criticizing each other and then they even started fighting with each other. Not to mention the slaps, they fought so much they even starting hitting each other with sticks and throwing stones at each other. In that fight many of the sevadars were wounded. The man in charge of the seva, one of the leading sevadar organizers, said, "Okay, let us all go to the Master. The Master will go from this side to His house so there I will ask Him to stop and see you." That man wanted to take them to Master Sawan Singh to complain about the fighting that they had done.

When Master Sawan Singh came past He saw them but He did not stop to meet them even though some of them were bleeding because they had been hit. He did not stand there, He did not want to listen, He did not want to talk to them. When the man in charge came forward and told Master Sawan Singh what had happened, the Master said, "They are the children of the same Father, but still they fight with each other. What will other people think who see that they are satsangis and still they are fighting with each other? What more punishment do they deserve? Can I give them any more punishment than what they themselves have got? I don't want to talk to them, I don't want to listen to what they have to say."

I was a witness to this incident; just imagine how much of Master Sawan Singh's displeasure they had earned that He did not even want to look at them or talk to them! Just imagine how much ill-feeling the new people who were around at that time had when they saw the sevadars fighting with each other!

The teaching of Master Sawan Singh was that while doing the seva you should be very careful that you are doing it lovingly. You should respect and love the other satsangis whom you are serving, because this is the main thing taught in Sant Mat. Many people come into the *sangat* and each sevadar should set such a good example, such a loving example, that the other people may carry that example back and remember how much love and devotion the sevadars had while doing the seva.

I had the opportunity to spend a great deal of time in the presence of this great Master and I saw that when people lived with the Master day after day, often their yearning for the Master gradually got less and less. I saw that many of these dear ones would not want to obey what the Master would ask them to do and they would even compete with the Master. What benefit can that kind of people get from being with the Master? Those dear ones who live at the feet of the Master, if they argue with each other, if they backbite, if they criticize each other, and if they even hit each other, what worse can they do, and what punishment can the Master give to them?

After some time Master Sawan Singh returned and asked the dear ones what the problem was. They all said whatever they wanted to say, and they all said they were right. No one admitted that he had made a mistake. They all were criticizing the others. Master Sawan Singh said, "When all of you say that you are right and that the other person has made the mistake, when nobody is ready to admit to a mistake, it means that all of you are innocent. Then why are you fighting with each other? If anyone has made a mistake, he should apologize and the other person should forgive. Don't you have any forgiveness?"

Then Master Sawan Singh told them to sit for meditation and He told people to watch over them. He said, "After meditating, come to me and tell me what you feel then." When we sit for meditation, it is the mind's habit that he will at once realize his mistakes. So when those dear ones sat for meditation, they realized their mistake and they all came and apologized to Master Sawan Singh. He told them, "Listen, you are all the children of the same Father. You should not fight with each other."

Guarding the Kings

O man, you have to remember the moment of pain, as you have very little time, very little time.

You are engrossed in the business of the world.
You were supposed to remember, but you have forgotten God.
Without the Naam your life will be ruined. You have very little time.

Mother, father, sister, brother — no one comes near you.
In the Court of the Lord there is no support except the Master.
Every single moment is going to be counted. You have very little time.

In the womb of the mother you lived hung upside down.
Do not forget how you were protected there.
The Master protects your honor from beginning to end. You have very little time.

O Beloved Satguru, forgive our faults.
O Giver Sawan, forgive our sins.
Listen to Ajaib — it is his hearty plea. You have very little time.

— Dukha Vali Ghari

While I was in the Army, I had the opportunity to meet eight heads of state in the Punjab. The kings in India at that time were very powerful and very strong, but I did not see anyone who was free of fear. Even though many soldiers would guard their palaces, still, if there was a little bit of noise in the middle of the night, the alarms would go off and everybody would wake up and ask if the guards were alert or not.

I also had the opportunity of witnessing the death of three kings. Once we were posted in the fort of King Bhupinder Singh of Patiala. He became very sick and hundreds of soldiers, all armed, surrounded his palace. Every half hour the number of soldiers was counted and it was proclaimed how many soldiers were guarding that place. But the Angel of Death came and took that king away, and when that Power came It was not the least bit affected by the armed forces! Although many people were there, no one knew when that Power came, and no one knew from which direction It came and took the soul of the king away. We knew the Angel of Death had come only after the king was dead.

I was also in the army when the King of Kapurthala left the body. Karpurthala was a princely state in the Punjab. There were many soldiers there but when the king's endtime came, nobody knew from which side Kal, the Lord of Death, came and took him. There were so many soldiers with guns and ammunition, but it was all useless. Nobody could help that king, outwardly, at that critical moment.

The Queen of Karpurthala was an initiate of Master Sawan Singh. Before she was initiated she had come to Master Sawan Singh with a lot of wealth. She was proud of being a queen and since she was carrying a lot of wealth she thought maybe she would be welcomed by Master Sawan Singh and she would get a lot of honor and name and fame from Him. However, when she came to Master Sawan Singh He lovingly explained to her the theory of Sant Mat. He gave her some books on Sant Mat to read, and eventually she followed the Path of the Masters and became an initiate of Master Sawan Singh. After that she used to tell her husband, the king, that he should go and see the Master and take Initiation. He would reply, "I may go see Baba Sawan Singh, but since I am a king, what will my people say? 'He is a king and still he follows a Saint?' What will they think about me?" Other times he would say things like, "Well, I don't have the court ready now. I will go next Satsang," or "Well, today I don't have a good coat. Maybe later when I get new clothes I will go see Him." So he always kept on procrastinating and he never went. But death does not spare anyone, and when his time came the King of Kapurthala complained that the Angels of Death were pulling him with chains around his neck and he was in serious pain. He requested his wife, "Do something for me because now I am having terrible pain." The Queen said, "Didn't I tell you to go and see Master Sawan Singh? He is the liberator, He is the forgiver; He forgives everyone's sins. But you did not do that, so what can I do for you now?" But when the Queen realized how much the King was suffering, she requested Master Sawan Singh to help him and then, because of the grace of the Master, he was saved from the beating of the Angels of Death. I was posted as a wireless operator in his palace and I witnessed this.

The state of Karpurthala used to be called as the Paris of India. When that king died, I helped take him to the cremation ground. It was very beautiful, with so many beautiful trees all around. At that place we reduced him to a handful of ashes, and at that time I sang a bhajan written by Ravi Das, which says, "A day comes when a person comes into this world, and a day comes when he leaves this world. No one lives in this world forever. No one is permanent here."

Asking for the Forgiveness

Once an initiate of Baba Sawan Singh committed a mistake and in order to confess his mistake he blackened his face and put a garland of broken shoes around his neck and came to Satsang. I also was present during that Satsang, and when the Satsang was about to finish he stood up and requested Baba Sawan Singh to forgive him because he had committed a mistake. Baba Sawan Singh said, "Okay, listen to me," and He told this story to all the sangat. Once there was an old woman, and she had a goat and a monkey. Both animals were her pets. Once that old woman prepared many delicious foods, and before she was going to eat the foods she thought of going to the market to buy some yogurt. While she was away from the house, what did that monkey do? He went into the kitchen and ate all the food that the lady had made. He even drank the milk. Then he put some of the milk and some of the food on the mouth of that goat and he removed the rope from the neck of the goat. After some time, when the old woman came back, she did not find any food in the kitchen, and when she saw that the mouth of the goat was smeared with food and milk, she thought that the goat had finished all the food and had drunk the milk. The monkey, who was very clever, was sitting with his eyes closed, pretending he was doing meditation.

As a result of this, the old woman became upset with the goat and started beating her. She did not say anything to the monkey because he had successfully played his trick and she had no doubts about him. A man saw all this drama and he thought, "Look at the condition of that poor goat! She did not do anything, it was not her fault, and she did not eat any food, but still she is getting a beating. While the monkey who is the cause of all this play, who even enjoyed the food, is now pretending to do the devotion of the Lord, and he is not getting any beating."

The meaning of this story was that our mind does all these tricks, our mind makes all the mistakes, but our body and our soul have to suffer for it. Master Sawan Singh did not even ask that person what bad deed or karma he had done. He said, "Okay, you sit down. The One Who is to forgive you is also within you and you are forgiven. You should not repeat that mistake again."

Many times dear ones who had made mistakes or who had sinned would come like this and in front of the sangat ask for forgiveness. In the sangat Master Sawan Singh would ask, "Is there anyone from the sangat who is willing to take on the karmas of this person?" Who could say yes? It is difficult to bear the load of our own karmas, so how can we even think of carrying the burden of other people's karmas? So when nobody would come forward to share the sin of such dear ones, Master Sawan Singh would lovingly say, "It is only the Master who takes on the burdens of our sins. In this world there is no one else who wants to share the burden of our karmas." Then Master Sawan Singh would always tell the person who asked for forgiveness, "Okay, you sit down. You are forgiven, but don't do it again."

It used to be such a unique scene in the Satsang of Master Sawan Singh. Many times during the Satsang the dear ones sitting there would stand up and they would ask such questions or they would make such comments. If any dear one would say more than he should have said, Master Sawan would say, "Don't tease me!"

Some Dear Ones of Sawan

When I visited the dera of Master Sawan Singh, I got to know some dear ones who were very devoted to Master Sawan Singh. There was one initiate of Master Sawan Singh whose name was Mahatma Chattardas who came from an area called Janawali that is now in Pakistan. Chattardas had left his family and gone into the jungle. He had done all the rites and rituals and had even performed the austerities. He had grown his hair long and he had even tried covering his body with ashes, but he did not find God by doing any of those things. Then he was told by someone, "God Almighty, for Whom you are searching outside, and doing all these things — you cannot find Him like that since He is within you." He was told that Baba Sawan Singh was the only one present in the world at that time who could show him the Beautiful One in his within. He came to the feet of Master Sawan Singh and became a very devoted initiate who manifested Him in his within.

In the same way, in the city of Ujain there used to live a holy man whose name was Hanuman and he had a brother who was called Japuti. Both of them went to Rishikesh, which is another holy place, in search of God. Hanuman had performed the austerities for twelve years, but he didn't receive anything from doing that. Finally he learned about Baba Sawan Singh and he and his brother went to Baba Sawan Singh. After they came to the door of Master Sawan Singh they did not leave it; they remained there for the rest of their lives. When I first met Baba Sawan Singh and He learned that I had performed austerities and that in search of God I had left my home and wandered here and there, He introduced me to Hanuman because he had done the same thing.

Gamblers are in contact with the gamblers, drunkards are in contact with the drunkards, because they think alike and their thoughts are similar. That is why they are always in contact with each other and they like to be with each other. In the same way, those who have done the rites and rituals, those who have done the austerities, those who have gone to the places of pilgrimage — those who have done all these outer things — they always like to be with and share with the people who have done the same thing. Whatever rites, rituals and religious deeds those two mahatmas had performed, and whatever hunger and thirst they had suffered in their lives, I had done the same things and had experienced the same things. That is why we became very close and I had much contact with them since they had done all the same things that I had done.

Those people did not have any house or room in the ashram of Master Sawan Singh. On the bank of the river they had dug out some cave-like places and they lived there. Whenever I went to see Master Sawan Singh I would spend many days with those people.

Mahatma Chattardas, whom I mentioned before, was also a very famous poet of the Urdu language. Very often he would recite a particular couplet in front of Master Sawan Singh, which would say, "Many people leave their homes, they go into the jungle to search for God Almighty. They do not realize Him there, because they are doing that following their minds. Beloved Lord is within us in the form of

Master Sawan Singh walking along the banks of the Beas River

Shabd, and we can have His darshan only after going within." He would also say, "He is the disciple, he is the true lover, who understands himself as the dead one when he does not have the glimpse of the Master. That breath in which the Beloved is not seen, that breath is full of sufferings."

Master Sawan Singh often used to give opportunities to such poets to come up and sing their poetry in front of the people. So on one occasion Mahatma Chattardas recited his poetry in which he said, "You are our very old friend, and now we have recognized You, and now we have embraced You." He went on saying things like that. It was very pleasing to Master Sawan Singh and He was smiling and laughing. When Chattardas was through, Master Sawan invited another poet up who had only one eye. He was one-eyed, but usually he would wear dark glasses so that no one would know that he had only one eye. But on that day he removed his glasses. When Master Sawan Singh looked at him, He asked, "What happened to your other eye?" That poet replied, "Well, Master always in the Satsang You say that we should become one-eyed, that we should close our two eyes and open one single eye in the within. So now this is only one eye — since You said to make one eye, that is why I have made one eye."

Hearing all this Master Sawan Singh and everyone in the sangat laughed very much. How could those people who were sitting there control their laughter after hearing such a humorous thing? Even now whenever I remember that incident, whether I am alone or even if I am traveling in a train, I cannot control my laughter.

Bhai Lehna Throws His Bomb

In the days of Master Sawan Singh many gentlemen would come nicely dressed and sit in the front of the Satsang because the people who used to make the arrangements for the Satsang knew the rich people well and would allow them to come and sit in the front row. There were many poor people however who never got this opportunity and who had not even once got to come close to the Master; they would always sit in the back. Regarding them Master Sawan Singh said many times in Satsang, "If the farmer is watering the fields, he does not look in the front part of the field where he is watering; he always looks in the back of the field, just to make sure how far the water has reached. In the same way, the Master does not pay a lot of attention to the people sitting in front. He always pays attention to the people sitting in the back because He knows that they are the poor, humble ones. He always looks in the back to the poor people to make sure they are able to see Him."

Master Sawan Singh had one disciple named Lehna who was a *harijan*, an untouchable of very low caste. Lehna was always in dirty clothes and did not look like a gentleman, and he was not allowed to sit in the front row at Satsang. Nobody would even let him touch their bodies. He was one of those poor, humble people who never got an opportunity to come close to Master Sawan Singh, but would always go and sit in the back. However, he was a very advanced disciple, progressing very much in meditation. Master Sawan Singh knew that he was never allowed to sit up front, so once He called him and said, "Lehna, you come and sit in the front row." When he did that the gentlemen who were used to sitting in the front row did not like that because they did not want to touch his body. They got up and went away from the front row, moving a distance from him, some even going to sit in the back. After Satsang was completed Master Sawan Singh invited him to speak; He said, "Lehna, now you come and throw your bomb." So Lehna came and he said to all the people, "For the sake of such a Master you have all gathered here, and you are always trying to have one brief glance of the Master. I don't want to say anything, but I just want to tell my brothers who do not like me, who do not like me sitting in the front, that they should know that the Master Whom they love and for Whom they have come, that Master resides within me day and night. He is always residing in me and He is happy to come and reside in this poor humble body that you are hating." Then Master Sawan Singh said, "Bhai Lehna, that is enough; that is all for today. Now you sit down."

Mastana Ji, the Intoxicated One

During this time I also came to know a dear one called Mastana Ji. His name was Kem Chand, but the name Mastana, which means intoxicated one, was given to him by Master Sawan Singh. While at the feet of Master Sawan Singh and while going to His Satsangs I met Mastana Ji many times and had many opportunities to spend time with him. He was my old friend and we had a lot of love for each other. He was a lover in the true sense. He used to call Master Sawan Singh as Sawan Shah, the emperor, and he used to remember Him with his every single breath.

Mastana Ji was from Baluchistan, an area that is now part of Pakistan. He was fond of Spirituality throughout his life. In the beginning of his search for God he used to worship *Sat Narayan*, one of the Hindu gods. He was so fond of worshipping the idols and doing the devotion that, using his own money, he made one idol of Sat Narayan out of gold and he would worship that idol. He never got the darshan of that god Sat Narayan but he got a lot of praise from people that he was a good devotee and was very devoted to that god. But Mastana Ji thought, "Well, I didn't get the real Sat Narayan; I am only getting the praise that I am a good devotee." A voice came to him from within saying, "Kem Chand, you go and search for the perfect Master, otherwise Kal will trouble you and peel off your skin. You go and find the real and perfect Guru." After hearing that, he came to India in search of the real Guru. He went to many places including Multan, Sanglah, and Montgomery, and spent his life searching. He became the disciple of nine different gurus, but none of them were perfect and so he didn't get any satisfaction. At last Baba Sawan Singh appeared to him within and told him, "I am sitting in Sikanderpur, in the Punjab; you come here." So Mastana Ji started searching for Master Sawan Singh and he came to Sikanderpur. There he met Master Sawan Singh Who, at the time they met, was out in the fields of His own property, looking after the people working there.

Master Sawan was all-conscious, and He knew that Mastana Ji had come, and that he had been worshipping the idol of Sat Narayan. So He told Mastana Ji, "First you go and destroy that temple that you have built in your house and bring me that idol of Sat Narayan, that dead Sat Narayan. Then I will give you the living Sat Narayan, the living God, Who will do your every work." So Mastana Ji went back to Baluchistan, which was five or six hundred miles from Beas, and he smashed that temple he had built in his home. He brought that gold idol of Sat Narayan and he gave that to Master Sawan Singh. After that Master Sawan Singh initiated him.

After receiving Initiation, Mastana Ji went back to Baluchistan, and his mind started troubling him, saying, "Now I will trouble you and will not let you do the meditation." But Mastana Ji was a very firm man and he said to his mind, "Okay, you have not met a firm man like me. I will also teach you a lesson." Then the real battle started. At that time in India it was considered shameful to ride on a donkey. So Mastana Ji blackened his face, put a garland of broken shoes around his neck and started riding around on a donkey. He hired a drummer to beat the drum, and with that drummer he rode all around the city. Many people began to laugh at him and abuse him, and he went on distributing sweets to all the people who were abusing him. Finally he went out of the city after getting a lot of abuse and then he sat for meditation in the remembrance of Master Sawan Singh. He used to meditate a lot; for many days he would do the meditation. He would remain hungry and thirsty for many days, and he would practice what Master Sawan Singh had taught him.

Master Sawan Singh used to say that those who have been shot with the bullet of love give up everything. They throw the account books into the well; they become useless for the world because they always remain in the love of the Master.

I got many opportunities to be in Mastana Ji's company and I got much love from him. He was an intoxicated *fakir* of Master Sawan Singh, and he was an illiterate. He did not even know how to sign his name in Punjabi, but in Sainthood he was successful. He was a true lover of the Master and he brought glory to the name of Master Sawan Singh in that part of India.

Mastana Ji

Mastana Ji Crosses the Border

When Mastana Ji used to come to have the darshan of Baba Sawan Singh he had to cross the border between Baluchistan and India. Once it so happened that Mastana Ji was coming with many other initiates, and they were stopped by the customs people and the police inspector. Mastana Ji said, "You should not stop us because we are doing the *haj* (pilgrimage) and our Master Sawan Singh is perfect. You should not stop us." That police inspector didn't care about that and he put all of them in jail. Mastana Ji told all the other initiates to sit for meditation, and as soon as they sat that police inspector came and he said, "Please leave this jail right away, because I am dying. I feel like my life is going to go out." That was the Will created by Master Sawan Singh, so that the jailer was compelled to set all those people free. Then Mastana Ji said, "I told you in the beginning that my Master is perfect and you should not stop us."

Mastana Ji Jumps in the Well

At the place where Baba Sawan Singh used to live there was no electricity in the Satsang hall. In the summertime they used to have large fans that the sevadars would move using their hands. One time, when I was present, one person was fanning Master Sawan Singh in this way and Mastana Ji was also there. Mastana Ji had the desire, "Let me go and fan my Master." He thought, "Is that person fanning the Master superior to me, or has he more right to my Master that only he is allowed to do that seva? Why shouldn't I go and do that?" However, there were many other people there who would not allow Mastana Ji to go in front of Master Sawan and do that job. Mastana Ji became very upset and thought, "Baba Sawan Singh always says in the Satsang that a dear one should never be stopped by anything, even if he is living in a place where there are many snakes or many lions and tigers — no matter how many obstacles there are in the way, the dear one should never be afraid or let anything stop him when he is going to have the darshan of the Master. When Master says all these things, why should I worry? Why should I just stay here? I should kick out that person with the fan and do that seva." Somehow he made his way to the front and he pushed that person and tried to get the fan from him. However, the other person was also very stubborn and did not give the fan to Mastana Ji and they both started fighting. Both of them were very strong and neither wanted to let go of the fan, so ultimately both of them fell onto Baba Sawan Singh Who was sitting there on the bed.

Baba Sawan Singh became upset and He said, "Well, Mastana, why don't you give him the fan?" Mastana replied, "Master, that person is not giving me the fan. Why should I give the fan to him?" So when both of them continued to fight over the fan, Baba Sawan Singh became very upset and He said, "Mastana Ji, you go jump in the well. You are disturbing me a lot."

Mastana Ji wanted to hear some words from the Master; he wanted to hear the order of the Master. So when Master Sawan Singh said, "Go and jump in the well," he at once went to the well that was near the Satsang Hall and jumped into it. When Master Sawan Singh came to know about that, He at once ran to the well and had a rope thrown into the well. Master

Sawan Singh told Mastana Ji to hold that rope and come out. But at the same time Master Sawan Singh was protecting Mastana Ji, and from underneath the water He was holding Mastana Ji up and not letting him drown. Mastana Ji knew that and so he said, "Well, I will not hold the rope and come out. I am obeying Your order. You told me to go and jump in the well, and so now why are You trying to rescue me?"

Anyway, when Mastana Ji came out, he used to say, "One should never get stopped by any obstacle when he is going to have the darshan of the Master. Even if one has to sacrifice a very big thing on the way to the Master, for having the darshan of the Master he should understand that sacrifice as the little one, and he should never let anyone stop him from going to have the darshan of the Master."

I told you earlier about Mahatma Chattardas, another initiate of Master Sawan Singh. In his writing, he wrote that the Master is not bothered by the world, and because He is in the love of His Master, He does not care for the love of the people. For this reason, usually He does not let many people come near Him. But the disciple, the dear one, the lover of the Master, even if he gets the opportunity to have the darshan of the shadow of the Master from a distance, still he understands himself as the most fortunate one. If somehow he gets the opportunity to have the darshan of the Master face-to-face, even from a distance, he will understand that he has gotten a very big treasure and that he is one of the most fortunate ones.

Dance, O Mind, Dance in Front of the Satguru

Dance, O Mind, dance in front of the Satguru.
Sing the praises of Satguru so that you may cut the sin of birth.

There is no liberation without the meditation of God; dwell on Him within your body.
You are not leaving gold and women — why are you involved in this Maya of the three gunas?
Without Satguru, no one is your companion — neither the son nor the father.

The market of greed and egoism is set up;
The drum of the god of lust is being played and Dame Attachment is dancing.

Breaking your love with the five thieves, do the remembrance of the Satguru.

Gorakh Nath and Machinder were defeated when Maya's eyes flashed in anger.
Maya climbed up on Gorakh Nath and applied the spur, making him her horse.
And then she said, "Hurrah! Hurrah! My beautiful horse is dancing by himself!"

Brahma, Vishnu and Shiva Ji were defeated when Maya showed her beauty.
Disguising herself as Bhasma Sur, she caught Shiva Ji and shook him.
Shiva's trident — the mightiest weapon — broke when he was pushed by the god of lust.

Siringi Rishi and Durbasa Muni were also defeated after doing their austerities.
Many great and mighty men came into this world, but were stalked by the Hunter, Kal.
Ved Vyas asks Para Rishi, "Should I call you 'Father' or 'child'?"

In one moment Narada lost the fruit of the austerities which he had performed for sixty thousand years.
When he was hurt by the god of lust, he cried, holding his head.
Then he caused his own face to be made into that of a monkey — and he cursed Vishnu.

In this dark Kali Yuga, the True Satguru, the True Power, has come.
O Living God of the Param Sant, You caught Maya and made her dance.
Mastana Ji says, "Deal in the True Merchandise: Truth knows no fear!"

— Nach Re, a bhajan of Mastana Ji

Mastana Ji used to tie anklets with tiny bells on his feet, like the dancers have, and he would dance in front of Master Sawan Singh. He would dance in front of Him, saying, "Here is God!"

I was also very fond of dancing in those days, and in that mood I had written this bhajan. These bhajans have Mastana Ji's name on them but were in fact penned by me. After Mastana Ji left the body he did not leave any successor but there was one person who took these bhajans and started writing his own name at the end, saying that he had written those bhajans. Because of this I did not feel comfortable, after Mastana Ji left, to delete his name and add mine. But in fact the bhajans that have the name of Mastana Ji were written by me.

In this bhajan it is shown that the rishis and munis — those who came and did meditation or devotion — were all caught in the trap laid down by the Negative Power. They were all deceived and they all fell down. However, those who practiced Sant Mat and became Saints never fell down. Mastana Ji used to say, "O Man, you are dancing in front of your wife, you are dancing in front of your children, you are dancing in front of your family, community, religion; you are dancing in front of your worldly work — but it would be better for you to dance in front of the Satguru." Here "dance" doesn't mean that one has to go and move one's body and dance in front of the Master. "Dance" means to deal with Him, to work for Him. Mastana Ji used to say, "I am saying this by God: that he who knows the trick of pleasing the Master, with him God cannot be displeased." So in this bhajan on one side the rishis and munis, those who lengthened their lives and lived for 60,000 years or more and did the austerities, are talked about, and on the other side it is said, "Hail the Satguru. Thank your Satguru, and be grateful to Him. In that way the Angel of Death will not come near you."

At that time when I wrote this bhajan, in the presence of Master Sawan Singh I said, "Just as Ranja (a great lover in Indian folklore) said, 'Come with me all those who want to become a fakir — because I neither got married, nor will I get married, and there is no one in this world who will mourn my death.' So those who want to become a fakir should come and follow me."

Master Protects the Souls at the Time of Death

Once in the Satsang of Master Sawan Singh one young girl stood up and thanked Master for taking care of her grandmother's soul. She said, "I thank You, Master, very much because when my grandmother died You came and took her soul up. As she was leaving the body she said,

'Master Sawan Singh has come and I am going with Him.'" Master Sawan Singh said, "Thousands of grandmothers are dying and always Baba Jaimal Singh Ji is coming and taking them up. It is not a new thing."

At that time Mastana Ji was also there and he had brought two bags of ashes and bones of many people who had left the body because of a cholera outbreak in Baluchistan. In India it is a tradition that when anyone dies they are cremated and some of their ashes or left over bones are taken and immersed in the waters of some holy river like the River Ganges or Jamna. Mastana Ji had brought such ashes and bones, but instead of immersing them in the River Ganges or Jamna he had brought them to Master Sawan Singh, because he used to say that Master Sawan Singh is the most holy place of pilgrimage. So when Master Sawan Singh said to that girl that Baba Jaimal Singh Ji was always coming, Mastana Ji stood up and said, "That is not true. All these people whose bones and ashes I am carrying, they all said, 'We are leaving and Master Sawan Singh has come to take our soul.' You say that it is Baba Jaimal Singh coming to take their souls, but they reported that Master Sawan Singh had come to protect their souls." Master Sawan Singh said, "Mastana Ji, you are brave." By saying this, He meant that those who are the brave *satsangis,* the meditator satsangis, they see their Master functioning everywhere.

Tulsi Sahib said that it is very difficult to understand a Saint. Even if you sit in front of the Saint and tell Him, "You protected us; You did this, or You did that for us" — still He will never agree. He will always say, "No, that is not me. I have not done anything." He is a very innocent being, He is a very serious being, and He will never say that He has done anything. It is very difficult to understand the Master.

Gurumukhs are so competent in Their work of Spirituality that if They are doing Satsang at one place physically, at the same time, They appear at another place and take care of the souls of the disciples. They are so very competent that, if They are traveling in this part of the world, at the same time They may be giving darshan and Satsang to other dear ones in other parts of the world. And yet They are very humble and always give the credit to Their Master. Whenever the dear ones have such experiences, they go to the Master and tell Him, "Master, You gave us darshan at this time." When such things happen, the Masters don't become proud of that and They don't accept any credit for Themselves. They always say, "It is all the grace of Baba Ji."

Supervising the farm work in Sirsa

With Baba Sawan Singh at Sirsa

When Baba Sawan Singh was developing the land at Sirsa, He stayed for a long time in the house of a Rajput gentleman named Madhu Singh. When He used to go to Sirsa where He had His farm, not everyone was allowed to go there. He used to say that when He went to His farmhouse, He was playing the role of a family man with His family; He was like a worldly person, and the satsangis should not come and disturb His worldly activities. So not many people were allowed to go there. However my commander, Lieutenant General Bikram Singh, was an initiate of Master Sawan Singh and was fond of seeing Him. He was allowed to go and see Master Sawan Singh whenever he wanted. As my commander's wireless operator, I also had the opportunities to go and see Master Sawan at Sirsa.

Master Sawan Singh was a very successful farmer and whenever He would visit His farm, He would visit the sevadars who were working at the farm and take them food. Every morning He would distribute among them as *parshad* the chapatis left over from the previous day and also give them sugar that was made from the sugarcane juice produced on the farm. Once when Master Sawan Singh went there to give food to the people, some gentlemen were there who were very worried about their clothes. Because of that they were not

Distributing chapatis as parshad to the sevadars at Sirsa

interested in doing the seva of carrying baskets full of mud. They were even complaining and telling the other people to stay away from them, because when the others were carrying the baskets of mud the dust would come and get their clothes dirty. At that time Master Sawan came, and those same gentlemen told the sevadars that they should go away because the dust was blowing towards the Master and spoiling His clothes. But Master Sawan Singh Ji said, "No, don't do that, because this dust of the sangat is very precious to me. It is very sweet and nectarful to me, and I like it because it is from the sangat."

Mastana Ji of Baluchistan was also there, and he crawled to the place where Master Sawan Singh was standing. He did not worry about his clothes; he did not even worry about his body. Master Sawan Singh told him he should walk and not crawl, but he said, "No, I would like to crawl on the sand where You have put Your feet, because it is like parshad to me."

At that time I was also present, and I was wearing a sheet, a small piece of cloth that was not very expensive, just an ordinary piece of cloth. When Master Sawan Singh came there to give parshad, there wasn't any chair or any other thing on which He could sit down. So I put that sheet down on the ground and He sat on that. I felt very fortunate that He sat on that sheet. I valued that sheet very much, I kept it and preserved it.

Who will appreciate the Master and the things of the Master? Not everyone can have this kind of appreciation, but only he upon whom the grace has been showered and only he who has the understanding of the glory of the Master. When Guru Teg Bahadur, the ninth Sikh Guru, was on His way to Patna from the Punjab, He came to the city of Kashi where Kabir Sahib used to live. From there He took the loom on which Kabir Sahib used to weave the cloth, and also that piece of wood on which He used to keep the cloth after weaving. Guru Teg Bahadur carried that all the way from Kashi to Patna, which is a very long distance, especially in those days when there were no good means of transportation. There were no trains or buses, and people had to walk. The dear ones who were accompanying Guru Teg Bahadur offered to carry those things, but He said, "No, this is something which I have to carry, because these are the things which were used by God Almighty to earn His livelihood when He came down to this world."

"Let us all go to Sirsa — Let's go, let's go"

Let us all go to Sirsa.
I am in the pangs of separation of the beautiful Beloved
  — let's go, let's go.

You always remain with the Lord and we suffer pain day
  and night.
Every moment we deaf ones are being washed away in
  sorrows. We are neither on this shore nor on that
  shore.

Fortunate are those souls that live with You every moment.
We have been bearing millions of sufferings by sitting and rubbing our knees.

In every conversation we feel pain and the whole world looks barren.
Come soon and show Your face. I am in pain without Your darshan.

My hope and wish is not fulfilled and I am sitting outside the boundary crying.
Without You, O Beloved, I am dead while alive. I offer my life to You.

O Beloved Sawan, where did You go? I, the prisoner, am spending my life weeping.
I sit and count the stars at night. In the day I spend my time looking at the road for You.

Hundreds of times I dreamed, O my Lord, You have forgotten me.
Why did You bring me close to You by telling me nice things?

O Dear Sawan, without You I am dead. Without Your darshan I have gone crazy.
I cry, O Sawan, please come out of the curtain now and have conversations of love with me.

Your shoes are much better than I. They are always with You. I wander around in hot sand.
Please come soon; I am surrounded by death. I am in pain for want of the darshan of my Beloved Sawan.

— Bhajan of Sant Kirpal Singh
Chelo Ni Saiyo Sirsa

On another occasion, I went to Sirsa with my general and while we were there at the feet of Baba Sawan Singh, I heard this bhajan: *Chelo ni saiyo Sirsa nu chaliye.* It was sung by one woman, Bibi Hardevi Ji, who later on was known as Tai Ji. This bhajan was very sweet and very attractive, but I did not know at that time that it was written by the Master who would later initiate me. During the time I was at the feet of Master Sawan Singh, I did not meet my future Master personally, I didn't have any communication with Him, I didn't know Him. In fact I had the opportunity to hear many bhajans that were written by Him, which were sung by Tai Ji, but I did not know that those bhajans were written by that great Master who was going to bring coolness to my heart in the future. I did not know that Tai Ji was so close to that Master or that she was so close to Master Sawan Singh. Hearing those bhajans, one felt coolness in the soul; they cooled down the soul.

In fact those bhajans were the messages from that great Master for His Master, Baba Sawan Singh. When Tai Ji used to sing these bhajans, she was conveying these messages, because that was a time when that disciple was not able to go and be with Master Sawan Singh. When Master Sawan Singh was developing His farm at Sirsa, He had given very strict orders that nobody should come there because it was His family place. He said that all those who wanted to meet Him should only come to the dera. However, for the dear one who has united himself with the Master inside, it is very difficult to remain away from the physical form of the Master. Such a one cannot live without having the darshan of the physical form of the Master. But since the order was given by Master Sawan Singh, that Beloved disciple could not go to Sirsa and so He wrote this bhajan to serve as a message. Tai Ji acted as a mediator between Him and Master Sawan Singh and the poems He would write as a message to Master Sawan Singh, she would sing those in the form of bhajans to Master Sawan Singh on His behalf.

You see how much humility and yearning there is in this bhajan. He says that Your shoes are much better than me, because Your shoes always remain with You. We cannot live with You all the time, but Your shoes always remain with You. We wish that we had become Your shoes, because if we had, we would have remained at Your feet.

The Beautiful Inner Form of Baba Sawan Singh

Since I saw Sawan I have hidden Him in my eyes.
I have never forgotten the way Sawan smiled.
Sawan is beloved. Sawan is beautiful. Sawan is the owner
  of my heart.

He was the Radiant Form Who lives in the eyes.
*His style was unique. His glory was unique. Still I have
    not understood.*
Every day I cry. Every day I sing. People call me mad.

White beard, broad forehead, tying a turban He came.
*Even the fairies bow down to Him. And the moon has
    come out in the sky.*
*The world searches for Him outside, but He has given
    everyone the slip!*

"Let us all go to Sirsa," Kirpal proclaimed.
*Ajaib also sang, "Gracious Sawan has caused the drizzle
    to shower."*
Come, let us all have the darshan of the Radiant Form.
    — Sawan Sawan Duniya Kehendi

In these pages I have just been talking about the outer meetings with Baba Sawan Singh. I had many meetings with Him, maybe more than a thousand. His face was so attractive, so beautiful that I can never forget Him. Whoever was given that smile by Master Sawan Singh could not forget it all his life. I was also a fortunate one to get that smile, and I still remember that, I cannot forget it. However, it is not the body, the outward physical form of the Master that the Masters always describe as the most beautiful one, it is the Inner Form, the Radiant Form of the Master. If one sees the Inner Radiant Form, one can never forget that. As far as the inner meetings with that Radiant Form, for me it was daily.

The bodies of different Masters are different. Someone is tall, someone is short. The body sometimes becomes weak because of sickness and things like that so it is not the physical body that Masters often talk about as the most beautiful form, it is the inner Radiant Form that we can see only after going within. The Shabd Form of the Master is so beautiful, so attractive, that once you rise above and see that with your own eyes you will never forget that Form and you will always want to look at that Form again and again.

When we withdraw all our scattered thoughts and attention by doing the Simran and come to the Eye Center, to the Third Eye, the physical veil is removed from our soul. When we go to this place and have the darshan of the Radiant Form of the Master, after that, no matter if the whole world says, "He is not the Master, He is a deceiver," you will not believe them. You cannot leave that Reality once you have seen it with your own eyes. History tells us that those great devotees who saw this Reality about their Master with their own eyes, they preferred to climb the cross, they preferred to get their body cut into pieces, but they did not leave the Reality.

> *Sawan is like the moon. He is the most beautiful one in the world.*
>
> *I sacrifice my body and life for You.*
> *Without You the world seems empty.*
> *I have to touch the moon in the sky.*
>
> *I always have the thought of Sawan.*
> *The whole world says that You belong to them, but You are mine.*
> *I have to tell You the condition of my heart.*
>
> *The mole looks so beautiful on the fair face.*
> *Ajaib is not content, even after seeing it many times.*
> *There can be no one like Sawan in this world.*
>
> — Sawan Chan Varga

When we cross over the plane of the stars, of the moon, and the plane of the suns, and when we manifest the Form of the Master, the Form of the Master is so beautiful, so loving — that Form cannot be described in words. In the writings of the Masters that very Form is praised and it is said that He is so beautiful that whenever we see Him, we feel as though the moon is coming out. Guru Arjan said, "May I always behold the beautiful Form of the Master. If I don't see Him, I lose my senses."

You know that when the moon rises and comes out, the moon bird goes on looking at the moon. He does not move his body and he keeps moving his neck as the moon progresses overhead. Even if it becomes very painful for him, he does not bother but still he goes on looking at the moon. He does not want to give up looking at the moon, even for a moment.

The condition of the disciple who has manifested the Master within becomes the same. Once you manifest the Radiant Form of the Master, you always want to look at Him. Once you manifest the Radiant Form of your Master within yourself, it doesn't matter if you go to America, to India, or to any place — even if you sit in a closed room — still He will always be with you. Just as the moon bird does not want to give up looking at the moon, the disciple who has manifested the Form of the Master within himself does not wish to give up looking at the Form of the Master even for a moment.

> *The Form of the Master is very beautiful — Within the sunlight is shining.*
> *The honeybee becomes happy, when the lotus blooms — he loves it.*
> — a couplet of Swami Ji Maharaj

When the disciple reaches the Form of the Master, his condition becomes like the condition of the honeybee. When the lotus blooms, the honeybee starts wandering around the lotus. It doesn't go away from the lotus even for a moment. He is so much in love with the lotus that in the evening, when the lotus closes, he stays within the lotus and he dies there. Just as the honeybee becomes crazy for the fragrance of the flower, in the same way, the disciple becomes crazy for the darshan of the Master.

I am not saying these things from hearsay. Whatever I have experienced or have seen, with the grace of the Master, I am talking about only those things.

The Partition of 1947

Once Master Sawan Singh was talking with some Akali leaders, Thara Singh and Udham Singh Nagoke, who were very famous religious leaders. At that time the commander of my army unit was there and I was also present. These religious leaders asked Master Sawan Singh, "We know that in your horoscope it is written that you have a life of a hundred years. Is that true?" Master Sawan Singh replied, "Yes, that is very true. But I will live to a hundred years only if the dear ones will allow me to work peacefully. If they do more meditation and ask only about the spiritual affairs, there is some chance I might live for a long time. However, if people bring worldly questions to me and do not meditate, if they throw their difficulties and problems on my head, and if I have to shed my blood to save the people, then I will not be able to live that long."

Saints do not like to shed Their blood for no reason, but They are helpless because They are very gracious on Their souls. Whenever

They see that the people are fighting with each other, They at once go to that place and rescue them. The grace of the Saints is not limited to just His city or state or country. His grace is extended to everyone who remembers Him with love and affection. Even a worldly father is affected if he sees that his two children are fighting with each other. He also feels sick. In the same way when the Saints see that the people are fighting with each other and killing each other, They also feel very sad for them and They intervene in their fight, and in that process They have to sacrifice Themselves. Saints do not perform any miracles and They do not use Their supernatural powers, but it is true that during such happenings, Nature itself takes up the form of the Saints and goes to rescue the people.

In the partition of India in 1947, India and Pakistan were formed as separate countries. At that time it was like a bloody storm because everywhere people were killing each other. People belonging to one religion were killing people of the other religion. In the place that is now Pakistan many Sikhs and Hindus were killed and in India many Muslims were killed. Many girls were raped and everywhere very tragic events occurred. People were not thinking about whether what they were doing was good or bad. They were not even paying attention to whether the person who was being killed was old or young, man or woman. In the name of religion they were killing people of the other religion, and it is possible that at no other period did India have to face such a hard time, such a terrible time, as it did during this time.

I witnessed all that happened from a very close distance because I was in the army and it was my duty to work where these things were happening at that time. The things I witnessed made it one of the most painful times in my life. I have visited many forests and I have gone very close to the lions and tigers and even poisonous cobras, but even they don't attack you unless you bother them. If you just leave them alone, they will not bother you. You can go your way and they will go their way. But when human beings become barbaric, they become like demons, and they don't have any mercy or sympathy for other people. Just imagine the condition of the innocent people who become victims of the barbaric acts of such people. Just imagine what that is like. Imagine you are going on a road and somebody comes and attacks you and kills you right there. You cannot ask for mercy, as he will not have any sympathy for you. What to talk about the men, this was done even with the small children, those who had not done anything wrong.

During that partition people were forced to leave their homes and property because they were always afraid of the people of the other religion who were coming to kill them. They would form a group and travel from their home area to another part of the country where they would be safer. During those difficult times, Master Sawan would welcome everybody at His dera and He would give them refuge and take care of them. To Him, it made no difference whether they were Hindu or Muslim. He would tell them, "This is your ashram, and you should not worry because God who protected you before, here also He will take care of you." Many Muslim people coming from India went to His dera and He protected them and fed them. He protected and took care of them without being concerned for His own safety or His own comfort.

Once Master Sawan was on the way to Amritsar for a treatment and on the way He saw the Muslim army coming. He told His driver to take Him to the Muslim soldiers, but the driver said, "They are the opponents of the Hindus and they will kill us." Master Sawan Singh said, "No. Nobody is going to do that. Nobody is our enemy." So when Master Sawan came to the military officer in charge of those soldiers He said, "In my ashram, in my dera, there are three or four hundred Muslim brothers, and if you can help me, we can do something for them." With the help of those soldiers, the Muslims who were staying at the ashram were also saved.

At that time, when the people were suffering, Master Sawan Singh not only provided outer help, but He was also the only One Who took on the karmas of the people. He took the suffering of the people onto His body. At that time I was living right next to the dera, and I saw that the people were coming from Pakistan in very bad condition. All their belongings had been plundered before they left and many of the members of their community had been killed. Many people reported that some old man had been protecting their group, staying up all night long protecting them from the people of the other religion. When these groups would come to the dera, they would see Baba Sawan Singh and at once they would recognize Him as the old man who had protected them. Even the young children, the infants carried by their mothers, who had never had the darshan of Baba Sawan Singh before, they would fold their hands to the Master when they saw Him, saying, "This is the Baba who protected us from the enemy. This is the Baba who was guarding us during the nighttime when the other people were coming to kill us." This would even happen to those who had not been satsangis, and this would happen to those who had never seen Baba

Sawan Singh before. They had not known about Him and they had not prayed to Him for protection, but still, since Baba Sawan Singh was one with God, He had that element of grace and kindness for all mankind. Because of that, even without being asked, He protected all the souls He was seeing.

During the time of the partition, whatever account of Kal the Master had to settle, Master Sawan Singh did that. In many places He appeared in His physical form to save people's lives and in many places He appeared in the form of Shabd to save the people. The True Master is a gracious being. He not only helps and eases the sufferings of the satsangis, but He also helps and eases the sufferings of those people with whom He does not have any outer connection. He helps those who ask God for help. So at that time Master Sawan Singh went to many different places and saved the lives of many people but in that process He had to give a lot of blood from His body. He had to give His blood in order to save those innocent people whom Kal was going to kill. He had to give His own blood in exchange for their lives.

The Masters are great souls and They do not come into this world only for a few disciples or only for those people who come to see Them, or for those who believe in Them. They do not belong only to one nation, religion or community. Since the Masters are very gracious and have a big heart, They take on the karmas of the people even without their asking. The souls working in the Master's form are very great. How can we understand the Masters?

Before 1947, even though he was very old, Master Sawan Singh used to say, "I do not feel old, and from within I am very active and I am very young." Only after these events that occurred during the partition, when He had to give a lot of blood from His body, only then He became chronically sick and very old. In His last days physically He became very weak, He had to remain in bed for a long time and He always needed somebody's support to move. His body became emaciated and He became thin like a stick. For many who had seen Him when He was healthy, when He was younger, they knew that He had been the most beautiful person in the world, and when they saw Him when He was sick, they were feeling very sorry. However, I had had the opportunity of having His darshan when He was in good health and also of having it when He was in His last days. There were many people there who used to only look at the body of the Master, but since I had the opportunity to have His darshan, I would see in His forehead that the radiance of the Power that He had was exactly the same as when He was younger. The experience one had depended upon one's receptivity, upon the feelings one was having when getting the darshan of the Master. For me there was no difference there.

In a way, the Masters become very old outwardly. Physically They become weak and They must suffer from many diseases. Physically and outwardly Their bodies may become very old and They may not even have the power to move. However, once the Shabd is manifested within Them and once They get the Divine Knowledge, internally Their attention, the *surat,* is always young. That is why, no matter how They behave outwardly, within They are always young and in Their full senses and old age makes no difference to Them.

Master Takes on the Karmas of the Dear Ones

Once, when Master Sawan Singh was suffering this sickness, my commanding officer went to see Him and I accompanied my officer to that meeting. When we went to see Him, He took about two hours to tell us about His sickness. At that time He told the person attending Him, when He was losing the blood, "Let the blood flow in both the east and the west" — because in the west there was Pakistan where there were many Hindus being killed by the Muslims and on the east side there were Muslims being killed by the Hindus.

At that time, there was a person who, seeing that Master Sawan Singh was suffering a great deal, did not have faith in Him and did not believe in what Master Sawan Singh was saying. Instead of understanding the reality after hearing all that Master Sawan Singh said, his faith was shaken and he did not believe in what Master Sawan Singh was saying. He started to have negative thoughts about Master Sawan Singh. He thought, "He is the Master and still He is suffering so much?" So he asked Master Sawan Singh if it was His own karma that He was paying off by giving a lot of blood from His body. Master Sawan Singh just smiled and said, "No dear one, it is not my karma, it is the karma of one of my dear ones." Master Sawan replied that it was not because of His own karma, because Saints are free of karmas. He said to just imagine the condition of the father whose sons are being burnt in the fire. Will he not feel anything when he sees that his sons are being burnt in the fire? Saints have the love of more than thousands of worldly parents put together and so, in order to save Their souls, They always have to shed Their blood or in some other way suffer with Their own bodies the karmas of the disciples.

In fact, at that time He was suffering the karmas of that very dear one who had asked that question. Saints are free of all kinds of karmas and diseases, but still when They come into the human body, how much They have to suffer. It is only the Saint who suffers on account of other people's karmas. He is the only One who burns Himself in other people's fire. Otherwise, who on the earth would want to burn in other people's fire? Who wants to carry another person's karma?

After some days that disciple was shown within that on that day Master Sawan Singh had been suffering on account of his karma. He realized his mistake and came and expressed his appreciation and thanked Master Sawan Singh for taking on that karma.

Even though the Masters carry the karmas of the people, still They do not let them know that They are carrying their karmas, They always remain very quiet, and very humbly and graciously They take on the karmas.

The Unique Humility of Master Sawan Singh

O Master, I am a grave sinner.
My friendship is with lust, anger, cleverness and deceit.
I am wearing greed, attachment, egoism, jealousy and praise.
I am deceitful, indulgent, a liar, violent — such sins I have
  done.

I cannot bear the pain and insults —
I am full of the desires for happiness and respect.
I crave for the taste of delicacies.
My mind always wants such foods.

I have made wealth and women dwell in my heart;
I am full of expectations from wife and children.
This sinner gets different types of pains;
Still he does not give up this act.

I am a lowly one full of doubts;
I don't fall in love with Your Feet.
I am full of incurable diseases —
Who besides You can do the treatment?

Whatever You wish, You can remove them in a second;

The Mauj (Will) of grace and mercy is unique.
Again and again I request and pray to You.
I do not see anyone other than You; You are the only Protector.

I am bad, I am bad, again I am worse and worse;
However I am, I have come to You.
Now You have to protect my honor;
O Radha Swami, remove my calamity.
— an excerpt from a bhajan of
Swami Ji Maharaj

This hymn of Swami Ji Maharaj is full of humility. When Almighty Lord Sawan became sick towards the end of His life, He used to make His pathi sing this bhajan. Whenever His pathi would sing this hymn He would become very happy and He would shed tears in the remembrance of His Master. We people, who lived near Him and were around Him at that time, were surprised how this Master, Who had become the Lord Himself, was calling Himself "the one who is full of faults."

Master Sawan Singh had worked very hard; He had done a lot of meditation. He had stayed up many nights doing the meditation but He had a unique humility within Him. He would always call Himself a sinner in front of His Master. What can we the worldly people understand of the Saints? Nobody can understand the Saints. Tulsi Sahib said, "Those who say that they can understand the Saints, beware — I touch my ears — it is not possible, because no one can understand the Saints." God has sent the Saints into this world with a lot of humility, a lot of meekness and a lot of love.

We do not see our own sins and because of that we don't believe we are sinning and so we don't want to give up those sins. But very easily we go on looking at other people's faults and sins, and we even talk about their sins and faults with other people. Saints lovingly tell us that if you want to look at faults, you should look at your own faults, you should look at the sins that you yourself do and always look at the good qualities of others. One should try to adopt those good qualities in oneself. Master Sawan was the form of God; He was one with God Almighty. He was free of all the sins and faults, but just to make us, the forgetful souls of this world, understand, He called Himself as the one who sinned or who made the mistakes. He lovingly told us, "Love everyone. Don't look at anybody else's faults; look at your own faults."

The Passing of Master Sawan Singh

Earlier I told of the meeting of Baba Sawan Singh with the religious leaders, in which He said it was true that He was supposed to live to be one hundred years old. However, those that meditate know that because of the burden that He had to carry, He left the body ten years earlier than He was supposed to leave. He left the body at age ninety, on April 2, 1948. My troop was still stationed at Beas at that time and I was there at His cremation also.

Towards His end, when He was suffering very much, the sangat was praying that Baba Jaimal Singh should allow Baba Sawan Singh to stay in this world a little more time. The sangat also asked Baba Sawan Singh to request Baba Jaimal Singh to shower grace on Him, but Baba Sawan Singh said, "No, I cannot do that, because that will make a difference in my discipleship. I have to do the work that my Master has given to me, and Baba Jaimal Singh has to do the work that He has to do. If you want, you can continue with your prayers."

With the grace of God I saw Master Sawan Singh as a great God. Even outwardly also I saw Him as God. However, I never saw or heard Him make any prophecy about any other person leaving the body, "He will leave at this time," or "He will leave at that time," nor did He ever talk about His own leaving. In fact, Master Sawan Singh used to say that those who make prophecies, do that only because they crave name and fame, only so that other people will come and praise them. He used to say that we should never believe in such prophecies.

Whatever pains and happiness, whatever comforts or discomforts, come to the Masters in the Will of the Lord, They always accept them and They do not make any excuses in going through the sufferings. They do not say, "But" and They do not say, "Why?" They always accept them gladly and lovingly. They always live in the Will of God Almighty and They teach us the same thing.

Just imagine that if the Masters were to give such hints, or were to make such prophecies about Their leaving, how do you think those dear ones who have been blessed with unbreakable love for the Master would be able to live? They would die just thinking about it; they would die from the grief of it. I saw that when Master Sawan Singh left the body, there were about two hundred people who ended their life. Some jumped from the walls, some jumped into the river and some jumped into the wells, because when they learned that their Master had left, they could not bear the pain of separation.

SEVEN

In the Bushes of Rajasthan:
Cultivating the Two Words

Baba Bishan Das Leaves the Body

Shortly after Master Sawan Singh left the body, I left the army and returned to my parents' home in the Punjab. There I worked on their farm, and continued to go and see Baba Bishan Das. I would go to see him and bring all the earnings I got from working in the fields.

One day around 1949 Baba Bishan Das came to my home. He came to me while I was working in the fields, and he told me, "Ajaib, I want to give you something." He held my neck and told me, "Look into my eyes." In the way of the Saints, eye gives to eye. Nectar is flowing through the eyes of the Saints. Everything is done with the eyes and everything is given only through the eyes; there is no other medium through which Spirituality can be given. So whatever power Baba Bishan Das had, he gave me through the eyes; he gave me everything that he had. He did not hide anything that he had from me. At that time he initiated me into the first Two Words and he gave me instructions for meditating on them.

At that time he told me, "The One who has to give you the rest, He will come to you by Himself. He will come to your place to give you more." He also told me that I should not claim possession of his ashram. He had made an ashram that was mostly made with the money I had given him, but he told me, "You have come into this world for Spirituality, not for my dera, not for buildings, and you should not create any disputes over that ashram. You should not claim possession of the ashram and you should not even go to look at that place. I do not want to attach you to the bricks because this is not your goal. Your goal is a higher goal. You should continue your search until the time when the One who has to give you the higher thing comes to you by Himself." He also told me I should go to Rajasthan, because He who was going to quench my thirst was going to come to Rajasthan. He told me I should do farming in Rajasthan to earn my living and that I should never remain idle but should always earn my own livelihood.

Just two days after he told me all these things, Baba Bishan Das left the body. At that time he was 80 years old. Before he left the body, people used to joke with him and say, "Baba, you don't have many disciples. Who is going to serve you in your old age? You don't even have anyone who can give you a glass of water in your old age. You have left your sons and family and you don't have any disciples to take care of you." He would always reply, "I don't need any disciples. I don't need anyone's seva, because I will catch the train while I am still in my senses." He meant that he would leave the body when he was still able to function properly. Baba Sawan Singh had promised that He would take his soul up, because Baba Bishan Das had perfected the first two planes and he had reached the third plane. Baba Sawan Singh had told him that he did not need to do any further meditation, He would take him up right from there. It all happened just as He said. Baba Bishan Das did not suffer any pains of old age. He left the body while he was still able to function properly, and Master Sawan Singh came at the time of his death and took his soul.

Baba Bishan Das did not have any disciples other than me, so after he left the body there was no other successor who could take care of his ashram. Many dear ones of the village where he had built his ashram came to me and requested that I should come to live in that place and take care of it. I said, "No, these are not the orders of my Master. I cannot do that." Then they told me that since there was no controversy there, and there was no other disciple of Baba Bishan Das, if I did not want to go there, I should nominate someone who could take care of the property. However I said, "Well, if I nominate anyone in my place, it is the same as if I was going and staying there. I will not nominate anyone; it is up to you. You can decide whatever you want to do."

So I did not go and get myself attached to that place; I did not even go and look at it. Since Baba Bishan Das gave me those orders I did not get attached to it. That ashram still exists in that village – Chana, in the state of Nabha in the Punjab. It is a very great, very beautiful ashram.

Rajasthan: "the Land of Mahatmas"

After Baba Bishan Das left the body I did not go to Baba Bishan Das' ashram but instead I left my parents home in Punjab and went to Rajasthan. The state of Punjab was very developed and furthermore, as I have said earlier, the home that my father had made for me in Punjab had all kinds of comforts and conveniences. There was a very big building, there was a garden, and every possible comfort of the world was there. However, Baba Bishan Das had told me to go to Rajasthan, because the One who was going to come to quench my thirst was going to come to Rajasthan, so I left my home in Punjab and went to Rajasthan.

Once I was reading the story of Hir and Ranja, two great lovers in India. Hazrat Var Shah, who wrote the poem about those two great lovers, also wrote a lot about the inner world. In this story Ranja was a very wealthy person, but because of his love and attachment for a girl named Hir, he left all his wealth and property and went to live in the home of Hir, becoming a shepherd. He left all his comforts and conveniences only because of his love for Hir. Reading that story, I cursed my mind. I told my mind, "See, Ranja left all his property, all his comforts, just because he wanted to get Hir, who was just a woman. How much will you have to sacrifice to get the Almighty Lord? Can't you sacrifice as much as Ranja did to obtain Hir?" Such were my thoughts at this time.

Nowadays Rajasthan is very green. There are many canals, many gardens and fields and a lot of food is grown there. However, when I moved there it was nothing like that. When I first went to Rajasthan there was nothing but bushes and sand. The sand would blow so much that if a man was sleeping outside in the night time, no one would be able to find him in the morning because he would be covered in sand. It was very dry and very hot, and there was very little water. Bhagat Namdev once visited Rajasthan, and when He saw the scarcity of water, and the love that the people there had for water, He wrote in His bani, "As the people in Marwar (another name for Rajasthan) love the water, in my heart I have love for the Almighty Lord." In those days, if anyone would greet the native people of Rajasthan, they would not return his greetings. Instead they would say, "You must be thirsty, that is why you are greeting me." There was no water in many areas, and people used to go twenty or twenty-five miles to bring water for drinking. After moving there I myself would live one full day, twenty-four hours, in summer on just two liters of water.

So at that time, it was very difficult for someone who had all the comforts of Punjab to leave there and come to Rajasthan, but that is where Baba Bishan Das told me to go.

However, while Rajasthan was a very poor area, it is also called "the land of the mahatmas." India has given birth to many great Saints and mahatmas, rishis and munis. Many mahatmas, rishis and munis spent their lives in India and they taught many people to do the devotion, and that is why India is called "the land of rishis and munis." Out of all of India, Rajasthan is the place where the greatest number of mahatmas have taken birth and spent their time and that is why it is called the land of mahatmas. Because of this, when I went there, the people of Rajasthan were very religious-minded and very righteous. The part of Rajasthan I went to was part of a state called Bikaner. In that area the people did not kill goats or cows and they did not hunt animals for eating. They did not drink wine, and no officer would take any bribe; there was nothing like corruption in this state. There were no movie theaters and there was no bad literature published there; there was no worldly means of entertainment. Everybody used to live a very simple life and they were all devoted to God. They were all very truthful and there were no thieves or robbers. People did not even lock their doors, and if anyone lost something, he would find it at the same place he had lost it as nobody would take someone else's belongings.

The reason that Rajasthan had such a pure atmosphere at that time was that the king of that state was King Ganga Singh, who was a very good and just king. He was a very righteous person who was a devotee of God. He had done a lot of austerities and he also did meditation. He used to understand the people of the state as his children and he used to protect them. He used to have a weighing balance on the table and whenever he would sit in the court and have to judge the cases he would say, "I weigh the justice and then solve the problems of the people. I weigh the justice and give equal justice to the people." Whenever he would see any officer dressed up very well, he would at once ask, "From where have you gotten this good dress? You definitely must have taken a bribe." He used to say, "God may forgive a corrupt officer, but I will never forgive a corrupt officer. I will not forgive any corrupt person, even if he is my son." Because of that, in those days if you left anything somewhere nobody would come and touch it, because people knew that in the kingdom of Ganga Singh they were not supposed to do that. He did not even use any money from the treasury for his own livelihood. He used to do farming to maintain his family and himself. That is a very rare thing that the leader in a country earns his own livelihood by working wholeheartedly and honestly.

India has had many natural calamities such as floods. There has been civil unrest and many innocent people have been killed, the worst example of which was the partition of India and Pakistan. However, Rajasthan was not affected by those things. Always there was peace and the law was maintained. Nobody was murdered there and the natural calamities that affected other areas did not affect the people there. Rajasthan is the land of religion and many great devotees were born there.

When Saints come and give out the message of Naam, They say, "Meditate on Naam and in that way the atmosphere in which you are living will become good, and there will be nothing in this world that can affect your place and its atmosphere." Such a place becomes the land of religion and Nature also becomes pleased with that place. So Rajasthan was considered to be the most religious area, and that is why Baba Bishan Das told me to go and live there.

Meditating in the Solitude of Rajasthan

I came to Rajasthan after getting the Initiation into the Two Words from Baba Bishan Das, and for the next eighteen years I did the meditation of those Two Words. When my beloved Baba Bishan Das left the body it affected me very badly. It made a hole in my heart and the pangs of separation from him tormented me. After getting instructions from him, I did that work which he had given me to do. Day and night I sat in remembrance of that Master, that Power Whom I had never seen but Who was going to come there and give me further knowledge. I would go on praying always that God should hear my cry and come to me, and I did not waste even one minute of my time in worldly pursuits. I always gave first preference to meditation and then to worldly responsibilities. I never wasted any time gossiping or socializing with people. I never went to visit places or people; I always remained devoted to meditation and during that time I only meditated.

I have described how in my life I had done many rites and rituals.

However, when Baba Bishan Das gave me the secret of the Two Words, all those rites and rituals that I used to do lost their taste, they lost their glory. Baba Bishan Das did not have to tell me to give them up. I left them myself once I got the secret of the Two Words.

The area in which I settled had only a few people living in it. It was very secluded, and all my life I have been very happy to live in secluded places. You can read the life histories of Saints and Mahatmas and see that They loved solitude and loved being alone. Baba Jaimal Singh sat on the banks of the River Beas only because it was a very quiet and lonely place. In solitude one can give up all the worldly thoughts and think only about meditation and the Satguru.

Baba Bishan Das had given me the work of meditation to do, and I felt that until I became successful in that I could not rest. I left sleep and rest on one side and I gave importance and priority to the work which my Master had given to me. I went on increasing the Light, and I would go on meditating six or eight hours every day. During the day I would work very hard in the fields doing my farming but I would stay up at night and utilize the nights for doing the meditation. At the place where I was living I built an underground room, and I would meditate in that room. I would go on sitting for many, many hours without coming out from my meditation place. Sometimes I would sit for the entire day, and sometimes I would sit for the whole night also. I would not meditate sitting on any kind of cushion; I never even put a gunnysack under me. Instead I would have only some sticks or hay underneath me, or sometimes I sat on a flat wooden platform.

Meditation is just like a battle, a battle with the mind. The purpose of meditation is to control the mind, and just as in a battle between two groups, the cowardly group will run away and the brave group will remain there and not run away. The purpose of the mind is to prevent us from doing the meditation; it induces laziness and pains, and tries to make us get up from the meditation, but in meditation one has to sit there and fight with the mind. During this time, if I did any mistake I would punish my mind so that it would not repeat the same mistake. I used to get up at one o'clock in the morning and if I would get up late, say ten or twenty minutes late, then I would punish my mind by bathing in cold water, even in the months of December and January when it is very cold in Rajasthan. Then I would sit outside in an open place, in the cold, for meditation. If we fight the mind and control the mind, we find interest in the meditation, but if the mind controls us we cannot find interest in meditation. That is why one always has to do the meditation, and never listen to the mind. Mind is the only enemy; he will never let us become faithful to the Master, and he will never let us do the meditation. One should never listen to the mind, but we should always listen to the words of the Satguru and always do the meditation.

God is Love, and in order to get to that Love we need to be very brave, because our enemy mind is in the way, and he is very powerful. He has his army of lust, anger, greed, attachment and egoism, and they are also very strong. So in order to get to Love, we need to be very brave. Kabir Sahib says, "In the *Gaggan*, or the Eye Center, the drum is being played. Now is the time for the warrior to come to the battlefield and fight." In the olden days there were no atom bombs and there was no modern equipment like we have now. Nowadays people can attack their enemies while staying very far away from them, and the enemy does not even know that he is going to be attacked. However, in the olden days the warriors had to attack their enemies face-to-face and they had to fight with swords. So in the olden days the generals and commanders beat the drums and inspired the soldiers in many ways so that they would go and fight their enemies. Kabir Sahib says in His bani, "The drum is being played at the Gaggan and now is the time for the warrior to come to the battlefield. Only he can be called brave who doesn't leave the battlefield without killing the enemy." This means that only he is a brave one who doesn't leave the Eye Center without conquering the mind.

Where is our Gaggan? Gaggan is the place, just a little above the Eye Center, where the Sound of Shabd is coming, and hearing that Sound of Shabd our soul gets intoxicated. Only in the human body can we go to the Gaggan and conquer lust, anger, greed, attachment and egoism.

Earlier, I told how, when I was in the army, I volunteered to go into battle, even though it was not my turn, because I was not afraid of death. I always used to think, "If the bullet comes, I will just open my shirt and I will stand in front of the bullet, because when death has to come, it will come, so why worry about death? But when I started doing the meditation, then I realized that to fight in the war was easier than to sit for meditation. When we start doing the meditation, mind becomes so obstinate that he tells you, "Go fight in the war, but don't sit for meditation."

The Story of Sunder Das and His Madness

Shortly after I moved to Rajasthan I met a man named Sunder Das. Sunder Das was a very devoted initiate of Master Sawan Singh, and we became very close. After meeting him, he came and lived with me and we lived together for many years. The story of Sunder Das and his life is very interesting and worth relating.

Sunder Das was a disciple of Master Sawan Singh for many years. When Master Sawan Singh was making the Satsang Hall in Beas, He graciously gave Sunder Das the seva or service of supplying water to the workers. It took many years to complete that Satsang Hall and Sunder Das did that seva very faithfully. Because of this seva, Master Sawan Singh was very pleased with him and graciously He told Sunder Das what was going to happen in his future. He told him, "Sunder Das, your wife will die and your son and daughter will also get killed. Because all your family will die, your mind will get upset and you will go mad, and in that madness you will commit murder. As a result you will be sent to prison and there you should confess what you have done. People will try to help you and release you, but you should not accept anyone's help. You should go through the trial, not let them

Master Sawan Singh carrying the first basket of earth during construction of the Satsang Hall, January 29, 1934. He gave Sunder Das the seva of supplying water to the workers.

release you, and accept the punishment. You should confess your guilt and go to prison. You will be sentenced to jail for twenty years, but do not worry: have faith in the Master. If you always speak the truth, you will stay in prison only for six years and then you will be released. After that I will look after you."

It is a very interesting thing that when Baba Sawan Singh said all this, Sunder Das was not even married yet. However, since he used to do a lot of meditation and he was going within, and he was very close and devoted to Baba Sawan Singh, he took whatever the Master said as the truth. When he came to know about his future, he thought, "Well, I won't get married. Then I won't have any children and all those things won't happen." But the circumstances were such in his life that he had to get married. Since he knew all these things about his future, when his family told him to get married, he told them he didn't want to get married. But they said, "Either you get married or we will all jump into the well and commit suicide." There were five people in his family and they all threatened to commit suicide if he did not agree to get married, so he gave in to them.

Eventually, in God's Will, whatever Baba Sawan Singh had told him about his future happened. He got married and he had a son and a daughter. First his son was killed in the prime of his youth, then his wife died, and after that his daughter was killed, and with that he went mad. In his madness he killed someone. Master Sawan Singh had told him, "The King of Faridkot will try to set you free, but you should not take his help and you should confess." The King of Faridkot was a dear friend of Sunder Das as Sunder Das belonged to a very high family, and when he was brought in front of the judge, that king tried to help him. The king knew that when Sunder Das committed the murder he was not in his senses, so the king thought, "This old man has suffered a lot, and I will help him." He told the judge that Sunder Das was not in his senses and had done the murder in his madness and he should be set free. Many other people also requested the judge to forgive him on the same grounds. However, because Sawan had told him not to accept anyone's help, Sunder Das didn't agree with that. He said, "No, I am not a madman. I have done this murder and I am guilty. Why don't you punish me? If you don't punish me, you are the mad one." Then he told the judge, "If you want to check whether I am mad, I will recite the *Jap Ji Sahib* and you tell me if I make any mistake in my recitation. Or else you recite the *Jap Ji Sahib* and I will point out your mistakes. If I am mad I will not be able to recite the *Jap Ji Sahib* very well.

Thousands carrying basketloads of earth as seva while building the Satsang Hall. Master Sawan is seen in the forefront, center.

Beas Satsang Hall under construction, 1934 – 1937

I am not mad. Why are you not giving me the punishment? Why are you not sending me to jail?" Baba Sawan Singh had told him that he should always speak the truth and that is why he denied he was mad. He confessed his guilt and he was given a sentence of twenty years and went to prison.

He was so devoted to the Master that he remained faithful even though so much happened to him. All those things he lived through even made him crazy, but still he did not lose his faith in the Master. He used to go within and he knew that everything that happened to him was according to the karma which he himself had to pay, and he knew how much Baba Sawan Singh was helping him. After exactly six years of imprisonment India became independent. All the prisoners who were supposed to be in prison for twenty years or more were set free and Sunder Das was one of them.

When he came out of jail he was still a madman and he wandered here and there in the streets carrying bones and doing different kinds of crazy things. At that time he came near where I was living and as he was coming down the road the children were throwing stones at him because he was doing crazy things. I was coming from the other direction and as soon as he saw me he threw away the bones. He fell down at my feet and said, "Now I have received peace of mind." After that he behaved like a good man, and after that he didn't have any problem of madness. Because he had full faith in the Master, and because he did whatever his Master told him to do, that is why the disease of madness was removed from him.

Living with Sunder Das

After meeting me in this way, Sunder Das came and lived with me and he lived with me for a long time. He was very devoted to his Master and had a lot of faith in his Master. He used to meditate a lot and he used to go very high up in meditation. We lived in the same house; we used to eat together and meditate together. I saw that he would always get up at exactly the same time each night, at one o'clock. He used to say that if he did not sit for meditation, he would feel as if his body became heavier and heavier, and he would feel much pain in his body, and that is why he would meditate daily. If someone would tell him that he was an old man and he shouldn't meditate that much, he would say that if one procrastinates and misses the meditation for one day, one will go on procrastinating and miss it for twenty-one days. How will one be able to fill up the gap which is created by not remembering the Master for that many days? So he used to say that he would never miss his meditation for even one day. It was his habit to always get up early in the morning and first do his meditation, and then he would go on to his other jobs.

Nowadays there are tractors and other machinery to plow the fields, but at that time we had only one camel and two bullocks with which we used to plow the fields. We both used to work together, plowing the fields and growing the crops. Both of us used to work very hard and we never allowed any third person to come and live with us, because Sunder Das would say, "If we let another person live here he will create problems and then we will not be able to do anything." So just he and I were living there together and between us we used to finish all the farm work, and along with that we also used to do our Bhajan and Simran. At that time I had the Initiation into the Two Words and I used to meditate on those Two Words. Sunder Das, being an initiate of Master Sawan Singh, had the knowledge of all Five Words, and he used to do the meditation of the Five Words. We used to do our Simran and we used to do our meditation without missing it, and we also used to do a wonderful job at farming.

We did not find that doing all that physical work interfered with our meditation. In fact, the more physical work we did with our bodies, the more it made us fresh and the more we were able to do the meditation. We not only did the work that was needed for our own fields, but we would also do the work that was useful for other people. Back at that time, there were no canals and people had to go in their bullock carts to get the water from many, many miles away. In the summer months, when the sandstorms would come, mountains of sand would form and it would become very difficult for the animals to walk through that sand. When this would happen, Sunder Das and I would take shovels and we would remove that sand so that it would be easier for the bullocks to walk on the path. We didn't have any personal interest in doing that work, and people would call us mad for doing this. Still, for the good of our meditations, we did that physical work because we understood that whatever work we would take from our physical bodies, that was all good and that would bring more freshness to our bodies.

The people who lived around us would hide and try to listen to what kind of conversations we used to have. When they heard that we only talked about the Master and about the love of the Master, they were very impressed and they wondered how we had so much love and devotion for our Master. Some people would even say, "They do not have any worries. They have no worldly things to do, that is why they are always talking about the love of the Master." Sunder Das was an old man, so people used to say, "His family has died and that is why he doesn't have any worries. The other person," they would say, referring to me, "He never got married so he has no family to take care of. That is why they are always devoted to their Master and they are doing the devotion of God."

Right from my childhood people always used to come to see me, saying that I was a Saint, and they wanted to meet me. Even though we did not allow people to come to see us, but still, as the Masters say, "Even if the perfume seller does not want to sell his perfume, sometimes one of the bottles of perfume remains open and that attracts people." So sometimes the people would come saying that they wanted to see the Saints they had heard so much about. They would see me working in the field in my work clothes and I would be carrying a plow or something like that and they would not think that I was one of the people whom they had come to see. They would say, "We want to see the Saint." I would say, "Okay, let us sit here and wait and he will come." Then they would start talking to me and they would realize that I was the person they had come to see. I never wore good clothes and I never pretended that I was a mahatma, even though people used to call me a mahatma. I always remained very simple and I used to do all the worldly things like the farming. Still our Simran and Bhajan was going on and we never missed our meditation. Many times if there was too much work to do, we would stay up in the night and finish that work, but we never allowed anyone else to come there and we never missed our meditation. We did our meditation and we also did all the worldly work.

Sunder Das' Experiences with Master Sawan Singh

Sunder Das had had the opportunity to spend much time at the feet of Master Sawan Singh and he told me many stories about his experiences with the Master.

Once Baba Sawan Singh went to the village of Ghuman, where Baba Jaimal Singh was born, to give Satsang. Before starting the Satsang, He wept very bitterly. Sunder Das saw that with his own eyes, and he told me that Baba Sawan Singh wept so much in the remembrance of Baba Jaimal Singh that some of the dear ones asked Him, "Baba Ji, if Your condition is such, what is the hope for us? If You cannot control Yourself, how can we control ourselves?" Baba Sawan Singh replied, "No doubt, Baba Jaimal Singh is with me all the time in the form of the Shabd, but if He would come in the physical form even once, I am ready to give up everything that I have. I up ready to give up everything and go with Him."

On another occasion Master Sawan Singh was talking about how Guru Ramdas would meditate, tying His hair up He would meditate for many hours. At that time Sunder Das, who used to meditate for eight hours at a stretch, said laughing, "Master, Guru Ramdas had to liberate the whole world. Why do we have to meditate for so long? We know that we are going to get liberation from You, so we do not need to meditate for so long." Nevertheless Sunder Das used to meditate a lot; he was number one among the meditators. However, he understood that those who have taken refuge at the Master's feet should not try to imitate the Masters, they should just obey whatever commandments they receive from their Master.

Once Master Sawan Singh was sitting with a group of disciples, about twenty or twenty-five people, and Sunder Das was among them. Master Sawan Singh was in a very jovial mood. He was so happy that a lot of light was coming out from His body. Then, feeling much pain and becoming very emotional, Master Sawan Singh said, "The dear ones become very lazy and that is why they make this Path very long for themselves. What can I say about how forgetful the souls are? There are many dear ones in this group who were initiated by Guru Nanak, but because of their laziness they have made their Path very long. Even that person who made the sons of Guru Gobind Singh get arrested by the police and who caused the sons of Guru Gobind Singh to be buried in the wall, even he is sitting here in the Satsang."

Imagine how those people present at that Satsang felt in their hearts. Sunder Das said, "All the dear ones who were sitting there were awestruck. They all wondered, 'Have we done so many faults?'" For the forgetful souls the Master has to come back into the world again and again, to take those souls Home.

Intoxicated in the Love of God

While we did not allow anyone to come and live with us, at that time there was another person who used to come to see Sunder Das and me at our ashram every night. One time I was talking with Sunder Das and we were having very loving talks about the Masters and about the Path, and both of us were very intoxicated in the love of God. We were talking as if we were drunk. When that person heard us talking, he thought that maybe we had taken something to make us intoxicated. We were talking about God in such a way that he got the impression that we were not in our senses so he just sat there, expecting us to come back to our normal state so that he could talk to us. He sat there for an hour or more, but when he didn't see any change in us he left. Before leaving he looked everywhere, even under the beds, to see if there were any empty bottles of wine, but he didn't find anything, so he went back to his home. The next morning he came back to us and apologized. He said, "Last night I came and I thought that both of you were drunk, and I had terrible thoughts about you. Please forgive me."

So you can see that just by doing the Simran of the Two Words there was so much intoxication that the other person felt that we had taken some intoxicants. Just imagine how much more intoxication one can get if one has the Simran of the Five Words and if you do that Simran sincerely.

Sunder Das and His Astrology

Once four pundits came to our ashram, saying, "We are palmists. We will tell you everything about your past life and your future." Sunder Das was living with me at that time and he was also present. Hearing what the pundits had to say, Sunder Das took out a long stick and started giving them a beating, saying, "Well, were you knowing about this? Were you able to predict that you were going to get a beating from me?" Sunder Das was not afraid of anything.

Once a fortune teller or astrologer went to Master Sawan Singh. At that time Sunder Das was living with Master Sawan Singh, so Master Sawan Singh said, "I also have one astrologer. We will compare your competency." He called Sunder Das and said, "Come on, Sunder Das, show your astrology." Soon Sunder Das came in with a stick, and that astrologer, seeing that, said, "Maharaj Ji, please forgive me." So I always thought that Sunder Das was a very good astrologer.

The Injured Dog

There was a pet dog of a family who lived near my ashram; he was a very good dog. Once he went to the house of another person and that other person shot him in the back. He was injured very badly and both his legs were broken so that he could not walk, but he did not die. At that time, with his wounded body, he dragged himself back to the door of the family who owned him, but they did not pay any attention to him. When they learned about his injury they did not help him or pay any attention to him, because they thought, "Now he is going to die soon, and he is not going to be of any use to us." They just left him on the street without even giving him water to drink.

It was very hot, and that dog spent the whole day in the street without getting any medical treatment or any water to drink. After spending the whole day in that condition, that evening he got the inspiration to start coming towards my ashram, which was about three hundred yards from where he was lying. Since he could not walk he started pulling himself. His front two feet were working so he starting pushing and pulling himself towards the ashram. However, about one hundred yards away from the ashram he broke down and stopped as he had no strength to continue.

In those days there was one dear one who used to come to see me every night, and when he was going back to his home he saw that there was a dog lying there in the road, without any trace of any man. He thought that maybe somebody had left the dog there so he came back to the ashram and he told me that there was a dog lying near my ashram. We went there, thinking that we should try to see the footprints of the person who had left him there, so that we would know who had left him. But we did not find any footprints; it was the dog himself who had come there. I looked at him and saw that he was not dead and I figured out that both the rear legs of the dog were broken and that is why he could not walk.

Through his eyes he conveyed, "Please take care of me; give me some water." So at once we went back to the ashram and I brought a pan of water and put his head in the water. It took him about two minutes to realize that he was near the water and then he started to drink it. All day long he had not had any water to drink, so when that water went into his stomach, life also started coming back into him, and then he started responding. I did not let him drink a lot of water right away as that would not have been good for him. After that we carried him back to the ashram and there I gave him some milk and ghee, clarified butter. I did this because in the villages where doctors are not available whenever anyone gets injured the first things the villagers give are milk and ghee that give a lot of strength. So we gave that dog the milk and clarified butter, which brought some strength to him, and then we removed the bullets and made dressings for his wounds.

After that for three months we nursed him and gave him a lot of nourishing food and with that care he gradually became stronger. Sunder Das was living with me at that time and he helped in taking care of that dog. Although his wound healed he did not heal completely and his rear legs did not work, so he could not walk or move by himself. Still he stayed with me in my room, and he was such a smart dog that whenever he had to go out to attend the call of nature, since he could not move his body himself he would tell us in his own way that he wanted to go out. He would cry or make some kind of sign to tell us that he needed to go outside and we would carry him outside. He lived for five years after that and I kept him in my room during that time. He never made my room dirty and he always remained clean.

Sunder Das and I understood him as a present given to us by Baba Sawan Singh. You can imagine who was the one who guided him to our place. Who told him, "You should go to this place where you will be taken care of. Over there the people will serve you."? It was God Himself, and when his time had come, he got the inspiration from God Himself to come toward the ashram. If he had gone to some other place, nobody would have taken care of him, and in that condition he would have died.

When the people who used to own that dog found out that the dog was with me, they started making fun of me, saying, "He is a madman; he does not have any other work to do and that is why he is taking care of such a useless creature." But why did I take care of that dog? I took care of that dog because many times in Satsang I had heard from Baba Sawan Singh a story about Rabia Basri, a Muslim Saint. Once when she was going on a pilgrimage to Mecca, on the way she found a dog whose four feet were broken and that dog was crying for water. There was a well nearby but there was no rope or anything by which Rabia Basri could bring up the water. So she cut off her hair and made something like a rope from it, and using some leaves of a nearby tree as a bucket she brought up some water, and gave the water to the dog and in that way she saved the dog's life.

It is said that Mecca, which was seventy miles away from where this was happening, came all the way to Rabia Basri because she had saved the life of one of God's creatures. When people went to Mecca they could not find it there and they started wondering where Mecca had gone. It is said that in the sky there was a sound saying, "Now I am near Rabia Basri because she has saved one of my creatures. I reside in all men and animals and I am pleased with her and that is why I have gone to welcome Rabia Basri."

Because I had heard that story from Baba Sawan Singh many times, I was inspired to take care of that dog. I understood that we get the opportunity to serve God's creatures only if we have good fortune. So I always considered myself as the most fortunate one when I was taking care of that dog.

Celebrating the Bhandaras of Sawan

The bhandara of beautiful Emperor Sawan has come.
Becoming the support for the suffering ones, He has come.

The land where the unique light has come is the fortunate place.
He has flashed the radiant darshan.

After becoming a man, the All-Owner has come.
He has hidden Himself within man. He who has loved has got the vision.

He shared the pains of the suffering ones. He showed the glimpse to the true dear ones.
He installed the fountain of nectar where he wished.

The talks of Your love are kept within the heart. The rays of Your light are embedded in the soul.
O Beloved, You gave the hint of True Naam.

O Giver, day and night I sing about Your favors. O Giver, take the souls across the Ocean of Life.
Poor Ajaib has come to Your door.
— Sohna Sawan Shah Da Bhandara

There were not many initiates of Master Sawan Singh in the area where I was living. There were only about eleven initiates in the whole district and they used to live about twenty or twenty-five miles away from the village where I lived. I would go to the city where those initiates lived for the *bhandaras,* the birthday celebrations of Master Sawan Singh; I used to celebrate Baba Sawan Singh's birthday with full enthusiasm. I would travel those twenty miles to be near those initiates and in those days there were no good roads and no canals or water. It was very dusty and very sandy and it used to take five or six hours to travel those twenty miles. Nevertheless I would go there and spend all the money I had for the celebration of Master Sawan's birthday, making all the arrangements for the food and everything else required for the celebration. I remained fully devoted to Master Sawan Singh and I had complete love and faith in Him.

One year we wanted to celebrate a bhandara on the second of April, the anniversary of the day Baba Sawan Singh left the body. So I met with one of these initiates who were also intoxicated in the love of Baba Sawan Singh and we made all the plans for this bhandara. We got some pamphlets printed and we gave them out to people in the city. We also hired some people to beat the drums and announce that we were going to celebrate this bhandara. In the announcements we said, "We will make *gulab jamans* (a popular Indian sweet) and other sweet things and people will be fed with all these good foods." We were mad in the love of Him, and that is why we celebrated Master Sawan's bhandara in that way, even though I was not an initiate of Master Sawan Singh at that time.

They were very loving and devoted souls, but sometimes when making the arrangements for these celebrations, the initiates would have disagreements and start criticizing each other. When I would hear them criticizing and disagreeing with each other, I would tell them, "This is not good; you should not criticize each other. You should obey the orders of Master Sawan Singh and you should do the meditation." When I would say this, they would get angry with me and would say, "How do you know anything about Sant Mat? You are not even an initiate." Then they would spank me and say that I did not have any knowledge of Sant Mat. I would suffer the spankings of those dear ones, but then I would tell them, "Yes, I am not an initiate; I don't have any knowledge of Sant Mat, but at least I know what Master Sawan Singh used to say about doing the meditation and not criticizing each other!"

"Are You a Sadhu or a Swadhu?"

Hearing about me, a disciple of Baba Sawan Singh whose name was Dharam Chand, came to meet me and in front of many people he asked me, "Are you a sadhu or *swadhu*?" Swadhu means "the person who is always craving delicious foods." It has been my habit every since my childhood that whatever I have in my heart, I say. So I told him in front of all those people, "I am neither sadhu nor swadhu. If I were a swadhu I would not have left my home in Punjab. In my home there was everything in abundance. My father was fond of very good food and I could have stayed there and eaten and enjoyed the worldly things. But I am not yet a sadhu either, because Baba Bishan Das has given me knowledge only up to Brahm, and he has told me that one becomes a sadhu only after going above Brahm."

When Dharam Chand told me that he was a disciple of Baba Sawan Singh, I loved him very much and after that we had a very good loving relationship. He used to visit me often and he became one of my best friends. He used to do the Satsang and I used to do the chanting of the banis, for his Satsang, and this went on for many years.

Meditating with the Initiates of Sawan

Sometimes the other initiates of Master Sawan Singh in our area would come to meditate with me. Together we would be about ten or twelve people and we would meditate together. We would always have one person standing up, while the others were meditating, to check the other people. If anyone was falling asleep in meditation or if he was trying to move, the person who was in charge at that time was told to slap the person on both sides. No one was allowed to make tea and no one was allowed to sit in meditation after drinking tea. No one was allowed to bring any kind of food to be distributed as parshad, because we used to think, "He who brings parshad and distributes food to the other people wants to take away the meditation of the others, and that is not fair." So this was a very strict period of meditation, as only the brave, courageous people can do meditation, and only those who have real love and faith can become the real meditators. So all of us in this small group had a very deep relationship. We used to get together and we loved each other very much. Because I had had the darshan of Baba Sawan Singh and was very fond of Him, I always enjoyed being in the company of the people who were initiated by Him.

Later on, there were many more people coming to see me and to meditate with me. We used to have meditation programs in which we would meditate just like the Sikhs do the non-stop reading of the *Guru Granth Sahib*. If there were three hundred people attending the meditation program we would divide that group into three different groups of one hundred people each. Then one hundred people would do the meditation and the moment they would stop meditating the next group of one hundred people would take over from them. In that way the meditation would always go on happening. Because I had the habit of meditation, that is why I started this system of the groups and doing the meditation. There is no better opportunity to perfect the Simran than in such groups. When we see that other people are meditating, that encourages us, that inspires us, to sit in meditation also.

"Pour This Tea on My Head!"

As I told you, this group of initiates would get together and arrange for Satsang. Once we collected some money, rented a hall in the city of Ganganagar and invited a mahatma to come there to do the Satsang. That mahatma was an initiate of Baba Sawan Singh and he was very famous. He would go to people's homes to do the Satsangs and wherever he went people would go and listen to his discourses because he used to give a very good Satsang. He would say that he was the sevadar of the sangat and he had come to do the seva of the sangat. The people used to love and respect him a lot.

So that day he gave a very good discourse about peace of mind and how to go within and do the devotion of the Lord. It is the usual practice of the Indians that when they have a function like Satsang, afterwards they prepare some tea or food for the sangat. So when the Satsang was over we thought that we should respect this Baba and we should take him into a separate room to serve him tea. We thought that first we would serve tea to the sangat and then take the mahatma into an inner room and talk to him privately and serve him tea there. While he was still sitting in the front tea started to be served to the sangat and the sangat started to drink. When the Baba saw that he was not offered tea first, and that the sangat was given tea before him, all the coolness vanished from him. He thought, "I am greater than everybody and I should have been served first." He became very angry and he started changing colors just after giving such a beautiful discourse about peace of mind.

At that time we became worried and didn't know what to do but after some time we came and requested him to come to the inside room to have his tea. But he was so much controlled by anger that he could not speak a word. When we saw that he was getting so angry we told him, "All right we are bringing the tea for you here." I went into the kitchen and brought the tea to him right there on the dais; I thought that maybe he would drink it. But he was so controlled by anger that he removed his turban and told me, "Now you pour this tea on my head!"

The people who were looking at him saw all this happening. The satsangis knew how the mind plays tricks on us and how he makes us fall down. They knew the condition of the mind so it was not a very unusual or surprising thing to them. But for the non-initiates it was a very unusual thing, because just a few minutes before he had given a very beautiful discourse and he was teaching people how they should control their mind, how they should not fall into the traps of the mind, and how they should always be peaceful and quiet. Now what was he doing? He was not doing what he was preaching, so it was a very surprising thing for them. They all laughed and clapped their hands and went away, saying, "Who is this mahatma who has come here to do Satsang?"

Those who have surrendered themselves to the Master know the tricks of the mind and they never allow their mind to play such tricks on them. However, those who have not surrendered themselves to the Master, even though they talk about the peace of mind, they can easily be tricked by the mind. If that mahatma had been doing the meditation and the Simran along with doing the seva of the sangat he would not have acted like that and he would not have become the subject of mockery. Many of the new people there were not initiates, and when he said, "Great is the Guru of the Radha Swami faith," they all left without having any faith in the Path. Master Sawan Singh used to say, "Many times our mind creates this kind of deception — that outwardly he makes us have humility, but inwardly he craves name and fame. Outwardly he goes on telling people, 'I am nothing, it is all the Master who is doing it, Master is making me do all these things,' but inwardly he is always looking for name and fame and the praises of other people."

Mastana Ji, the Emperor of Baggar

During this time I also had many opportunities to meet again with Mastana Ji, the intoxicated lover of Master Sawan Singh. After Master Sawan Singh left the body, Mastana Ji had also started living in Rajasthan. He lived in an area named Baggar, which was a part of Rajasthan near where I had settled. He was a very dear lover of Master Sawan who was successful in Spirituality, and He started giving Satsang and started giving Initiation in this area. He brought glory to the name of Master Sawan Singh in our area of Rajasthan.

Earlier, when Master Sawan Singh was alive, as Mastana Ji had grown closer to Master Sawan Singh, some of the people around Master Sawan Singh at Beas became very envious of Mastana and they even started hating him. When Master Sawan Singh saw this, He said many times in Satsang, "Mastana Ji, should I make you a Master? Should I make you the king of Baggar?" He would say this when all the sangat had gathered, in front of 60,000 to 70,000 people. Mastana would reply, "What do I have to do with becoming the owner of Baggar? I have only You and I need only You. I don't need to become the owner or king of any place." Furthermore, when Master Sawan Singh used to speak in this way in front of all the sangat, nobody believed Him, for when Saints or Masters prophesy, at that time nobody believes them. Only later, when that prophecy is fulfilled, do people realize that whatever Master said was true. In the same way, when Master Sawan Singh used to say in front of all the people, "Mastana, now I am making you the king of Rajasthan," nobody understood what He was saying and nobody believed that what He was saying would come true. They started asking, "How can Sawan Singh make Mastana Ji the emperor of that area of Rajasthan?"

Baba Sawan Singh saw how the Beas people hated Mastana Ji so much that sometimes they even put boiling water on his body. When He saw the condition of Mastana Ji, Master Sawan Singh Himself had a cave made, a kind of underground room, two hundred miles away from His dera for Mastana Ji to meditate in. He told him, "Mastana, now you go and do your meditation there and you should not come to the ashram, even to see me. You should not even come to my cremation when I die. These people will weep because they are doing very bad things to you, but I am giving you such a thing which will do all your work." Mastana Ji did that, he went to that underground room and did the meditation and he did not even come out for the funeral of Master Sawan Singh. Later I myself got the opportunity to be in that meditation cave and to meditate there.

So after Master Sawan Singh left the body, Mastana Ji stayed in the area of Baggar. He was an intoxicated fakir, and He did not make any ashram. One day He would build a hut to stay in, and the next day He would destroy that hut and move to another place. He didn't go out of the area of Baggar and He didn't go into any other part of India. He used to say, "I have the orders for only this small area." He always obeyed those orders and gave out the Naam only in that area, but still when He started giving the Initiation He had a very large following. He never used to go outside that area, but if people would come to Him from outside, He would initiate them. Whenever He would give Satsang people would come in great numbers; many thousands would come. There were many initiates of Baba Sawan Singh who went to Mastana Ji and they saw the same form of Master Sawan Singh in Mastana Ji. They served Mastana Ji with their mind and their body, for they saw that the same Power was working there.

Mastana Ji Distributes the Money

Saints do not perform any miracles, but sometimes through Their disciples They make things happen so that the people may know that when a disciple of a Master can do so much, what can the Master not do? This area of Rajasthan was very poor and so for twelve years continuously Mastana Ji went on distributing money, clothes and other things to people. He would do many other miracles to help the poor, like sweetening the water in the wells where the water was salty or spoiled, and planting dry sticks in the ground which would then grow into trees. He would sit among thousands of people and go on giving them money, fresh currency notes, starting in the morning and going on until late in the evening. There was no estimate of how much money He gave out.

There was a reason He started giving out money to the people. Master Sawan Singh bought His property at Sirsa, after selling His own ancestral property, which was near the city of Ludhiana where He had been born. The property in Ludhiana was sold at a very high price and the property in Sirsa was bought at a very low price, so that the new property was much bigger than the property that He originally owned. When people came to know that Baba Sawan Singh had bought this huge property, they were surprised. You know the Saints are always bothered by the people of their society, and people started criticizing Baba Sawan Singh, saying that He had bought this land using the money of the sangat. The Akali people printed many pamphlets against Him and even published a book in which they claimed that He had done this and that He was not a true Master.

Baba Sawan Singh clarified this matter in front of the whole sangat. He said, "This is the grace of Baba Jaimal Singh. I got a very good price for my land near Ludhiana, and I got this property at a very low price, and that is why I bought so much of it. It is true that I have bought the property, but I have not used the sangat's funds for it."

Mastana Ji, the intoxicated lover of Master Sawan Singh

We know that when someone criticizes a dear soul he will tolerate it and bear the criticism when it is directed at himself, but when it comes to the criticism of his Master he will never tolerate it. So when the people started writing those types of things, Mastana Ji could not bear it. He also did not like it that Baba Sawan Singh should feel the need to clarify such matters in front of the sangat because He knew His Master was perfect. Master Sawan Singh had not misused the sangat's funds and whatever He was saying was true. Mastana Ji did not like the way people were criticizing His Master, and He wanted to show the world the truth. He wanted to prove that His Master was the perfect one, that He was not a beggar, that He was the giver of all riches.

Mastana Ji used to say, "You people say that Master Sawan Singh has bought property with the money of the sangat, but I will show you what the truth is. I am not even capable of calling myself a dog of Master Sawan Singh; even His dogs are better than me. I am just a lowly being of His, but you people don't know what Sawan Singh is. You don't know what Power He has brought into this world. You have only seen Him outwardly and you don't know how He works. I will show you what He is and how He works." Only to respond to the people's criticism of Master Sawan Singh, Mastana Ji used to give out money. When giving out the money He would say that this is the gift of Sawan *Shahenshah,* the Emperor of Emperors, and it will never end.

People could not find out how Mastana Ji was doing that, so they would come to Him and ask how He made the money. He would reply, "How can I explain to the cobblers how I make money? This is all the Will of Master Sawan Singh. You also go to Sawan Singh and ask Him how I do it." Many times the Indian government officials tried to find where He was getting all the money from. The police suspected He had some sort of printing machine with which He was printing the notes and they tried very hard to find out whether this was true. Many times they searched through His home and through all His belongings but they could not find anything except pebbles and stones. They even put Him in prison. I remember once that He was arrested and He was in handcuffs, and the people asked Him, "Now tell us where you are printing this money which you are distributing!" He replied, "What can I say to the cobblers? Cobblers are interested only in the skin, and you are like the cobblers. Because you are worried about the skin, the outer appearance, that is why you do not do the meditation. Come to the Eye Center and you will see how Sawan Shah's Will is working there, ready to give out gold, silver, pounds and any other thing. What am I giving out? I am giving out nothing in comparison to what Master Sawan Singh is giving out! Come to the Eye Center and see how His Will is working there."

I have seen myself that while doing all this, He Himself would wear only old, torn clothes, and torn shoes also. Showing these torn clothes and shoes, He used to say, "The poor Mastana has only these things. Such is the play of Master Sawan Singh: the poor Mastana doesn't have anything more than these torn shoes and clothes." Mastana Ji wanted to show them that if a lowly disciple of Master Sawan Singh can give money to the poor, why would such a Master beg from the people and misuse the funds? He used to say, "Sawan Shah is a very great Power and I am His dog. What can the Master not do in this world, the Master whose dog is giving out money to people?"

Mastana Ji Makes Me Describe the Beauty of Master Sawan Singh

The sangat of Mastana Ji was new and they had not seen Master Sawan Singh. Since I had seen Master Sawan Singh, very often Mastana Ji would ask me to speak to His sangat about Master Sawan Singh. Whenever I would visit Mastana Ji, in front of His whole sangat He would call me and say, "Okay, now tell people what Master Sawan Singh was like; How did He look?" I would describe the glory and beauty of Master Sawan Singh to all Mastana Ji's sangat exactly as I had witnessed it.

I would tell them how beautiful Master Sawan Singh was and how He had a very attractive form. He had a very broad forehead, His face was very pink and full of beauty. It always seemed as though there were two lights burning in the forehead of Master Sawan Singh. Whenever He used to talk, even the birds and animals would stand still. Even the sun, moon and clouds were under His control and whenever He wanted, the clouds would go and cover the sun. I would tell them how whenever He would laugh, it would feel as if His whole being was laughing and it would feel as if flowers were coming out from His mouth. He was so beautiful, so handsome, that even the fairies used to pay homage to Him, because even the fairies were not as beautiful as Master Sawan Singh.

Whenever I would describe Master Sawan Singh, Mastana Ji would become very happy, because he who is the gurumukh disciple becomes happy hearing the praises of the Master and he who is the real disciple of the Master always talks about the form of the Master. Mastana Ji was very intoxicated in the love of Sawan Singh and He used to love me a lot.

Mastana Ji Tells Me about the One Who Will Come to Initiate Me

Once, when I saw Mastana Ji in a very good mood, I asked Him, "Are you the One Who is going to give me the Initiation?" I wanted to confirm what Master Sawan Singh told me when I went to see Him with Baba Bishan Das. Master Sawan had told me that the Power who would give me Initiation would come to me by Himself, and I wanted to know from Mastana Ji whether He was the One Who would come and give me the Initiation. When I asked Him, He told me, "No, I am not the One. He is a very Powerful One. He has done so much meditation that if two groups of people are fighting with cannons that are blowing fire, if He puts up His hands He could stop the cannons from firing. When the time will come, that Power will come to your home by Himself and give you the Naam Initiation, and you have to appreciate Him." He said, "I have Master Sawan Singh's grace on me. Whatever I am is due to the grace of Master Sawan Singh. I have not done any meditation and whatever I have here, I have not earned it; it is a gift of Master Sawan Singh. However, that Power Who is going to come to you, He has done the meditation. He has really earned the blessings of the Master, and those who want to see the fruits of meditation should go to see Him. Master Sawan Singh was the Living God and the One Who is coming to you is the Son of God."

Mastana Ji Leaves the Body

After giving the Satsang and the Initiation in that area of Rajasthan for twelve years, Mastana Ji left the body in 1960. When His end time was coming near, He took some of His disciples and showed them the tombs of the Mogul emperors. He told them, "You see how the birds are making this place dirty? Nobody even cares to sweep this place." After that He took the disciples to Gurdwara Sis Ganj where Guru Teg Bahadur, the ninth Guru of the Sikhs, was martyred. When He brought His disciples there, He told them to see what was going on there; people were very respectful, cleaning their feet before entering, distributing parshad, and meditating in the temple. He said that the Mogul emperors had made many buildings and the army at that time had saluted them at many different places, but now there is no one who cares enough to keep the buildings of those emperors clean; even the birds are making them dirty. But at that place where the Gurdwara was located, where one sadhu was beheaded by the Emperor, 300 years later people are worshipping that place! Saints say that time always tells the Truth by itself, that Saints have the Truth within them and eventually people realize that Truth. That is why Mastana Ji would say, "To meditate is the best." The fragrance of the meditation spreads all over the world —

even after one's death — for many, many years. So the Saints and mahatmas who were given many troubles by the worldly people of their time, now all the people go to the places where they were cremated or born and in the memory of those Saints such places are made into memorials.

After Mastana Ji left the body, nobody was commissioned to be His spiritual successor. On the contrary He made a writing on the wall saying. "I am not allowed to say when I will leave the body and after me there will be many people fighting to become gurus. But you have to be in His Will and you have to meditate. Otherwise Sawan Singh will peel you, just like a banana is peeled. He will give you a severe punishment."

Practicing Ayurvedic Medicine

During this time, when I was meditating on the Two Words, I also used to practice *Ayurveda*, an Indian form of medicine, and I learned a lot about it. In that system people are healed using herbs and natural remedies. Because we have taken up the body it is natural to suffer pains, but when God created the creation, He also created the herbs and natural medicines. To make people aware of these things He sent the great people, the rishis and munis, who had the power of understanding the use of herbs and plants. The first doctors and healers were taught by the rishis and munis how to heal people and how to use herbs. The rishis and munis also taught them, "It is very important for you to have good character, because only then will the healing which you are doing be beneficial to the patient. If your character is not good, your treatment will not give any benefit to your patient. But if you have good character, if you are chaste, then it can have a direct effect on the patient, and even if you only give him a little medicine, he can become all right." They taught that it is very important for those who are healing others to have a very good character and that a lot is transferred through good character.

Nowadays medical science has progressed a great deal and it has led to the creation of many machines and other inventions, and because of them many people are getting benefit. In the olden days there were no x-rays, but still the rishis and munis were able to detect what was in the body. This was only because of their spiritual practice. Their mind, their body, their very existence was very pure and that is why they were able to detect that. Just by putting their finger on the patient's veins and counting his heartbeat, they were able to say what the patient had eaten even six months ago and what it was that was bothering him. Moreover, there is the saying in India, "Even if the sadhu gives a little bit of ash as medicine, then it will work." If one has good character, even if one doesn't have so much knowledge of the diseases, if one gives the patient just a little bit of medicine, the radiation of one's good character will help them.

Once a person came to me and he was suffering from very severe diarrhea. It was caused because once he ate some meat and one piece of the meat was not digested and somehow it got into his large intestine. It didn't go out with the bowel movements, but got stuck there and because of that he got diarrhea. Whatever he would eat would just come out and he was having a lot of pain. For one year continuously, he went to all the doctors he could find, and he got many treatments, but he was not healed. When he came to me, I put my hand on his head and I told him, "I don't know what is there, but you have a block somewhere in your large intestine and this is what has caused all this suffering." I told him, "I cannot say for sure, but if I give you some strong laxative and that thing is removed, then you will be all right." So I gave him some laxatives and after a couple of days he became all right. Today, people are detecting such things using x-rays, but in the olden days, when there were no x-rays, people used to detect such things because of their experience and because of their spiritual practices.

The healing that occurs because of such radiation is not done using one's spiritual powers; it occurs because of one's purity. On another occasion, in the village called Manjhuvas there was a boy who was in a very serious condition. His parents had taken him to many big cities to get him cured, but he did not get better and he was very close to death. His doctor used to give him good medicines; he was a very good doctor who used to come to see me also. When they were tired of going to so many places and being given all sorts of medicines, one of his relatives told the parents to invite me there. When I went there I told them, "I cannot guarantee that he will not die from some disease sometime, but I am sure that if I give him the medicine which he has been taking from the doctor he will survive." People were ready to take him to the cremation ground, he was so close to death, but when I went there I removed all the people from the room and the boy asked me, "Are you sure I will survive?" I said, "Yes, I am definitely sure that if I give you with my hands the medicine you are already taking, it will work. You may die from some other disease, at some other time, but if I give you this medicine with my hands, you will definitely be healed." And it happened that when I gave him the same medicine his doctor had been giving him, with my hands, he was completely cured, although he didn't start walking, moving and functioning normally for twenty or twenty-five days because he was very weak and had lost a lot of weight. At this time I didn't use my spiritual powers and I didn't lose anything spiritually; it was only because of my purity that it worked. If you are pure and with your pure hands you give anything to anyone, it will carry the best effect and that person will definitely get healed. So it was my personal experience that if there is any doctor who has a chaste life, who is doing even a little bit of meditation, no matter what medicine he gives to the patients, they will get healed. Besides the medicine, the doctor's own charging will also work to remove the sicknesses. If there is any complicated sickness, it may take time, but if the doctor has a good life, if he is chaste and if he has good thoughts, all these will have an effect on the patient also.

Worldly Thoughts at the Moment of Death

Because I was practicing Ayurveda, I would be called to see people when they were about to die. Once there was a businessman in the city of Padampur who never got married. He always had the desire to get married and always used to think about it, but somehow he never did it. When he was about to die they took me to see him. When I held his arm to feel his pulse, at once he woke up and asked me, "Are you tying the wedding band on my wrist?" In India it is a custom that when a boy gets married they tie a thread on his wrist, so he thought that I had come to tie a thread on his wrist to get him married. He was ninety years old and he was on his death bed, but still, because of his unchaste thoughts, he was thinking that he was going to be married. I thought, "Brother, now you are preparing for the journey to the beyond; how can we get you married now?" Whatever simran, or remembrance, he was doing throughout his life, he remembered that at the time of his death and he spoke out from that.

Another time I was called to see a dear one when he was about to leave the body. This dear one had many good houses and had collected a lot of wealth. When I got there he was calling the name of some poor person who did not own any house. He was requesting God Almighty, "God, if you want to take someone, why don't you take that person who does not have any home? I have worked very hard in making all these homes."

Lovingly I told him, "Dear one, it doesn't make any difference whether one has made a house or not. The person whose time has come, only he will be taken by God. Just because that person whose name you are calling out does not have any house, it does not mean that he will be taken by God."

On Abortion: Adopting the Baby Named Gopi

Because I was practicing medicine, sometimes people would come to me asking me to perform an abortion. Because my thoughts were very religious and very godly, I would always reply, "No. If I have learned the medicine, it is for saving the lives of people, not for taking anyone's life."

Just think, when life is put into the body, at that time the baby is very helpless and the baby cannot do anything. When the baby is aborted using chemicals or other things, when the baby is killed in the womb of the mother, it is very painful. Just imagine if you were in that situation before you were born. If someone were to kill you, what would you feel? Would you feel happiness or pain? So even though those souls who experience this, who are aborted, have very hard karmas to pay off and that is why they meet their end this way, still, after all, sin is sin and those who do that deed get the punishment for it. An account will be asked of every single deed and we will have to pay for it, as that is the punishment for the sins. For this reason I always abstained from this kind of deed. Indeed, throughout my life I have had the habit of trying to help anyone who is going to have an abortion so that the abortion doesn't happen. Many times I even sold my property to help such people.

In Ganganagar there was one lady civil surgeon who was an initiate of Master Sawan Singh. She was very well respected there because she was very sympathetic to all the patients who would come to her for treatment; she was very popular. Once a married couple came to her to get an abortion and since it was against the teachings of the Path and since that lady surgeon had a lot of sympathy for all the people because she was an initiate, she advised them not to do it. She said, "If you had taken some measures before the baby was conceived then it would have been all right, but now that your wife is already pregnant you should not do this thing because it is like a crime." Those two were also initiates of Master Sawan Singh, but still they insisted on getting an abortion.

That lady civil surgeon understood and remembered the teachings of great Baba Sawan Singh so she called me in, as I also knew that couple, and I knew that lady doctor. She said, "The parents are initiates and I am also a satsangi. This is not a good thing to have happen," and she requested me to advise them and somehow convince them that they should not do that serious thing because it was neither healthy nor good.

I tried my best to advise them. I suggested many things to them but they were not willing to accept any of my advice, and they wanted to get that abortion done. Finally I had to make this offer. I said, "Whether it is a boy or a girl, when the baby is born you should give it to me and I'll take care of that baby. If you are afraid of the expense, don't worry; I'll take care of that too." In India usually people don't like to have daughters because when one's daughter is married one has to spend a lot of money. In many cases one has to spend the earnings of a lifetime just to get one daughter married, so people are afraid and don't want to take the responsibility of raising a daughter. So when I told them, "Whether it is a girl or a boy I will look after that child," then they agreed.

When that baby was born, he was a boy, very beautiful and very loving. I gave him the name Gopi, because the *gopis,* the girl devotees of Lord Krishna were beautiful, and he was also beautiful. I took care of him, I adopted him and he came and lived with me at my ashram.

The True Renunciation

During this time I met two brothers from the village of 77 RB, Gurdev Singh (who later came to be known in our sangat as Pathi Ji) and Darshan Singh. They were seekers after truth and came to love me very much. At that time Darshan Singh used to serve a mahatma who would not look at any woman and who wanted to have no contact with any woman. He did not even like to see women and he would always keep a very great distance from any woman. Both of the brothers used to serve that mahatma before they met me and they were under his influence.

Whenever I went to 77RB they used to talk about that mahatma.

They said that he was such a great mahatma and that he never likes to see women or have any contact with them. That mahatma's teaching was that you should not eat food that was cooked by a woman; he was so strict about all these things. So once they were talking to me about how good that mahatma was, and I asked Darshan Singh, "Tell me one thing, what was wrong in that mahatma, why did he not want to see any woman?" He replied, "Because the mahatma says that if he sees women he cannot preserve his vital fluid in his dreams." I told him, "Darshan Singh, if just by looking at the women he cannot preserve his chastity, then what would happen if sometime some woman would go near him? And still you tell me such good things about him, that he is very good."

It is a very funny thing that at that time, while he was following and serving that mahatma, Darshan Singh became the father of seven children. So I asked him, "Tell me one other thing, about your children. How did you manage to have all these children when you were following such a strict mahatma who did not even want to look at the women?" He did not have any answer to that question, and he just kept quiet.

If we have renounced all these things outwardly but from within we are holding on to them, it is nothing but hypocrisy. Such hypocrisy, such renunciation, can be very misleading. If we are not maintaining chastity in our thoughts, the chastity which is maintained in the body does not have any importance, it does not have any value, because all day long, twenty-four hours a day, our mind is thinking lustful thoughts and having fantasies. If this is our condition, instead of becoming a chaste person, we become the most indulgent one.

Regarding celibacy — it is a great privilege and it is a matter of great grace of Almighty God if one can maintain celibacy. If one can maintain chastity all through his life, if he can remain as pure as he was when he came out of his mother's womb, and maintain that purity all through life, that is a great thing. But this can happen only if that person has the gracious hand of Almighty God on his head. I was a very fortunate one to be able to do that.

People say, "We are celibate, we are the mahatmas," and talk about maintaining celibacy, but it is very difficult to do that. I have met many mahatmas, many so-called religious people, who say that they are celibate, that they are chaste. However, it is very unfortunate that they cannot even maintain their vital fluid. They lose their vital fluid even in their sleep. So those men whose condition is like this, that they cannot maintain chastity even in the state of dreams, if they have women at their disposal do you think they will be able to control themselves? Or if they are women and they have men available, will they be able to control themselves? It is not possible, because if you cannot maintain chastity in thoughts and in the state of dreams, how is it possible for you to maintain it physically?

The other brother, Gurdev Singh, was also married. He had spent his life in a good way, and he did not go to other women or spend his time in bad company. However, he was married and he used to be with his wife. He didn't know that one has to abstain, to remain in control, even in married life. Because he was enjoying with his wife, he always remained sick. He would always have his children walk on his body or give him a massage or rub his head. All day long he would work in the fields but his body was very weak and he would always have people working on his body.

When he met me, I lovingly asked him, "Can I give you a remedy for this?" When he was receptive, I told him to just maintain chastity. He did that and he no longer had any problem. He didn't have to go see the doctors, he didn't get sick, and he didn't need to make people walk on him. The person was the same, but when he obeyed these teachings and maintained chastity he completely changed and he no longer had those problems.

The Disease of Anger

There was a friend of mine named Chaudi who lived in the same village as I did, but he had the misfortune of being very much controlled by anger. In the villages people kept their animals in the same courtyard where they themselves lived, and once when he was entering his home through the courtyard his buffalo touched him. He became very upset at this and he took a big piece of wood and hit that buffalo on the head and at once the buffalo died.

When the buffalo died and fell on the ground, there was a camel there that saw this and he started making some noise because he saw the buffalo dying. When my friend saw that the camel was also complaining, he took the same big stick, hit the camel and also killed the camel right on the spot.

When his mother and his wife saw all this they were very frightened. They did not want to say anything because they knew that if they would speak up he might come and hit them also, so they kept quiet.

After that he went to the kitchen and sat near the fireplace. The fireplace was burning so he felt a little more heat than he could bear, so he took that piece of wood and he smashed the fireplace. Afterwards he went to his bed and he lay down there.

I was also in the same village and it so happened that right at that time I thought, "Let me go and see my friend." I did not know that all this was happening. So I went to his home but I did not notice the buffalo and the camel dead over there. I went into the house and asked his wife where Chaudi was. She replied that he was at home, but he had a cold and so he was not able to come out to see me. In those days I was practicing Ayurvedic medicine, and I thought what was the point of practicing Ayurveda if I did not help those who were sick, so if my friend was suffering from a cold, I should go and give him some medicine.

However, that dear one was so embarrassed by his misdeeds, by his anger, that he did not want to face me and he hid himself in his bed. I went in and I removed the sheets from his bed and I saw that his body was burning like anything. His face was red, his eyes were very red and he was burning in anger. I asked what the reason was. He said, "Didn't you see the dead animals in the courtyard? I was so much affected by the wave of anger that I killed both animals on the spot. I would have killed my mother and my wife also if they had spoken anything, but it is good that they did not speak so I did not kill them."

So just in a moment he killed his two animals and he was about to kill his family also. Why did this happen? Only because of the anger. Anger was so terrible for him that he could not think about what was right and what was wrong and that is why he killed those two animals. Anger is such a thing that it won't leave you unless something very serious happens. Unless you have destroyed something it will not leave you.

All the Saints have talked about anger and they all have said that it is a spontaneous madness and the only way to get rid of it is meditation. One can increase anger within oneself as much as one wants and one can decrease it as much as one wants, but the blood of the person who has anger in him gets burned and many problems and diseases are brought in the body by becoming angry. The person who has anger within him always remains upset, there is no peace in him and he bothers all the people who are around him. I saw how much damage anger could do, and I understood why in the literature of Sant Mat anger is referred to as a very low thing.

The Problem of Caste and Untouchability

In India the Saints have had to struggle very much against the belief in the caste system. Rajasthan is also affected by this problem and even now people believe in the high and low castes and in untouchability. I was the first person in Rajasthan to speak against the belief in untouchability and in high and low castes. I was the first person who brought people from different high and low castes and from different religions and made them sit together and eat together. Many people came to me, delegations of pundits, and told me, "Everything is fine — your teachings, your sayings — but there is only one difficulty, that you bring people from different castes and walks of life and make them sit together and eat together. You treat everybody alike and that is not acceptable."

Once a pundit came to me as a leader of one delegation. The other pundits had told him that he should come and talk with me about this. However, he used to smoke tobacco, so I told him, "Pundit Ji, these souls whom you call low caste are not as bad as your tobacco."

There were some native farmers of Rajasthan who were present there and when I said this, since they were addicted to tobacco they asked me, "Is it really so bad, the tobacco?" I told them, "Yes. If you don't believe me you can read in the *Puranas,* the ancient scriptures, where it says that when Rishi Narada was given the knowledge of herbs and vegetation by Lord Brahma, when he came to the tobacco plant, Lord Brahma said, "This is such a thing which will not be used in the Golden, Silver and Copper Ages, but when the Iron Age comes, people will start using this to a great extent and those who use it will go to hell. If anyone who is called a pundit or Brahmin uses the tobacco, he will be born as the pig of the village and those who give donations to such a pundit will also go into the body of the pig." So when the farmers came to know the reality, they opposed the pundit who had come there to debate with me and they asked him, "Why didn't you tell us earlier that tobacco was such a bad thing?" Later on some of these same farmers became satsangis.

Meditating on the Two Words

As I told you earlier, Baba Bishan Das had the inner knowledge up to the top of the causal plane. He had the knowledge of the first Two Words, and he had done that practically. Whatever knowledge he had,

Sant Ajaib Singh, circa 1963

and whatever he had done practically, he gave me that.

Our soul is the resident of Sach Khand, the Real Home, our origin is Sach Khand, but after coming to the Eye Center, the soul has spread all over. The soul joins the company of the mind at the Eye Center, and after that the mind is controlled by the desires, and the desires are controlled by the sense organs. In that way the soul is controlled by all these things. The soul is spread everywhere; she is attached even to the things outside the body, and she is controlled by the attachment to parents, to the community and to the country in which she lives. In this way, after coming down from the Real Home, Sach Khand, the soul has gotten dispersed in the world.

When the soul came down, first of all the causal cover was thrown upon her and she lost some of her brilliance and her light became a little less. When she came further down, the astral cover was thrown upon her and she lost a lot more of her radiance; the light became less. Finally, when she came down further, the physical cover was thrown upon her and she lost all of her light. When we concentrate at the Eye Center, we become successful in removing the physical cover from our soul. The Masters give a very beautiful example to make us understand this. They say, "Suppose there is a lamp which has many thick coverings on it. No doubt the lamp is burning and it is giving full radiance, but because of the covers, the room in which the lamp is put is not bright. If we carefully remove the covers one by one, we will find that the room will become brighter and brighter, and when we have removed all the covers, the room will become full of light. Similarly, when we come to the Eye Center and concentrate our attention there, we become successful in removing the physical cover from our soul."

When the soul starts hearing the sound of bells her dirt starts going away and she becomes more and more pure. Then she reaches the astral plane, whose owner is *Jot Niranjan*. At the top of the astral plane the soul reaches *Sahansdal Kanwal,* where there is the light of 1000 flames burning. When this light is lighted up, the whole of the within is lighted up. Over there is the nectar. Before we get there, because we are not doing the meditation, our soul is outside, spread all over the world and since our soul is outside, our soul is not drinking that nectar. Instead of our soul drinking that nectar, lust, anger, greed, attachment and egoism are drinking that nectar. But when we go within, our soul starts drinking that nectar. When we go within, one by one all these five passions: lust, anger, greed, attachment, and egoism, leave us and then we ourselves start drinking that nectar. In the place of lust, anger, greed, attachment, and egoism, the good qualities are manifested within us. We get continence, chastity, discrimination, forgiveness and all the good qualities within us. All the opposing forces leave us alone and in their place come all the good qualities.

After reaching the top of the astral plane the soul then has to go to *Trikuti,* or the causal plane. There is a kind of tunnel that connects Sahansdal Kanwal and Trikuti called *Bank Naal*. In the Bank Naal, first the soul has to go straight and then she has to go very deep, very far down, and then again she has to come upward. In Trikuti one has to stay for a long time and meditate because there our karmas have been stored from ages and ages, from many previous births, and they get paid off when the soul stays there and meditates. It is very important for the soul to stay there for a long time and pay off all these karmas, so that she can continue her journey. After paying off all the karmas the soul can leave Trikuti and reach up to the peak of Brahm.

Baba Bishan Das had perfected his meditation to the point that he had journeyed through the astral and causal planes and he had reached the top of Brahm. With the grace of Baba Bishan Das I also became successful in my meditation up to the point where I had traversed through those two planes. The great thing about Baba Bishan Das though was that he knew that there was something beyond the causal plane, beyond Brahm. Many times mahatmas who have attained the position of the causal plane believe they have achieved the complete God and that is why they do not teach people about the other planes. They always think there is nothing beyond what they have achieved. They think that they are all in all. But Baba Bishan Das knew that there was something beyond that, and that is why he always remained humble.

Hearing the Sound Current

After rising above the mind and the organs of senses, when we listen to the Sound Current, the Shabd *Dhun*, then it seems to us that this Sound can be heard even by people who are living twenty or thirty miles away, although that is really not the case. The Sound Current is so loud that we feel that many other people can hear it, but the reality is that only the meditator is able to hear it, and not the other people.

It is like that special kind of musical note that the hunters often play to attract deer. Usually the deer do not like to go near men, but when the deer hears that sound to which he is attached, he also becomes intoxicated. He is attracted to that and he comes and places his head at the foot of the hunter. So when you gain the concentration and you hear the Sound Current, you become so intoxicated and attracted that it may seem that it is being heard all over. However, that is not the case; it is within you and only you are listening to it.

Even the sounds of the lower planes are very loud. When I was initiated by Baba Bishan Das into the first Two Words, he gave me the knowledge of how to reach up to the causal plane, and when I used to do that meditation I used to hear the sounds from there. Once in the month of June, which is a very hot month, especially in Rajasthan because the sand heats up very quickly, I was sitting for meditation, listening to the Sound Current. Suddenly the Sound Current came very loudly, and it was so melodious that my heart was attracted to it and my mind was fascinated by it. At that time I thought that some musicians had come and were playing their musical instruments near my house and I felt like coming out from meditation to see them. After some time, when I couldn't stop myself, I came out and for an hour or so I went on searching for them. The sand was very hot, but I was not aware of it because I was still hearing the Sound Current. There were some noises outside also, but I was not aware of them, because the Sound Current was so loud and it was so melodious that I wanted to meet those musicians.

For one hour I searched for them. There was a farm there and I went into the field, but I couldn't find anybody. When Sunder Das came to know that I was out of my cave and was searching for somebody he found me and asked me what I was doing. At that time I came back to my consciousness and I became aware that I was out of my meditation place and that there were blisters all over my feet because the sand was very hot. I told him that I was looking for those people who were playing musical instruments, but he told me that nobody had come there and nobody was playing any instruments.

Mahatmas tell us, "This body in which we are living for a long time, have we ever gone into this body and seen how God Almighty has kept the precious wealth of jewels there, or how many jewels and precious things are within us?" Swami Ji wrote,

> *You will behold the radiance of the Light within*
> *And listen to the wonderful Melodies in the Inner Sky*

When we concentrate the streams of the mind and soul, which are scattered everywhere, at the Eye Center by doing Simran, then we can easily catch the Sound of the Shabd, which is coming from above, at the Eye Center. Our mind gets intoxicated by the outer music, and just as a snake dances to the tune of the music, in the same way our mind also starts dancing to the tune of the outer music. However, our soul becomes intoxicated and our soul starts dancing when we hear the Inner Music.

"Do Not Lose Heart, Do Not be Disheartened"

Even though I did meditation for eighteen years continuously, still towards the end of that eighteen-year period, in my last days of meditating on the Two Words, my mind started playing a very great trick on me. At that time I was about to get the perfection in those Two Words, and then the thoughts started coming within me, "You have been meditating for such a long time but where have you reached? What have you received? You have been meditating for so many years, but still you have not achieved perfection. What are you doing? This is all useless. This is just a waste of your time." Thoughts like that started coming and bothering me.

So one part of my within was saying, "Get up; don't meditate," and like that, but the other part was saying, "No, you should continue doing it." One time it so happened that I obeyed the one part that told me to get up, and I came out from that underground room and started walking. When I had walked about one hundred and fifty yards, a voice came to me, from where I don't know, and it said, "Do not lose heart. Do not be disheartened. Do not lose your enthusiasm; go back to your room and do the meditation." At once I realized it was a trick of the mind that had brought me out from that underground room and I knew I was supposed to go back and start doing the meditation. So I went back and I continued my meditation. At the end I perfected those two stages, those two planes, into which Baba Bishan Das had initiated me. I achieved that only with the grace of my first Master, Baba Bishan Das.

The Master is sitting within us, He knows everything that we are doing and He is the One Who makes us do the meditation. That is why, even after receiving the experiences, we should not think that we have done anything or that anything happened because of our efforts. One should always be grateful to the Master, because in fact Master is the One Who is doing the meditation. He is the One making us sit; He is the One Who is giving us all the experiences. Instead of giving an opportunity to the mind to create negative thoughts within us, we should be grateful to the Master and have His constant remembrance.

Dharam Chand Asks Me to Become a Guru

The result of my meditation was that thousands of people started coming to me. Once I became successful in what Baba Bishan Das had given me, Satsang started going on at our ashram, and the means for conducting the Satsang and supporting the sangat were established there. However, since Baba Bishan Das had told me that this was not the ultimate, that there was something more beyond that, I did not become the Guru of anyone and I did not initiate anyone even though there were so many people following me.

When Dharam Chand was convinced that I had become successful in the first Two Words, in the meditation of the first two planes, and when he saw that thousands of people were following me, he thought, "Since many people follow him and in appearance he looks good, why not make him the Master?" He suggested that I should become the Master and he would start telling the people about his experiences with me and he would work as my agent. I told him, "I don't know how to hold Satsang." He told me that I should not worry about that because he was a very learned person and knew *Gurmat Siddhant* by heart. He said, "You don't worry about it; I will do the Satsang."

So I told him that in the Sikh history I had read a story of Guru Hari Rai. Once, when He was taking a walk with some of His disciples, He saw a cobra that was being eaten up by some ants. The cobra was not dead, but he had no power to remove those ants. The disciples asked Guru Hari Rai why that cobra was suffering so much, and what karma he was paying. The Guru told them, "In his past lifetime he was a fake Master. He mislead the people and that is why he has become a cobra. The disciples have become ants and are eating their Master while he is still in the body, and the condition of the Master is such that he has no power to remove the ants."

So I told Dharam Chand that whenever I remembered that story, I felt frightened because I know that those who become false Masters and mislead the people have to pay for it. I told him, "Dear one, you are telling me to become a Guru? I have not yet become a disciple."

O My Beloved, Do Not Delay!

I have written the letters and I am sending them to Sawan.
O Beloved, do not delay.

Please come at once. O Resident of Anaami, come to my country.

The month of Sawan has come, and the friends have erected the swings.
Your remembrance is bothering me. O my Beloved, come home, do not delay!

Every day I am hoping for You. I am waiting for You. Even in the orchards the mangoes have ripened.
This is very joyous weather. O my Beloved, bring the happiness, do not delay.

When in the sky the clouds are full of rain and when the cuckoo birds sing the song,
The friends are swinging on the pipal tree. O Beloved, You also come and give me a swing, do not delay.

Today from the sky it is raining, but my Beloved One is far away from me.
Again the spring has come. O my Beloved, You also come, do not delay.

My anklet is singing; may someone come and unlock the mysteries of my heart.
O Beloved, listen to the melodious song of the anklet of Ajaib, do not delay.

— Likh Chitthiya Sawan Nu

In this bhajan it says "I have written the letters and I am sending them to Sawan." This does not refer to writing the outer letters, with outer paper and pen. To do the Simran day and night, to sigh cold sighs in His remembrance, and to remove our attachment to the pleasures, that is writing the true letter. Our mind becomes intoxicated by hearing the sounds of all the outer instruments like the violins or harmoniums, but our soul becomes intoxicated when she listens to the drum of the Sound Current inside.

In this bhajan the anklet does not mean an outer anklet. It means the anklet of the soul. The bhajan is conveying, "The anklet of my soul is sounding day and night, and this is the call, this is the yearning of my soul, this is the yearning of my heart. Listen to its melodious song." In India, in the month of Sawan, the month of the Indian calendar that is the same as July, the clouds form in the sky and peacocks dance in their joy. In the same way, our soul becomes intoxicated and dances when she hears the Sound of the Shabd. Then from within the heart, the true prayer comes from the soul. The soul says, "The sound of my anklet is such, my yearning is such, that only You can come and quench my thirst."

So after I was initiated by Baba Bishan Das I did the meditation of the first Two Names for eighteen years continuously. I did that meditation regularly, without understanding it as a burden, for eighteen years. I did not waste even one minute of my time in worldly pursuits; I only meditated during that time. Baba Bishan Das had told me, "Your Goal is a higher goal, and the One who has to give the rest of the thing, He will come to you by Himself." So I was sitting in remembrance, waiting for my long-separated Lord to come to my ashram, to give the Bread of Life to this hungry one, and to give me that nectar for which my soul was thirsty.

Master Kirpal Singh (1894 – 1974)

EIGHT

The Meeting with Kirpal

The Story of Harnaam Singh

There was a man named Harnaam Singh who used to work in the fields at my ashram in Kunichuk. He was a low caste person, a garbage collector, and he used to smoke and use other intoxicants also. Once around the year 1966, Harnaam Singh went to the city of Abohar, which is about fifty miles from Kunichuk. He was standing on the side of the road in that city and that great Master Who was going to come to me drove by him. He was passing through that city on His way to Delhi and for just a moment He gave darshan to Harnaam Singh. Harnaam Singh exchanged glances with the Master and he absorbed the darshan of that great Master with his eyes. He was not initiated, he knew nothing about that Master and you can imagine how little of the Master's darshan he could have had, because Master was in a car and you know how fast a car goes. Still Harnaam became so absorbed in that brief darshan that a unique kind of awakening happened within him and after that he remembered the beautiful form of the Master. Before he had had the darshan of the Master, he was not a very good person; he did not have any spiritual qualities. He used to drink, smoke, and do all kinds of bad things. However, as soon as he had the darshan of the Master, he decided to give up all the bad things he had been doing.

When Harnaam came back from Abohar he told me, "You always talk about spiritual things, and today I have seen such a great spiritual man — I don't know Who He is, but I have seen Him all dressed in white. He had a white beard and He was all pure, all holy, and I cannot forget those eyes. I still remember the eyes and the form of that spiritual being and from now on I have decided that I will give up all the bad things that I have been doing." I was very surprised to hear this from him, because he did not have a very good past. He lived for one year after that incident and he never touched any bad thing; he became a very good person.

The Master did not explain anything to Harnaam Singh — He did not say to him, "You should give up drinking, you should give up smoking," etc. It was the grace of the Master which created that awakening within him so that he gave up all those things without anyone explaining to him. He did not get Initiation, but still he remembered the form of the Master and he never forgot the eyes of the great Master.

One year later Harnaam Singh, along with forty other workers, was in my fields harvesting gram, a type of chickpeas, and he seemed to be in good shape, very healthy. Suddenly he felt very nervous and he lay down on the ground. His son came and told me about his father's condition, saying "I don't know what has happened to my father; he has become very ill." I went there, but before I reached the place where he was he had become unconscious, and I felt very sad. But soon he came back into the body for a few moments. I put his head on my lap and I asked him, "What's wrong, Harnaam Singh? What has happened to you?"

He told me, "Nothing has happened to me, but now I am going, because that spiritual power, that person Whom I saw one year ago and told you about, now He has come. That old Sikh man, with the white beard and all dressed in white clothes has come to receive me. He has come in a plane and now He is taking my soul up to the Real Home; it is all His grace. One year from now He will come to your place by Himself; you should prepare for Him, and welcome and respect Him, and He will do everything for you." After saying these things he left the body.

Even though Harnaam Singh was not initiated and knew nothing about the Path, because he had had the darshan of that great soul once, he was liberated. Everyone looked down on him all his life, but that beloved Master didn't look down on him, and He came to protect him.

The Master Sends the Message that He is Coming

*Ajaib remembers Kirpal in the bushes of Rajasthan.
Giving up the palaces and mansions, He became a fakir.
The pain of separation of the devotees is unbearable.*

> *Ajaib's mother gives him this advice, "O Son, enjoy the happiness of wealth and power."*
> *The disease will not leave the body of those who have been bitten by the cobras of these bushes.*
>
> *The pains do not go away without Kirpal. The doctors of the veins of love are not available.*
> *Attaching your eyes to the Saint's eyes, extract the nectar as the mill extracts the juice.*
>
> *After hearing the true voice of the suffering Ajaib, the locks of the treasures of Kirpal were opened.*
> *When He heard the cry of Ajaib, it pierced through His heart. Finally Kirpal came, giving up His throne in Sach Khand.*
>
> — Ajaib Kirpal Nu Yad Karda

When he left the body, Harnaam Singh told me that in one year that Master would come to my place by Himself, and it was around that time, one year before I met Him physically, that I started having the darshan of that Master internally. He started appearing within me and giving me His gracious darshan. At that time He started coming within me in the form of Swami Ji Maharaj (the Master of Baba Jaimal Singh); He had short hair and His mustache was also trimmed.

Six months before He came, in the remembrance of that Master I started preparing my ashram in order to welcome Him, because I knew that someday soon He would come. That place was developed in His remembrance, and I was waiting for Him, because there was a hint from within that something big was going to happen in my life; "Someone is going to come and give me His grace." For that reason I was building the ashram with full enthusiasm. Day and night people were working there, and I was telling the people who were helping me with the construction that a Master was going to come there. I didn't know who that Master was, but I told everyone that a Master was going to come, and we were waiting for Him.

When that Master first started appearing to me within, He first came in the form of Swami Ji Maharaj, but gradually that form changed, until towards the end, a few days before He met me physically, I started seeing Him in His own form. Then He Himself sent one of His devotees to me with a message that I should stay home because He

Swami Ji Maharaj (1818 - 1878)

was going to come to see me, He was going to visit me at my ashram.

Even though I was sitting there waiting for Him, searching for Him, I did not know anything about Him. I had never heard of Master Kirpal Singh. I had not met any critic of Master Kirpal Singh, nor had I met anyone who had praised Him. I didn't even know that there was a Saint called Sant Kirpal. I didn't know whether He lived in Delhi or Calcutta or some other place; I didn't know whether He was learned or not, whether He was married or single. I don't know who told Him that I was there, that I was living in that village. But He knew that somebody was sitting in His remembrance, and that is why He sent one of His dear ones to me with that message. He sent His representative who told me that Master Kirpal wanted to come and meet me. I asked that representative whether He was the real Mahatma, and she said, "Yes, He is the real Mahatma." Then I said, "He is most welcome. He will sit in my heart and I will go by every word of His commandments."

It was the grace of Almighty God working at the human pole of that Beloved Master that He came for this poor soul, because He knew which soul was sitting in His remembrance at which place. Since my childhood I had been sitting in the remembrance of Almighty God and I had always been craving for Him, and thinking about those fortunate souls who were able to sit at the feet of the Holy Masters. I was living in the hot burning desert and I was suffering from the heat. I had the burning desire in my within and I was suffering like anything. He knew within whose heart there was yearning and who was sitting in His remembrance, so that is why He Himself chose to come to me. He answered that prayer, that request, which was coming from my heart. My inner longing was communicated to Him heart-to-heart, and He came all the way to my place, traveling five hundred kilometers through the desert, and He met me. He came down into this world, He came down to the desert, and He cooled the heated heart and quenched the thirst that I was having ever since my childhood.

When such a great yearning is created within us, that Ocean of Grace starts flowing towards us. It is exactly like the father who cannot bear to see the sufferings of the son. It does not matter that the son is suffering because of his own faults and mistakes, still, because the father is full of compassion and mercy for his son, he makes every possible sacrifice to remove his suffering and bring happiness to him. In the same way, when the souls are suffering in this domain of the Negative Power, the Master Power cannot bear to see the suffering of the souls. Even though the sufferings are caused by the souls themselves, still He has so much compassion for them — as the souls are of the same essence as He is — and because of His compassion He comes down into this world to remove their sufferings.

So this is my personal experience, that the Beloveds of God are the All-Conscious Ones, and They know who remembers Them with a sincere heart. They definitely reach the place where someone is remembering Them with sincerity in his heart. That is why I have written, "When He heard the prayer, when He heard the voice of poor Ajaib, it went through His heart, and giving up His throne in Sach Khand, finally He came down to meet Ajaib."

The Master Arrives

There were thousands of people following me at this time. The Satsang was already going on, but because I knew there was something more, beyond what Baba Bishan Das had given me, I did not initiate anyone. When I got that message that the Master was coming on a certain date, I went ahead with extensive arrangements for the occasion, and sent word to all those who visited me often, to come and see that Master for Whom I had been waiting. On that day when He came, there was a big group of people, many thousands, sitting there.

Before the Beloved Master came, the dear ones sprinkled water all around on the road to keep down the dust, because that land was very dusty, and they even covered the road with sheets so that the car of the Master would not touch that dust. From the entry point, where His car was to park, to the middle of the courtyard where He was to sit on the dais, they spread embroidered linen. I felt that my soul was to meet her husband — the Oversoul — and, feeling shy, like a bride I observed the age-old Indian custom and kept away from the entry point where He was to arrive. Instead I requested my friend Sardar Ratan Singh to receive and welcome the Master at the gate. The Most Holy One came, and on His arrival inquired as to where I was. On being called to Him, He overwhelmed me with His love-filled glance; only He knows about that first meeting, why He showered grace on me. I was completely lost in His darshan, and I was not aware whether a man had come or whether God had come.

Master Kirpal Comes Like the Groom, and He Marries Me

O friends, my beautiful Satguru is Kirpal. He is merciful on the poor.

I was separated for so many births and was searching for the dearly Beloved.
May I meet the perfect Master so that I may go across.
Now I have got the Husband, the Emperor, who takes care of me.

O friends, wandering from door to door I became very crazy.

I did not get any Knower of the heart. No one heard my plea.
O friends, now I have got my Beloved, the support of my heart, the treasure of Shabd.

I did the practices of water, performing the austerities, and bathed in the places of pilgrimage.
I worshipped in the temples and holy places, but no one shared the pain.
O friends, my Beloved has come and has put me on the Path, and makes me see Him.

Listen, O Beloved Kirpal — make everyone have the beautiful darshan.
The life of Ajaib is full of bad qualities. Take him across!
O friends, the True Saint has come — my Husband has come — and He loves me!

— Satguru Sohna Mera

Right from childhood I had had the desire that my groom should come to marry me. I had the desire that the Form of God Almighty who was going to marry me should come to my home Himself like the groom does. Even though my mother had told me that a man does not get married to another man, still I had that desire. So Kirpal came, and at that time He came like a groom. In India when the groom goes to marry the bride, he brings clothes and ornaments. In the same way, when Kirpal came, He brought a ring for me, which was made by His own earnings, He brought clothes for me, and He married me. He did everything that was required according to the Indian tradition. He gave me that ring, He gave me the clothes, and in that way He fulfilled my desire, He quenched the thirst which I had had for ages and ages. The Male, the Almighty Lord for Whom I was waiting, came in the Form of the Shabd and He married my soul.

As I said, I had not known about Master Kirpal. I had not known anyone who had told me about Him. But when He came and I exchanged my glance with Him, I knew that He was my Beloved Husband. I became overwhelmed in His love and joy, and I told Him, "Master, as I was born from the womb of my mother, still I am the same. I am as pure as a virgin and I have come to You with all my purity and virginity." Then this yearning came to me, "How can I make myself acceptable to Him?"

In India the wives are taught that it is up to the husband how he wants to keep his wife. The wife always has to surrender to the will of the husband. They are taught that no matter what the husband does, the wife always has to accept whatever comes from the husband, and she should separate from the husband only when death separates her. So like that, when I met my Beloved Husband, this yearning came to me, "How can I be His wife? How can I make myself acceptable to Him?" I did not ask Him anything. I did not even care whether He was a renunciate or He was married. But as soon as I saw Him, I knew that He was the One for Whom I had been yearning since my childhood. Then I thought, "What should I do? How do I make myself acceptable to Him? Will He like me or not?"

He was the Husband of my soul, and what can I tell you about my union, my meeting with Him? My condition was like what Guru Ramdas described in His writing, where He says, "O Lord, I am Your disciple and I have fallen at Your feet. I have taken refuge in You, and my soul is indulging with the Oversoul, and I am getting so much pleasure and happiness." The union of the husband and wife in this physical plane leaves only unrest and dissatisfaction, but the happiness and pleasure one gets when the soul is meeting with the Oversoul cannot be described. When the soul goes and meets with the Shabd, that happiness, that satisfaction, cannot be described outwardly; it is something worth experiencing.

The stories of love are untold. One cannot tell the stories of love because when love comes into the heart, the lips close, one cannot say anything. It is something worth experiencing.

If one is yearning for someone from one's very childhood, and if one had gone to so many different places and done so many things looking for that person — if that person appears and one meets Him, just imagine what one's condition would be! How can one describe that moment? One will only be amazed, one will only be surprised and one will find no words to describe that meeting, that moment when one meets one's Beloved.

"I Do Not Believe in Any Wahe Guru, I Believe Only in You"

Even now in the villages of India the old customs and traditions are prevailing and it is the custom there that when a girl is married, with whatever name her in-laws call her, she will be happy and not mind; she has become of her husband. For that reason she doesn't mind being called by any name that her in-laws call her. In the same way, in the Path of the Masters, when one has become of the Master, when one has become the dear disciple of the Master, one should be pleased with whatever one's Master calls you. One should be satisfied and content with whatever the Master gives. Whether He gives one pain or happiness, one should be happy in that. The Master always tries to give as much happiness as possible, but if any pain comes from His side, even then one should not complain and one should always remain happy like that girl who does not complain when she is married. In the Path of the Masters, loyalty to the Master is needed most.

In Rajasthan, even now, it is the custom that if a married woman is coming from one direction and she sees that a man is coming from the other direction, and if it is likely that his shadow might be cast upon her body, she would wait for one minute so that she does not even take the shadow of another man. In the same way, the disciple should also remain loyal to the Master and should always remain content with whatever the Master gives. So when my beloved Master came, I told Him, "Master I have neither seen the Wahe Guru nor have I seen the *Akal Purush,* the Timeless Lord. I have not seen anyone and I don't care to see anyone because I have seen You. I do not believe in any God — I believe only in You. I know that You have come in this desert to quench my thirst and ever since childhood I was longing for You. Now I want to catch hold of You and I want to be of You. Whatever You tell me I will do that, and whatever You give me, I will be content with that." In truth, when we come to the Master we should become like that girl. We should catch hold of the Master like that girl catches hold of her husband and does not mind how her in-laws treat her. In the same way, when we come to the Master, we should catch hold of the Master, and we should be content in His Will. So in that way, I felt that if I understood the Master, if I did what He told me to do, then everything was with me.

My Mind, My Heart is Empty

When I first saw Him, when we first exchanged glances, I also told Him, "I do not know what to ask from You, what to say to You, because my mind, my brain, my heart, everything is empty. I do not have any questions." I did not ask Him any question, I did not even care to ask him whether He was married, whether He had children, or what He did.

I said, "Master, somebody asks for milk or worldly riches from You, somebody asks for sons and children from you. But I only ask for Your darshan. I only ask for Your grace."

Master smiled and became happy and said, "I have come here only because I saw that your within is empty, your mind is empty. There are so many people around me who are mental wrestlers." He used to call the learned people mental wrestlers, and He said, "There are so many of them around me, but I have come all this way only because I saw that there is an empty place. There is a heart which is for me, and that is why I have come to you."

This is the reality that at that time my Beloved Master embraced me. The people who witnessed that came and they touched my body, and they sang this hymn, "Fortunate are those souls, fortunate are the jivas, who are embraced by the Master." So, because I was hungry for His grace and He had the grace, He showered grace on me. I was burning like a fire and He had Naam with Him. He caused the rain of Naam to shower and He cooled down my heated heart.

He Asks about My Meditation

When beloved Lord Kirpal came, the very first thing He asked me was "How is your meditation?" He did not talk about any worldly thing, He didn't ask me about anything except my meditation. Hearing that question I felt very overwhelmed and I was very moved, for I was meditating strictly on the Two Words and it was the first time in my whole life that someone had come to me and asked how I was doing in meditation. Before I met beloved Master Kirpal many of my relatives had come to see me, but they all had their own desires, and they all wanted me to fulfill their desires. Nobody listened to me and nobody cared for how I was doing. Even though I tried to tell them, they were not interested in how I was doing. Instead they all told me about what they wanted and how they were doing.

I had a habit of writing poetry ever since my childhood, so when Master Kirpal asked me that question about my meditation, I replied in the form of poetry. I told Him, "Up until now many guests have come to me and they all sang their own songs. They all talked about their own selves, they all tried to impose their own teachings on me, but nobody asked me about meditation and nobody made me do meditation. But today is blessed, and today I am feeling as the most fortunate

Sant Kirpal Singh early in His mission

one. Today my fate has been awakened because I got such a guest who cared about my meditation, who has come to make me meditate more."

The Master is the only one who asks about our welfare. He is the only one who asks about our meditation and our soul, because He becomes happy and is pleased knowing about our soul. As Master Sawan Singh used to say, even though the Master knows everything, still He is very pleased when the disciple tells the Master what experience he is having.

I Ask Master about Seeing Him as Swami Ji

As I said earlier, for one year before He came physically, Master Kirpal had been appearing within me in the form of Swami Ji Maharaj with His hair cut short and His beard trimmed. Only a few days before I met Him physically did He start appearing to me in His own form. So at that time when I met Him, I asked Him, "Master, first You were appearing within me in the form of Swami Ji Maharaj, and after that You started appearing within me in Your own form. Why didn't you appear within me before in Your own form?" Master said, "I didn't do anything. This is Master's grace. This is all because of the grace of Master Sawan Singh."

Then I told Him about Harnaam Singh and how he was liberated by Master even though he was not initiated, but had had His darshan at Abohar for just a few minutes. Master said, "This is all Master's Grace. Master Sawan is doing all these things. I am nothing."

When perfect Masters come into this world, They do everything for the disciples. They even take the suffering and pains of the disciples, but They never exhibit Their qualities to Their disciples. They never say, "We have done this for you." They always give credit to Their Master. It is very difficult to understand a Saint and it is very difficult to understand the words or teachings of the Masters. Tulsi Sahib has said, "If anyone claims that he has understood the Master, God forbid, I touch my ears. It is not possible."

Master Kirpal Offers Me His Ashram

When that gracious Kirpal came to me, He offered me His ashram. He offered that I could come with Him to His ashram and take care of things there. I wept and told Him, "Master I was looking only for

You. All my life long I have searched for You and I have been waiting for You. I have all this ashram here; what do I have to do with bricks? I don't need anything. There are many bricks here. Do I have to go and hit my head on the bricks?" I told him I had many buildings and things in Punjab, that Baba Bishan Das had also made a big ashram and that there in Kunichuk I had made a very big ashram in His remembrance while waiting for Him. I said, "My Lord, I don't need any ashram. I have looked only for You and now that You have come, I have found You, because I asked only for You. I need only You and nothing else."

He who wants to do the devotion of the Lord does not hesitate in sacrificing anything for the Master. In this Path, even the biggest sacrifice is the smallest.

Master Stays and Gives Grace to the Sangat

When Master Kirpal came that day, He planned to stay only an hour and a half because He had to go further. This time went by without Master having a chance to meet the sangat. When He told me He had to go, I told Him, "You have pulled me using the hook of love. Now where are You going to go?" I told Him, "Just look out there." There were 20,000 people waiting for Him, not one of whom was initiated. When Master Kirpal saw the yearning of those souls sitting there, He felt very gracious and He stayed for five or six hours. He showered much grace on them, so that everyone saw Light instead of Master there, and everybody said that it seemed to them that Master was talking only with them. That was very great grace that Master showered on them all.

When Master came, a lot of happiness was expressed by exploding firecrackers and things like that. He told me He was not pleased with that. I told Him, "I understand that You are not happy, but at least look at our happiness — how happy we are." Then He said, "Yes, all right; I am happy in your happiness."

Seeing the Master as Light

During the very first Satsang that He gave there, one non-initiate person saw Master Kirpal Singh sitting on the dais in the form of complete Light. He said, "This Master is not a human being; He is not a man. He has just assumed the body of a man but in fact He is God." There was another non-initiate person who had never seen a picture of Baba Sawan Singh before that, but He said that he saw an old man wearing white clothes, with a white beard and carrying a stick in His hand, standing behind Master Kirpal Singh.

At that time the minds of the people in Rajasthan were very pure, as there were not many good roads, there were not many canals and there were not many television sets or radios. They were innocent people and just by giving them a little impetus, just by giving them a little understanding, they would start doing the devotion of the Lord because their minds and their thoughts were not spread very much into the world. That is the reason that when Master Kirpal came to my ashram for the first time all the people there said that they had had the darshan of the Master in His Real Form, the Form of Light. They saw the Master turning into Light, all Light.

A Message for My Soul

During that Satsang, through the words of the holy *Guru Granth Sahib*, Master Kirpal sent me a message. He gave me a hint. In the *Guru Granth Sahib*, Guru Arjan Dev Ji has written, "He Who has sent you into this world, now He Himself is calling you. So, very happily and easily, through me you can come back Home." When Pratap Singh Ji, who was Master's pathi or chanter, sang this particular line of the *Guru Granth Sahib* during the Satsang, I understood that it was a direct message for my soul, for my Self. I understood that now God Almighty, Who had sent me into this world, had come in the form of beloved Lord Kirpal to take me back.

If we get lost in this world — suppose we have taken a wrong road or gone astray — and we meet someone who knows us and puts us back on the right track, just imagine how grateful we would be. In the same way our Real Home, our country, is Sach Khand and we don't know how much time has passed since we have been separated from our home. We are lost in this jungle of pains and pleasures and we are wandering here and there away from our home.

With every single breath this poor soul thanks the Master Who showed him the way home. I was wandering here and there; I had wandered off the right path. I had gone very far from the shore, and He invited me to come back home. He not only invited me and showed me the True Path, but He helped me walk on the Path. He helped me come

Master Kirpal Singh giving Satsang, with His pathi, Pratap Singh

back to His Home. That is why I am always indebted to Him and I am grateful to Him.

Kirpal Tells Those Who Want to See God to Close Their Eyes

Master Kirpal in the Satsang asked people if they wanted to see God. Everybody raised their hands and said, "Yes, we want to see God." I also raised my hand, and some even raised both their hands to make sure that they would not be left out. Then Master told them, "Those who want to see God, close your eyes." Everybody closed their eyes, but I didn't close my eyes. At that time some dear ones complained to Him that I was not closing my eyes. He called me and asked why I was not closing my eyes. I replied, "Master, You said that those who wanted to see God should close their eyes. I want to see God, but when I am able to see Him with my open eyes, then why do I need to close my eyes? I don't understand anybody else as God when You are in front of me. I am seeing the six foot tall God moving and talking in front of me. Why do I need to close my eyes?"

Master smiled and said, "Yes, that is true. He has understood my teachings."

"Today is the Auspicious Day and It Has Come with Good Fortune"

Today is the auspicious day and it has come with good fortune, for we had the darshan of our beloved Satguru.

One who is entangled in the this world; one who is always forgetful in this world;
One who has gone many times up and down; and one who is stopped in this world; one who was caught in the superstition and the blind faith of the world,
He has been taught the teachings of Satguru, and Satguru has put him on the Path.

Today He speaks some of Light, some far and near; and other matters are coming on His lips like waves in the ocean.
He has awakened our within by saying some incidents of past days, some of the present days, some of the coming days, and He has told us many good things.
Thus He has awakened our within.

He who is the Beloved and worthy of worship in this mortal world, He is free from all the temptations.
He is the star of this dark world, and He has removed the sins from the world — from me and you.
And He has cleared up the difference between the liar and the truthful one — between the low and the high.

One who is to get the hell, gets heaven if he comes to His Path.
This is in one's own hands.
One who does this (meditation) whether today or tomorrow — will never die out of the hunger of Naam — because coming to this Path, many sinners have turned into devotees.

God is not achieved by going in the mosque, nor is He in the temple.

> *He is not in the wilderness, but He is within everybody.*
> *When we close our outer eyes and walk on the Path shown by Master, and when we do the Simran of Master's teachings — Master Himself unites us with God after bringing us to the Path.*
>
> *From the shadow of the clouds, and from behind the drops of rain,*
> *From the cold of winter and the fire of summer, Master's teachings, Master's grace and Master's sayings have liberated millions of sinners*
> *Who have remembered His Naam only for once.*
>
> *This is the determination of Ajaib — always be attached to Kirpal. Always be happy in His Will — whatever He gives, always be contented with that.*
> *This is your Path. And if you go away from the Path, you will go astray — you will suffer.*
> *Because those who have forgotten their Satguru have not been happy.*
>
> — Aj Shub Diharda E

In India there is the custom that when during the wedding the groom enters the home or when we bring some new thing into our home, before that thing enters the door, some oil is poured on the gate, and it is considered to be an auspicious occasion. However, Guru Nanak Sahib says that the moment or the day when we meet our beloved Master, only that moment is counted and considered to be auspicious in our life. The moment when we are able to meet our Master is the most auspicious day, the most auspicious moment.

In search of happiness and peace we cross the oceans; we climb the mountains. We go all around the world; we collect all the riches and the wealth of this world. We even acquire power and we become rulers. We create children and we do so many things in this world to achieve peace and happiness. However, even if we become the owners of all the mountains, even if we collect all the riches of this world, still we won't get any peace and happiness.

This is my personal experience, that one gets happiness and true peace only twice in his lifetime. One time is when we meet the physical form of the Master. If we have that great yearning and love for the Master, when we are able to meet Him on the physical level, on that day our mind that is wandering here and there stops wandering, and we get the real peace and contentment. The second time when we get real peace, contentment, and happiness in our within is the day when we are able to withdraw from all the nine openings of the body, when by doing the Simran we are able to rise above our body consciousness, come behind the eyes and see the Radiant Form of the Master. These are the two days when we get real happiness.

On the day that Master first came to my ashram, I sang this bhajan to Him that says, "Today is the auspicious day and it has come with great good fortune because today I am having the darshan of my beloved Satguru." I sang that bhajan because that was the fact of my life; it was the truth of my life. I understood that moment, that second, when I met Almighty, Omnipotent Master Kirpal as the most auspicious moment. I had never seen such an auspicious day before and moreover, I was not sure whether I would have that opportunity again or not. That is why I called that as the most auspicious day and I sang this bhajan to Him.

Even now, many years later, whenever the dear ones sing this bhajan it refreshes my memory of those moments, those first moments when I met my Beloved Lord. If one reads the words of this bhajan one will find hundreds of secrets hidden behind every single word.

On the same day I also sang the bhajan that says, "God has come in the form of man," because that was also true. Truly speaking at that time I was half-mad, because my Satguru Kirpal came into my house. He was the owner of that Hidden Power; He was all in all. Master listened to those bhajans and He paid a lot of attention to them. After listening carefully to each and every sentence, after listening to each and every word, Master was very pleased and I was gaining His pleasure. The way I sang those bhajans to Him was so devoted, was full of so much yearning, that I was able to drink a lot of nectar from Him. After each and every word He was saying, "Yes, *tik hai, tik hai* — this is good, this is good." He was pointing at me and He was very much happy. Moreover, there were many people present there at that time to share in that happiness.

After becoming a man, God came.
After coming, He awakened the world.

*For many births the souls were stuck here. For millions
    of miles the souls wandered astray.
He Himself made this union.*

*Millions of sinners have come to His door.
With one glance He liberated them. He took their raft
    across.*

*Those who received His Grace and Mercy came and met
    Him with no delay.
They got His Secret.*

*In Satsang He made this proclamation, "Oh Man, why
    did you come into this world?"
And He showed the Path of Love.*

*He showed the Path of Simran and Bhajan;
He made us leave all the rites and rituals, and do the
    repetition of Naam.*

*Ajaib says meditate on Naam; God Himself will come
    and be Gracious;
He distributes the true happiness.*

— Banda Banke Aaya

During that time when I was singing to my Master He gave me His darshan the way Kabir Sahib gave His darshan to Dharam Das, His disciple. Dharam Das came to Kabir Sahib only after much searching and only after losing all his wealth in his search for God. At the time Kabir Sahib was giving him Initiation, Kabir gave him the inner darshan and told him about his previous births. He made Dharam Das realize that He had always been trying to get Dharam Das to Sach Khand in his previous births. At last, in this birth, it happened that he had come to Kabir and he got the Initiation.

In the same way, when Master Kirpal met me He showed me very clearly that He was looking for me and that He was waiting for me to come to Him to get Initiation and go up. So that is why when He came to my ashram I sang these two songs. He liked those bhajans, and when a lot of satsangis were sitting in front of Him I said, "Master, at least for today You should give Your darshan openly to all the dear ones so we will not have to struggle day and night for Your inner darshan. If You don't want to give us this blessing daily, at least for today, because today is the most auspicious day in my life. You should give Your inner darshan to me and to all the people so that everyone will know that God is only One and He neither resides in the temple nor in the mosque nor in the church. He resides in the hearts of the devotees."

I told Him, "Give us Your darshan openly, so that the priests in the temple as well as the *mullahs* in the mosque may all realize that God does not reside in their buildings, but He resides within the devotees of God. If You give Your real darshan to everybody, if You reveal Your secret to everybody, all the confusion and illusion that people have spread in the world will go away." I told Him, "In this way, O Kirpal, all the fighting which people are doing in temples and mosques — people say, 'Our temple is good,' or 'Our mosque is good'— all the conflicts that arise from this, all the delusions, will also be resolved. Then the people will realize that the manbody is the real temple or mosque within which Kirpal is residing, within which that Kirpal is God."

Still I remember that happiness, and at that time my soul confessed within me that this is the long-separated God. This is my old companion. This is my beloved Kirpal. At that time I was sure that everywhere there is Kirpal. In the water there is Kirpal, in the air there is Kirpal, on the earth there is Kirpal, in the sky there is Kirpal; everywhere there is Kirpal and there is only Kirpal everywhere. Kirpal is the protector, and Kirpal is the destroyer. Guru Nanak has written in His writings, "If Sant Kirpal (the Gracious Saint) is showering *kirpal,* is showering grace, then even the sinners, even the critics, can be liberated with the other people."

> *O Beloved Kirpal Guru, my love with You is very ancient.*
>
> *I am lying at Your door. I am standing with my hands stretched out.*
> *The eyes are thirsty; make me have Your darshan. Shower grace, O Lord. Take me across.*
> *O Friend of the miserable ones, the Ocean of Compassion, how do You forget me?*

Showering grace, You liberated the Saints. O Satguru, You have liberated even the sinners.
You ate the contaminated fruits of Shivri. You embraced all those who came into Your refuge.
You have erased everyone's difficulties; You have known everyone's pains.

O Satguru, I am in Your refuge. You are an Ocean and I am Your drop.
You are my mother and father and brother. I am a beggar; You are the Giver.
O Ajaib, this is the tale of lives. This is the story of birth after birth.

O Beloved Kirpal Guru, my love with You is very ancient.
— Tumse Tumse Meri Prit Purani

All the Great Souls come from the same plane and They know each other very well. However, They do not come into contact in the physical world until Their destined time has come. Before They meet physically, the yearning that the disciple has for the Master is such that He always feels that something is piercing through His heart. He always feels that something is lacking within Him, that something is missing within Him. Right from His childhood, He is always longing to meet the Master, because He knows that Great Soul, because They have both come from the same plane.

For such disciples also the time is predetermined when They are supposed to go and meet with Their Master. Even though They Themselves are the enlightened ones, but still Their time is predetermined and when that appropriate time comes, They go to the Master. When They come to Their Master and They look into the eyes of the Master, They realize that He is their old friend and for Them that is enough. When They come to the Master, just within moments, in the first exchange of glances, They understand that this is the Master and from this Soul, They have to receive Spirituality.

Such a disciple feels happiness only when He comes across the Beloved of God, when that Saint gives him Initiation into Shabd Naam and when He gets the opportunity to do God's devotion. When such Souls who come into this world with this feeling of yearning, with this pain of separation, meet Their Master, when Their glances are exchanged, when They look into the eyes of Their Master, the intoxication They receive at that moment cannot be described. They become so much absorbed in the love of Their Master that even if They were to be cut into pieces, still They would not complain. They would not hesitate if it were for the love of the Master. No matter what they are offered in this world, no matter how many difficulties They have to go through, once They go to the Master, Their enthusiasm, Their passion, Their love for the Master never decreases. Instead it goes on increasing with every moment.

Receiving the Initiation

Whether You recognize me or not, come to my courtyard.
I sacrifice myself on You, come to my courtyard.

For me there is no one like You. I have searched for You in forests, seashores and deserts.
I have searched for You in the whole world.

His parents called Him "Pal," people call Him "Sant Kirpal."
You are my faith and morality.

Leaving my parents I have caught hold of You, O Emperor Kirpal, my beloved.
Maintain the honor of those who are attached to You.

I have searched for You in all the cities; which messenger should I send?
My heart is throbbing as I have climbed onto the sedan chair of love. O husband Kirpal, catch hold of my hand.

We want Your darshan always — by any means.
O True Emperor Kirpal, the Lord, You are my support.
Poor Ajaib has met beloved Kirpal, and I thank Him millions of times.

Master Kirpal at a roadside stop

> *Countless sinners have crossed over by remembering Kirpal Singh.*
> *Ajaib says never give up the support of Kirpal Singh.*
>   — Bhave Jan Na Jan

Master held Initiation in the city of Ganganagar on that trip, and at that time I received the Initiation from Him. The opportunity was given to me by Master Kirpal to sing a hymn to Him before getting Initiation. I sang this hymn when He told me to sit on the dais and say something. In this bhajan I told Him, "It is all right that your parents used to call You 'Pal' and people are now calling You 'Sant Kirpal.' But for me, You are my religion, my morality, my everything. So please come to my door." I requested of Him, "I have waited for You, and now You have come. Please reside in my eyes so that You will not go away from me and I may not see anybody else. I left my parents, and now I have taken refuge in You. You are my Emperor of Emperors, You are my Giver, You are my everything. Now that I have taken refuge in You, You should take care of me. If You will not take care of me, what will people think? People will call me mad, because I left my parents, property and everything. After doing that, if I still don't get You, people will think, 'For whom has he left all this, if he is not getting anything.'" So in this bhajan I requested that Emperor of Emperors, "You are my everything, You are the Giver. Please take care of me because I have come to You and taken refuge in You. I left everything and now I have only You. You are my husband and I am Your wife; please take care of me."

In this bhajan, I begged that Kirpal, "Searching for You, I went to many cities, many forests, many rivers. But I didn't know what Your address was or where You were residing, so how could I write You any letter? How could I send any message to You? Now You have come here." When I used to read the banis of the past Masters, how sitting in the sedan chair of love They went to Sach Khand, my heart also throbbed and I felt the same yearning. But I used to think that I had used up this manbody, because a lot of time was spent in His search but still there was no hint of Him coming. So I requested Him, "I am afraid that this manbody has gone. Hearing that people could sit in the sedan chair of love and go to Sach Khand, I am very afraid that maybe I will not be able to do this. So I am requesting You, Kirpal, now that You have come, take care of me, hold my hand and make me cross the ocean. I am not asking any worldly thing from You, I only want Your darshan by any means. I want Your darshan always — I want You never to go away from me."

I conveyed to Him, "You are the Emperor, and people call You 'Emperor Kirpal,' and there is no doubt about that. You are the only support, the only way for me to realize God. You Yourself have said that You are the only way for me to realize God. But I do not understand You as the way; I understand You as Almighty God. Tonight I will sleep because today when You came I found peace. I was separated from You for ages and ages and I haven't slept; tonight when I have found You, I will sleep a very deep sleep. Now all my worries are gone."

When I understood that I had found God, I became grateful to Him and thanked Him thousands of times. I was very happy because that Kirpal, Who was separated from me for ages and ages, had come to my courtyard, and now I was seeing my God.

I had been meditating on the Two Words for the last eighteen years since my Path had been opened to me, so He did not feel the necessity to explain the theory to me. He took me into a separate room and initiated me there. He looked into my eyes, and with His grace He took my soul up, and for whatever time He felt appropriate, He kept my soul there.

In the other room where the other people were being initiated I saw that they were given diary forms.* So I requested, "Please give me the form so that I can also keep the diary." But Master replied, "Your life is your diary."

---

* Master Kirpal Singh gave His disciples a daily diary form to record the meditation they did and to identify ethical lapses in thought, word, and deed.

NINE

At the Feet of Kirpal

The Instructions of Master Kirpal

After showering grace on me, after giving me the Initiation, before Master went back to His ashram, He gave me the duty of keeping quiet and doing meditation constantly. He gave me the order to do Bhajan and Simran, to just sit in meditation and do my practices. He told me, "You are not to worry about the world. You are not to come out in the world. You are to close your eyes to the world and do your meditation. You should not even come to see me; you should only do the work that I am telling you to do. You don't need to come to any conference or any meeting. Whenever you will need me, I will come to visit to you. I will come on my own to see you. You do not need to open your eyes, for whenever I want I will come and make you leave off the meditation."

So, because I was in His refuge, I started doing the meditation without caring about the people. He gave me the duty of meditating constantly, so I always stayed in one room and meditated. I became cut off from the world and I never went anywhere. I never went to Delhi, I never went to any place; I always concerned myself only with my meditation. Before Master Kirpal came to my ashram, I had thousands of people following me and I used to see people and talk to them and do all kinds of things like that. After meeting with Master Kirpal I stopped doing all of that and started doing full-time meditation. I left all the world and did not meet anybody from the world.

It is very important to obey what the Master says. Often I have said that I got the habit of obeying the commandments and keeping the discipline from the army, because in the army it is a rule that first you carry out the work which you have been given, first you obey the orders, and later on, if you have any doubts or questions, you can ask them. I remembered the time when I was in the army, and how I was able to please my worldly officers just by obeying their orders, and thought, "Is it not just as important to obey the order of God Almighty, the Master Himself, in Sant Mat?" It was only because of this habit of obeying the orders and keeping the discipline that when Master Kirpal came to my ashram I was able to obey Him.

Master told me that He would come there by Himself, and He did shower grace in that way. When He went on tour to Rajasthan, He would come to see me, and stay with me. Moreover, when I was doing the meditation, many times He would come physically in His private time to see me. That was a distance of 500 kilometers, but many times, in His sickness even, He used to come there by Himself to take care of me, to see how I was sitting in His Remembrance. He used to say, "The owner of the cattle knows what the cattle need. Whenever a cow needs water or anything, he comes out by himself and gives that. The cattle do not have to ask for it." In the same way, because I was also tied up at the door of Beloved Kirpal, He was worried about me and He used to come to take care of me. I relied on Him and He kept His promise, He kept His word, and He used to come to see me.

The Love Which Master Kirpal Gave Me

When my beloved Master would come to visit me, He never allowed me to sit in front of Him, He would never let me sit on the floor. He always gave me the honor of sitting right next to Him. He would never allow me to bow down to His feet, but always He was embracing me. Many times He allowed me to be with Him and He would make me sleep in the same room with Him. Many times I got the opportunity to eat with Him, and as a father feeds his child, in the same way He would feed me – He would even feed me with His own hands. He loved me as a father loves a child. He would even make me sit in His lap, just as a child sits in the lap of its father, and I got the opportunities to play with His beard also. What to speak

Ajaib Singh and Master Kirpal in Ganganagar

about cleverness, at that time I was half mad. I was not even aware of what I was doing, for when I was with my beloved Master, even though in respect to age I was grown-up, in my within my thoughts were very innocent, like a child's.

The people who used to see me with my Master used to say, "Kirpal is fond of Ajaib" because of the way He would treat me, the way He would express His love for me in front of other people.

He would not make me sit in His lap when alone only, but in front of all the people, and the people who were standing there would sing this hymn which said, "Blessed are the souls whom the Guru embraces, very blessed are those souls whom Master allows to touch His body."

When He would embrace me or make me sit in His lap, I would have such peace and happiness which I cannot describe in words. Whenever He would embrace me, I would think that it is as if God Himself is embracing me and I am sitting in the lap of God and God's hands are on my back. The happiness that I received is beyond any description. I consider myself the most fortunate one that Master Kirpal chose me. He gave me this human body, He Himself came in a human body to meet me, and He chose me for His devotion. He did every possible thing for me and He gave me so much love that I cannot forget that happiness. As Kabir has said, "If you make a dumb person eat rock candy and then ask him about its sweetness, he cannot describe it in words because he cannot speak. He can only dance and show his happiness." In the same way, I cannot describe outwardly, in any words, the happiness that He gave.

I had never gotten such love in my life and I can never get such love again in my life. I cannot describe the love that I received from Him. He would give me so much love that many times I would weep, and I would ask, "How come You are giving me so much love? You are *Sat Purush*, the True Lord, and I am just a worldly jiva. Why are You showering so much grace on me?"

Singing the Bhajans for Master Kirpal

I got many opportunities to sing bhajans in front of Master Kirpal and He always used to like it very much. He would listen to my bhajans with much affection and love and He used to become very pleased with the bhajans I would sing to Him. He would pay a lot of attention to every single sentence of the bhajans. In fact, He would nod His head with every single line of the bhajans I would sing, and He would get so intoxicated in the bhajans that He would point at me and say, "Yes, that is correct." Saints are also attached to the love of Their Masters, and in the bhajans the love of the Master is very much present.

He never allowed me to sit in front of Him and sing to Him. He always made me sit right next to Him on the dais, but still from there I would sing bhajans to Him. I did not prepare for singing the

Master Kirpal on the dais, listening to the bhajans

bhajans; it was not that I would write a bhajan and then sing it to my Master. The bhajans would come instantly; they came out from my heart and they were the voice of my soul. In fact it was He Himself who would make me sing the words in His praise.

In the beginning I had to gather courage to sing in front of the Master, but gradually, later on, the love that I had within me started coming out and my bhajans were very sweet. Master used to love them because in my bhajans there was a lot of love for the Master and humility too. Masters are not hungry for our love, because They are already attached to the love of Their own Master, but Masters always like to hear loving bhajans from the disciples. So that is why when we sing the bhajans, if we do it lovingly, then the love comes out. Since I have always liked to sing the bhajans or write the bhajans, even from my childhood, whenever I would sing in front of my Master I would get so overwhelmed and so intoxicated that many times I would even have tears in my eyes and the dear ones listening to that bhajan would also have tears in their eyes. It was the very best of times for me because I was able to open up my heart and I was able to express what I had in my heart for Him. It was a very precious time, a very beautiful time. The grace that I received at that time is beyond description.

When singing the bhajans in front of Him, many times I used to feel like an infant, and many times I would feel like I was His wife. A child holds the beard of his father, and even if he holds it tightly, the father is not upset because the child has love for its father. Gradually, slowly, lovingly, the father removes the fingers of the child, but he does not get upset. In the same way, there is nothing like embarrassment or shame between a husband and wife. In love, whatever they do for each other, neither of them will mind. In one bhajan I said, "I have met the beautiful husband Kirpal and now this Ajaibo has become His." In India the name Ajaib is masculine and Ajaibo is feminine. In that bhajan I have not called myself as a male, I have called myself as a female, as the wife of Kirpal.

So when the love for the Master is created within us, when the desire to please Him is created within us, no covering is left on the soul. The soul becomes free of any kind of embarrassment, and there is no hesitation in expressing the love for the Master.

Like Lord Rama Came to Shivri, Lord Kirpal Came to My Home

O Guru Kirpal, come to my home.
Just like You are fond of Sawan, so I am fond of You.

Whoever has meditated or remembered You, with a true heart, even for once —
With both Your hands full You have given him Your love.
My string is in Your hands — You are the companion of my life.
You are the devotee of devotees, and it is not good for You to reject me.

O Dear One, You enjoyed the contaminated berries of Shivri.
Giving up the good delicious food of Duryodhan, You preferred to eat the simple food of Vidur.
I am not only Your servant, O Satguru; I am the servant of Your servants.
Just like You have protected the honor of everyone, protect my honor also.

O Satguru, how do I call You? I do not know, I do not have any knowledge.
I do not have any style. I do not know . . . It is not in my hands to call You.
O Guru Ji, moment after moment my eyes are thirsty for Your darshan.
This is the request of Ajaib, "Please do not let me suffer anymore."

— Guru Kirpal, Mere Ghar Aana

There is a place in India named Pampasur that in the Silver Age was believed to be a very good place for meditation. Many great rishis and munis used to live there and do their spiritual practices. They had many good ashrams and they were proud of their ashrams. In that place there was also an old woman who was of very low caste, a dark-skinned untouchable, named Shivri. The rishis and munis were so proud of their devotion, of their practices, that they did not like her at all. But Shivri was very devoted and, in the name of God Almighty, every morning she would clean the path on which they walked, and she would do whatever she could do to serve them. She was doing all that in the name of God Almighty.

When Lord Rama went into exile he went to that place; when the yogis living there learned that Lord Rama was coming, they were sure that Lord Rama would come to their houses, for they were all very proud of their *japas* and *tapas*, rituals and austerities, which they did daily. On the other hand that low caste woman, Shivri, also had very much love and was very devoted to Lord Rama. Since she was also a very great devotee and she always had the desire to serve the Saints and Mahatmas, when she heard that Lord Rama was going to visit Pampasur, she thought, "What if Lord Rama decides to come to my poor humble hut? What would I present to him if he came to my hut? I don't have anything to give

Master Kirpal and Sant Ji at Kunichuk Ashram

him to eat. I will go and bring some berries from the forest." So she went into the jungle and picked some very good-looking berries. When she came back home she thought, "What if these berries are not sweet? What if they are sour?" She thought that she should taste them ahead of time, to make sure they were sweet. She tasted all the berries, but she was so intoxicated in the remembrance and love of Lord Rama that she forgot that, according to Hindu ritual law, she was contaminating those berries by tasting them.

When Lord Rama came to Pampasur, he did not go to the ashram of any of the proud rishis or munis. Instead he went straight to that small broken hut of Shivri and he ate those "contaminated" berries. With so much love for her he did that, and by doing so he gave honor to and glorified that poor Shivri, and those rishis and munis who were proud of their practices started weeping because God was not pleased with them.

There was a pond in that place whose water was dirty. The rishis and munis did not allow that old lady to take water from that pond because they understood her as a low caste person. They requested

Lord Rama to remove the dirt of that water by blessing it. Lord Rama wanted to teach them a lesson and break their egoism, so he told them, "You are very good mahatmas, you are doing a lot of practices; you should bless that water. You should put *your* feet in that water." They did, but the dirt was still there. Then Lord Rama himself put his feet into it, but still the dirt was there. So Lord Rama said, "No, I can't do it either. However, let us try that old lady." Shivri was invited and when she put her feet into the water it became very pure. In that way Lord Rama taught the rishis and munis a lesson; that in the court of the Lord, only love and devotion are counted.

This is a very old story from the scriptures, but the reality is that there were many learned and wealthy people around Master Kirpal Singh. There were many people who held very high posts, and many great people used to go to Him. However, He chose to come to this poor one, just as Lord Rama chose to go to Shivri. In the same way, Almighty Lord Kirpal chose to come to my home, and He blessed and glorified my home.

In the same way, in ancient times the town of Delhi was called Mastinapur, and the Pandavas and Kauravas were ruling there. When they started fighting with each other, Lord Krishna wanted to go there, to mediate between them and stop the war. They were cousins and Lord Krishna thought that if they fought, the world would experience a great loss, because they were the entire ruling family of India. Duryodhana was king at that time and he was very proud of his kingship. He thought, "I am a very important person so Lord Krishna will come directly to my house." However, there was one low-caste servant, a sweeper, named Vidur. He was a devotee of Lord Krishna and he also had the desire that Lord Krishna would come to his house. Even though Duryodhana was proud and thought that Lord Krishna would come to his house, when Krishna came, seeing the devotion of Vidur, he went straight to the house of Vidur.

Vidur was not at home when Lord Krishna arrived. Vidur's wife was there, but she was bathing. When Lord Krishna called the name of Vidur from outside the house, she became mad in the love of Lord Krishna, so much so that she forgot to put on her clothes, but came out of the bath completely naked. Lord Krishna told her, "Crazy woman! You are not even aware that you are naked! Go and put on your clothes."

Lord Krishna came into the house and sat there, waiting for Vidur to come. Vidur's wife wanted to serve Lord Krishna by giving him food. However, there was nothing in the house except bananas. She took a banana from the cupboard and peeled it, but instead of giving the fruit to Lord Krishna, she gave him the skin and threw away the fruit. However, Lord Krishna didn't complain and he ate it. When Vidur came in, he saw that his wife had given the skin to Lord Krishna and had thrown away the fruit. He rebuked her, saying, "Have you left your senses? What are you doing? You have given the skin to God and have thrown away the fruit!" She brought another banana and he peeled it, gave the fruit to Lord Krishna and threw away the peel. However, Lord Krishna replied, "Vidur, the sweetness that I had in that peel is not in this fruit."

Then she cooked vegetables for Lord Krishna, but forgot to put salt in them. Lord Krishna ate that dish, but never complained. However, when Vidur ate that food, he became very upset. He told his wife, "What has happened to you? Have you gone mad? First you gave the skin of the banana to Lord Krishna, and now you are not putting salt in the vegetables! What is wrong with you?"

However, Lord Krishna told him the next day, "Oh Vidur, you don't know the sweetness of that vegetable which she made for me. That vegetable dish was sweeter than kheer (rice pudding). She made that vegetable dish with so much love, and when I ate that food made with love it was very helpful to me; I spent all night in meditation. Because of that love and the sweetness of the vegetables, I was able to meditate for a long time."

The next day, when Duryodhana came to know that Lord Krishna had stayed overnight at a servant's house, he was very upset. He spoke with Lord Krishna very sharply, saying, "You don't like our palaces. I know you went there to eat very sweet delicious food because they have very sweet things for you. However, you did not remember that they are of low caste. They are not people of our caste." However, Masters always say, "God never looks at the caste. He looks only at the love and devotion."

Since my childhood I had been reading the bani of Bhai Gurdas, which says that if we are able to feed a Gurumukh, if we are able to put even one grain in the mouth of a Gurumukh, we get the fruit of performing millions of yajnas, a type of religious deed. So I had this very old desire that sometime in my life I would meet a Gurumukh and I would feed Him from my sincere earnings. I had this desire that when my Master would come to my home I would have the opportunity to feed Him. As it happened, when I met with

Beloved Lord Kirpal, He told Tai Ji that from then onwards the clarified butter, or ghee, and the wheat that they would use in His kitchen should come from me. Graciously He gave me the order to send those things to Him.

This was a very old desire of mine and He fulfilled that desire. Just as Lord Rama went to Shivri's home and He did not go to any other place, in the same way Lord Almighty Kirpal came to this poor one's home, and He blessed me with His presence. Master listens to everyone's prayer, but to whose home does He come? When we make our heart full of yearning for Him, when we make a place for Him, He definitely answers our prayers and comes to our home. Just as when a child calls for its mother, the mother cannot delay – she leaves everything and she comes to pick up the child – in the same way, when we call for our Beloved Master, leaving everything, He at once comes to us.

The Master is so gracious, He is so kind and merciful that whoever has remembered Him with a true heart, He at once comes to him. He doesn't even care, He doesn't even remember to wear His shoes, but at once, as soon as He hears the call of His dear one, He comes, because the sincere call of the devotee moves Him very deeply.

Even though I had many people working at my farm, still I myself used to plow that one acre of land where I grew the wheat for my Beloved Lord. I watered that field myself and I used to take care of it. I did not allow anyone else to go near that field; I used to grow the wheat for Him myself. In the same way, I used to take care of the cow that gave the milk to make the clarified butter for the Master. All the time I was doing that, I did the Simran and I always felt grateful to the Master. I considered that seva higher than the kingdom of the heavens, and I always felt that I was the most fortunate one because Master had given me such an opportunity to do that seva. I would always wonder, "What good deed have I done, because of which I have been given this opportunity to serve my beautiful Master?"

Controlled by the Love of the Disciple

O Beloved Satguru, improve my life.
Suffering by karma, I am calling at Your door.

I have not even a little control over You.

> *Except You, in this world, nothing else is mine.*
>
> *I have come to Your shelter – don't reject me.*
> *I have got much suffering – no more agony!*
>
> *Cool my heart which is heated by pain.*
> *O Beloved Satguru, improve my life.*
>
> — Satguru Pyare Meri

When I sang this bhajan in front of my beloved Master, which says, "O Master, I do not have even a little bit of control over You," He said, "No, don't say that; that is not true. Those who meditate definitely have power over the Master. Like the Master has all His control over the disciple, if the disciple loves the Master, if he goes within, he also gains control over the Master. The obedient children can even tie the father with ropes; they can do anything, because they have controlled their father in their love." In the same way for the obedient disciples there is nothing impossible because they have manifested the Master and they have controlled the Master with their love. Those who meditate and go within, they have the power over the Satguru. Whatever they want, Satguru will do for them.

> *Come, O Guru Kirpal, the Sangat is calling You.*
> *In Your hands is the key to the whole world.*
>
> *Folding their hands, the Sangat is calling You.*
> *Where did You go, O Giver, leaving the sangat?*
> *This is my prayer, that You may always show Yourself*
>   *to us.*
>
> *O Protector of the Sangat, don't delay.*
> *Hearing our voice, come soon.*
> *All the Sangat is sitting, waiting to have Your darshan.*
>
> *O Doctor of the Sangat, the medicine is in Your hands.*
> *Somebody else locked the door, and You applied the*
>   *key.*
> *You saved Joga by becoming the guard.*

When Nanaki called, You came at once.
Lovingly You ate the chapati of request.
In that way, You come and don't forget me.

From the very beginning You have been hearing the requests.
You made the ship of Makhan the trader come to the shore.
Save the Sangat – this is the request of Ajaib the Sadhu.

— Kirpal Guru Aaja, Kirpal Guru Aaja

Satguru knows what is there in our hearts, because He is sitting within us. Once I had made some chutney and I had even prepared food, and then the thought came into my heart that when Nanaki, the sister of Guru Nanak, had made a chapati, when that chapati turned out very beautiful and very good, she thought, "My brother, Guru Nanak, should come and eat this." Even though at that time Guru Nanak was living far away, but still He appeared there to eat the chapati because His sister had remembered Him with love. So I thought that like Guru Nanak came to quench the thirst of His sister, is it possible that my Master may come and fulfill my desire? I had the desire that my Master should come and eat the chutney which I had made, and eat the food which I had prepared. And it is true that after that, Master sent one person whose name was Ramlal. He came and informed me that Master was coming there for lunch. Because I had desired that Master should come and eat the food there, even though there was no schedule for that but still Master came and ate that chutney and ate that food. Then Master told me, "Your chutney is very delicious, and now that I have eaten your salt, I will have to be true to your salt, and I will have to give you something." I was a very fortunate one that Master, Who was residing within me, heard my plea and knew my desire, and He came and fulfilled my desire.

Master Kirpal's Love for His Master

As I have told you, I got many opportunities to sit at the feet of my Master and sing bhajans to Him and whenever I would sing He would listen to the bhajans very attentively. Since I had a lot of

Master Sawan Singh with Master Kirpal

yearning, and when a yearning soul sings a bhajan to the Master it is so deep and so full of yearning that the ocean of love which is in that yearning soul comes in its full force and it breaks all barriers. So when that kind of love would come up in the bhajans, Master Kirpal would also shed tears.

He would remember His times with His Master Baba Sawan Singh. Even though He had become the form of the Almighty One, He still had so much love for His Master, and He had the pain of separation from Him. Even though He was One with the Almighty Lord, physically He was separated from Him and that is why many times, in the pain of separation, He would shed tears.

Whenever in my words of poetry, in my bhajans, the name of Master Sawan would be mentioned, at once tears would start rolling down His cheeks and He would start weeping.

They are the most fortunate people in the world, they are the best people in the world, who have this kind of crying and who can shed this kind of tears. Master Kirpal used to talk about the love that Master Sawan Singh had for His Master. He Himself told me that once Master Sawan went to the village Ghuman where Baba Jaimal Singh was born and lived in His childhood, because after Baba Jaimal Singh died, Baba Sawan Singh had promised to give a Satsang there. Just as they were entering the village, at the boundary, Baba Sawan Singh got out of the car and, kneeling down, bowed down on the ground and paid homage to that place. He said, "I sacrifice myself for this place; this is a holy place because my Master was born here." Afterwards, when He went to do the Satsang, He could not talk. He started crying in remembrance of His Master. He wept and wept and the tears would not stop. He wept so much that the sangat who was accompanying Him could not resist and they started weeping. When Master Kirpal saw His condition like that, He said, "Beloved Master, if Your condition is like this, what is the hope for us?" Baba Sawan Singh could hardly say anything, His voice was choked, but He did say one thing, He replied, "I have so much pain of separation from my Beloved Master that I am ready to sacrifice everything for Him. If Baba Jaimal Singh were to come in His physical form in front of me even once, I am willing to give up everything that I have. Just to have His darshan will be enough for me." His enthusiasm, His pain of separation, His feeling of yearning, had not decreased even after so much time. His affection, His love, His yearning for the Master was still the same. Such was the love of Baba Sawan Singh for Baba Jaimal Singh. All the Saints have so much love for Their Masters.

So I have seen this with my own eyes that whenever Master Kirpal Singh would mention the name of His beloved Master Sawan Singh or whenever He would hear someone talking about Baba Sawan Singh, the tears would roll down His cheeks. I remember on one occasion we were in the town of Hanumangarh and the sevadar named Harbans Singh was singing bhajans in remembrance of Baba Sawan Singh. I was sitting with Master Kirpal Singh, and with every single line sung of that bhajan Master Kirpal would shed tears. He would weep and He would even point His finger, saying, "Yes, that is absolutely right." Such was the love and devotion He had for His Master.

The Humility of Lord Kirpal

Once in Ganganagar, the district collector, the superintendent of police and other prominent people with high positions came to see Master. They all knew me and when they learned that my Master was coming, they all had the desire to see my Master also. They wanted to honor Him, because they already had much respect for me. When they came there, I introduced everybody to my Master, and they had many garlands and flowers and they wanted to garland Master. However, when Master saw that basket full of garlands and flowers, before they could garland Him, He took those garlands and put them around their necks and He put some flowers over their heads. He gave them the honor that they wanted to give Him. Master said, "You came here with the desire of garlanding me, but I also have that desire. I am also fond of respecting people. I want to show my happiness – how happy I am to see you." In that way, He respected them.

God has sent Saints with so much humility that even if the humility of the whole world was put together it could not equal the humility, the gentleness, that the Saints have. This gentleness, this humility, is not a sign of weakness. It is Their big-heartedness that gives Them this quality of being gentle. This is the highest quality, for if one is standing on a lower place all the water will come to you. In the same way, if one is humble and lowly within himself he gets everything. Kabir Sahib says, "He who is always very humble, and he who always speaks humble words, only he realizes God Almighty, because God Almighty always resides in the heart which is very humble." Supreme Father Kirpal used to say, "If you want to go to the Almighty Lord, you should take humility with you, because He has everything except humility. Why should God have humility when He is the Owner of the whole creation? That is why He likes those people who are humble in their hearts, and who bring the gift of humility to Him."

Master Kirpal knew a lot about the world and about the different societies and religions. On another occasion a pundit came to put a sign on His forehead, as many pundits do, expecting that the person on whom they put that saffron-like sign will give them some money. Before the pundit could do that to Master Kirpal, He put the mark on the pundit's head. Then, in addition to that, He gave the pundit two rupees, and said, "Now we are both happy. Whatever desire you came with, that is fulfilled, and I am also very happy to see you." Another time a Muslim person of a very low caste came to see Master Kirpal at my ashram. At that time Master was sitting on the bed. He did not let that person sit on the floor; He called someone to bring him a chair. He said, "He also has a soul in him and he should get the honor of sitting in the chair."

Master Kirpal was so sweet; He was the abode of humility. His humility cannot be described in words. One could go on telling stories that show His humility. It would become a very big book, because there were so many incidents in which it was clear how humble He was.

If I would try to glorify Him, and if I would try to sing His praises, He would not be pleased with that. He would not get inflated like a balloon. He would always be very quiet and very kind, and whenever anybody would try to praise Him or glorify Him, He would not be pleased. He would say, "This is all Master Sawan Singh's doing. This is all the grace of Master Sawan Singh." He would never say that He was any power. He always used to say, "I am a pipe; I only give the water which I am receiving from Master Sawan Singh." He would give the credit to His Master. Sometimes I would call Master Kirpal "True Emperor" and when I would do that He would always catch my ears and say, "Be careful! Don't say that again!" He never wanted anyone to praise him. He was never happy when anyone praised Him. He always remained in humility and He would become very pleased when He could remain in humility.

Master Takes Care of This Lowly One

Kirpal worries for you – why do you worry?

He is the All-Owner of the whole world.
He is merciful to the poor.

Except devotion, no worry works –
Even if you think a million times.

My Lord makes the high from the low.
He listens to everybody's voice.

Giving up "me, me," do "Thee, Thee."
The Protector protects you.

> *In the Court of the Lord is the support of the Master.*
> *The mighty Kal moves back.*
>
> *He always protects*
> *Those who are clean and true within.*
>
> *Reducing the gallows to a pinprick,*
> *He cuts the trap of attachment and Maya.*
>
> *O Benefactor Master, I thank You a million times.*
> *After coming You have taken care of Ajaib.*
> — Teri Soch Kare Kirpal

When Master ordered me to remain in meditation He told me that I was not to come out and that He would come to see me. He told me He would take care of me. After that He used to come physically to see me and also when any dear one from my area went to visit Him, He would ask them about my well-being and ask them how I was. There was no satsangi in Rajasthan who went to visit Master without Master first asking him, "Have you seen him before coming here?" Master was very concerned about me from within but outwardly also He was very concerned about me. Only for this poor one Master Kirpal called the head of the Congress Party of Ganganagar and only for this poor one He ate lunch with him and told him, "This is your task, to take care of Sant Ji."

I did not care for myself as much as my Master cared for me. This is true, that as long as we go on saying that we care for ourselves, we do not get the complete protection of the Master, because we still think that we are taking care of ourselves. However, when we surrender ourselves to the Master, all our worries become His worries, and then He takes care of us and He protects us.

As long as a child understands that he is capable of taking care of himself, and as long as he does not rely on the parents, as long as he does not surrender himself to his parents, the parents remain busy doing their work and they do not pay complete attention to the child. But as soon as the child starts crying and calls for help, at once the mother comes running, leaving all her work behind. So when we surrender ourselves completely to the Master, then the Master comes running and He takes care of us.

When the disciple manifests the Shabd Form of the Master within him, only then his pride disappears. This is because when the disciple

Master Kirpal giving darshan

reaches there, he sees how many more gurumukh disciples are already there, how many better disciples have already reached there. He finds himself no one as compared to the other gurumukh disciples who have already reached the Master. Guru Arjan Dev says, "Over there, there are so many souls superior to me. Who knows my name over there?" To that Form the soul says, "I will not find even one like You, whereas You will find millions like me." This poor soul also said the same thing to his Master: "O my Master, I will not find even one like You, but You will find millions like me."

Asking Only for the Darshan

O Giver, show us the glimpse of Your darshan.

Since a long time the thirst has been felt in the heart.
In the chest the wounds of yearning are caused.

O Giver, extinguish the burning of life.

In Your love I have become mad.
In Your remembrance I lost my life.
O Giver, make the True Satguru come and meet me.

We are separated in the illusion.
You are sitting in Sach Khand.
O Giver, remove the veil from our mind.

Kirpal Ji, come and make us have Your darshan.
Cool Ajaib, making him drink the nectar.
O Giver, make us drink the nectar of Naam.
— Dikhade Dikhade Dikhade Data Ji

Guru Ramdas has written, "If someone would make me meet my Beloved, I am ready to sell myself for him. I am ready to sell myself for him, not in order to get the worldly kingdom or the worldly name and fame, but I am ready to sell myself for him to have the darshan of the Lord." Similarly I never asked anything of a worldly nature from my Master, but many times, standing in front of Him, I used to say, "Somebody comes to You asking for milk, somebody comes to You asking for a son, but this lover asks only for Your darshan."

Whenever I would see my beloved Master pleased, in my innocence I would say this couplet, "O my Beloved, O my Beautiful One, I wish that I may always have You with me so that I can go on having Your darshan all the time. I wish that I could make You sit in front of me all alone, and I could go on looking at You." When I would say that to my beloved Master, He would try to reach my ear to twist it, but I would quickly move my head and I wouldn't let Him do that.

Whenever I was in front of my beloved Master, in my heart I used to say, "Your eyes are the color, the dye: my eyes are that piece of cloth which needs to be colored. My eyes are serving Your eyes, and they do not expect anything but the sight of Your eyes." Those who have real love for the Master serve the Master without expecting any rewards. They have only one expectation, the darshan of the Master, and they never get satisfied, no matter how much they have had.

Master Kirpal adjusts His turban

"I Wish I Were Your Mirror"

One day when Lord Kirpal came to my home I saw that He was adjusting His turban, looking in the mirror. From the very beginning I have had this habit of writing the poetry, so I composed these couple of lines. I said, "O Lord Kirpal, I wish that I were a mirror and You would look at me, You would adjust Your turban and You would make yourself up looking in my mirror. I wish that I were Your mirror and You would hold me in Your hands and You would look at me like You are looking at the mirror. Now, if I call You Maharaj or if I call you the True Lord, if I praise You or if I say anything to You regarding Yourself, You get upset at me, but if I were Your mirror then I could say anything I wanted. I could have even found faults in You. I could have said that You need to adjust Your beard, You need to adjust Your turban, You look like this and You look like that, and at that time You would not even mind."

The Stolen Bus

> *Your love has made me mad. Now I have no control over it.*

> *People say that love is easy, but its attack is like that of the tiger.*

> *It is the poisonous black cobra. The soul trembles and becomes perplexed.*
>
> *I feel your love in my bones. When I take a step my heart throbs.*
> *From within the string of love vibrates. The soul dives into the love.*
>
> *Your face is like the moon and our condition is like the moonbird.*
> *The trap of love is very strong. Our soul weeps.*
>
> *Listen, O Satguru Ji Kirpal, what is our condition, the suffering ones?*
> *Forgive us, O Satguru, gracious on the poor ones — the soul makes this request to you.*
>
> *He who wants to earn the love should first sacrifice his head.*
> *Ajaib says, Then he gets the darshan of his beloved. So says the Bani.*
>
> — Tere Prem Bavari Kita

Master Kirpal used to say that when He was going to Baba Sawan Singh's ashram to see His Master, He would become half mad. He told about His own experience when once He felt like going to have the darshan of His Master. At that time it was the month of August, the hottest month in India, and it was noontime, and Master Sawan Singh was resting. On one hand, Master Kirpal was worried about the health of Master Sawan Singh and so He didn't want to disturb Him, but on the other hand, the fire of separation was burning, and He was feeling like going and having the darshan of His Master. However, those who have real love for the Master within them, that love is respectful, and they remain within limits. So Master Kirpal told me that He stood there on the hot burning floor all day, waiting for Master Sawan Singh to open the door and come out and give Him darshan. In the evening He was satisfied when Master Sawan came out. When Master Kirpal came down from Master Sawan Singh's room, after having refreshment, He again felt like going and having a quick glance at Him. He again went back and Master

Sawan Singh rebuked Him saying, "Are you mad, that you have come again? You just went and now you have come again to disturb me?" So Master Kirpal said that only He knows within whom the fire of love is burning, only He knows who has created that fire, and only He who has created that fire can extinguish it.

Once when He came on tour, Master was staying in Ganganagar which was only 25 minutes drive from Kunichuk Ashram. At that time I went to the Kunichuk Ashram to get milk for Him. Although it was only 25 minutes since I had seen Him, I felt so much yearning to see Him again that I didn't wait for the bus driver to come and take me back to Ganganagar. Instead, with one other person, I kidnapped that bus and without the notice of the bus driver we took that bus to Ganganagar. When Master Kirpal saw that a bus had come to the place where He was staying, He thought that maybe a lot of people had come to see Him. But when He came out, He was surprised to see only two people coming out from the bus, and I told Him, "This bus is always meeting with accidents, so I advised this person who is with me to come and request You to please bless this bus." Even though we had stolen that bus, still we said, "This bus has been brought here to get Your blessing."

People say that love is very easy. However, it is not; it is very difficult. Those who are shot by the bullet of love, only they know what it is like. They become useless for this world. Mahatmas say, "People understand love as easy, but it is very difficult." Once the poisonous snake bites, the person who was bitten loses all consciousness of this world and enters the next. When the tiger grabs any animal, one grab is enough; the animal is killed. The love of the Master or the love of God is like the bite of the snake and the grab of the tiger. Once the Master gives His love to anybody, He makes him useless for the world. Towards the world he sleeps; towards the Master he wakes up. He within whom that love arises is not aware of the world; he always has the inspiration of love, and always from his tongue the name of his beloved comes out and nothing else.

You know that if someone is yearning for the darshan of the Master, he cannot get satisfied until he has it. He who has this pain of separation, who has the yearning to have the darshan of the Master, cannot resist and he will do every possible thing to have His darshan. Master Kirpal Singh was such a powerful Master and His love was such that He used to trap the souls in His love. It was all His grace that He made me sit in meditation. If He had not done that with me, I would have done many things like stealing that bus to go have His darshan. He was great, and because His love was so powerful, I could not live without His darshan. He was the Power who controlled my soul, and right from my childhood, I always had this innocence in front of Him. When I met my Master I did not use any wisdom in front of Him; I was like an innocent child of forty days old before Him and even today I have the same attitude.

I Understand Myself as the Guilty One in Front of the Master

O Guru Ji, there is no good quality in me; I am full of bad qualities.

You have all good qualities — I have none.
How could the meeting with the Beloved happen?

I have neither beauty nor attractive eyes.
I have neither good ways nor sweet words.

We are sinners — we are full of bad qualities. We have fallen at Your door.
Except for You we find no refuge at any place.

Understanding us as orphans, attach us to Your feet.
Do not involve us in the cycle of 84 lakhs again.
Whatever has happened with us in the past has happened.

We have given up all support except You. O Beloved One, dwell in our hearts.
Folding our hands we make this request.

I am the sinner, full of bad qualities. Poor Ajaib is Your slave.
Without Kirpal there is no shelter.
— Mere Vich Na Guru Ji Gun Koi

If you would look through the eyes of Ajaib, if you would look through the soul of Ajaib, you would know how much he has suffered in his past lives. What to talk about past lives, even the suffering of this life cannot be counted, and only he knows how much he has suffered and only he knows how much grace Lord Kirpal has showered grace on him. He has made a sweeper, He has made a maid, as the queen of Sach Khand. What can Ajaib tell Master Kirpal? What can he tell the All-Owner? Can he tell Him, "I am the best of all, I am the king, I am the emperor. There is no one else in the world like me," when he knows that it was all the grace of Master Kirpal? It was the grace of that Almighty Lord who made it possible for this lowly one to go to Sach Khand and finish his birth and death. What can he tell Him except expressing his humility, except expressing his gratitude for all the grace He has showered on this poor soul?

Kabir Sahib says, "The Path of God, the Path on which we have to go back to our Real Home is very thin, about one tenth the size of a hair, but the mind has become very big like an elephant. How can he walk on that Path? How can he go back to the Real Home?" The mind says, "I am intelligent, a learned one; I have this, I have that." Because of all these I-hoods he has become very large. How can he walk on that Path? He has to become as thin as the Path, he has to develop that much humility within him.

Once when Master Kirpal came to my home, I wept a lot and I requested Him to let me wash His feet and drink that water. I told Him, "That water will bring a lot of peace to me, so You should allow me to do that." However, He wouldn't let me do that. He didn't let me have that opportunity. Instead He involved me in talking and in the end He embraced me, and in that way He quenched my thirst.

"How Beautiful You Seem to Me"

Once when Supreme Father Kirpal came to my place, He was wearing a lightweight blanket like a shawl and He was looking very beautiful. In Punjabi a shawl is called by the word *kumbli* and it has a spiritual significance. So I said a short line, " 'Kumbli, kumbli,' everybody says, 'kumbli,' and I see that You are the one with the kumbli. Ask my heart and You will know how beautiful You seem to me." When I said this, He was very pleased and He embraced me. Whenever I would say anything like this He would embrace me. He would become so happy and He would caress me like the father caresses a child of forty days old. He would make me sit on His lap and He loved me very much.

He was very beautiful. No doubt there are many beautiful people in this world but the beauty that my Master had was incomparable. Nobody else in this world had that beauty and that is why I always used to call Him "the Beautiful One." I never called Him using the word "Master" or "Hazur" but I would to call Him "the Beautiful One." I always used to say that my Master is the only beautiful one; He is the only beautiful person in this world.

Hazrat Bahu said, "May every cell of my body become an eye so that I may behold the form of my Master. And after looking at my Master so much, still I will not get any contentment." Further, He said, "If every single hair of my body becomes an eye, and if I get the opportunity of looking at the Master with so many eyes, still I will not get any satisfaction; still I will find one more way to have the darshan of my Master, because for me the darshan of my Master is worth more than millions of pilgrimages."

When we manifest such a beautiful Master in our within, after that we are not attracted to any worldly thing. We have no attachment in our within because there is nothing in this world which can attract us as much as our beautiful Master attracts us. No one is as attractive as He is and no one is as beautiful as He is.

Tear Up the Paper of the Account of My Sins

Once Master Kirpal was visiting Karanpur and there were many satsangis there who remembered how Master Sawan Singh used to give out chapatis with His own hands to the dear ones. They asked me to go and request Beloved Master that He do the same thing with us, that He, like Master Sawan, give us parshad with His own hands. I was very excited about that and I went to Beloved Lord Kirpal and told Him that the dear satsangis were requesting this. He was very gracious and He agreed. He told me to go and get the basket full of chapatis, which I did. He then gave the parshad, the blessed chapatis, with His own hands to all the dear ones, and everyone was very happy.

It was at that time that I wrote this bhajan which says, "O Beloved Lord, tear up the paper on which the accounts of our sins are written."

> *Tear up the paper of the account of my sins. I don't*
> *ask for anything else.*
>
> *You can do everything, You are All-Conscious.*
> *I am the one who makes faults and I am not true to the*
> *salt.*
> *Becoming the philosopher's stone, liberate this iron.*
>
> *We cannot know Your Glory,*
> *Nor can we recognize the Divine Light.*
> *Shoot the arrow of grace into our hearts.*
>
> *One day we have to leave this foreign country.*
> *The body is false, the maya is false.*
> *O Lord, holding us by the arm, take us across.*
> *We are the sinners, we are the ones who make mistakes,*
> *O Lord, forgive us — we are the poor souls.*
> *Remove the pains of egoism.*
>
> *Shower grace on us and make us give up the sins.*
> *Make us do Simran and Bhajan.*
> *O Kirpal Ji, liberate this suffering Ajaib.*
> — Mera Kagaj Gunah Vala

Saints take away the paper of the account of the soul's karmas from the Lord of Judgment, and after understanding the account of the soul's karmas, Saints tear up that account. There is only one thing that the Masters have put on as a condition and that is that the disciple should never understand the Master as a human being. He should never think that the Master is like other human beings and he should never in his life lose his faith in the Master.

If we are able to maintain the faith that Master is God Almighty, that He is All-Knowing and All-Conscious, then riding on the Shabd that is sounding in our forehead, we can easily go back to our Real Home. No forces of the Negative Power can bother or stop the disciple on his way back to his Real Home, because on the very first day, when the Master gives Initiation, He takes away that paper of the account of the disciple's sins from the Lord of Judgment and tears it up. As Guru Arjan Dev says, "The Master has taken the paper of the account of the disciple from the Lord of Judgment and He has torn it up."

So after giving us Initiation, the Master erases our account, and after that He tells us that we should not write a new account; we should not make a new register of our bad deeds. After receiving the holy Initiation, a satsangi should never fall into the evil things. He should never commit any mistakes, consciously or unconsciously. Becoming a brave warrior, he should always keep a strong guard against his mind. If we keep polluting ourselves, if we keep making our garment dirty, all the grace we receive from the Master is used only in cleaning us.

In writing this bhajan, I remembered the time when I was in the army. When someone is recruited into the army, on the very first day his sheet roll, or service record, is made. In that sheet roll, it is written from where he has come, what his qualifications are, and what are the things that he can do. That kind of account is maintained for every recruit when he joins the army. All the mistakes and all the deeds that he does are recorded in that sheet roll. When he gets an opportunity and does something brave, that is also recorded in his sheet roll.

When the time arrives to give rewards or prizes to the army men, the officer calls for the sheet roll of each person. If someone has made his sheet roll dirty by doing only the faults and the mistakes and has not done many good deeds, then the officer is regretful and says, "Why did this person not maintain a clean sheet roll?" Even though the officer may want to reward him on account of one or another good deed, the officer cannot do that if the soldier has not kept his record clear and if he has not lived his life very clearly and cleanly. In the same way, our sheet roll or account of deeds is also maintained.

We should never think that there is no one keeping the account of our deeds. The One Who watches over us is not outside; He is not far from us. He is within us and He sees what we are doing. Therefore, if one is clever and wise, he does not write the black words on his soul. He looks within himself and makes sure that he is not doing anything wrong. So thinking about all these things, in writing this bhajan, I did not ask for any worldly thing from my Beloved Lord, I only asked Him to please the finish up the accounts of the bad karmas or sins which I had done in my life.

Accompanied by the Master

There is a village along the Rupur canal in Punjab named Dabwali where some relatives of mine used to live and once I went there to visit them. In the evening I went out for a walk and along the canal I saw that there was one Udasi sadhu with long hair sitting there with many other people listening to him. He had done a lot of austerities like the jaldhara practice and other japas and tapas. It was the last day of this period of austerities for him and when the sadhus complete a period of austerity they do a final reading of the *Guru Granth Sahib* and many people get together and offer their homage. When I saw many people going towards him, I also became curious. I thought, "Why not go and see him before continuing my walk?" I also felt like paying homage to him because, as you know, before meeting the Masters I also had done the rites and rituals and performed the austerities. Even though I did not get anything from that, still I always had the appreciation for those sadhus who had really done austerities, because it requires a lot of devotion and very hard work to do them. So when I saw him I at once remembered that I also used to perform austerities like he was doing, and I thought, "Let me have the darshan of such a sadhu who has done such practices."

That sadhu was sitting on a rope bed and his followers and the people who had come to see him were sitting on the ground. When he saw me coming towards him, he at once got up from his bed. He welcomed me and told me to sit with him on the bed. I said, "No, it is not good for me to sit on your bed, because you are a mahatma and I am just a poor farmer. It is not a good thing for me to take your bed or take your seat." I tried to sit on the floor, but he said, "No, don't sit on the floor, come and sit with me on the rope bed. I can see someone with a white beard and white clothes who has come with you. He is very tall person, with a white beard and a white turban and He is some great Power. He is very impressive and He is behind you." I told him, "No, I have come alone, there is no one with me." I didn't want him to make me sit on the bed in front of his sangat. I wanted the sangat to respect him as they were doing before. I gave him much respect and I told him, "No, please let me sit on the ground like your followers. I am like your servant and I have come to have your darshan. You have done very good devotion; you have done very hard work doing these practices. You should be sitting on the bed. It is all right; I don't want to sit there." But he didn't let me sit on the ground and he insisted that I sit on the bed.

When I told him so many times that I wanted to sit on the floor, finally he told one of his disciples to bring a mat and he made me sit on the mat. While I was sitting there he would talk to the other people and after talking to a couple of people he would again tell me that he was seeing Someone dressed in white with a very great personality. He told that to his followers also, that there was Someone, some Power, accompanying me. Again and again, at least ten times, he said that, and when he told me that repeatedly then I realized how my Master was always protecting me and always accompanying me. I became very grateful to my Master and I told the sadhu, "Yes, that power was accompanying me." I knew it was by the grace of God Almighty Kirpal that the sadhu could tell that the Master was accompanying me. Who knows where Master Kirpal Singh was physically at that time but still that Udasi sadhu in Punjab, who was doing a little bit of devotion sincerely, was seeing the presence of the Master with this poor disciple. When you attain that high position where the Form of the Master is manifested within you, the people who do a little bit of meditation and go up a little bit, even they can see that the Form of the Master is with you.

So the Master is always present with the disciple and He always accompanies us like a shadow. No matter where you are, even if you go in the forest, He is always present with you but we do not believe in this until we have true love and devotion for Him and we manifest Him in our within. Once we manifest Him in our within, then we become sure and then we see Him going with us everywhere. Then not only we, but also the other people, those who can see, they bear witness, they say that the Master is accompanying us.

Saving the Dust from Under Master Kirpal's Feet

O Giver, I need no one except You!

The world fights, but still does not become successful,
No matter if they get millions or billions.

PRINTING DEFECT

Dear Reader:

During the printing of these books, something happened to the printing plate for one set of pages. The result is that certain letters in some words did not get enough ink to be easily readable, making the affected words a puzzle if not completely unintelligible. Please refer to the following list of pages with sentences and paragraphs printed correctly, if you have any trouble reading your copy of the book.

Sant Ajaib Singh, July 1996

We sincerely apologize for this problem, which was only discovered after the books were all printed and bound.

— (continued on back)

Page 283

> *O Giver, wherever You send me, I go there. I always eat what You give.*
> *I am the puppet — in Your Hand is the string.*
>
> *I wandered in every corner — I got Your radiance everywhere.*
> *I saw no one else except You.*
>
> *Wherever I go I sing of You. I carry Your message.*
> *You have installed the lock, and You Yourself turn the key.*
>
> *Beautiful Emperor Kirpal has become gracious on Ajaib.*
> *May my love become like that of the moon and the moon bird.*
> — Menu Tere Bina Kise Di Na Lor Datiya

Often, becoming pleased with me, Master Kirpal would allow me to ride with Him in the car, and I would become very glad. I would become very pleased because at that time I would feel as if I was riding in the ship of His Naam, and I was going Home. At that time He would also become very pleased, and He would tell me many things of this world. He would tell me many things that had happened to Him, and He told me many things that were going to happen in the future. Those things, those matters, were not of the worldly nature for me, they were the spiritual matters, and I enjoyed those talks very much. He told me many things of the past and He told me many things of the future, and in that way He touched my heart.

* * *

Page 290

through meditation the physical cover is removed from our soul we reach the first inner plane, the astral plane, or Sahansdal Kanwal. When we go on meditating, the astral cover is removed from our soul and we reach the second inner plane, the causal plane, or Trikuti. After removing all three covers, physical, astral and causal our soul reaches the third inner plane, Par Brahm, and our soul comes to realize her reality. She comes to know she is just a soul. She is neither a woman nor a man; she neither belongs to America nor any other spiritual region of *Bhanwar Gupha* and then the purely spiritual region of *Sat Lok* or *Sat Naam*.

* * *

Page 291

The soul says, "With the grace of the Master, after going to Sahansdal Kanwal, now I have come to the court of Trikuti, which I have won. From there with the grace of my Beloved Master, I have gone into the Beyond." When, by doing the Simran, we are able to collect our scattered thoughts and attention, and we are able to vacate these nine openings of the body, and after we remove the physical, astral and causal covers from our soul, then our soul reaches Sunn or Par Brahm. There the soul picks up rubies, diamonds and pearls, and bathes in the place called *Triveni,* or the three rivers.

* * *

Page 294

is sitting?" All the Saints Who have reached that place have become quiet, because over there, there is no talking. All those who have reached there cannot say anything, They just become quiet, because it is the region of peace and quietness, and who wants to go back into this world and talk about it? Kabir said, "It is like some salt; if the salt wants to know about its origin, it goes into the depth of the ocean. But when the salt goes there, it is dissolved in the water of the ocean. So how can the salt come back and tell others about its origin?"

> *I embrace those Feet, what can I say of that Akam Bani (which cannot be talked about)?*
> *Now I have completed my arti (worship), I have told you the secrets of Agam.*
> *Kissing the dust of the feet of Radha Swami, I have come to my own Home.*

Masters give us the hints and They tell us about that place. They tell us, "Dear Ones, come along with us and see the Reality with your own eyes."

God is so gracious that He came as Christ, He came as Kabir, and He came as Guru Nanak. He came as beautiful Emperor Sawan, and He came as Almighty Gracious Kirpal. We are the most fortunate ones to have had the glimpse of Almighty Kirpal, whose name is sung by the entire creation. He took the lost orphan Ajaib and carried him in His lap. No one can compare to Him.

Come Kirpal Guru, I celebrate.
I beg of You to give me Your darshan.

* * *

— (continued from front)
Because there is so much about this book that is wonderful and readers have waited so long for it, we elected not to reprint the entire book. We hope this insert will clarify the text in those books where there is a problem.

If you feel disappointed with our "solution" we will gladly accept your returned book for full credit, including postage.

We appreciate your patience and understanding.
— Sant Bani Publications

IN SEARCH OF THE GRACIOUS ONE
An Account in His own Words
of The Spiritual Search and Discipleship
of Sant Ajaib Singh

compiled by Michael Mayo-Smith

Published by Sant Bani Ashram, Sanbornton, New Hampshire
September 2007

*O Giver, wherever You send me, I go there. I always eat
what You give.
I am the puppet — in Your Hand is the string.*

*I wandered in every corner — I got Your radiance everywhere.
I saw no one else except You.*

*Wherever I go I sing of You. I carry Your message.
You have installed the lock, and You Yourself turn the key.*

*Beautiful Emperor Kirpal has become gracious on Ajaib.
May my love become like that of the moon and the moon
bird.*

— Menu Tere Bina Kise Di Na Lor Datiya

Often, becoming pleased with me, Master Kirpal would allow me to ride with Him in the car, and I would become very glad. I would become very pleased because at that time I would feel as if I was riding in the ship of His Naam, and I was going Home. At that time He would also become very pleased, and He would tell me many things of this world. He would tell me many things that had happened to Him, and He told me many things that were going to happen in the future. Those things, those matters, were not of the worldly nature for me, they were the spiritual matters, and I enjoyed those talks very much. He told me many things of the past and He told me many things of the future, and in that way He touched my heart.

When the disciple is in love with the Master, he has this desire that maybe once, at least for once, he may sit in the ship of the Master and he may travel around with the Master. He always has this yearning to be with the Master and enjoy with Him.

Many times I also got the blessed opportunity of walking along with Master Kirpal in my own field and it was something very enjoyable. I always liked it very much. It was very pleasing to me because to walk with Him was like walking with God Almighty. I cannot forget those times when He used to take walks with me, and how He would pat my back, and how I would look at Him like the moonbird looks at the moon. I would try to bow down to Him and touch His feet, but He would never let me do that. How can I forget all those scenes?

Guru Arjan Dev said, "May I always behold this enchanting, beautiful, attractive form of my Beloved, because when I look at Him, when I go to see Him, only then do I remain sane; otherwise I go insane."

One time when He was visiting my place, we both went for a walk and we happened to be walking on a sandy road. It was not very solid; it was sandy. Suddenly it came in my mind, "Why not take some dust on which He has just put His foot, and why not preserve that, because it is a very precious thing for a disciple if he can get the sand on which his Master has just stepped." So, at once, I tried to get some sand from the place where He had just put His feet. I tried to do it in such a way that He would not notice it, that He would not see it, because sometimes our mind tells us that the Master is not seeing this, that He does not know about this. But He is All-Knowing, He is All-Conscious, and He can see everything. Even if we are very careful, still He can see everything. So when I did that, Master Kirpal saw that and He got upset. He did not like that because the Masters always want the disciples to go within and get attached to the inner feet of the Master. They want the disciples to get attached to the inner dust of the feet of the Master and not get attached to the outer things. So Master Kirpal said, "Don't do that. Now you will go on bowing down to this thing again and again. If other people see you doing that, they will also try to imitate you and that is not a good thing." I had this habit right from my childhood of making up the poetry. So at that time, when Master was telling me not to do that, I made up one brief verse. Tears came into my eyes, and in all my love I said, "O My Beloved, I have picked up the fresh sand from Your very fresh footprint and I am bringing it close to my heart. O Beloved One, Your Five Shabds have pierced through my heart and They have liberated me."

It is true that I have preserved that dust of the feet of my beloved Master very safely and with much respect. I still have that with me. Earlier I also told about the time I had a sheet that had the honor of being used by the Great Lord, Master Sawan Singh. I also preserved that and have that with me.

When beloved Master Kirpal came to my place, at that time I spread out the same piece of cloth, that same sheet which I had protected. When

Master Kirpal came there, He looked at that very ordinary, inexpensive piece of cloth. He looked at it and He smiled and instead of sitting on it, He took it and put it on His head. Only He knew what that piece of cloth was. So I still have that piece of cloth, on which two forms of God Almighty have showered Their blessings.

The purpose of preserving those things is that whenever I see those things it makes the memory fresh. Even now, whenever I feel sadness, I take out that dust and I bow down to that sacred dust. Master Kirpal also gave me one coat, and with much respect I often wear it.

This is the glory of the dust of the outer feet of the Master. Those who value the dust of the outer feet of the Master, those who value and appreciate the outer things of the Master, those who respect them and make such outer things of the Master an essential part of their life, only they get this yearning to go within. Only they get the yearning to remove the cataract from their eyes, to open their inner eyes and to see the Radiant Form of the Master within. They are just like Guru Arjan Dev who did not ask for any worldly wealth from His Master. He did not ask for any successorship. He did not ask for any sons or daughters. He asked for only one thing, "Nanak says, 'I have only one desire, that You make me the dust of the feet of the Masters.' "

I Ask Master How He Made Me His Wife

The Satguru has come — the beautiful, jovial Kirpal!
He is the knower of my heart. My own Husband has come.

In my heart I have yearning for Him. I speak like the rainbird.
I was tired from looking for Him. O friends, I searched for Him day and night.
He has come — my jovial Husband.

O friends, His glimpse is more unique than the sun.
He has cooled down the burning world by making them do the repetition of Naam.
He came, told the secret, and became the means for the suffering ones.

> *He is the child of Mother Gulab Devi; He is the Owner of the Sangat.*
> *Congratulate Father Hukam Singh! The unique light has come.*
> *He, the store of vigorous devotion, has come into the world.*
>
> *O friends, He is the Son of Emperor Sawan. His name is Kirpal.*
> *He became gracious on the foreigner Ajaib.*
> *He, the beautiful and confident One, has come in the home.*
>
> — Aaya Satguru Aaya Ni

One night Master Kirpal was sitting with me and He was very happy. His eyes were glittering very much; the Light was coming from His eyes. The reality was that from every single cell of His body, from every single hair of His body, the Light was coming and He was very happy. In my innocence I asked Master, "Master, how have You made me Your wife?" He said, "Don't you know? When I gave you Initiation, when I connected you in the within, in the form of the Shabd I went around with you and I took the circles." In the Indian marriage ceremony the husband and wife circle around the fire four times, and that is known as taking the circles. So He said, "Don't you know that when I connected you in the within, I had gone with you in the Form of the Shabd and I had circled around, and in that way I made you my wife? Now no one else has any right over you, no one can touch you, no one can take you, and I can take you whenever I want." He cannot be called as the husband whose wife is taken away by somebody else. It is the responsibility of the husband to protect her, so Master said, "Now it is my responsibility and I will protect you. No one can touch you, no one can touch even your finger, and no one can take you anywhere."

In one of the bhajans I wrote, "The beautiful husband Kirpal is met, and now Ajaib has become His. Ajaib is like a wife of Kirpal, and she has been sold to Kirpal for no money, for nothing. Now she has become of Kirpal."

It is very difficult for one to understand himself as the wife when he is male. However, when we become conscious within, when we realize the inner knowledge, then even if we don't try, still these words come out from within us, "whether You know me or not, I am Your wife and I am sacrificing for You thousands of times." Those whose inner veil is lifted, their worldly love goes away and true love for the Master remains there. At that place no attachment or love for the world remains, only love for the Master remains. Such a person whose veil is lifted does not have any will of his own. Whatever he does, that happens in the Will of the Master; he works according with the wishes of the Master.

Masters have always referred to themselves as female beings in front of their Masters. In Their writings, in Their poems or songs, They always refer to Themselves as the female beings, like the wife of Master or God. Some women satsangis once asked Master Kirpal, "Whenever You say things to the dear ones, You never say, 'This is for the women' or 'This is for the men.' Why is that?" Master said, "Those who do not go within, do not know who is male and who is female." In fact we are all female in front of the Almighty Lord. He is the only male, and the difference between male and female comes to an end when we enter into the third inner plane, *Par Brahm*. Before we enter there we are either male or female, but when we go into Par Brahm we see that we are all souls and God Almighty is the only one whom we can call as a "male being." So unless we meditate and go within, unless we rise above body consciousness and enter into Par Brahm, we cannot understand all these writings of the Masters.

The Fight with the Mind

When Almighty Lord Kirpal showered His grace upon me, when He gave me the Initiation and told me to sit for meditation, at that time the mind created so many things to intimidate me and made it very difficult for me to sit in meditation. On the battlefield the bullet will come and hit you, and at once your body will cool down; but in meditation there is no bullet. In meditation one doesn't have any weapon, one doesn't have any bow and arrow. The only thing one has is the Master and the shield of the Shabd Naam that the Master has given. As Tulsi Sahib has said, "O Tulsi, to fight in the battlefield is the work of a day or two, but to fight the mind is a continuous struggle in which you do not even have any weapons."

Those who have struggled with their mind, only they know what the tricks of the mind are. Only the Mahatma who has struggled with the mind knows how much power the mind has. Vashist, the Guru of Lord Rama, once said, "If someone tells me that there is a man who has lifted up the Himalayas, even though it is unbelievable, still I might give a thought to it for a moment. And if someone says that someone has drunk the entire ocean, even though it is not believable, I might believe it for a second. But if someone says that he has controlled his mind, I would never believe it, because it is not possible." Master Sawan Singh used to say that the mind would rather stand in front of a roaring cannon, prepared to die, than sit for meditation. When Baba Sawan Singh did His meditation, He also realized how difficult it was to fight with the mind. He also worked very hard in meditation. Whenever He would be bothered by sleep, He would stand up. He had a wooden stand, called a beragan, and standing with the support of that beragan He used to meditate. He would stand all night and meditate like that. For many days He would not come out of the meditation room. He worked very hard in His meditation according to the orders of His Master, Baba Jaimal Singh. When our True Lord, Great Emperor Kirpal did His meditation, He also witnessed the same things and He also said it was not an easy thing to fight with the mind. When He was a disciple, Master Kirpal had made the bank of the River Ravi the place for His meditation. He would go there and He would stand in the waters of the River Ravi and He would meditate like that. He worked very hard, stayed up many nights and did a lot of meditation. He also did what Baba Sawan Singh asked Him to do.

So when Master first told me to do the meditation, I also had some difficulties. Until we take our mind to its real home, mind will never become our friend. He will bring many types of difficulties in our meditations. Looking at the materials of the world our mind has gone crazy and that is why it rebels. If you try to control any crazy man, in the beginning he will fight with you and it is very difficult. However, if you give him medicine and give him good advice, when he becomes all right, he also becomes a very good friend and he becomes grateful to you. In the same way, our mind has gone crazy looking at the materials of the world, but when we take it to its real home, it will become all right.

Although it is very difficult to struggle with the mind, this does not mean that up until now nobody has controlled his mind. God Almighty sends into this world His children, His Saints, Who struggled with Their mind and became successful. Since They have struggled with Their mind and have become successful, They tell the dear ones, "If you will also work according to the instructions of the Master, if you will also take the grace of the Master and struggle with your mind, you can also control him."

So if one wants, one can become successful in this Path, but one has to make one's heart strong like iron. Therefore, whenever these difficulties or problems would come, I would always remember this vow which I had taken, "O my heart, O my mind, you have taken this promise that you will never be discouraged." With a lot of love and faith in the Master, this poor soul did the meditation and working hard, I became successful.

The Journey Within

Earlier, I told how Baba Bishan Das had initiated me into the first Two Words, and meditating on them for eighteen years, I became successful in my meditation up to that level, up to the level of the third plane. However, Master Sawan Singh had assured me that the time would come when that Power, Who would give me the Initiation into the Five Words, would come to my house by Himself. Baba Bishan Das also told me, "You will get the real thing, and the person who will give that thing will come to you by Himself." So this is the blessing of those great souls that the Shabd came in the form of Kirpal and met me. When Master Kirpal came, He gave me the Initiation into the Five Shabds, and opened the way further up.

The coming of a true sincere soul, a true disciple, near the Master is like bringing dry gunpowder in contact with fire. As soon as the dry gunpowder comes in contact with fire, at once it explodes. On the other hand, if the gunpowder is wet, it will take some time. First it will need to become dry and then it will explode. In the same way, if the disciple is not prepared, then it takes time for him to develop receptivity. However, for the souls who have prepared themselves, it doesn't take much time for them to develop receptivity and get grace and intoxication from the Master. When the true disciple — who is like the dry gunpowder — comes, it does not take much time for the Master to put whatever He wants within him.

Our soul has to go through five great planes, and it can transcend the five planes only by climbing on the Sound Current. On our soul there are three covers, three bodies, physical, astral and causal. When through meditation the physical cover is removed from our soul we reach the first inner plane, the astral plane, or *Sahansdal Kanwal*. When we go on meditating, the astral cover is removed from our soul and we reach the second inner plane, the causal plane, or *Trikuti*. After removing all three covers, physical, astral and causal our soul reaches the third inner plane, Par Brahm, and our soul comes to realize her reality. She comes to know she is just a soul. She is neither a woman nor a man; she neither belongs to America nor any other country. She is only a soul, the essence of God. Going on, the soul passes through the plane of dense darkness, or *Maha Sunn,* and reaches the purely spiritual region of *Bhanwar Gupha* and then the purely spiritual region of *Sat Lok* or *Sat Naam.*

Right now we are sitting in the physical body and functioning through it, and we see the Master also in His physical form, through His body giving us answers to our questions outwardly, explaining things to us and inspiring us to go within. When we rise above the physical body, remove the physical cover from our soul, and go to the astral plane, then we see the Master in the form of the Shabd. There the Master is functioning in His astral form. Further when we remove the astral and the causal covers and reach Par Brahm, then we see the Master working in the form of pure Shabd. As we go on progressing upwards in the inner planes the form of the Master goes on changing from pure to more pure and in Sach Khand we see the most pure form, the *Sar Shabd* form of the Master. Often I have said that Sant Mat is not a fairy tale; it is Reality, and those who work hard and go within see all these things with their own eyes.

In the following hymn, Swami Ji Maharaj describes the ascent of the soul.*

> *Swami (My Lord) has made me brave and has made*
>   *me win the battle.*
> *I have conquered mind and Maya*
>
> *All the treasures of deceit have been ruined.*
> *The army of passions has run away.*
>
> *Climbing on the fort of Trikuti, I have won it.*
> *I have beaten the drum (proclaimed the victory) at the*
>   *peak of Sunn.*

---

* In this excerpt from a Satsang, Sant Ji comments on a hymn of Swami Ji Maharaj.

The soul says, "With the grace of the Master, after going to Sahansdal Kanwal, now I have come to the court of Trikuti, which I have won. From there with the grace of my Beloved Master, I have gone into the Beyond." When, by doing the Simran, we are able to collect our scattered thoughts and attention, and we are able to vacate these nine openings of the body, and after we remove the physical, astral and causal covers from our soul, then our soul reaches Sunn or Par Brahm. There the soul picks up rubies, diamonds and pearls, and bathes in the place called *Triveni,* or the three rivers.

Only with the grace, mercy, and blessings of my Master was I able to obey the orders that He gave to me. Only because of that was I able to see the real glory of my Master. I was able to see what position He has in the inner planes. Even now He is coming through those inner planes and going back, and the disciple who goes within and sees the glory of the Master in the inner planes, only he can know how great his Master is. When the Master comes to the lower planes, which we call "heaven," wherever He goes, all the gods and goddesses and angels who have reached up to those lower planes treat Him with great respect. They give Him a place to sit; they all give Him a lot of respect and appreciation. All the gods, goddesses, and angels who are stuck there beg Him for liberation. They all beg Him, "Kindly take us along with You." He loves those souls also, and He tells them to be patient. He tells them that it is the law of nature that only when you are given the human body can you get Initiation into Naam and liberation lies only in the Naam. When they say that they did not appreciate the human birth when they were given it and it will be very difficult to get liberation, Master tells them to be patient and to wait for the time when they will be given human birth. So only the disciple who goes within knows how much respect and appreciation the angels, gods, goddesses, and other spirits who are in the inner planes give to his Master.

Suppose a session judge is walking on the street in a city. He may be wearing ordinary clothes and he may be wandering here and there. He may buy vegetables from a shop, and the people may not realize that he is the session judge because they don't know him. But if someone knows him, and recognizes that in his speech or in his pen there is great power, that person who knows the judge will respect and appreciate him even in the place where no one else has recognized and respected him. In the same way, a Saint or mahatma is seen by millions of people in this world. Many people look at Him and for them He may seem to be an ordinary person. But those who go to the inner planes and who know the real glory and position of the Master, when they see a Saint, even in His ordinary outfit, still they appreciate and respect Him. They know how much power God has given to Him and how many rights this Saint or Master has received from Almighty God and what He can do. Only that dear one who goes within and sees the Master's Real Form is aware of the glory of the Master in the inner planes and only such a person can have real appreciation and respect for the outer form of the Master.

In another place Swami Ji Maharaj has said, "Through millions of practices the mind will not come under your control, unless you will make him hear the Inner Dhun." He says the only thing which will control your mind is the inner music; make him hear that and he will come under your control. Some mahatmas, like Kabir, have called that inner divine music the Shabd; some Muslim Mahatmas have called it the *Kalma,* and Guru Nanak calls it *Hari Kirtan* or the Song of God. When do we hear that Kirtan? Only when we remove the physical, astral, and causal covers from our soul and reach Par Brahm. When our soul and our mind become free from these covers, only then is the mind able to hear the sweetest melody of all; it is attracted to that melody, and only then does he come under our control.

> *The river of Maha Sunn was in my way, which I was made to cross with the grace of the Satguru*

Further the plane of Maha Sunn, the plane of dense darkness, comes. The radiance of the soul who has reached Par Brahm becomes equal to that of twelve outer suns. However, in the plane of Maha Sunn, it is so dark that even that much radiance does not work, and the soul cannot go through that plane by herself. At that place the radiance of the Master is required. That is why in all the Hindu *Shastras,* the Hindu scriptures, it is written that Guru is the One Who manifests Light in the darkness. So the soul, even though she herself is a very radiant one, still she cannot manage to go through that place of dense darkness by herself. It is only the Master Who takes the soul with Him, and in His own radiance, in His own Light, He takes the soul across that plane. So that is why Swami Ji says that after she reaches Par Brahm, the soul goes beyond Par Brahm only in the company of the Master. Guru Arjan also said, "Even if there is the radiance of hundreds of moons and thousands of suns, without the Master, still it is all darkness."

All the rishis and munis – those who have tried to go within without the guidance of the perfect Master – they are stuck over there; they cannot go further. So that is why Swami Ji says that, after Par Brahm, you will be able to cross the darkness of the Maha Sunn region only if the Master goes with you, and you will be able to cross that region only with the Light of the Master.

> *I have dwelt in the palace of Bhanwar Gupha.*
> *Getting to Sat Lok, I am astonished in surprise.*

Now the soul comes to Bhanwar Gupha. This is the plane that does not fall away in the grand dissolution. There the Shabd sounds like a flute. Swami Ji Maharaj lovingly says that when the soul crosses over the region of Bhanwar Gupha, even the Great Negative Power — the *Maha Kal* — nods his head and says, "Now this soul has gone beyond my control; now I do not have any control over this soul." Beyond Bhanwar Gupha is the region of Sat Lok, the region of Truth, or Sat Naam. When the Masters give us the Initiation, They do not connect us with Themselves; They connect our soul with the Sat Naam, the Sat Lok. It is the duty of the Masters to take our soul to the Sat Naam – the place where They have connected our soul. All the Mahatmas who have reached there have written about the melodious sound of the Shabd over there. They all have said that the Sound in that region is very melodious; it is like the *vina* or bagpipe.

> *The Soul is decorated in the Alakh Lok.*
> *From there in a moment she ran to Agam Lok.*

Then the soul goes to *Alakh Lok*, or the untraceable plane, and from there to *Agam,* or the unreachable plane. Guru Nanak Sahib also says that he who goes beyond the Alakh and Agam planes, only after going there, gets or recognizes the Sat Lok, because beyond that is the true place of God where the perfect Masters reside.

> *What can I say in glory of the throne made of flowers,*
> *Where Radha Swami has cast His Feet.*

Swami Ji Maharaj says, "What can I say to describe that throne upon which my Beloved Master, Who is the Form of God Almighty, is sitting?" All the Saints Who have reached that place have become quiet, because over there, there is no talking. All those who have reached there cannot say anything, They just become quiet, because it is the region of peace and quietness, and who wants to go back into this world and talk about it? Kabir said, "It is like some salt; if the salt wants to know about its origin, it goes into the depth of the ocean. But when the salt goes there, it is dissolved in the water of the ocean. So how can the salt come back and tell others about its origin?"

> *I embrace those Feet, what can I say of that Akam Bani (which cannot be talked about)?*
> *Now I have completed my arti (worship), I have told you the secrets of Agam.*
> *Kissing the dust of the feet of Radha Swami, I have come to my own Home.*

Masters give us the hints and They tell us about that place. They tell us, "Dear Ones, come along with us and see the Reality with your own eyes."

God is so gracious that He came as Christ, He came as Kabir, and He came as Guru Nanak. He came as beautiful Emperor Sawan, and He came as Almighty Gracious Kirpal. We are the most fortunate ones to have had the glimpse of Almighty Kirpal, whose name is sung by the entire creation. He took the lost orphan Ajaib and carried him in His lap. No one can compare to Him.

> *Come Kirpal Guru, I celebrate.*
> *I beg of You to give me Your darshan.*

> *Come Satguru Ji, I am requesting You.*
> *I am carrying the water for Your sangat.*

> *Even the sun is embarrassed by Your glimpse.*
> *No one finds the limits of Your importance.*

> *I have come and stood on Your words.*
> *O Lord, protect my honor, as I have become Yours.*

> *You are the benefactor – give the alms.*

*The beggars have come to Your door. Don't send them
away empty.*

*You Yourself are the support of Your sangat.
Poor Ajaib has come to Your door.*
— Aa Kirpal Guru Mai Sagan Manondi Ha

People Call Me Mad

The lotus is fond of the sun, and when the sun rises the lotus also blooms and expresses its happiness. In the same way, one who has had the darshan of the Inner Radiant Form of the Master, he also becomes very happy and looking at him, the other people also feel the same happiness. They wonder what has happened to him. They do not know what that person really has, because they only see the joy and happiness on his face.

In my case, when I met with Beloved Lord Kirpal and when He showed me His Inner Form, when He showered grace on me, my condition became like that. I was intoxicated in His love and the people around me were astonished. They were wondering what had happened to me, because for them I was different. They were seeing something different in me. After meeting with Master Kirpal I started doing full-time meditation and this was a sudden change. Before Master Kirpal came to my ashram I had thousands of people following me, and I used to see people and talk with them and do all kinds of things like that. But after initiating me, Master gave me the duty of meditating constantly, so I always stayed in one room and meditated. Suddenly I became cut off from all the world. Because of this many people taunted me. They told me that they believed me to be a great man, but they couldn't understand why I had become an initiate of Master Kirpal. They said, "Before you were free and now you are bound." Many dear ones even thought that I had gone mad. They thought that maybe this Kirpal Singh who had come had put something in my head. They said, "Kirpal of Delhi has done some magic on his head and that's why he's gone mad and changed his position. That is why this wise man, who was doing well before Master Kirpal came, has now gone mad." However, smiling I would say to them, "Doing the Simran of Kirpal Singh, remembering Kirpal Singh, millions of sinners have been liberated. Ajaib says that you should also follow Kirpal." When I said this, they would leave without any other argument.

Gracious Sawan Has Caused the Drizzle to Shower

Gracious Sawan has caused the drizzle to shower.
At least come out in this intoxicating weather and see.

In the sky there are colorful swings,
At least set the swing of love to its peak and see.

Understand the melody of the songs sung by the cuckoo,
At least sing one song of love and see.

You will get the happiness of heaven here itself.
At least come under the shade of the hair and see.

I'll make You drink through the cups of eyes.
At least exchange Your glance with me and see.

I will write my whole life in Your Name.
At least for once get in love with me and see.

Today the nectar is showering from the skies.
At least for once create the yearning and see.

Coming into the intoxication of the month of Sawan,
At least shoot the arrow of Your glance and see.

Ajaib has become Yours for no cost.
At least for once You try me and see.

— Sawan Dayalu Ne

The Master expects only the meditation from the disciple. He does not expect the disciple to bring gifts to Him. The only thing that He expects from the disciple is that he may bring Him the meditation. So, as the Master is expecting only the meditation from the disciple, here the disciple says, "I do not expect anything from You. I have becomes Yours free of cost, and at least for once, You try me and then see."

If we are working for somebody and expecting the reward for it, that cannot mean that we are doing the devotion. We are working. Kabir Sahib also says, "If the Master is living off the wealth of the disciple, then He is the greedy one; and if the disciple is doing the devotion of the Master expecting rewards from Him, then he is also a greedy one; and they both are playing their games." But this is not the case between the true disciple and the Master. As the Master expects only meditation and nothing else, in the same way, the true disciple does not expect anything from the Master. He only does the devotion of the Master. So that is why here the disciple says, "Ajaib has become Yours for no cost. Now at least for once, You try me and see."

As the disciple is the lover of the eyes of the Master, in the same way the Master is also the lover of the eyes of the disciple. As the disciple gets a lot of satisfaction and intoxication by looking into the eyes of the Master, in the same way, if the disciple is true and if he is doing what the Master is asking him to do, the Master also becomes the lover of such a disciple.

The story of the Master and the disciple never comes to an end. For forty-five years Master Sawan went on telling the stories of the Master and the disciple. For twenty-five years of His life, Master Kirpal Singh went on giving the teachings to the people. All the ten Sikh Gurus and all the perfect Masters Who came into this world went on telling us stories of the disciples and the Masters. They wrote many great scriptures and holy books, but still the stories of the love of the Master and the disciple never come to an end. The more one talks about it, the more one tries to obtain it, the more one gets. There is so much more I could say as love is such a thing that never finishes.

One Should Never Love a Foreigner

Your face is beautiful and You have a beautiful attraction.
The soul is so happy that it is flying in air.
Come really and give us darshan, O Giver.

O Giver at least once enter my home, so that I can relate the sorrows of my heart to You.
Like the rainbird I am saying, "O Giver, for once reside in my eyes.
And then I will never open my eyes again."

Again and again I have been into many births.
When my fate awakened then I came to Your feet.
O Giver, come and protect me now so that I may never waiver.

Sawan and Kirpal are true and pure.
Ajaib the poor one has come to Your door.
Millions of times I sing Your praises. I sacrifice my life at Your door.

— Sohna Sohna Mukhra

This is a fact, that when the Beloved Master visited my home, I used to get so overwhelmed with happiness that I would not even remain aware that I was putting my feet on the ground — I would feel as if I was floating in the air in happiness. I would be like half-mad.

When He would leave, my condition would become like that of a *chicori* or moon bird. The condition of the moon bird is such that as long as she can see the moon, she is all right, but when the moon sets and goes away then the moon bird does not have any peace. Such was the condition of this poor soul. When He left my home, as long as I could see His car going, I would feel life in my body, but when I stopped seeing His car, I would feel that He had taken my life with Him also. After His departure, for many days I would not feel comfortable or be able to do anything of this world. I would remember His beloved form and suffer that pain of separation until I saw Him again.

Similarly whenever I would go to see Him at the place where He was staying on tour, when He would find out that my jeep had arrived He would at once come out of His room to greet me. After seeing Him, when I would go back, He would come out to see me off and wait there, keep standing there, as long as He could see my jeep. It was His grace and His greatness that whenever He had to say good-bye to me He would stand at the door as long as I would remain in sight.

Whenever Master would get ready to leave, after completing His tour, or whenever I had to go away from Him, I would feel the yearning, the pain of separation, and I would recite this couplet in front of Him, "One should never fall in love with a foreigner, no matter if he is worth millions." I would say that now I have come to realize that it is not a good thing to love the foreigner even if he is very valuable and very loving "because the foreigner always has to go back to his home." Master would complete that couplet by saying, "It is better to have love for the foreigner, because when he is not around you, whenever you remember him, you weep for him, so your love is maintained."

When the lotus flower blooms, the honeybee comes there and he is so attracted to the lotus that he always stays there. At night when the lotus closes the honeybee does not remember to go away from the lotus; he is closed in the flower and he dies. But still, he does not want to give up the company of the lotus. The disciple of the Master who has manifested Him develops such kind of love.

I have seen this with my own eyes, and I say this: that He was great, He was All Truth and He came into this world to give. As He used to say, "Saints always come for giving." He did not have a limited amount of grace to give to a limited amount of people — He had grace for everyone. People got from Him according to their receptivity, according to their vessels. If everyone had become receptive to His grace, everyone would have gotten a lot of grace from Him because He brought a lot of grace to this world.

TEN

Kirpal the Gracious One

Kirpal, the Giver of Grace

Shower Grace on everyone, shower grace, shower grace.
O Guru Pal, remove everyone's pains, remove the pains, Guru Pal.

We are Your children – You are our Father. Who except You can reshape our distortions?
Remove the darkness, O Master, manifest the Light. We are wandering; show us the way.
Who will take care of us if You will forget us?

May we live becoming men, and create heaven on earth.
May the black cloud of sins disappear, and the stream of Naam's nectar flow.
May the honor of the Sangat increase – may everyone be blessed.

Whoever has Your Form in his mind and whoever has Your Naam in his mouth,
All his works are accomplished in the wink of an eye.
May You shower grace on me and may I accomplish my work.

> *O Kirpal Guru, give me only this boon – make my body, mind, and wealth pure.*
> *May I be liberated from all the dualities, and may I see Your beauty in everyone.*
> *Ajaib sings Your praises with a sincere mind.*
> — Sab Par Dya Karo Guru Pal

How can I describe the glory and grace of my Beloved Master Lord Kirpal? I cannot describe His greatness enough through words. When He wanted to shower grace upon the dear ones, His grace knew no limits; His grace did not have any beginning or any end. He showered so much grace upon all the dear ones who came in contact with Him.

The reality is that whenever God wishes to shower grace on the souls, He Himself comes down in the form of a Master. Guru Nanak says, "God Himself takes the form of a Sadh. Whenever He wants to shower grace on the souls He comes down in the body of a Sadh." Kabir says, "The Creator is speaking through the human body." No doubt the Master has the human body, but still He is more than man and He is above all men. There are many people sitting in the Satsang. Some of them are clever and some are not, but still they are all called humans. The Master also has the human body, but He is above the limits of man and He is above the limits of mind and matter. So Master Kirpal was such a giver of grace that no words can describe His greatness.

The meaning of the name Kirpal is "one who showers grace." In His bani, Guru Nanak had already written that if Sant Kirpal – the Gracious Saint – showers grace, then along with the devotees, even the critics will cross over. In every home, Master Kirpal, with firm determination and faith, spread the Naam of His Master, and that is why today all over the world the name of Kirpal is shining.

Masters Come for the Sinners

Master Kirpal Singh used to say, "The perfect Masters are like the washermen. The washerman accepts the clothes of the gentleman as well as the baker and the oil merchant, because he knows that he can clean the clothes of anyone. In the same way, the perfect Masters know that under the smog of maya, and under the burden of the sins, there is a pure soul within everyone, and with His grace He can make all the souls pure."

Kirpal, the Giver of Grace

In my area there used to live a very good person from the Hindu religion. He would not eat meat, he would not drink wine, and he lived a very good life. In the same area there also lived a prostitute. Both of them came to Master Kirpal Singh. Master Kirpal accepted that prostitute for Initiation and He did not give Initiation to that Hindu even though he was a very good person.

How was that prostitute inspired to go to the Satsang and get Initiation? It so happened that she used to live about one kilometer from my ashram. In the night time when she would hear the sevadars at the ashram singing the banis, she would come out on the bank of the canal and she would sit there and listen. When she heard the words of the Satsang, she asked people to take her to the ashram. However nobody wanted to bring her because they thought that they would also get a bad name if they accompanied her because she was a prostitute, so no one brought her to the ashram.

One day she herself came to me and she asked me, "Last night I heard you saying, 'If the gracious Saint showers grace, even the sinners can get liberation along with the virtuous persons; Nanak says this.' Is it true? Is it possible for a sinner like me to get liberation?"

I said, "Yes, it is possible for you also." She then asked about the Master and asked me would I inform her when He comes. I replied, "Yes, I will send the message very happily and you can come here." So she came there and along with that Hindu person, went to Master Kirpal. Master Kirpal very happily accepted that prostitute and gave the Initiation to her, but He did not accept that Hindu person.

This made the people of that area criticize Master Kirpal a lot because they started wondering what was wrong with that Hindu person. They wondered why Master Kirpal didn't give him the Initiation and why He chose that prostitute for the Initiation. What was so good about her? I told them, "Only time will tell us why Master made that decision." Even though people criticized Master Kirpal throughout a very wide area when He did this, still Master Kirpal did not care for their criticism and He happily and lovingly gave the Initiation to that prostitute. I told the dear ones to wait for some time and to see whether she continues to be a prostitute or whether she changes herself.

Master Kirpal used to say that when any person comes to the Master to become a disciple, the Master sees the karmas, and every intention very clearly, just like we see cardamom seeds placed in a glass jar. They know how much affection that person has for the Master, how much desire he has for doing the Path of Spirituality and for what purpose he has come to the Master. Those who have the real yearning for doing the Spiritual Path, and a real yearning for God, Master not only gives them their reward, but He also gives them His own earnings. He tells them, "This is all for you. I have earned all this for you and now you take care of this." Those who are not willing to do anything but just talk, and who come to

Master Kirpal at an Initiation

Master for name, fame and honor only, they get nothing from the Master because the Master knows for what purpose they have come to Him.

It happened that after that woman got the Initiation she gave away all the wealth that she had collected by doing that business of prostitution. She gave up being a prostitute and she started earning her livelihood by honest means. She started living a very normal and simple life. She died some years later, and from the time of her Initiation until her death she lived a very good life.

Master Kirpal did not care about the criticism of the people and even though she was a prostitute, He forgave her sins, forgave her faults. He welcomed her and gave her the Initiation. He always used to say, "Masters come for the sinners. We are the sinners, we have all the bad qualities, but it is because of the grace of the Master that we are attached to His feet and we are on this Path."

In the beginning people used to criticize me also. They used to ask, when I myself was a very good person, why was I involved with these kinds of bad people, and why was I allowing these kinds of people to be with me? However, because of the grace of Master Kirpal and the color which He had given me, I was able to color those people who were around me in the same color in which I was colored. It was not in my hands, it was not up to me to do that. It was only because of His grace that I was able to save myself from the sins and I was able to love the sinners and later on have those sinners change into good people.

When we meditate and come to the Eye Center and start remaining there, when we start going to the inner planes, even the lower planes, we learn about our bad qualities and the bad deeds which we did in our past lifetimes. We learn how many bad deeds we have done, not only in this lifetime, but also in our past lifetimes. When we go further up in the higher planes then everything becomes as clear as an open book. At that time we realize all the bad deeds that we have done in many of our past lives and then we realize how dirty we were and how very gracious our Master was. It was only because of His grace that He cleaned us up. We were dirty, we had done a lot of sins and it was only because of His grace that He made us pure.

Just as the prostitute had done many sins, there was also a famous dacoit in Rajasthan who had committed many murders. He came to Master Kirpal Singh, and when he came there Master asked him, "What is your profession?" He replied, "All my life I have been a hunter of men." Master asked him, "Now what is your idea?" He replied, "That is all over; now I have come to repent and take refuge at Your feet." Master Kirpal gave him Initiation and he became a very good man. In the same way, Udham Singh was a very famous robber of Maza. He used to torment the disciples who were coming to see Master Sawan Singh, and sometimes he even drowned them in the river. However, when he learned of the importance of the Saints, he came to Master Sawan Singh and got initiated by Him. After that he used to praise Master Sawan Singh constantly in front of the sangat. When Master Sawan Singh told him to stop doing that, he would say, "Let me remove all my sins, because with this mouth I have criticized You a lot; now let me remove those sins by praising You."

Kirpal Tells Us to Remember Death

O man, meditate on the Naam of Master, as one day the slumber of death will come.

O Kabir, what can the sleeping one do when he does not get up and remember the Lord?
One day slumber will come and he will have to stretch out his legs.

All your life has passed sleeping and still you are not awakened.
In the end you will repent when Yama hits you.

You forgot to meditate on Naam and the Negative Power spread his snare.
You became intoxicated in the pleasures and Maya deluded you.

"You will not get this time again," explained the Satguru.
"Your good fortune has awakened and you got the human birth."

In the court of the Lord no one will listen to you except the Satguru.
Ajaib says, "Without Kirpal we do not get any other support."

— Bande Naam Guru Da Japle

In His Satsangs, Supreme Father Kirpal Singh, while mentioning death, used to recite this couplet in Urdu, "No one is aware of his death, no one knows about one moment but he is collecting things for a century." He was telling us that we, the forgetful souls, have forgotten death and forgetting it we have collected the material things for centuries, even though we do not know whether the next breath will come or not. Master Sawan used to say that the amazing thing is that we carry our relatives and friends to the cremation ground and consign them to the fire, but we have never made our cunning and foolish mind understand that such a day has to come to us also. One day all of a sudden, we will have to leave the market of this world. We are not aware of that moment.

My Beloved Master told me, "Look here, we have not come to live in this world forever. The time which has passed will not come back." So that is why in this bhajan it says that the time which has passed does not come back; this is what Kirpal makes Ajaib understand. All the Saints Who come into this world awaken us, the ones who are sleeping in the deep sleep of attachment. They come to awaken us and They tell us, "You should do the work for which you have come into this world. You have not come here to live forever. You are like a traveler, and this is an opportunity which you have been given to do the devotion, so you should get up and you should do your devotion."

The Death of My Father

As I said earlier, my father was a very religious-minded person and he always used to involve himself in the rites and rituals of the Sikh religion. No doubt he was a very good person but he did not like it when, as a child, I would sit down in meditation with my eyes closed. He was against me when, right from my childhood, I expressed the yearning to meet some Master who could give me the knowledge of God. Because my father was religious-minded and liked the rites and rituals, he didn't like my idea of going into the shelter of a living Master; he wanted me to do the things which he was doing. Whenever I would leave the house to search for a living Master, he would taunt me and say, "I will see which living Master is going to come to your rescue. I will see when your devotion will liberate me."

It was not only my father who opposed my devotion. In the beginning, when I was starting my search for Saints and Mahatmas and was visiting many Mahatmas, much unrest was created in my family. My relatives came to me and gave me a very hard time. They told me, "By going to the Saints and Mahatmas, you are bringing a very bad name to the family. What do you have to do with going to the Saints?" Later on in my life I went to Punjab to do Satsang, and sitting in that Satsang was one of my uncles, although I did not know that. He was hiding himself and he came only to see what I was doing there. After Satsang, he saw that I did not collect money from anyone and that people were coming and going after hearing my Satsang. He felt very sorry for me that I was unnecessarily doing service for people without taking anything from them, so he came to me. He couldn't bear that people were not paying me anything, so he asked me, "Without getting any payment, you are working for the people?" I told him, "Uncle, when I do not take anything from the people, then you say, 'You are not doing a good thing.' If I start taking money from the people, then you will say, 'You are begging, and you are bringing a bad name to the family!' How can I please you? Because either way you are not pleased. Tell me the way in which I can please you." So it was not only my father who was unhappy over my devotion; many of my relatives were also opposed to what I was doing.

After I met Master Kirpal, I told my father firmly, "You will see that at the time of your death, my Master will come to take care of your soul." He would ask me, "Really? Will He really come to take my soul up?" I would tell him, with firm determination, "I am sure that He will come to take your soul up." At that time my father was very old and he was unable to travel and have the darshan of the Master, so I said to Master, "Master, my father is very old and has not seen You. He often taunts me and says, 'I will see when your devotion will liberate me.' Whether or not You give Your darshan to anyone is not my business. But at least You should give Your darshan to my father, because I have promised him that You will come to take him. So please have mercy on me and take care of his soul."

My father was 95 years old when he left the body and his body had become very weak. When his end-time came, no act that he had done in his lifetime came to his rescue. None of the recitals of the holy book and no priest came to rescue him. However, three days before he left the body, he started telling people how he was seeing two old men with white beards and white clothes, and that they were telling him to prepare for the higher journey. He told his experience to hundreds of people who came to see him, and he sent me a cable, saying he was almost ready to leave the body. At that time I was living in Rajasthan and my father was living in Punjab. When I got to his home, he caressed me and loved me very much. He told me, "Tomorrow I am going to leave the body at 12 o'clock, but now I understand that your devotion is the true one, because now I am seeing two people in front of me, and they have come to take me up. They have white turbans and white beards and they both are wearing a special type of pants." He was very happy. I also was very delighted when I showed him the picture of Master Sawan

Singh and Master Kirpal Singh, and he said yes: They were the two men he was seeing, and They were saying, "We have come to take you." I told him, "Yes, you will meet one more. When you go up you will see one more; that is Baba Jaimal Singh. He is the Master of the Masters." Then he understood what the Master is. He realized that my devotion was going to liberate him. And then he told the people, "Today I realize that the devotion which my son is doing is true, and the Master Whom he is following is also the True One."

The next day at 11 o'clock he called me and told me to sit with him. He took me in his lap and caressed me, and he told me, "I made a great mistake. In the beginning I told you not to do the devotion, but now I am seeing that your Path is the true one and whatever you are doing, that is the Truth, because your Master is here. I am seeing Him in front of me and moreover within me I am also seeing Him. Today I know that your devotion was worthwhile and because of your devotion I am also getting the liberation." So I was very glad to know that at least at his end-time he had accepted his mistake and now he was believing in our Master. When he left the body, and Master came to liberate him even though he was not an initiate, the other people in the family who were present there also praised the Master. Even that uncle who I had told you about earlier was also present there, and he said, "Now I believe in you: you are doing a good thing and your Master is perfect," and later all those relatives went and got Initiation from the Master.

Even though he was not an initiate, but because of the strength of the satsangi in his family, my father received the grace of the Master. Master Sawan Singh used to say that the Master is going to liberate the satsangis, but He also has to liberate the relatives of satsangis. He also used to say that it is a very big thing that Masters take care of the relatives of the satsangis, but more than that, They even take care of the birds and animals who are taken care of by the satsangis.

Performing the Rites and Rituals after My Father's Death

Even though Masters Sawan and Kirpal showered so much grace on him, because he did a lot of rites and rituals all through his life, my father still had the desire that when he left the body I would take his remains to a holy place named Gaya and perform the rites and rituals over there. He even said, "Over there, when you offer rice balls and the other foodstuff, the departed souls stretch out their arms and receive the offerings." So I promised him, "Yes, I will do that. I will perform the rites and rituals there, because in that way I will also know whether the departed souls receive the offerings by reaching out their arms or not. But, mind you, I will give them those things only when they themselves stretch out their arms, only when they themselves come to receive the things. So when you go, you better tell all the departed souls that they should stretch out their arms when I go there to perform the rites and offer the foodstuff."

So after my father left the body I went to that place with his remains. However, at that place I saw the hands of many who were nothing but robbers, someone saying, "Give here" and someone saying, "Give there." There were many of those, but there were not any hands of the departed souls, nor was there any hand of those who could say, "You give us these things and we will liberate the soul." Only the hand of the Master is capable of doing that. The Master's hand is the only one that gives us liberation. So this is why it is written in the *Guru Granth Sahib,* "What should you do? All the rites and rituals are contained in the meditation of Shabd Naam, so you should do the meditation of Shabd Naam."

Sunder Das Burns His Leg

Sunder Das and I would sit in the field to meditate and we would sit for eight hours at a stretch. During the winter we would build a fire nearby and would sit near the fire in order to keep warm. One day we were sitting like that and during that sitting a piece of burning wood slipped and fell on Sunder Das's leg. That piece of wood burned his leg but he was not aware of that. You know how painful it is when your body burns but he did not feel any pain because his soul was withdrawn, and when the soul is withdrawn and is enjoying the inner planes it is not aware of pain and other sensations like that. Afterwards, when he got up from that meditation, he told me, "Today I have gotten such an intoxication in meditation; I have never gotten such an intoxication before in my whole life."

He told me that during that meditation both Baba Sawan Singh Ji and Master Kirpal Singh Ji had appeared to him and Master Kirpal asked him if he had ever seen Bhikha Ji and Sarmad Ji (two well-known Masters of the past). When he replied that he had not, he had only heard of them, Master Kirpal told him to look into His eyes; and when he did so, Master Kirpal took him up with His own attention. Sunder Das saw Dharam Rai (the Lord of Judgement), Who asked him why he had come, as no one was allowed entry to that place. Sunder Das replied that he had been sent by Master Kirpal Singh and was going to see Bhikha Ji and Sarmad Ji. When Dharam Rai heard the name of Master Kirpal Singh, He felt very happy and asked him to sit down and tell Him something about the Master, as He was happy to have met a disciple of Baba Sawan Singh. Sunder Das said that he was not allowed to sit there and that he would tell Dharam Rai about Master Kirpal Singh some other time. Dharam Rai then ordered that four *devtas* (goddesses) take Sunder Das in a sedan chair and transport him to their boundary. They did this, and told him about the further way which would take him to Bhikha Ji and Sarmad Ji. As Sunder Das was flying, he came to a place where there was an extremely beautiful and charming old man with a majestic face, who asked him where he had come from and where he was going. Sunder Das replied that he had come from the material world, and was going to see Bhikha Ji and Sarmad Ji under the instructions of Master Kirpal Singh. The old gentleman said that he could be of no service to him, but that the airplane he was traveling on would take him to those personalities.

This "airplane," not made of worldly perishable matter but of Shabd Naam, started flying again, and took him to the place where Bhikha Ji and Sarmad Ji lived. There was a watchman there who inquired where Sunder Das wanted to go, and was told in reply that he had come from the material world on the instructions of Master Kirpal Singh to see Bhikha Ji and Sarmad Ji. The watchman told him to go up a staircase, above which there was a big courtyard where both those personages would be found. While going up the staircase, Sunder Das heard every step of the staircase shouting and proclaiming loudly that "Kirpal" was the "Mightiest and the Savior"; even the sun and the moon were shouting like that, and every step had numerous lights on it.

When he arrived at the top of the staircase, Baba Sawan Singh also appeared and asked one of His attendants to take Sunder Das to Bhikha Ji and Sarmad Ji. The conversation did not take place through the tongue but through thoughts. When the attendant took him to the place of Bhikha Ji and Sarmad Ji, the door opened and he had the pleasure of having the darshan of the two divinely radiant personalities to his heart's fill. Afterwards, when the attendant brought him down, Sunder Das realized that he had come back to the body and then all the pain and suffering started.

At that time his leg had been burned quite badly so we took him to a doctor in Ganganagar. The doctor said that his leg was so badly burned that it needed to be amputated because the poison was spreading in his body. This worried Sunder Das very much, but I told him that he should not be worried because the One for Whom we were working would take care of us. At that time Master hinted from within that we should apply the juice of leaves from the neem tree on that burnt leg and it would be all right. We did that for a few days and his leg healed.

A few days later Master Kirpal came to my ashram to visit, and along with all the other dear ones who came with Him, He was told about the incident. When He heard about it, He said, "You see, this is the devotion, this is called meditation. Is there anyone who does meditation like this? Is there anyone among you who forgets his body and everything, and remains attached to the Feet of the Master in meditation like this?"

Master Kirpal Shows Sunder Das the Fate of the False Masters

One time Master Kirpal came to visit my ashram and while we were sitting with Him, Sunder Das requested that he might be shown the areas where false gurus, those who act and pose as Masters and commit many sins in the name of Spirituality, are punished. Master Kirpal asked him to close his eyes, and when he did so He took his soul to the hell where about five hundred false gurus were collected and were being given a new punishment every day. Some of them were made to stand on burning iron pillars, their tongues were being pulled out and tied with chains carrying huge stones, and there were enormously big stones on their heads. *Yamdoots* (messengers of death), in the form of animals with long beaks, were pulling and biting their flesh.

Here and in an adjoining hell, he saw the false gurus suffering many types of extreme tortures. On inquiring from the Lord of Death as to who were the souls who were being punished so mercilessly, Sunder Das was told that those persons had become gurus in the physical world, even though they did not engage themselves in intense meditation and were not able to carry on the spiritual work; they had deceived their disciples by sheer acting and posing, with the help of parties, and were reaping the reward for their malicious actions. The animals with long beaks were the disciples who had been misled by them; they were settling past scores.

After this, the soul of Sunder Das came down; he opened his eyes and narrated to Master Kirpal what he had seen inside. Master Kirpal smiled and said that those who deceive others will inevitably have to suffer for their deeds, but those who are initiated by perfect Masters will always conquer [all obstacles], if they have love for the Guru and live by His orders. Disciples of a perfect Master cannot be molested inside, so long as they remain the disciples of the Guru; even poisonous snakes will feel happy coming under the feet of the disciples of a perfect Master.

Hundreds of dear ones were present when Sunder Das went through all this. It was not as if Master Kirpal gave him a sitting in a closed room and made him see all these things; it all happened in public. He was sitting there at my house with hundreds of people present, and he was asked to relate whatever he had experienced inside in front of them.

There was a lawyer in that group who had witnessed all that. He stood up, trembling, and told Master Kirpal, "Master, I have heard so many Satsangs of Yours, and I was never afraid. However, today what You are making this dear one say — You are not saying all this Yourself, but You are making him speak the truth — makes me tremble. My heart is trembling because now I have realized that the Negative Power is also a Power." He understood that the Master is a Power and there is also a Power to whom we have to give an answer, to whom we will have to give an account of our every single breath.

Sunder Das was a very good meditator of a very high order. He used to go within, and once you go within, no doubts exist. Once you go within, the Path becomes as clear as an open book.

Sunder Das Leaves the Body

At that time Rajasthan was a very backward area and there were not many cars, jeeps or motorcycles there. So once a man told Sunder Das that he should learn how to ride a bicycle. Sunder Das replied, "Why should I do that? When God has given me two legs to walk on, why should I use them for learning to cycle? When I see anybody riding a bicycle, I feel like giving them a big blow with a stick, because they are not using the legs given by God the way they should be used." When he said this the man asked him, "What will you reply to Dharam Rai, the Lord of Judgment, when He asks you why you didn't learn to ride a bicycle?" Sunder Das replied, "Well, what do I have to do with the Lord of Judgment? I am not worried about Him because I do not have to go in front of Him. My Master is perfect and when I die He will come to take me. I don't have any concern with the Lord of Judgment." Sunder Das was such an interesting man, and indeed when his end-time came Master Sawan Singh did come to receive him.

As it happened six months before he left the body Sunder Das told me that he was going to leave the body on a certain day. He told me that if I wanted to commemorate his death — to distribute food or do anything like that — I should do it while he was still alive, because he wanted to see it. Twenty days before that day arrived he purchased his coffin and made all the arrangements for his departure from this world. He even told me that I should bring the clothes that he would wear after he left the body, so I did that and he kept them with him. The day before he left the body he told me, "Now the call has come from the court of the Lord and now I'm ready to go."

The day that he was going to leave was the day of our monthly Satsang and so we got together with a lot of the sangat. We gave a big feast to all the satsangis who were there, making halvah and other very good food. All those who came there got filled with good food, and looking at that he said, "Yes, now Master is very happy because everything is happening in His Will." About two hours before he was to leave the body, he said, "Now all the three Masters — Master Sawan Singh along with Baba Jaimal Singh and Master Kirpal Singh — have come to take me and I am going with them." There were hundreds of people there and he told all of them that the Masters had come and he was going with them. At that point he told us to take the halvah and distribute it to all the sangat, which we did.

Just a few moments before he was to go, I asked him, "Sunder Das, do you have any desire? Tell me. Don't take any desire with you." He said, "No, I don't have any desire. I don't want anything — except one thing — that my sister should also be taken at the same time I am. Master Sawan Singh should take her with me also, and she should leave the body with me." He had one sister who was older than he was. He was ninety years old when he left the body and his sister was a little bit older, about ninety-five. She was in very much pain and was suffering a lot because of her old age. She didn't have Naam Initiation and she had become so weak that she was not able to walk without the support of a stick. So when Sunder Das was about to leave the body he told me, "It will not make any difference to the Master to shower grace on my sister, but if she can be released at the same time, I will leave peacefully. I am worried about her." So when he said this I looked at that old woman and asked her, "Are you ready to go?" When she heard that I was asking her whether she was ready to go with Sunder Das or not, whether she was ready to leave this world or not, at once, with a lot of pain, she got up somehow and tried to stop Sunder Das from requesting that. She became very afraid of death and using her cane she left that place. I asked Sunder Das, "Is your sister ready? If you think that she is ready to go then you should stop her." But she was not ready, she was not stopped and she left the room. Then Sunder Das said, "The time is really up and now I have to go. Now sprinkle the water because Master Sawan Singh has come with Baba Jaimal Singh and Master Kirpal Singh and I am going with them," and then he left the body. He left the body in his full glory and all the three Masters came to liberate him.

After he left the body his sister came back. Holding the hand of Sunder Das' dead body, she started weeping, saying, "Brother, why didn't you maintain the religion of brotherhood? Why didn't you take me with you?" But I told her, "He maintained his religion, he wanted you to go with him to the court of the Lord, but you were not ready. When he was telling you to come, you were afraid of death, and now you are not telling the truth."

Master Sawan Singh used to tell a very interesting story about one old woman whose granddaughter became sick. That old woman would always pray, "O Lord, take me from this world instead of my granddaughter, because I am old and I have seen this world a lot, and I don't have any interest in living. May the Angel of Death come and take me instead of her." Once it so happened that a cow came in from outside and it was looking for some food in the kitchen. She put her mouth into the pots, one after another. Somehow she got her head stuck in one big pot with a black bottom. When the cow's head was in the pot, she could not see anything and becoming afraid she frantically rushed here and there in the kitchen. When the old woman saw her, she thought that it was the Angel of Death and she at once said, "No, no, I am not the person whom you should take — she is lying in that bed!" So from outside we may say that we are ready to go, but when the time comes it is seen that nobody is ready to go. Sunder Das' old sister spent the rest of her time in great pain and she left the body in a lot of pain. At the time when Sunder Das was asking for her liberation, she was also in pain, but she was not ready to leave this world.

After Sunder Das left the body, we cleaned his body up and we dressed him in white clothes. His body looked somewhat like Baba Sawan Singh's body. He had a sharp nose like Baba Sawan Singh had, and he had almost the same eyes and the same long face. After we dressed him in the white clothes we made him sit in the cross-legged position. To those who had the privilege of seeing Baba Sawan Singh, we said, "You can look and see if there is any difference between Baba Sawan Singh and Sunder Das."

So you can see the faith of Sunder Das, and how much faith he had in the Master and how devoted he was to Master Sawan Singh. Earlier in his life, because of his faith and because he followed the instructions of Master Sawan Singh, all his sickness, all his madness, was removed. Master Sawan Singh had promised that He would come to liberate Sunder Das, that He would come to take his soul up. He not only came, but He came with Baba Jaimal Singh and Master Kirpal to take him. So this is the result of having full faith in the Master and being devoted to the Master. Master Sawan Singh used to say that at their end-time the meditators become more pleased and they experience more happiness than they would have at the time of getting married. If there is any pain, it is to the body, but the soul does not have any pain. Those who have done the meditation, they are prepared even before God Almighty calls them, and instead of becoming afraid, they become happy.

Jagroop Singh Leaves the Path, But Still Master Kirpal Comes to Liberate Him

Hear our plea, O Guru Kirpal, and divert our minds from the bad deeds.

The mind does not come to Satsang. It doesn't feel embarrassed doing the bad deeds.

> *O Gracious Lord, have pity on the souls and attach our hearts to the Feet of the Master.*
>
> *We are the suffering ones from birth after birth. We are the unchaste, angry, deceitful, indulgent ones.*
> *O Guru, You Yourself take care of Your souls and break the veil of mind.*
>
> *The mind is afraid of Parmarth. Leaving meditation he presents excuses.*
> *He has been wandering for many births – shower Grace and unite him with the Lord.*
>
> *The honeybee loves the fragrance of Your flowers. He always waits for Your Grace and Mercy.*
> *Hear the plea of Ajaib the sinner: attach the mind in Simran.*
>
> — Tusi Araj Suno Kirpal Guru

There was an initiate of Master Kirpal named Jagroop Singh. After taking Initiation, he left the Path and started eating meat and drinking wine. Once another initiate in his village accidentally ate meat and drank wine, but afterwards he realized his mistake. Ordinarily people have this habit of finding fault with others; they don't think about what they are doing or have done, and so when Jagroop Singh came to know that that other initiate had taken meat and wine after Initiation, he taunted him and said, "Either leave the Path or don't eat and drink these things." That other dear one replied, "I did this by mistake and now I realize it. You should not taunt me like this, because you also eat meat and drink wine. You have also made a great mistake." Jagroop Singh said, "Yes, I have also done that, but it is not a mistake. I left the Path and then I started eating meat. You should also leave the Path."

I happened to hear this conversation and I said, "Jagroop Singh, you should not talk like this. You say you have left the Path, but Master has not left you. Definitely at the time of death He will come to take you. Then you will realize that this was your mistake. At that time you will be so ashamed that you will not be able to look at the Master. You say, 'Bring the promissory note and I can write on that that I have left the Path.' However, in reality Master will never leave you because when Saints initiate any soul, They always stay with him. They never leave him until the end of the world." When I said that, he replied, "No, I don't believe in that. This is all bogus." After that, whenever I would see him, he would say, "I am waiting for that day. Whatever you said, it is all false." But I would say, "No, wait for the time and you will realize this."

It so happened that he murdered a person and was sent to jail and it was in jail that he left the body. Because he had made that mistake, he was given punishment on his body and before leaving the body he got sick. There were many locks and guards there, but still Master appeared at that place to liberate him at his death. At that time Jagroop Singh said, "Now my Master has come, but with which face can I stand before Him? How can I reply to Him?" But still Master came there, for once a Master has initiated any soul, no matter if he has done bad deeds, still the Master comes at the time of death to liberate him.

When this thing happened, many prisoners who saw it were very impressed. They understood the importance, the greatness of the Master Power. They wrote me many letters saying they wanted to take Initiation when they got out of jail.

The Death of My Young Relative

One cannot describe the glory of the Master. It is a matter of experience; only those on whom He is gracious can know about His glory. It is also a matter of faith; the more faith one has in Him, the more one can see of His glory. There was one boy who was a relative of mine who left the body at the young age of fourteen. In those days in India the disease of smallpox was very severe and many people used to die because of it. Now it has been eradicated from India, but in those days it was very bad. That boy got smallpox and he suffered from that disease for many days before he left the body; he was in terrible pain and he would even become unconscious.

However, whenever I went near that boy, he would ask me to sit with him. Whenever I sat with him, he would say, "Before you came, I felt as if insects were biting and eating my body. The pain which I was having, I cannot describe. In addition I see many evil faces and they are frightening me. But when you come, all those things go away and I feel comfortable." Whenever I was sitting with him he would say that he felt some relief, and he would request me to stay longer with him.

Since his mother had faith in the Master, Master gave her an experience and she saw the Master in a dream. In her vision the Master told her, "Since your son is suffering so much he won't be able to live in this world. He will die. But don't worry, because on the third day from now at midnight I will come to take him up. You should make tea then, and after he drinks tea I will take him up. But take care that you do not weep after he leaves the body, because now his soul is under my protection. He will be born again in a human body and he will become a man." In that village there were four or five other satsangis and Master was so gracious that He also gave darshan to all those other satsangis and told them that on the third night He would come and take that boy at midnight.

The lady became very happy that the Master was going to come and protect the soul of her son. It happened just as He had said. Three days later two of the other satsangis of the same village were going to sleep about eight o'clock when they had the experience of seeing Master's car coming there, and Master told them that He had come to take the soul of that boy. Both of them came to me and told me that they had seen Master and that very soon He would be coming to take the boy's soul. So we were prepared for that and that night we all sat there in meditation.

At 11:30 that boy asked for tea and his mother went into the kitchen to make some. She was not at all worried about her son's departure, as she was feeling very happy that Master was coming to take him. She knew the boy would not leave the body until he drank the tea, so she wanted to delay, and she started singing hymns in the kitchen. At 12:15, when I saw that she was delaying his departure, I called her and said, "Why are you not giving tea to him?" Then the son shouted out, "Mother, bring the tea as soon as possible. If you will give me a spoonful of tea, it's okay. If you don't want to give it, we will go without drinking the tea." So at once the mother brought the tea and as soon as he drank two spoonfuls, he said, "Now Master has come here and I am going with Him." He shouted out in a loud voice, and because I was sitting very close to him, he put his hand on my chest and left the body. Even though he had had so much pain in his last days, his passing was peaceful and he had no pain at that time. Master came there to protect his soul, and He took his soul up.

When that boy left the body nobody wept for his departure, because everyone knew that Master had taken care of his soul. His parents did not weep because they had faith that the Master had protected his soul. The family was criticized by other people in the village, for if anyone loses his young son, it is a matter of great sorrow. When the parents did not weep, people started talking about them, "Look at them, they are not even sorry to have lost their young son." But since the parents knew what the reality was, they did not weep. They were very grateful to Master Kirpal for coming to take care of their son.

Master always takes care of the souls of the disciples. Even if one is not initiated, but still if he has faith in Him, Master comes and takes care of that soul. Master Sawan Singh used to say, "Masters always come into this world to protect the souls of the disciples." If you have faith in Him, He will definitely come to take you and give you a better place. So how can we sing the praise of that great Master Kirpal?

The Dear One Who Listened to Criticism

Once a dear one came to Master Kirpal in our ashram, and he asked Master why he was not having good meditations. Master asked him if he was having the problem of lust. He said, "No." Master said, "Maybe you are having the problem of anger?" He said, "No, I don't have that problem." Master asked him about many basic problems, but none of them applied. Finally Master asked him, "Are you involved in criticism? Are you criticizing anybody?" He said, "No, I don't have such habits." Then Master asked him, "Are you taking part in hearing criticism? When anybody else is criticizing someone, are you present there?" He said, "Yes, I have a habit of hearing criticism." So Master said that whether you criticize or hear the criticism, it's the same. The one who criticizes and the one who hears the criticism both are sinners and they both lose.

Master Sawan Singh used to speak about criticism very strongly. He would say, "There is no taste in speaking ill of others. There is taste or pleasure in the sense enjoyments, but where is the pleasure in finding fault? But even so we do not stop it; we are always doing it." He used to say, "If you criticize someone, your good actions will go to his account, and his sins will come to your account, and in that way he will get the blessing." Master Kirpal also used to say, "If a satsangi criticizes other people, he will not be forgiven, but if a non-initiate criticizes others, he may be forgiven. A sat-

Master Kirpal in a small group darshan

sangi knows that this is bad, while a non-initiate does not."

If we criticize the Saints, They do not imitate us. They do not respond to our criticism. Mean persons always present excuses to justify themselves and to prove that they are true, but wise men always wait for time to prove that they are true. Saints always wait for time, because They know that time will tell people what is the truth. One may attend the Satsang of any perfect Master or read His writing, and you will not find even one single line of criticism of other people. They don't criticize others because They have love and respect for all.

No Light Due to Lust

Once a dear one came to Master and told Him that he didn't get any experience of Naam during the Initiation. Master told him to sit in front of Him and close his eyes, and when Master was just about to touch his forehead, that dear one realized that it was his own mistake and he confessed. He told Master, "What can You do? I myself have turned off the Light which I had in my within by enjoying lust so much in my life. Now my forehead is blackened, there is no Light there. How can You manifest Light there? I have done this by myself." So Master was also very sorry for him and told him that from now onwards he should maintain chastity and then everything would become all right.

Guru Nanak has said that when we preserve the vital fluid, Naam gets manifested within us by itself and Light also gets manifested within us by itself. When we preserve the vital fluid, the mind, which is making us wander here and there like a swift horse, becomes still and remains quiet. Light gets manifested in our forehead and we meet the Indestructible God who is present everywhere. If we preserve the vital fluid, if we are celibate, then we will be able to sit for five, seven hours continuously and we will come out from that position only when we have to attend the call of nature. There will be no question of getting tired. Our thoughts will not go to any other place, they will not go out of our body. Like the blossom of a rose, our heart will always remain in bloom and be happy.

People Who Tried to Deceive the Master

When Master Kirpal would put the dear ones into meditation, afterwards He used to ask what they saw inside. However, I remember that when He would initiate people after coming to my ashram, at the same time He would make some other people sit for meditation on a different side of the tent. Those people would not sit for meditation during the Initiation as they were told to do by the Master, but instead they would talk with each other, make jokes and do things like that. When they knew that it was time for Master to come, at once they would sit up in meditation with their eyes closed, pretending that they had been meditating right from the beginning.

Afterwards, when Master would tell them, "Okay, leave off please and sit comfortably." He would ask the people what they saw inside. He would ask, "How many people saw stars, how many people saw moons?" and so forth. The people who talked during the Initiation and did not meditate then, but closed their eyes only when Master was about to come back, those people would raise both their hands to show that they had seen stars, moons and things like that. Since I used to see all this, I felt very bad. I did not like it very much

Master Kirpal asking about meditation experiences

because I thought, "Why are these people deceiving the Master? Doesn't Master know what they are seeing and what experience they are having?" It affected my mind so much that since then I don't like to ask people what they see. Because of that one incident I do not feel comfortable asking people about their experiences because I feel that sometimes people try to deceive the Masters by lying about what they have seen in meditation.

Master Sawan Singh also did not ask people about their experiences. Guru Gobind Singh said, "All the Saints have Their own Will. They have different Wills. Even though They come from the same plane, even though Their meditation is the same, They come from the same Light, Their instructions are the same, but still They have different Wills, They have different ways of doing things."

Donating in the Spiritual Cause

There was an initiate of Master Sawan Singh who used to live in my area. He was a businessman and he had very large losses in his business. He owed people a lot of money. He was so disappointed with his life that once when I was going to Karanpur in the jeep, he lay down in front of my jeep. When I saw him there I stopped the jeep and asked him why he was doing that. He said, "I owe people so much money —

more than the number of hairs on my head — and I have lost my reputation. Unless I get the money to pay the people back I am not going to survive. I am going to commit suicide. Please help me."

I told him, "If you had come to me last night I would have made some arrangement, but I cannot do anything right now. I have to go to see the Master. Give me some time and tonight I will sell one of the squares of my land and I will give you something like five or six hundred rupees and you can pay back your debts. Then you won't need to worry about anything."

That person listened to me and he knew I would do that because I had so much love for him and he knew that I would give him the money. After telling him all this I went to see Master Kirpal. After seeing Master Kirpal I was in a rush, as I had to come back and arrange to sell the land so I could give the money to that dear one. When I asked Master's permission to leave He asked me why I was in such a rush. I told Him about that dear one. Right then another dear one had come to see Master Kirpal and he had given Him a huge amount of money, a large donation. At once Master Kirpal gave me that money and He told me, "You can sell the land later on, but take this money and give it to that dear one. Maybe he can use this money."

However, I am sorry to say that before I reached the place where that dear one was, he had already committed suicide. He did not wait for me. His son met me in Padampur, about sixty kilometers from that place, and he told me about him having committed suicide.

The dear one who had come to donate that money to Master Kirpal Singh must have thought that Master had accepted that donation because He needed the money. But Master did not keep that money with Him even for a second. He gave it to me to use for that other dear one. It is possible that if I had reached there in time, if it was meant to be, then that other person's life would have been saved. In that case the person who had given the money would have earned a good karma for having saved one person's life. But it did not happen. It is possible that Master wanted the money to be utilized in some other cause.

Swami Ji Maharaj has said, "Master is not hungry for your wealth but He is accepting it for your benefit. He is using your money for the benefit of the hungry and thirsty. He is feeding the hungry and thirsty with your money and in that way He is utilizing your money in the right place. In that way, when you are giving money to Him which He gives to the poor and needy people, you are gaining His pleasure, and when He is pleased, Sat Purush is pleased." Kabir Sahib also said,

"Those who move the rosary without the guidance of the Master and those who give the donations without the guidance of the Master, all their efforts are useless, because only the Master knows what place or what practice will bring benefit for the dear ones." The Masters know which is the right place that Their disciples should donate the money, and that is why when the money is donated under the guidance of the Master, only then does it bear good fruit for us.

Saints are not interested in running big langars (free kitchens), and They are not even interested in building big buildings. They do that only because They want to utilize the money of the dear ones in the right place for the right purpose. Master Sawan Singh used to say, "In the langars of the Master the rich people donate from their earnings which is distributed among the poor and rich equally. In that way the earnings of the rich people become successful, if used at the right place."

My personal experience was that many people wanted to give money to Master Kirpal but only the fortunate ones were allowed to do that. Many other people who had money and wanted to give it to the Master were not allowed.

There was another dear one, an initiate of Master Kirpal Singh, who was an inspector on the police force. He was a very truthful man. He would not accept bribes and he would always do his job in a good way. Unfortunately these days it is the habit of the leaders that unless you accept bribes from people and share with them, they always keep you moving from one place to another, and they make trouble for you with such things as false lawsuits and things like that. They do not like it if you do not take bribes and share it with them. So that police inspector was the victim of poor leaders and there was a false lawsuit brought against him, because he had been determined not to take bribes. When that false lawsuit was brought against him, he thought of committing suicide, thinking that there was no use living in such a world where people don't appreciate the truth.

Since he was a very good person, an initiate, he came to my village to discuss all this with me and he wanted to seek my advice about whether he should commit suicide. When he told me his story I lovingly told him, "Why do you feel like this? Why do you consider committing suicide? You will definitely get whatever is written in your fate and if you want anything I have fifty kilos of land here and this house which I can give to you." I touched his feet and told him, "Don't try to end your precious life."

When I told him all these things and when I offered him the land and the house, he was soothed and he gave up the thought of committing suicide and he again started living his normal life. Many years later, after a period of fifteen years, he came back to visit me after having been promoted to the District Superintendent of Police, and he brought with him many of the other policemen. The people who used to live with me at that time had seen him as a police inspector, which was a lower rank, but when he came as a high officer along with the other policemen, they did not recognize him. So he asked the people here, "Do you recognize me?" When the dear ones said that they didn't, he replied, "I am the person who was offered the land and the home by Sant Ji. His offering changed my life and I am here to see him. You can imagine how much it affected me that He offered me all those belongings."

The Boy Named Gopi

Earlier I had told you about the couple who were initiates of Master Sawan Singh who were going to have an abortion when the wife was pregnant. In order to prevent that, I offered to adopt that child, and I did so. He was a beautiful boy to whom I gave the name Gopi and he came and lived with me in my ashram in Kunichuk. There I used to live on the second floor, and since he used to live with me he also would stay on the second floor and we would sleep up on the terrace. Up there, there was no provision to go to the bathroom and so every night whenever he wanted to go to use the bathroom he had to come downstairs. Since he was small and very young it was difficult for him to go down during nighttime to use the latrine, and he would always complain that he was afraid of the dark, because there was no electricity there.

That young boy was very loving, very beautiful and very devoted to Master Kirpal. He used to imitate me in sitting for meditation and I used to tell him stories about Master Kirpal. I used to tell him that he should not be afraid of anything because Master was always with him and that no power could attack him and no power could destroy him if he would remember the form of the Master. He was very fond of Master Kirpal and he was very interested in listening to the stories of the Master. Many times he would say that in the nighttime he saw Master Kirpal and he used to tell me about his beautiful dreams about Master Kirpal. After some time he stopped going downstairs to go to the bathroom at night. Instead he started urinating in the rainwater pipe that was on the terrace not far from where we used to sleep and which was near the latrine that we had made and reserved for Master Kirpal. When I asked him why he was doing that, he told me that Master Kirpal had given him darshan and graciously told him, "Gopi, you don't have to go downstairs to use the latrine. You can pee right here in the rainwater drainpipe." When a person says that he has been instructed by Master Kirpal to do that, how can I tell him no? So I told him, "Well, if Master has told you to do that, you can do it, and I don't have any objection." He continued to do that and as a result that rainwater pipe became very dirty.

Master Kirpal did not have any fixed time or program to come to see me. Whenever He would feel like coming, graciously He would come and give me His darshan. One day Master Kirpal came, but since we did not know ahead of time that He was coming, we had not done any cleaning or any other preparations. When He was going to use His latrine, He smelled that bad smell on the terrace and asked me, "What kind of smell is this? Who is making this place dirty?" I said, "This place is made dirty by Your disciple, Your child whom You ordered from within." When I told Him the whole story He laughed and He was very pleased with that boy. He caressed that boy very lovingly. Whenever He would come He would always give that boy a lot of darshan, and Gopi would tell us many things about the Master and about the many experiences that he had with the Master.

These events show the kind of souls that children have, and how, if they are inclined towards the devotion of God, how much grace of the Master they can get. They can get themselves connected with the Almighty Lord very easily. We grown up people have our attention so much spread in this world that it is difficult for us to concentrate, but since the children are innocent and their attention is not spread so much into this world it becomes very easy for them to receive the grace of the Master. In the family we should tell the children good loving stories regarding the love of the Master, regarding the sympathy of the Master and when we tell the children all these good things about the Master we will find that they will receive the Master's protection. Many times the children have to go out of their house into the dark night or go to some strange place, but if we have told them stories about the Master and they have love and faith in the Master, they will remember the

Master, and we will find that the Master has protected them even in the place where nobody else can go and help them. They develop such a remembrance of the Master within, in their mind, that every time they sleep or whenever they sit for meditation they always see the Master. So we should always tell our children about the Master and the love of the Master.

Master became so pleased with that boy Gopi that He gave him parshad and He also told me, "He is a very beautiful and loving soul, but unfortunately he does not have a long life to live on this earthly plane. He will hardly live up to twenty-five years and after that he will die." When He told me that I became very sad because he was a very loving boy, very beautiful and very devoted.

When he was eight years old, his parents came to me and said they wanted their son back because they did not have any other child as beautiful and as loving as he was in their family. I resisted; I told them, "You do not have any right to take this boy back because you have already given him to me," but still they wanted him back. I even called their relatives to see that justice was done, but still they did not listen to anyone and they took that boy. So I had to tell them, "You are taking this boy, but you will repent in the end, because my Master has told me that he does not have a long life to live. Whatever he is doing here with me is good for him and good for his soul and you should leave him with me." However, they did not believe that and they took the boy away.

About fifteen years later that boy spilled some petrol on his body and it caught fire and he had to go into the hospital. While he was in the hospital he did not have any pain. Whenever I went to see him, he regretted that his parents had not behaved justly with me and he blamed himself for leaving me. I lovingly told him, "Dear son, it was not your fault, it was your parents' fault that they took you away from me, but now it is okay." Finally, after remaining in the hospital of Bikaner for a year he left the body.

When he was in the hospital he always told his family that they did not do the right thing. He told them, "You should buy a special jeep and go to the Satsang every month. You should not miss the Satsang even once." When he was taken away by his family there was some tension between me and the family, and they stopped coming to Satsang. However, after he left the body the family started coming to Satsang again. Every month they would come to the Satsang, doing what Gopi told them to do.

The Elderly Disciple Who Asked to be Excused from Meditation

O mind, again and again I will tell you that this is the time for devotion, this is the time for devotion.

Don't forget the place where you were hung upside down. With the support of devotion the Master made you free. Now obey the Master.

Once the time has passed, you will not get it back. Without Naam, you will then repent. Your life is like sugar candy in water.

You came as a guest but sat controlling the place. You forgot the Home where you have to go in the end. This matter won't be taken lightly.

Whoever meditates with a sincere heart, at the end the Master helps him.
O Ajaib, become dependent on Kirpal.
— Tenu Varo Vari Aakhe

Once an elderly initiate of Master Kirpal wanted to ask Master Kirpal that, as he had become old, he should be excused from meditating. He requested that I arrange a meeting with Master Kirpal so he could ask that of Him. I did that and when he saw Master Kirpal he said, "All my worldly responsibilities have been taken care of. I have four sons and they own a very good grocery store and they are well settled, and now I have nothing to do. But I have become old and even the farmers forgive an old bullock. They don't take any work from him, but they feed him. In the same way, now that I have become old, I should be excused from meditation. I should not be told to meditate; I should be given this concession. You should take me without the meditation."

Master Kirpal laughed and said, "You are right that farmers don't make old bullocks work, but if all your responsibilities have been taken care of and you have nothing to do, then why don't you meditate all the twenty-four hours? From now onwards, you should meditate twenty-four hours; all day and night you should be meditating." That old man could not argue and he went back.

That old person used to have the habit of keeping a watch in front of him when he would sit for meditation. Since I knew that he had been told by Master Kirpal to meditate for twenty-four hours, I was surprised to see him using a watch – because when you are told to meditate always, then why do you need to have a watch? So I asked him in front of all the people in the sangat why he used a watch when he had been told by Master to meditate for twenty-four hours. After that he gave up that habit.

I have seen this many times that when Master Kirpal in Satsang would put a lot of emphasis on doing more meditation, when He would say that every satsangi should meditate at least two-and-a-half hours per day, that they should give up thousands of works to sit for meditation and hundreds of works to attend the Satsang, the people would just keep quiet. No one would even nod his or her head. However, when He would say soft words, like every satsangi should do the meditation even if only for two minutes per day, and they will get the benefit, they will get the liberation, then everybody would be very happy. They would fold their hands and say, "Master, thank you very much. We will try to do that." When people are told to meditate more, not many people appreciate that, but when they are told to do a little meditation or less meditation, they like it very much.

Once a girl asked Master Sawan Singh, "What is the need of doing meditation when Satguru is going to liberate us?" Master Sawan Singh replied, "There is no doubt that Master will take you, but at that time you will have much pain, because you will be involved in the habits of the world, and you will find much pain in leaving all that." Master Kirpal Singh used to say that if you want to take a piece of silken cloth off of a thorny bush there is a possibility it will be torn if you take it up at once, but if you take it off slowly, easily, it can be taken off without getting torn. I have seen with my own eyes that in my area the people who did not meditate after coming on this Path and who did not change their habits, no doubt Master came to take them at the time of their death, but still they could not stand in front of the Light, the glory of the Master, and they suffered much pain at that time.

If a child says, "My father has a lot of wealth, so why should I work?" that son's heart is dead. People also criticize him because he is idle. Similarly the disciples should try to carry their own burden. We should not give our burden to the Master. If we give all our work to the Master, it is not bravery on our part. Master Sawan Singh used to say that when people are repeating, "Master will take us, Master will take us," it is just like they are saying, "Give us the wealth, then give us the cart to carry that wealth; You should give us everything."

Praise Just the Master

Earlier I told how whenever any dear one from my area would go to visit Master Kirpal in Delhi, He would ask them about me. If the dear ones had seen me before going to Delhi, they would tell Master about my well-being. However, most of the people did not come to see me before going there and did not understand it was important to do that, and they would tell Master that they hadn't seen me. When He would ask about me, then they would realize that they should have come to see me.

When they would come back, I would ask them about Master, how He was and how His health was. They wouldn't reply to my question, but they would tell how this time in the Satsang there were thousands of people, how there were many loud speakers, how some people were working very hard doing this and that thing, and so forth and so on, but they wouldn't talk about the Master. So I would tell them, "Dear Ones, I am asking you about the well-being of the Master, but you are not telling me anything about Him. Instead you are talking about the loudspeakers there, about the thousands of people and about all of the sevadars. You should praise the Master Power which is working within all the people, within all the sevadars. Who can work on his own if the Master Power is not working within him?" I would tell them, "Why don't we just praise the Master Power, the Master who is working within everybody and because of Whom all this thing is happening. If there is no Master, nobody would have been able to do all this work."

Master Sawan Singh used to say that until you have perfected your meditation, you should never live in the ashram because when the people come to visit the ashram they praise you. They give you name and fame and they will tell you that you are very fortunate one to live here and things like that. You will get caught up in name and fame, and unnecessarily you will be caught up in the egoism and you will feel that you are a real sadhu. In that way, those who are praising you and thanking you for your service, they will take whatever spiritual wealth you have collected by doing the service. They will take all that and you will remain empty-handed.

I used to hear Master Kirpal say this, that "Those who are living near me, who spent a lot of time near me, are like the blood suckers on

Master Kirpal at the World Conference of Religions, February 1970

the cow's udder. Those who are coming from far away are like the calf coming from a distant pasture – they get milk from me."

If one praises any Mahatma or Saint Who has perfected Their meditation, if one praises Them to Their face, They never keep the credit to Themselves, but They always say that this is all because of the grace of Their Master. They always say, "I am a sinner, I am just a very lowly soul like you people, and I didn't do anything. This is all because of my Master." They always pass on the credit to their Master and they do not keep it with them. However, those who have not done the meditation, if one praises them what will they do? They will get puffed up with the praise that one is giving them and they will start thinking that they are something and that is why people are praising them.

The Conferences of Master Kirpal

Many great people, great kings, very learned people, and many other people used to gather around Master Kirpal. They all wanted to take advantage of being around Master because He was very popular and many politicians and other great people use to come to

Prime Minister Indira Gandhi listens to Master Kirpal Singh at the World Conference on Unity of Man, New Delhi, February 1974

Him. Master Kirpal also held many conferences and invited many people to attend, and many renowned leaders did attend. However, instead of getting inspiration for meditation and doing meditation there, the people got the desire of having their picture taken with one of those dignitaries or with Master Kirpal, and no one wanted to sit and do the meditation.

Up to a certain extent, Master's purpose in having the conferences was successful, because as He Himself told me, in India there are so many religions and communities and people fight with each other. One community fights with another community. So that is why Master Kirpal invited and collected the leaders of all the different religions in India. He hoped that by presenting the truth of Naam within them and by sewing them in the same thread of Naam, they would stop fighting with each other and accept the truth.

One time Master Kirpal, in front of a large gathering of the sangat in Ganganagar, said, "I wish, and I have suggested this to the government, that all the monasteries and so-called religious places should be sold and with the money they get from selling those places, they should do things for the public welfare. I will be the first one to sell my place to contribute in that work." However, He also said that the government did not wish to accept that suggestion.

As I said earlier, when Master first came to my ashram He told me that I should just sit inside my room and meditate, that I should not attend any conferences. It was not easy to obey that order, because who does not want to be praised and who does not want to be known in the world? Everybody who was around the Master tried his best to show other people that he was very intimate and close with Master Kirpal. At that time, the mind plays such tricks that nobody wants to sit for meditation when other people are being praised and are brought into the limelight. I was the very fortunate one that He told me I should sit in the room and do meditation, that He told me I should not come to attend any conferences. Masters say we should give up all our support and seek the support of the Master. We should turn our back on the name and fame, and praises of the world, and we should work hard. If quietly you close your eyes and let Master do His work, you will get a lot from the Master.

Master Takes on My Fever

Once Master Kirpal was going to visit my ashram and one or two days ahead of time He sent some of His dear ones in advance to my place. When they came to the ashram I had a very high fever. Seeing my condition, one of them went to Ganganagar and sent a cable to Master Kirpal saying that I was sick. That dear one didn't ask me anything and he didn't tell me that he was going to cable Master; without my approval he did that. As soon as he sent the cable my fever went away and on the other side, Master Kirpal started having a very high fever.

The next day that dear one came to me very happily thinking that he had done a great thing by sending that message to Master. He told me, "I cabled Master about your sickness and now you are free from it." I became very angry with him, because I knew that Master Kirpal had taken on the karma that I was supposed to pay off, and that He was suffering from that fever. So I asked him, "Why did you do this? I didn't tell you to do it!" and I was very upset with him. I told him, "Now Master Kirpal will not come today because He is paying off the karmas which I was supposed to pay." And it so happened Master Kirpal didn't come on that day. The fever was so high that He had to postpone His program. He suffered very much for this poor soul and He didn't come on the day we were expecting him, and He didn't come on the next day either.

On the third day Master did come, but His face was very yellow and pale. He was sick and very weak and He needed some help to get out of His car. In fact it was a very big karma that He was paying off. When He came, because I had told the dear ones that He was not going to come on that day but He would come after a couple of days, the dear ones thought that I was all conscious. They came to Master Kirpal praising me, saying, "We knew that You were not coming because he told us." Master Kirpal was very tired and sick and said, "He told you that I was not coming since it was only because of him that this happened." I apologized to the Master. I told Him, "I didn't want You to carry my karma but this man went and cabled you. Forgive me. I did not know that the cable was sent to You about my condition." Master Kirpal told me, "No, it is all right. Whatever has been done is done."

Sant Satgurus are free from all sufferings and disease but because They are in the love of Their disciples, whether the disciple wants the Master to take the karmas or not, They take over the karma of Their disciples. The Masters take the burden of karmas of the disciples on Their bodies because They are determined to liberate Their disciples in this lifetime.

Asking for the Worldly Things from the Master

O Guru Kirpal Ji, we cannot bear the pains.
Living in the world, we cannot control the mind.

Daily our mind goes on sinning and doesn't care. It never walks straight to the Satsang.
We cannot forget the desires of the mind even for a moment.

Save us from the five thieves, and spread the coolness within the heated souls.
We cannot remove the sins within us.

Hail Kirpal, Hail the Limitless Shabd, Who has liberated millions of souls.

> *Without You the sinking ships cannot be brought to the shore.*
>
> *O True Father, day and night I remember You. Waiting for You I count the days.*
> *Ajaib says, "We cannot forget the qualities of Kirpal."*
>
> — Kirpal Guru Ji Satho

There was a dear one in the village of Ganeshgarh who expressed a lot of love for Master Kirpal and he asked me, "Can you kindly bring Master Kirpal to see me in my home?" I was impressed by the love he had shown for the Master, and since he had invited Him with much eagerness and faith, Master Kirpal decided to go there. Even though Master knew why that man was inviting Him, and He knew everything that was going to happen over there, still He agreed to go. He said, "Okay, I will come to your home, because I have to fulfill your desire too." As it was only four or five miles away from my place, I also went.

So when Master Kirpal went to visit that home, there was one very old man there who had been on his deathbed for the previous eight days. He was suffering so much that his family wanted him to die very soon. As soon as Master entered their home, they all took him to the bed of that old man and requested Master to help him so that he might die peacefully and soon.

After that, they had a bullock that had gone crazy and was also very old, and now it had become very difficult for them to take care of him, so they wanted to get rid of him too. So they took Master Kirpal to the bullock and told Him to shower grace on that bullock also. Then they took Master Kirpal into their home to serve Him some tea. In India it is the custom that if anyone comes to your home, you offer them tea and things like that, and so they had arranged for tea. In fact, Master Kirpal was not interested in drinking tea as He had just had his tea before leaving my place. Still they compelled Him to drink the tea. Now that person who invited Master Kirpal had a little wound, a boil, on his leg and he had the desire that Master should look at that boil so that he could get some grace from Him. Before serving the tea, that person showed his leg to Master. He said, "Well Master, before You have tea, please cast Your gracious eyes on this wound so that it may become all right, and then You can have Your tea."

Masters are the perfect beings and They don't mind such things, but if there is any true devotee around, he won't like it. When something like that is happening in front of him, he cannot bear that. My beloved Lord was an Ocean of Love and I was a devotee of love. In my whole life I did not ask for anything but love from the Master, and since He was an Ocean of Love and I was a devotee of love, He gave me all His love. When I saw what that disciple was asking of Master Kirpal, I did not feel good about it. I could not bear what that disciple was saying, I could not control myself and I became so upset. I said to him, "Well, dear one, you just keep your tea. We don't want your tea. What kind of disciple are you? You could easily cure your wound by going to a doctor, you could buy two pennies worth of ointment and make your wound better, but here you are asking the Master to do that for you! God Almighty has come to your home and this is what you are asking from Him?"

Master sat there quietly. He didn't say even a word. So those people said, "Well, why do you bother? When Master is not saying anything, who are you to bother?" Master sat there quietly and took on His head all the karmas that they wanted Him to carry. When He came back to the ashram, only I knew how much He suffered because of all those karmas. When we came back Master's eyes were swollen. He suffered so much. He couldn't urinate and in that way He carried all the karmas of that family. Only I know this because I was present with Master and only I know how much Master had to suffer on account of those people's karmas.

So just imagine how much that cup of tea was worth! What was that disciple asking from the Master for that one cup of tea? Usually we people do not meditate, or we meditate very little. However, we have so many desires that we present to our Masters, and when those desires do not get fulfilled, then we lose faith in the Master. We cannot call this having true love for the Master. It is like we are working for the Master and asking payment for it. Guru Nanak Sahib has said that if we are asking for anything other than the Naam, it is like we are inviting all the sufferings and problems, because contentment, happiness and peace are only in the Naam.

There was a disciple of Guru Gobind Singh who had a horse that got constipated and became very sick. If that horse had died, it would have been difficult for that disciple for he did not have any other animals to do his work, and he would have become very poor. So he prayed to one of the ordinary gods and goddesses, saying, "I will donate two rupees in your name if you remove the sickness of my horse."

When he was praying to that ordinary god, another disciple of Guru Gobind Singh heard him. The second disciple said, "O man, you are the disciple of a Master, and still you are praying to an ordinary god to take care of your horse? Why don't you pray to the Master?" The first disciple replied, "I am praying to this god to remove the constipation of my horse, and I am saying that I will donate two rupees in his name. I will donate those two rupees only when he will remove the constipation of the horse. How can I ask my Master to do this dirty job, my Master Who is the owner of Sach Khand, Who is much purer than everything else in this world? How can I ask Him for this little thing, when I can make this god do this work for only two rupees?" So the true disciples of the Master, who appreciate the glory of the Master, never pray for such little things. If they are ever in any circumstance where they have to pray to the Master, they never do that because they do not want to use the power of the Master for their worldly problems.

Even when God rewards us for our good karmas by bringing us into the company of the perfect Saints and we get Naam Initiation from the perfect Master, what do we start doing? Instead of doing the devotion of God, we start asking for the worldly things. Someone says, "May I get this thing, may Master bless my son, may You cure my daughter or sister," and things like that. Instead of taking advantage of the human birth, instead of doing the devotion of God, instead of collecting the pearl of Naam, we go on collecting shells and in that way we do not take advantage of the reward of our good karmas.

Kabir Sahib said that the Master wants everyone, but no one wants the Master. When they come to see the Master, either they come for name and fame, or they come for worldly things. They always request, "Master shower grace on us, do this or that for us," but they do not come for the Master. They do not ask the Master for that true thing, that real gift, for which the Masters have come into the world. The Masters have come into this world to take our soul back to the Real Home, but no one comes to the Master asking for that precious gift.

In Ganganagar it became the practice that if anybody became sick, people would sit in meditation and pray to the Master to remove the sickness. I saw this for a couple of days and then I told people that it is a very bad thing, because we cannot carry our own burden, we cannot do the meditation and we want our Master to carry the burden of our little sicknesses also. When I said that, most of the people didn't like it, but some people who were real lovers of the Master, who loved Him very much, they accepted that.

On another occasion when Master Kirpal came to the ashram, a couple came with a young girl and they asked me if they could see Master because they wanted Him to shower grace on that little girl because she cried all night. I told them, "Either you should take this girl to a doctor, or you should see if she is hungry in the night. You should take care of her." I lovingly advised them not to put that burden on the Master, but they felt very bad and they thought I was not letting them see the Master. So this is our condition. We want the Master to take care of our sicknesses, we want the Master to take care of our children, we don't want to do anything ourselves, and we want our Master to carry all our burden.

Master Sawan Singh used to say that those people who ask for worldly things after coming to the Master, what are they going to get from the Master? It is better for them to stay home. In fact, when we ask for so many worldly things, we lose our faith. When we get sick, and if we are asking the Master to cure us, the Master knows what is best for us, what is beneficial for us, and He does not want us to come back into this suffering world again. If He were to listen to all our prayers and if He were to grant us all our wishes, He would never be able to take our soul back to our Real Home even if He were here for thousands of years.

The Naam that the Master gives us is like a philosopher's stone and our mind is like the iron. Master has given us this philosopher's stone so that touching the mind with the Naam we may remove all the impurities of the mind. However, instead of touching the mind with the Naam, we don't use the Naam; instead we go on asking the Master for the worldly things. After giving the Initiation the Master expects a lot from His disciples and He always looks forward to that time when the disciples will rise above the organs of senses and the mind and will do the meditation and purify themselves. This is why whenever the Masters come to the disciples They always expect to see the disciples in a better condition. But unfortunately, since the disciples do not use that philosopher's stone — they do not make their mind do the Simran, they do not rise above the tricks of the mind — they always remain in the same condition and that disappoints the Master.

Remaining in the Will of the Master

Two people came to see beloved Master in my home, but they had to leave soon because they were in the service. However, Master told them not to go back. It was very hard for them to accept that, because they were afraid of their officer. Later on we found out that the bus that they would have been riding on met with an accident, and no one in that bus was saved, or if they were saved, they had very serious injuries. Then they realized that Master wanted to save them, and that is why He told them not to go on that bus.

The Master knows better than us. The disciple should always be making this prayer, he should always be requesting the Master, "O Master, may I always live in Your Will." The reality is that we do not know what is good for us, whether riches are good for us or poverty is good for us, whether sickness is good for us or good health is good for us. We do not even know whether the pains are good for us or the happiness is good for us, even though outwardly we all seek happiness, we all ask for the comforts. We all ask for happiness, even though we do not know what is good for us. When we do not know what is good for us, then why not remain happy in His Will? Why not bow down to Him and His Will?

Earlier I told how in the Army there is a rule that whatever order you have been given, it is your duty to carry that out first, and only after having done the work can you ask questions about it. In the Path of the Masters, the same principle applies. In the Path of the Masters, whatever order you get from your Master, it is your duty first is to carry that out, and if you have any questions or complaints or if you want to say anything about that order, you should say that only after you have carried out that order. We should start doing the work even before the Master finishes giving His orders, and if we have any questions or complaints, we can come later and ask the Master. The Master never gives useless orders: He tells us to do only those things that are beneficial to us.

Master Showers Grace on the Souls

After coming He cooled the heated hearts by showering the rain of Naam.
The true Satguru has come to remove the pains of the suffering ones.

Master Kirpal Singh

*The place where Beloved Kirpal resides is blooming.
Time after time He planted the plants of Naam and gave
the water of Satsang.*

*Hail, Hail Beloved Kirpal! He attached the dear ones to
  His feet.
Showing the path of five Shabds, He united them in Him.
Removing the differences of duality, He taught only one
  Shabda.*

*Beloved Kirpal is present everywhere, absorbed in the
  eyes.
The Beautiful One who is present in all is obtained by
  the rare ones.
He taught One Shabad, after making us forget all the
  knowledge of the world.*

*Servant Ajaib makes this prayer, "Listen O Beloved Kirpal,
We have fallen at Your Door. Save our honor, O Giver.
Filling the jholi of Naam, He taught to fill the jholis of
  Naam.*

— Tapde Hirde Thare Aake

How can I describe the glory and grace of my beloved Master Lord Kirpal? I cannot describe His greatness enough through words. When He wanted to shower grace upon the dear ones, His grace knew no limits; His grace did not have any beginning or any end. He showered so much grace upon all the dear ones who came in contact with Him.

Once Master was giving Initiation in Ganganagar and there was a dear one named Bagirath who came to get Initiation. He sat there as the Initiation was starting, but after Master had given the instructions and given out the Words, he got up and came out of the Initiation. He told me that he felt as if his body and clothes were on fire and he could not stand it and that was why he could not continue. I told him, "This opportunity will not come again and you should try and sit here and take this Initiation." However he said, "No, this is not in my control and I am going home." I told Beloved Master about this and Master told me, "Okay, let him go."

A very muddy road led to his home that was about thirteen or fourteen miles away and one small bus used to run there. He sat on the bus and told the bus driver to drive very fast so he could get home as soon as possible because he was not feeling well. However, since the road was not good and the bus had to drive through the mud and the sand, it took him one hour to get to his village. As soon as he stepped into his home, he fell down and he told his wife, "Now I am going, and those who have come to take me, they have very dangerous faces. I don't know whether they are going to punish me or what. But I am also seeing one old man — the Master — with a white beard, white turban and black coat." He told his family all the signs of beloved Master Kirpal, and he said, "He looks very kind and He is going to help me. He has come to take me and now I am going." Then he left the body.

The next day when I came to know about him, I reported it to the Master. Master said, "It was not in his fate and God was not gracious on him, so he did not get the full Initiation. Even though he came here, was accepted, and sat here, it was not in his fate to get the Initiation in this lifetime. That is why he got up and left. But, he was taken care of by the Master. He had come in contact with the Master once, and he will not go below the human body. Once again he will get the human body in which he will get the perfect Initiation."

So that man was just given the Names, the Simran, and he was just told how to do the meditation, but he was not even given one sitting of meditation. He did not complete the Initiation, but still the perfect Master came to take care of his soul. All those who come in contact with the perfect Masters and get Initiation from Them, even if they die right after the Initiation, or even if the Master leaves right after their Initiation, they are under the protection of the Master and their soul is always taken by the Master. We cannot describe the glory of the Master in the full sense. When Master gives the Initiation He thinks about it very deeply and after understanding a lot, He gives the Initiation. Then He always takes care of the souls that are initiated by Him. We should never have any doubt about the graciousness of the Master, for the reality is that whenever God showers grace on the souls, He Himself comes down in the form of a Master. Guru Nanak says, "God Himself takes the form of a Sadh. Whenever He wants to shower grace on the souls He comes down in the body of a Sadh." Kabir says, "The Creator is speaking through the human body." No doubt He has the human body, but still He is more than man and He is above all men. There are many people sitting in the Satsang. Some of them are clever and some are not, but still they are all called humans. In the same way, the Master has the human body, but He is above the limits of man and He is above the limits of mind and matter. So Master Kirpal was such a giver of grace that no words can describe His greatness.

ELEVEN

Into the Underground Room:
My Soul Mingles With Kirpal

"Are You Awake or Asleep?"

Now my Master has given to me through the eyes.

I wander to door after door — no one cares for me.
I neither understand myself as living nor dead.
My Master has made me alive.

I am the ignorant one — I do not know anything.
I do not recognize the Glory of the Master.
He has converted me from dirt into gold.

I do not see anything with my eyes;
The night is dark and there is no way.
My Master has illuminated me.

Satguru has come to my home.
He has awakened my sleeping fortune.
Ajaib has been taken up by Kirpal Satguru.
— Ab Mohe Nainan Syo Guru Diya

As I have described earlier, Baba Bishan Das, my first Master, was very strict. Whenever I used to go to him, he would treat me very strictly. Whenever I would give him a donation, he would give me a beating, and he never allowed me to even have a cup of tea from his ashram. Baba Bishan Das made my life, because if he had not been so strict with me, I would not have maintained the discipline. I would not have improved my life, so it was he who made my life. However, when I met Beloved Master Kirpal, He was full of love. He was gracious and gave me all the love I wanted, all the love I was looking for.

Once He made me sleep in the same room with Him. We had a very big bed and I was lying down with Him but I was not sleeping. I was looking at Him, into His eyes, and He was looking at me. At about 1:00 or 1:30 that morning He suddenly asked me, "Are you awake or are you sleeping?" I told Him, "No, I am not awake. I have been sleeping for ages and ages." Then He called me near to Him, telling me, "Come on, come here." We had a chair there and He sat on the bed and He told me to sit on the chair. He looked into my eyes, very deeply. He was so gracious on me that, with only that one look, He awakened my soul. He showered so much grace that He awakened me for my whole life. Then He smiled and said, "The Satguru has come into this world and He is calling all the people, 'Awake, everybody should get up.'"

Guru Nanak says, "Whoever is liberated is liberated through the eyes." Master Kirpal always said, "Spirituality is always given and received through the eyes." In the Way of the Saints, eye gives to eye. This is the matter of Master and disciple. Everything is given through the eyes and there is no other medium through which Spirituality can be given. He was gracious; He gave me through the eyes and the soul of this poor one was awakened.

Master Kirpal Gives Me the Duty to Continue His Mission

Once Master Kirpal was going to travel from Ganganagar to Karanpur, which was a long way. I thought that maybe He should go alone in His car so that He could lie down and rest in the back seat. At that time He was not well physically and He was very tired. The night before He had spent all His time talking to people and all that day He had worked hard giving Satsang and meeting with many people, so I wanted Him to be able to rest in His car. However, Master called me and said, "I want to talk to you about something important." I told Him, "Master, please rest because You have given so much time to the other people. You should rest." I told him I would go in my jeep. However, He insisted, and He took my hand and took

Master Kirpal Singh on tour in India

me to His car, saying, "No, you come. I want to talk to you about something important."

For the next two hours He talked about the time when His Master left the body and what His own condition was at that time. He told me all about the circumstances in which He was given the work to do by Master Sawan Singh. He told me the things Master Sawan Singh told Him when Sawan Singh gave Him the orders to do the work of Naam Initiation. He told me that there are many orders that the Masters give to the disciples and the disciples obey those orders even though they

do not want to because it is for the good of the people. He said, "When My Master told me to do Initiation, I told Him that I could not do that, but He insisted and said that I would have to do it. He told me, 'Look here, Kirpal Singh, there will be many people who can explain the theory in a very good way, but just explaining the theory is not enough. It cannot take you above. Giving the Initiation is not only explaining the theory; it is taking on the responsibility for the souls. Because those who are only explaining the theory have not meditated, they will not have true knowledge and they will mislead the souls. It is difficult to find someone who has meditated and who can make others meditate. I don't want my teachings to be lost in the world; I am giving this job to You to make sure this perfect science does not disappear and so that my teachings remain alive and are given to the people. I am giving this work to You and You will have to do it.' At that time I did not say anything. I just bowed down my head in front of Him and accepted whatever He had to say."

When Master Sawan Singh gave this responsibility to Master Kirpal, He asked His dear ones to count and tell Him how many people were initiated. He was told that about 125,000 people had been initiated, hearing which Master Sawan Singh said, "Kirpal Singh, I have done half of Your work. Now You will have to initiate the other half."

Hearing this, Master Kirpal was surprised and He felt as if the ground was slipping from under His feet. At that time He wept in front of His Master and said, "Master, You be the one to do the other half. You do the rest of the work too." But Master Sawan Singh said, "No, You will have to do that." Master Kirpal replied, "Let me become the pipe and whatever water You will send to me, I will just let it pass through me and give it to the people. Whatever grace You will give to me, I will give to the people." Master Kirpal could not refuse the order of Master Sawan Singh, but He made this prayer to Him, saying, "Master, You please sit here. You live in this world, because You look very beautiful sitting on that throne."

During the last days of Master Sawan on this plane, His health was not very good. The sangat used to implore Him to cure Himself and to pray to Master Baba Jaimal Singh to keep Him in this world for the sake of the sangat. Master Sawan Singh used to say that He could not make this request, as this would affect His discipleship. Master Kirpal Singh would always pray to Master Sawan Singh that He should remain there physically and guide all the dear ones. He used to beg Master Sawan Singh, "We cannot bear the sufferings You have to suffer. Kindly shower grace on us and cure Yourself so that the blessings of Your physical presence may always remain on our heads." One day, looking at Master Kirpal Singh's love, Master Sawan called Him and asked Him to sit in meditation right next to Him. Master Sawan Singh said, "You always ask me to cure myself and remain on this plane. Today the decision is going to be made in Sach Khand. Come and sit in meditation here by my bed and see with your own eyes what is being decided for me in the Court of the Lord." When Master Sawan made Master Kirpal Singh sit in meditation right by His bed and made him see the decision which was being made in the Court of God, Master Kirpal saw that in Sach Khand all the perfect Masters who had been to this mortal world — Guru Nanak, Kabir, Shamaz Tabrez, Maulana Rumi, Tulsi Sahib, Swami Ji Maharaj, Paltu Sahib and others — had gotten together, because They all have so much love for each other, They are like good friends. They had gotten together there and They were all discussing whether Master Sawan Singh should be left in this world for some more time or not. All the Masters agreed that Master Sawan Singh could remain on this plane for some more time. But Baba Jaimal Singh did not agree to that and He was against it. He said, "No. Baba Sawan Singh has already taken so much burden on Himself. At present the conditions of the world are not favorable. No

Baba Sawan Singh presiding at Satsang, with His gurumukh son, Sant Kirpal Singh Ji, giving the discourse

more burden should be placed on Him and He should be brought back."

So when Master Kirpal Singh saw all that and when He finished His meditation, Master Sawan Singh asked Him, "Did You see now what They have decided for me?" Master Kirpal could not even say a word; He just bowed His head in front of Master Sawan Singh and accepted His Will. After Master Sawan Singh made Him see all these things within, Master Kirpal looked into the love-filled eyes of Beloved Sawan which gave Him so much intoxication that, as Master Kirpal said, "that intoxication cannot be described in words. At that time He lovingly cast His gracious sight on me — and that darshan was so full of love that it always remains with me. The peace and intoxication which I received at that time was more than I had gotten even after sitting at His feet for my whole life." Master Sawan gave Master Kirpal all His spiritual wealth, and after that the eyes of Master Sawan Singh closed and started looking within, and did not open again.

Master Kirpal was not happy to do that work. Those meditators who meditate and go within do not become happy when they are given this job, because they know the burden which the Master carries. They are not anxious to become the Master and do this work because they know what duty they will have to perform and how much burden they will have to take on their shoulders if they become the Master. Indeed it is very difficult to discharge this duty, and when the Master gives this order to the one who has to do this work, his soul trembles. He cries and begs at the feet of the Master that his Master continue in the physical body so the sangat may keep getting the benefit of His darshan. He desires and makes every possible effort to prevent the Master from giving him this job. Even the smallest thought of the Master's leaving is not less than his own death. He desires that His Master always remain over his head even on the physical plane. But when they are given the responsibility by the Master, when they are given this work, when they are given the orders by the Master, they cannot refuse their Master and they accept whatever comes in the Will of their Master. So Master Kirpal told me, "I did not want to do the work which I am now doing, but I had to obey the orders of Baba Sawan Singh and I had to do the work. My Master told me that I had to continue His mission. Otherwise I had no interest in it."

So the disciple who has been appointed by the Master to do the seva of giving Initiation knows that there is no other sin other than not obeying the commandment of the Master. Because they are bound by the love of the Master and because they have to obey the commandments of the Master, they bow down to the orders of the Master and they accept this responsibility. However, such disciples, who work in the place of the Master, never get involved in criticism and they never form parties and they never create any kind of divisions in the sangat. In fact they are full of humility and they have so much love for the Master in their within that this love is coming out from every single cell of their body. Even though they are not interested in doing that work which has been given to them by the Master, but because they are bound in the love of the Master, they have to obey that commandment of the Master and that is why they do it.

Only those people who do not meditate form the parties and desire to become the Master. They do not know that they will have to settle the accounts of the souls with the Negative Power and that they will have to take the karmas of the souls on their own body. Since they do not know what job they will have to do, they are anxious to become the Master, and that is why they form parties and criticize other people.

When Master Sawan Singh left this earthly plane and the physical separation from Master Sawan Singh happened it became so unbearable for Master Kirpal that He left everything. At that time He quietly left the dera of Master Sawan Singh at Beas; He did not quarrel over the seat of the Master and He did not quarrel over the property of the Master, but on the contrary He left His own house in the dera. Master Kirpal had made a very beautiful house in the dera of Master Sawan Singh, but Master Kirpal told me that He could not even look at the house that He Himself had made. He just bowed down to that place and peacefully He left and, in the remembrance of His Master, He went to the forest of Rishikesh where He did His devotion. The dear ones who went to Rishikesh to bring Master Kirpal back for the benefit of the sangat, only they know how difficult that was and how hard it was for them to convince Master Kirpal to come back to the world for the benefit of the sangat.

When Master Kirpal was telling me all those things, at that time my heart and my body were trembling and I felt as if the earth below me was moving away. I was wondering why He was telling me all these things. I asked Him, "Maharaj Ji, what kind of things are You talking about? Why are You saying all these things to me?" He said, "These very things will help you in the future." I got the hint that He was going to tell me the same thing, and I was so terrified that I felt like opening the door and jumping out of the car. However, He held me very tightly and suddenly He told me, "You will have to give out the message of Truth to the people."

I wept in front of Him and told Him, "Master, You know that I do not know anyone in this world. I do not have as much worldly knowledge as You do. When even You who are such a great being and You who own so much worldly knowledge, when You are opposed and criticized by the people, where do I stand? People will criticize me, and I do not have any worldly knowledge; how will I be able to do all this work? I request that You always stay with us, and that we may always enjoy Your grace. You remain here and do Your work, and we will be very happy just sitting with You." He embraced me and said, "No, you should not worry about that, because when a bad person does not stop doing his bad deeds, why should a good person stop doing his good deeds? You have to do this work." He told me, "Nowadays propaganda and preaching are at their highest, and educated people with the support of parties will become gurus. They will make true false and false true. They themselves will be in illusion because of not meditating and will lead others into the ditch of ignorance. To deceive someone's soul is the greatest sin." Emphatically He said that the Path of Truth must continue, so that the needs of those souls who have the real desire for God may be fulfilled and He told me, "Now you have to do this work. Be careful and don't let my teachings be destroyed in this world. You have to continue to spread my teachings in this world."

Only I know how I felt at that time, because I had not done the meditation to become the Master. When I was meditating on the first Two Words, and even when I perfected the meditation through the first two planes there was no question about being the Master and doing this job, because one who has perfected the meditation of the first Two Words cannot get permission to do this work as he is still not perfect. So at the time He gave me the orders to do this work, feeling very sad I told Him, "Master, I did not do the meditation for this sake. I did the meditation because I was a devotee of Your feet and I wanted to sit in Your lap. I wanted to be a honeybee of Your love and a lover of Your feet; I feel happiness doing that, and I do not want to do this work."

He did not look at my weeping. He did not look at my trembling, but He embraced me and told me, "Don't worry, I am always with you and nothing bad will happen. Your work is only to convey the Truth." He put His hand on His chest and He said, "It is my work to liberate, and I will liberate all those who will be initiated by you."

I say this from the depth of my heart, that if I were to impose my wishes, the wishes of my heart on the Master, I would not have been given the work of giving the Initiation. I would not have been given the seva of running His mission. I did not do the devotion to become the Master or to do the work that I was given to do. I did the devotion of God only because I heard that as the child is dear to the mother, in the same way, the devotees are dear to God Almighty. I just wanted to become one of the dear ones of God and that is why I did the devotion. I thought that when I did the meditation and perfected myself in it, I would meet God and that I would always remain connected to God. After that I would get peace and all my worries and problems would be over.

I did not have any idea of this seva when I was doing the devotion. I was very innocent and I did not know what was going to happen. I was not expecting anything like this when I was doing the devotion. I did not suffer hunger and thirst and do the meditation hoping to do this work. If I had known that I would have to carry the burden of the dear ones' karmas, and if I had known that Master would make me work as He did, I would not have gone inside and I would not have done the meditation. I was very sure within myself that my Master was perfect and that He would definitely liberate my soul and take me to Sach Khand and that there would be no question of coming back into this world again. But I did not know that after my inner vision was opened, that He would give me the responsibility of this work. If I had known that after perfecting myself in meditation I would be given such a big responsibility of taking care of the souls, of doing the Satsangs for the dear ones, of flying in airplanes, of having the restless days and nights going here and there to meet the people and do all this work, I would never have meditated in the way I did. If I had known that I would have been given such a big responsibility I would never have meditated.

But after I did the meditation, when He gave me the orders to continue His mission, only I know what happened within me and how I felt. Within myself I felt like a thief who is caught red-handed. He cannot run away, he cannot sit down. He is confused and he does not know what to do. He cannot do anything; he just waits there for the judgment to come. At that time I felt the same way.

Master Tells Me to Give Initiation, and I Ask Him to Show the Dear Ones His True Form

We have not seen anyone like our beloved Satguru.
My Satguru is great. We haven't seen anyone as great as Him.

He is the owner of both of the worlds; He is the One Who dwells in the hearts of the world.
He is the knower of all the hearts. He is the One Who knows the matters of all the hearts.
His form is the Form of the Shabd, such a Form we have seen with our own eyes.

He alone who is capable of seeing Him, sees Him. And when he sees Him, keeps seeing Him (becomes wonderstruck).

His form is loving, His face is loving, and the beholder becomes His after seeing Him.
He is the attractive one, the One Who is liked by the mind. Such a Beloved we all have seen.

Probably every eye saw Him, but of course through his own angle of vision.
But he who saw him lovingly, came out of this midstream.
He is a Great Ferryman. We have seen Him taking a fully loaded ship.

Dear one, Guru Kirpal is that Ferryman. He is the beloved of Beloved Sawan.
Dear one, Kirpal is the Ocean of Grace. Ajaib loves Him more than his life.
He is the most Beautiful One. One who saw Him became His.

— Hamare Pyare Satguru Jaisa

The first time Master Kirpal told me to give Initiation to some people, He asked me to explain the theory to them and teach them the Simran. I stood up and folding my hands I lovingly requested Him, "O True Lord, You are the True Emperor. In Your home there is no lacking of anything. Why don't You show them Your Real Form? You should give Your open darshan to all these people who have come here for Initiation."

I spoke those words remembering one very unique experience of my life. I can never forget that experience because it was the time that He gave me His open darshan.

At the time of that experience I had asked Master Kirpal, "Bulleh Shah called his Master the great deceiver. He said that if you want to do the robbery you should do it in the home of God, and if you want to deceive, the greatest deceiver is the Master. So why is this? Even though Inayat Shah, Bulleh Shah's Master was Almighty, He was the All-Owner of the whole creation, and Bulleh Shah knew that, why did he refer to Him as the great deceiver?"

Beloved Lord Kirpal answered that when the disciple goes within and sees the Truth, the Reality of the Master inside, then he comes to realize that the Master is the greatest deceiver. Is it not a great deception that He is one thing and He is telling you that He is something else? Outwardly we see Him breathing like us, walking like us and we see Him paying off all the karmas. We see Him going through all the sickness and disease, although those karmas, those diseases are not His own. He does it for the sake of the other people, but we see Him performing all the things just as we do.

But He is not what we see Him to be. He is the All-Owner, but still He becomes so small and humble in front of us. He tells us, "I am not your Master. I have just connected you with the Shabd. Shabd is your Master." But He Himself is the Shabd. Is that not the great deception? The deceivers say one thing, but they have something different in their hearts. In the same way, the Masters are something different than what They tell us. Outwardly They seem to be just like us, but inwardly They are not what we see, They are different.

At the time I asked Him this question, it was wintertime and in the winter the days are short and it becomes dark early. It was around 8:00 or 9:00 p.m. and Master Kirpal was sitting in a room wrapped up in a quilt. It was very cold and He was sitting wrapped up, as if He was feeling a lot of cold. So when I asked Him that question about Bulleh Shah, He removed His quilt. Even though it was so cold over there, and I was sitting on the chair and He was sitting on the bed, still I could feel the warmth, the heat, coming from His whole body. His whole body became full of light and His forehead and His eyes were also pouring out immense light. It was so strong, the light was so strong, that the whole room was filled with the warmth of that light.

I can never forget that experience because it was at that time that He gave me His open darshan.

Indra Mati was a disciple of Kabir Sahib. When she rose above the body and went in the inner planes she saw that Kabir Sahib was sitting on the throne of Almighty God. She bowed down at the feet of Kabir and said, "If You had told me earlier that You were the All-Owner, the Almighty One, why did I have to go through the hardship of doing the meditation and all those things? I would have just bowed down at Your feet at that time." Kabir Sahib said, "If I had told you earlier that I was the All-Owner, you would not have believed me. Now you can do whatever you want."

So when you see Who the Master is, what He is inside, and when you are also able to see Him outside in His great glory, then you become small and humble, because you realize that He is the greatest of all. He is the Owner of all Creation, and you realize that you don't have any honor, any name or fame, and you don't have any egoism, because you know that He is the greatest of all. When you have seen and realized the greatness of the Master, when you have seen how every single hair of His body is emitting light, every single particle of His body is full of light; do you think you can be proud of anything you have? All the pride and ego vanishes when you see and witness the Reality of the Master.

So, remembering that incident I said, "Why don't You give them Your open darshan? Because if You give them Your open darshan all the disputes between the pundits and mullahs will be finished and there will be peace all over. The saffron which the pundit has mixed to put the mark on people's forehead will just be left there and he won't use it. The mullah will forget to make people arise in the name of the Lord, and the bhai of the gurdwara will also stop what he is doing. In every home they will talk only about You. So if You do not want to shower Your grace on all this world, at least do so on these dear ones who are sitting for Initiation. Why don't You tell them Who You really are and why don't You give them the open darshan?"

At that time Master did not become puffed up, but with a very stern look He told me, "Don't make them tear off my clothes! Just do what I have told you to do."

"The Fragrance Will Come Out from Your Body"

At that time when Master Kirpal told me that I would have to keep running His mission after Him, He made many prophecies in front of the people. One evening He said, "The time will come when the fragrance will come out from your body, and that fragrance will cross all the oceans and people will be attracted by that fragrance. Many people will come from America and Europe and they will become your disciples. Those people will make you fly in the airplanes and you will go to many places and many people will come to you."

Hearing those prophecies, people started laughing and at that time nobody believed in His words. Some people said, "Master knows many ways of pleasing people, and He is just saying that so Sant Ji will be pleased." They asked, "How is it possible that the fragrance will come out from the body of a human being?" One man even said, "Master, You say that people will make him fly in an airplane, but now nobody is making him sit in a jeep!"

When Masters utter such words, at that time we people don't believe in what they are saying. Master replied, "Whatever is the order from the Court of God, I have said only that. It is up to you if you want to believe this. If you don't want to believe, it is all right, don't believe. But the time will come and then everyone will believe." If the people who were present there had understood what the Master was saying at the time, they would have been given a lot. People don't know that the Master has contact with God and whatever He speaks, in fact God Himself is speaking through Him.

Master Tells Me to Leave Kunichuk

As was mentioned before, in Kunichuk there was a lot of property that belonged to the ashram and I had made a very big, very beautiful building there. I had invested a lot of money in making that; it was a three-story building and even now there is no building in that area which can compare with it. When a Master makes a beautiful ashram, some of the dear ones forget the Master and they see only the ashram. In that way there were people who used to go there to see me who bothered more about the property and the house where I lived than they bothered about me. They would all look at those things more than they would look at me.

Because that place was on the highway, it was very convenient for the people to come there, especially for those using that highway. One time, a military officer going somewhere on that highway stopped there. We lovingly welcomed him and we offered him some food. He looked at all the buildings and things, and then when he was having the food, these thoughts came into his mind: "This Saint has such a large property and he has not gotten married. He does not have any child and has no successor or heir, so to whom is he going to leave this property after his death?" So after he ate the food, he said, "Baba Ji, one thought is bothering me. I do not see anyone here who could inherit your property, since you did not get married. I am wondering who is going to get all this property and who is going to be your successor? Have you written any will in favor of someone?" I laughed and in a humorous way I said, "I was waiting only for you. If you want I can give everything to you." Then I lovingly told him, "Dear One, you see that you came here and I served you selflessly, but you are looking at my property. Why are you worried about it?" So people used to come and bother me with questions like that.

Late one afternoon, in the evening, when Master Kirpal had come to the ashram to visit me, He asked how much land I had and how big the property was. I told Him to come with me onto the roof and I showed Him the boundary of my land was fifty *kilas* or thirty-two acres. I told Him that I owned all that property. Then He went all around and, wearing His glasses, inspected everything, all of the many buildings and all the things I had. Then very lovingly He said, "I am very pleased with all that you have, but you should leave all these things at once and go away from here." He told me that even the Saints make one mistake. He said, "Even after coming to the physical plane my Master Baba Sawan Singh made this mistake. I also made this mistake of making the big buildings. Even though I was fond of living in the jungles and I did not want to make the property or the buildings, but still I made them and now I see that you are also making the same mistake. So while I am still in the body, you leave everything here and go to the village of 16 PS and make your residence over there. Meditate over there. You do not need to come to see me. I will come there by myself whenever I want to see you."

Master Sawan Singh used to say, "The Master does not take anything from the disciple but at the same time He does not leave anything with the disciple." As I had requested Master to take my ashram, my wealth, my everything, I would have been very happy if He had accepted all those things. However, He didn't take anything from me, but then He didn't leave anything with me. He made me leave all those things. He told me, "Don't take anything from here. Whatever animals, cows and other things that you have, you should not sell them, but distribute them as donations to the daughters of the people, to be used as dowries. Don't take even a little thing from this place; go to village 16 PS and meditate." At that time I had taken off my turban that I had just tied and I just had a small piece of cloth on my head. When I went to the closet to pick up my turban, to put the turban back on my head, He said, "Didn't you hear that I told you to leave everything here? I didn't tell you to take even your turban." So with whatever piece of cloth I had on my head I left that place immediately and I went that same evening to 16 PS.

Baba Sawan Singh also used to say, "I touch my ears. God forbid, may the Master not put anyone to the test!" Just imagine if someone has come into your life, and if you have a very good house, if you have many acres of land, and if that person comes to you and he tells you, "Leave everything and go away from here," without assuring you that he will give you more, or that he will give you some other property, how hard it will be for you to obey that! Just imagine how hard such a test would be! At that time, when He gave me the orders to go to 16 PS, I saw that my mind hesitated. On the worldly level it was very difficult to obey that order and when He gave that order, for once the heart felt it, for once my heart shook. In my mind a lot went on happening, but at the same time, from within, I remembered the words of Master Sawan Singh, who used to say that when a potter is making a pot, he hits the pot from outside, but inside he also keeps another hand to give it protection, to give it support. In the same way, whenever the Master puts a disciple to the test, at the same time, from within, He is supporting the disciple, but only a few people can understand that. So then my soul said, "You have been longing for this person all your life. Now when you have met Him, can't you obey Him?" I thought, "Now it is up to Him. Whether He wants me to be in the shade, whether He wants me to be in the sun, wherever He wants me to be, now He is responsible. So whatever He is telling me to do, I should do that," and I left everything as it was.

Just as a goldsmith checks and tests the purity of gold by rubbing it on some kind of stone or some kind of instrument, in the same way the Masters also check the purity of the person within whom They are going to manifest the Naam. They want to know whether that person is greedy or not, whether he is able to sacrifice all or not.

You know that when a storm comes, even big trees get uprooted. In the same way, when the Master gives the order, it is not in the reach of everyone to obey the order, the commandment of the Master; only he on whom the Master is gracious can obey the commandment of the Master. So Master put me through a very difficult test, and it was by His grace and His own bravery that He made me pass that test. It was not my courage, my bravery that I was able to pass that test. He Himself put me to the test and He Himself made me pass that test.

The Orders to Meditate

After showering grace on me, He came to 16 PS and He Himself instructed me to make an underground room there in which to meditate. When He told me to make that small room, He gave me the duty of keeping quiet and doing meditation in that room. He put His hands on my eyes and closed them from outside. He told me that I had to close my eyes in respect to the world and I had to open them inwardly in respect toward God. He told me, "Dear Son, you are not to worry about the world. You do not have to come out. You have to sit there and meditate, and you should do the work that I have told you to do. Whenever I feel it appropriate I will come to see you by myself."

At that time, I folded both my hands to Him and from the eyes of this poor soul, the loving tears rolled down. Like an orphan, like a helpless person, I requested my Beloved Lord, "O Lord, You have to protect my honor because this is the kingdom of the Negative Power and the Negative Power is chasing me. He will create all sorts of difficulties for me. Master, how am I going to overcome all the difficulties; how am I going to face all these difficulties? I pray that You please always keep me in Your refuge, always continue showering grace on me, and always give me Your love. You have to maintain my reputation. You have to protect my honor." He embraced me and told me, "Nothing new will happen here." He said, "I promise that I will always be by your side and I will always come here when you need me. You should not worry about anything. You go and sit."

Meditating at 16 PS

So obeying the orders of the Master, at 16 PS I made an underground room and I made one simple house and a little tank for storing water. I had no program to expand that place so only those things were made. At that time I had only one sevadar with me. I told that sevadar that he should not bother me. I requested him to eat his food at his regular time but to just cook the food for me and leave it there. He was not allowed to call me for food, but whenever I wanted, I would come out and eat. I didn't have any scheduled time for eating and I was very pleased with him because he did not disturb me to tell me to drink tea or eat food. I did not eat very good foods, I always ate very simple food. In my underground room there was one wooden bench on which I used to sit. I never put a cushion or any other thing on that bench but simply sat on the wooden plank.

Often the sevadar who was with me gave up hope for me, because many times I would not come out for two or three days. I would not be aware of the time and I would sit for twenty-four hours or more; a meditator is not aware of when the day has passed or when the night has passed. Whenever I wanted to sit and do that type of meditation, for two days prior I used to take soups of vegetables like pumpkins and other light foods, so that I did not have to go again and again to attend

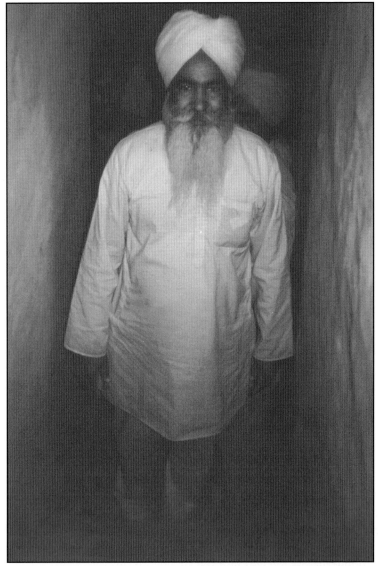

Sant Ji on the stairs to the underground room at 16 PS

the call of nature. In that way if I sat for two days continuously I did not have to go out and attend the call of nature. Doing this type of meditation, in the beginning the problems of hunger and sleep may bother you, but later on these do not trouble you.

According to the instructions of Master, I did the meditation there in the underground room at 16 PS. At that time I did not feel any responsibilities to go out into the world and do worldly things. It was a very isolated place and I didn't see many people and I didn't talk to many people. I never went to the nearby village and I never went to anyone's house. Every once in awhile I may have gone out, but otherwise I remained in the underground room and I continued doing my meditation. But the promise which Master made to me, when He told me, "Close your eyes and sit, and I will come to see you by myself," He kept that promise. Many times He came there to see me and He put His blessed feet on that place, those blessed feet for which even the gods and goddesses yearn. So that was the place where Master Kirpal showered all His grace on this little man. That was the place where He came and showered His grace on me. I was useless — nobody was ready to give a single penny for me — but then I met Master Kirpal Singh and my body became precious.

Opposed by the Negative Power

Earlier I told about the time when I joined the army. At that time Hitler was advancing and routing everyone. Many people preferred to go to prison for twenty or thirty years because they knew that if they would join the army and go into battle, death was certain for them. But at that time I was not afraid of death and I gave my name happily even though I was younger than 18 years old and it was not my turn to go to that war. I had so much enthusiasm, I was prepared to face anything, any challenge, and I was not afraid of death. But when the time came for me to go into the underground room, the Negative Power, or Mind who is the agent of the Negative Power — no matter what name you call that Power — that Power came in front of me in the form of a lion and he opened his mouth and did not let me go inside. He was adamant; he was determined he would not let me go inside the meditation room. It was very difficult for me to face that, and at that time I realized how it was easy to go into the army and accept death, but how it was more difficult to go into meditation and face the Negative Power.

This was not just my experience. Those who have struggled with their mind, only they know what kinds of forms the mind takes up when he tries to stop the devotee from doing the meditation. Only they know what the tricks of the mind are. Only the mahatma who has struggled with the mind knows how much power the mind has.

So, in the beginning, when I was about to go into the underground room for doing the devotion, I made this prayer to Almighty Lord

Kirpal, "O Lord, since my childhood I have not sought the support of anyone, neither of my mother, nor of my father. I did not seek the support of any of my brothers or sisters. I always looked to You for support. Even now I have only Your support. So I am going inside this room to do the devotion of God, having Your support, and with Your grace and help, I pray that You should save my honor. You should protect my honor and You should make me successful in the job for which I am going inside this place." With a lot of love and faith for the Master, this poor soul went into that underground room, and working hard, I became successful.

I Need Only the Grace of Kirpal

Master Kirpal used to give the example of the love between Laila and Majnu. He used to say that once Majnu was sitting in the remembrance of Laila and the breeze was blowing towards the palace of Laila. He thought, "This is a very good way of sending the message. Since this wind is touching the palace of Laila, I should send some message through the wind." So he said, "O Wind, you are going towards the palace of my beloved; tell her that I am sitting in her remembrance." You can very well imagine how deep their love was, even though they had the worldly type of love. The relation between the disciple and the Master is much deeper and if the disciple also feels the same love for the Master as Majnu felt for Laila, he can achieve anything, because the love and the relation of the disciple with the Master is even deeper than the worldly love.

Once Majnu was kissing the feet of a dog, and somebody asked, "Majnu, what are you doing?" He said, "This dog sometimes visits the palace of Laila and that is why I am kissing its feet." Bhai Gurdas has also written, "Meeting the dog from the palace of Laila, Majnu became fascinated and he loved that dog."

The cremation ground outside of my village was in the same direction from my house as Delhi. Usually the people from that area of Rajasthan do not like to make anything that is directed toward a cremation ground, because they think that it is bad luck. However, when I made my house at 16 PS, the door of the house was in the direction of the cremation ground. When somebody asked me why I had made the door of my house in the direction of a cremation ground, I told him, "Only my Beloved and I know this secret." As long as Master Kirpal lived in the body, I would always keep my face towards

Sant Ji sitting in the underground room

Delhi and I would always sleep keeping my face towards Delhi, and I did not even mind that the cremation ground was in that direction.

Once a woman came to me very sympathetically and said, "It seems as if some ghost is controlling you. Let me take you to someone who can repeat some mantra and can remove that ghost from within you." I told her lovingly that within me such a Satguru was sitting who can heal people by repeating the mantra, but He is so dear and such a unique one that nobody can control Him.

One evening when I was sitting in the remembrance of Master with tears in my eyes, I came out of my underground room and was sitting outside. That woman came with her son and they taunted me and said that nobody else was paying any attention to me. She said, "I can take you for treatment." I told her, "I will not be treated by anyone except Kirpal. For me, I need only one medicine and that is the grace of Master Kirpal. If Kirpal keeps showering grace on me, that is enough for me." When they saw the tears in my eyes, they were very impressed and they were also moved.

The true devotees, the true lovers, do not pay any attention if they are criticized or taunted by people. In fact they grow stronger in the devotion when they are criticized. It is like the wick of a lamp that gives off more light when it is trimmed off. In the same way, if the real devotees, the real lovers of the Master, are criticized by the people, or if they are given more suffering, they become more devoted to the Master. This is because the true lovers always tell their mind, "This is the reaction of your own karma; you are paying this for your own karma." They tell their mind, "Be grateful to the Master, because He is helping you pay off this karma in your lifetime." For this reason the real devotees, the real lovers of the Master do not mind if they have to face difficulties and problems, because they know it is coming from the Master.

> *I have found the beautiful beloved Emperor Kirpal.*
> *Except You I found no other support.*
>
> *O Lord, in Your remembrance I bore the separation.*
> *Searching for You, I visited every shore.*
>
> *I bathed in the all the places of pilgrimage and performed the austerities.*
> *I wore the colored robes, but did not find the Beloved.*

*I searched the whole world but did not find any support.
In Your search I checked every door.*

*Ajaib sings Your praise and meditates on the True
  Naam.
He seeks Your support and has left the whole world.*
— Sohana Shah Kirpal Pyara

My Relatives Offer to Take Me for Electric Shock Treatments

In the same way my relatives used to think that I was mad. They used to say that Kirpal Singh had done some type of magic on me. When I first moved to Rajasthan the area was very poor, but when the canals were built in the Kunichuk area the land became very fruitful. Life became more comfortable and I had a very good house there. However later, after I met Master Kirpal I made that sudden move from Kunichuk to 16 PS and I abandoned everything I had. They were wondering what had happened to me, because for them I was different. They were seeing something different in me, and that is why they thought I had become crazy.

My maternal uncles always used to bother me and would argue with me a lot about the Master. They used to tell me that what I was doing was not right, because people taunted them and told them, "Your son has become a sadhu." Because of that they would tell me that since I had become a sadhu I was bringing a bad name to the family and I was defaming them.

One day they asked me, "Have you seen God?" I said, "Yes, I have seen God who is walking and talking. He is six feet tall and I always see Him here. If you give me an opportunity I am ready even to broadcast it on the radio. I will stretch out my arms and tell the whole world that I have seen God. My beloved Master is my God."

Even though the Master has reached the final stage and He has achieved everything, He always hides that from the people. He does not go on telling people what He has gotten. However sometimes the disciples, in their emotion, do say such things, that their Master is God Almighty.

One uncle said, "You have sold yourself, you have sacrificed yourself for that Kirpal and you say that He is the most beautiful one. You say that He is the gracious one?" I gave him the example of Laila and Majnu. I told him that no doubt Laila was dark-colored. I told him that I had read in the history that Laila was of dark complexion and that Majnu was of fair complexion and that people used to taunt him; "O Majnu, why have you sacrificed yourself for Laila when she is not even beautiful, when she has a dark complexion?" He replied, "That is right, but you should see Laila through my eyes. People of this world see only one part of Laila but I see the complete beauty of Laila." So it is not the body that is beautiful. It is the love that is beautiful. The form of the Master is very beautiful because He has love, and love is that which makes this form beautiful. The Master has such a love that enchants your mind, that takes over your mind.

Once when I visited my mother's parents' home, again I met with my maternal uncles. They said to me, "We have seen your Master and there is nothing at all in Him like what you say about Him." I told them, "You people do not have the eyes through which I see Him. If you could look at Him through the eyes that I have for Him, you would want to leave your homes and follow Him."

I had one elder brother especially who was very much against the Masters. When I was first initiated by Baba Bishan Das, he was very much against Baba Bishan Das and later on when I came to Master Kirpal Singh, he was very much against Him also. He used to drink a lot of wine and shout, "I don't believe in any Kirpal or anyone like that!" We never got along and we never sat together in love. We never talked together in love because I would always try to inspire him to follow the Path and I would always talk about the Masters while he would always try to take my attention away from the Path of the Masters. For this reason we never got along with each other.

That brother even went to Kirpal and complained to Him, "You have done something to our boy and he has gone crazy." I was always upset with that brother who had said those things to my beloved Lord Kirpal. I felt very bad, thinking, "Why did he say those things to my beloved Lord? He doesn't know what my beloved Lord has given me; why did he say those words to my beloved Lord?"

Because that brother thought I was controlled by some magic that Master Kirpal had done and that I had gone mad, he came to 16 PS with some other relatives. For one last time they tried to persuade me to do the worldly things. They told me, "Why do you always go on singing the praises of Kirpal? Whether you are sleeping or awake, whatever you are doing, you always sing His glory, you always sing His praises. Maybe He has done some magic on you. We don't know what has happened to you but we think that Kirpal has made you crazy." With much sympathy for me that brother even offered to take me to Amritsar where there is a mental hospital and where they treat mentally ill people by giving electric shock treatments. He wanted to get me the electric shock treatments, and he thought that after that I would be all right.

I replied "The One who is giving me electric shocks, the One who is going to treat me, I have Him and I don't need your sympathy. Yes, Kirpal has put a lot in me. He has taken over my soul and I will lovingly tell you that remembering the name of Kirpal many millions of sinners have got liberation. If you also remember Him lovingly, if you also do His devotion, you can also get liberation." Lovingly I told that brother, "You know that I have surrendered myself to Master Kirpal and I have become mad in His love. I am mad and you are good people. It is not good to keep connection with a mad man and, if you think that I am mad, you should not come to see me. I don't have any connection with you, so you go." I told them that as Master Sawan Singh used to say, those who are hit with the bullet of love become useless for the world and the family. They forget all the accounts and they remain attached to the feet of the Master. I said, "I can live without you, but I cannot live without the Lord of my soul. Since He has given me the orders to remain here in the meditation, now I don't have any connection with you and I will stay here forever." So it was all Master Kirpal's grace that after that they stopped coming to see me and they did not bother me. After that I did not have any connection with them. I never went to visit them and they never came to see me.

When that brother left the body many years later, he didn't get sick before his death. He was healthy, but one evening, when he came back from his farm, some relatives were visiting him, and as soon as he entered the house he said, "There are four butchers who are holding me and giving me trouble." The people asked him what the butchers looked like, and he said, "They are the butchers of Kasur." Kasur is a place that is now in Pakistan and the butchers of that place were very famous. Then suddenly he said, "But now I don't feel any pain! They have left me alone because the Master of *Mahant* has come and saved me from those butchers." That brother used to call me Mahant, which means priest or holy man, so he said, "The Master of Mahant has saved me," and then he left the body right there. When he was saved by Master Kirpal he realized the power of Master Kirpal, and so before he left the body he told all the family members, "I made a grave mistake by not going to the Master and not getting the Initiation. Bring Ajaib to this house and all of you take Initiation."

If he had also seen the Inner Form of the Master that Lord Kirpal graciously made me see, he would not have said all the unkind words that he did to my beloved Lord. He also would have realized the glory and greatness of my beloved Lord. He got the glance of the Radiant Form of the Master in his final moments and that is why he told his family members that they should go to the Satsang and should not miss the Satsang even once. For many years I had no connection with my family, but since his death my family members come to the Satsang. They have received Initiation and they are doing seva. They bring wheat and fennel and other things that they grow for the langar and they are very regular in attending the Satsang.

If he had received the Initiation in his life and had done the meditation, and if he had seen the Radiant Form of the Master within, who knows how much he would have benefited from this life, and how much he would have improved his life?

If a satsangi is strong in his devotion, if he has a lot of faith in the Master — even if the relatives of such a satsangi do not believe in the satsangi, even if they do not come to the Master, still their souls will be protected by the Master. Masters not only protect the souls of the relatives of the disciple, They also take care of the souls of the animals and birds of the disciples. Sometimes the relatives of a satsangi will think about the Master to whom their relative is devoted and the relatives of a strong satsangi will always gain, they will always get the benefit from the Master. If a satsangi remains strong in his devotion, one generation of his family gets liberation. If he is a very good meditator he can liberate many generations. Master Sawan Singh used to say, "One generation of any ordinary satsangi gets liberated, and many generations of a satsangi who does a lot of meditation get liberated."

The Dear Ones Meditate with Me at 16 PS

When I was meditating at 16 PS, there were some dear ones who wanted to stay there and meditate with me. I had put a sign outside saying that only those who want to be crucified while living should come into this place. I put up another sign also, saying, "Rest is illegal. Those that want to rest, they should not come here." Therefore, those that wanted to stay there and meditate, I told them to sign a paper that they had to be up before three o'clock. Following that, each one signed a paper, some saying they would get up at twelve o'clock, some that they would get up at two o'clock, etc. At that place we were not ringing any bell in the morning to wake people up because there it was the responsibility of each one to get up on his own, because we were getting up for God. So if any dear one was not getting up according to his promise at the scheduled time, he was not allowed to sit for meditation. He was not even allowed to come again. We would throw out his bedding, saying, "You are not a lover of Hazur; you only know how to talk."

Once it so happened that the dear ones there asked me, "We are getting up early in the morning and we are staying up all night and meditating and doing so much hard work, but we don't know whether Master is aware of this or not." I replied, "This is my personal experience, that Master *is* looking at what we are doing. He is aware of every single minute that we are spending in His remembrance." They said, "How do we know that He knows whether we are meditating or we are sleeping? How do we know that He is always present here?" I said, "All right, if you want to have this experience, you will have it tonight. On your particular time, on the time you have agreed to get up, Master will come and wake you. Then during your meditation you will know that He is present with you." They asked me, "How will we know that He is present there and that He has awakened us?" I told them, "That depends upon your truth and purity. Whatever amount of truth and purity you have within, according to that you will feel His presence and you will see that He has come and awakened you."

So that night everyone sat for meditation. I was underground and the other people were sitting for meditation in another room. At whatever time they had fixed, Master came there and called them, "Now get up." When they got up and sat for meditation, whenever they felt drowsy and their head would tip forward, Master would bring their head back up. If anybody was falling over, Master brought him back to the right position. In that way three or four hours passed during the meditation time. Master was always present there and was always bringing them back to the right position whenever they were feeling sleepy. They were tired because of all these changes, because whenever they meditated before, if they leaned forward, nobody was there to bring them back, so they were at rest and very comfortable. But on that night, because Master was there and Master was always bringing them back, they got tired because they had to sit straight and they couldn't sleep in their meditation.

When they got up from the meditation, I came up and asked them, "Well dear ones, tell me, did you feel the presence of the Master here? Did Master come and do anything for you?" They said, "Yes, Master did come and He helped us in our meditation. But if He is going to come like this, then we are going to leave this place, because we cannot do the meditation like He wants us to do." So it is my personal experience that whenever we remember the Master, He is always there helping us.

My Soul Mingles with Kirpal

The importance or the greatness of that underground room in 16 PS lies in the fact that it was the place where this poor soul got the vast treasure of Spirituality from Supreme Lord Kirpal. It was the place Supreme Father Kirpal showered grace and He gave such a vast treasure of Spirituality which cannot be obtained by any power or by any force. It cannot be obtained anywhere else. Until the Master showers grace upon the disciple, one cannot get this Spirituality. In the beginning, many times we understand the Master as not more than a human being. However, when we go within and see the Master with our own eyes, then such a faith in the Master is developed within us that we can never think the Master is just a human being. Of course He is in the human body, but the Shabd has come in the human form, and the Master is above the human beings. He is not just a human being; He is the Shabd; He is that Power.

Guru Arjan Dev has described this moment like this: He says, "Just as water comes and mingles with, becomes one with, the other water, in the same way, the soul goes and mingles with the Oversoul." The light of our soul mingles and becomes one with that Great Light just as water mixes with other water.

Regarding this meeting, I describe it in the Punjabi style like this: "The Beloved One has embraced me, opening His shirt, and there remained no gap between Him and me. The sugar became one with the *patasa* (sugar candy) and there remained no difference."

God is an Ocean of Love, our soul is the drop of that Ocean, and the Shabd or Sound Current is the wave of that Ocean. As long as the soul is separated from God Almighty, she is called the drop, but when she gets in the wave and becomes one with the Ocean, she also becomes God.

So it was at this place, meditating in the underground room, where Master Kirpal showered His inner grace on me, and my soul mingled in His.

The True Disciple

When the Master sees that the disciple has obeyed His instructions and has become perfect, Master gives him all the treasure, all the wealth which He has collected. He even gives the disciple His own earnings in addition to the earnings of the disciple. He says, "This is all for you. I have earned all this and now you take care of this." Usually I say that it is a matter of great good fortune to get the perfect Master, but in the same way, it is a matter of great fortune for the Master to get a real disciple. Master travels a lot and goes through a lot of difficulty in search of the real disciple. He is ready to sacrifice anything for the true disciple because within the true disciple the Master has to sit with all His Power.

In fact the Mahatmas, Great Souls, are chosen by God and sent into this world by God Himself. But only to teach the people the Truth, They show us that without going to the Master one cannot obtain liberation and perfect oneself. That is why before They come to the feet of the Master physically They seem to search a lot, and it makes no difference to Them whether They are born in poverty or wealth. Unless They meet the Master physically, day and night They are restless, yearning for that moment when They can see and meet Their Master, so that after meeting Him, suffering thirst and hunger day and night, and working hard day and night, They would be able to do the meditation. Mahatmas always remember this purpose of Their coming into this world and unless Their purpose is achieved, They do not rest. That is why the Masters, both when They are in search of God and after They have met the Master, day and night, They work hard in Their meditation: to show other people that without working hard for God, He cannot be obtained. They work very hard and suffer a lot so that They can demonstrate to the other people that without working hard in the devotion, one will not achieve success. They come into this world to teach us about God and to develop the love of God within us.

Master Kirpal Comes to the Underground Room

Just before Master Kirpal left for His last world tour in 1972, He came to 16 PS, to the place where I used to meditate in the underground room. At that time when He came, I had been in deep *samadhi* for three days and I had not come out of the underground room. The sevadar who was living with me was afraid and worried about me because I had not opened the door and come out for the last three days. He had lost hope that I would ever come back into consciousness, and thought that I was dead.

As you know, when Master Kirpal told me to do the meditation, He told me, "I will come to see you myself. You should not come to see me." So during His last days, with His weak old body He came. The Masters can go to Their disciples whenever They want; no mountain and no ocean can stop Them, because the love of the disciple is such that the Masters will be dragged there. When one remembers Him like I was remembering Him at that time, He will always be in front of you. If you are hot, and if you are perspiring while sitting in His remembrance, Master will come there and He will fan you. When you have so much love and faith for the Master, then the Master will also work wholeheartedly for you. The Master takes care of the disciple, even without the disciple writing a letter to the Master, even without the disciple calling for help from the Master. The Master appears there; He comes to help the disciple.

When Master came, they broke open the door so they could get to me. Master had become very weak physically in His last years, and moreover at that time He had a fever and was not feeling very strong. The sevadar requested Him, "Master, please don't go down the stairs. Don't go to the underground room because You will have to go down the stairs and it is very dark there. Don't go there because You are very weak." But Master Kirpal replied, "No. Where Ajaib can go, I can also go." Master quoted the couplet, "Come on friends, let us go see the battlefield. Let us go to the battlefield and see where the warriors are fighting; when they are fighting and getting killed, they do not complain and they continue their fighting."

Nowadays it is the age of science and people can wage wars sitting very far away from the place where the fighting is going on. However, in the old days it was not like that. The two armies would go to the battlefield and fight there. The leaders of those troops would go there and fight face-to-face, using swords and other weapons. So the time spent in the underground room was like the fight in the battlefield. Master Kirpal gave this place the name of battlefield, and that is why He said, "Come on, friends, let us go see the battlefield where the lovers climb the cross. While they climb the cross they are not afraid of death, but they are very happy. Happily and joyfully they climb the cross and they do not mind it." In the battlefield people fight with swords, rifles and other weapons and they fight for name and fame, for worldly honor, and for things of the world. But in this battle, in the battle of meditation, one does not fight for anything of the world. One has to fight to free his soul, and in that battle there is no sword, there is no weapon. The Simran given by the perfect Master is the only weapon, and the grace of the Master is the only thing the disciple has with him. If we win this battle, the battle with the mind, Master gives us the supreme status. As the generals and brave warriors get medals from the kings and emperors, in the same way, the Master, Who sees how we are fighting with our mind, how the struggle is going, when we win this battle He gives us the highest status as the medal.

So in spite of His weakness He came down to my room. At that time I was in meditation and looking at me He said, "At least one has become successful." Master Kirpal put one hand behind my neck and one hand on my chest and graciously He brought my soul down because I had not come down for the last three days. He was very pleased looking at me and He embraced me. At that time He was very happy and I was also very happy to have such a Father who cared for me everywhere. He asked me if I had any pains, and He asked me what I desired. At that time I could only say, "O Master, You are very sweet." I told Him that I desired only Him and nothing else.

The disciple gets the perfect Master only if he is a very fortunate one. But this is my personal experience, that if the Master is fortunate, only then will He get a real disciple, a true disciple. It is not a little thing for a Master to get a true disciple in His lifetime. Master used to say, "God is in search of man, and when a person becomes a man, a true human being, then God Himself comes searching for him."

So when they took me out from the meditation in the underground room, at that time I remembered the times when I used to go from door to door searching for God Almighty. I used to call my search, "going from door to door," because when I was searching for God Almighty, I had gone to so many different communities and religions only in search for Him. So at that time I said this couplet in front of Master Kirpal, "I have gone from door to door praising people in the name of

"The True Disciple," a painting by Joseph Swan showing Master Kirpal Singh pulling Sant Ji out of deep samadhi in the underground room at 16 PS

God, and telling them to come and put the alms in my cup."

You know that the people who go from door to door always go on rousing people in the name of God. They shout aloud so that people may wake up and come out and give them the things that they are begging for. So I said, "My dear beloved Master, I went from door to door begging for the alms and I roused people in the name of God so that they would give me the alms. And when I roused You, when I came to Your door, You gave me the alms, You gave me the donation. Those who will give the donation to me, their desires will be fulfilled." This was a part of the couplet.

When I said this to Master Kirpal, He laughed and said, "What desires of mine can you fulfill, if I give you the things?" I told Him, "O Father, that is true, there is nothing I can do for You, Your desires are already fulfilled. But I am requesting You only to put the alms in my cup, because You are All in All, and You can do everything. But I want to say that the Master can get a true disciple only if He is the most fortunate one, just as the disciple gets the perfect Master only if he is the most fortunate one. In the same way, a Master also gets a true disciple only if He has good fortune."

> *The Light of God has come, everybody give congratulation.*
> *I am laughing heartily and telling everyone door to door.*
> *I am telling everyone door to door that the beautiful One has come.*
>
> *Today all the gods and goddesses are celebrating happiness and the fairies are singing bhajans.*
> *The whole world is congratulating in happiness and is celebrating festivities in the homes.*
>
> *The face can't help but smile. The brightness of the Light is overwhelming.*
> *The glare is in my eyes. The friends are getting together and saying the Divine Light has come, being different from the world.*
>
> *A Light has come in the home of father Hukam Singh and mother Gulab Devi.*
> *His name is Kirpal and He is a model for the world.*
> *He came and removed the darkness from Ajaib. I am happy to reside in 16 PS.*
>
> — Jot Rab Di Hai Aai

TWELVE

Separation from Kirpal

Getting the Hints that Kirpal Was Leaving, I Leave 16 PS

When Master Kirpal came on His last visit to Sri Ganganagar, which was before He left on His last world tour, He gave me many instructions. It was at that same time that He also told me that He would leave this world very soon. When He told me about His leaving, only I know the wound I felt in my heart, and only I know how I was crying at His feet. My first guru, Baba Bishan Das, also left soon after he gave me Initiation into the first Two Words, so when Master Kirpal told me He was to leave soon, I was not able to speak. I started weeping because the pain of separation was too much. I said only one thing, "O Lord, the owner of all this world, is only this written in my fate, that every time I have to weep, that every time I have to be away from my Master?"

About one or two months before He left the body, He started to give me very clear hints — warnings — that He was going to leave. He had already given me the order, "You do not need to come to see me because I will come to see you whenever I want." So on one side He had given me this order not to come to see Him and on the other side He was giving me these hints that He would be leaving soon. At that time I was in 16 PS and the dear ones who were with me know what my condition was at that time. I could not do anything but weep in His remembrance. Many times I would hit my head against the wall because I had nothing else to do. His orders

Sant Ji's meditation hut at 77 RB

were such that I had to obey Him. Yet on the other side I knew that very soon He would be leaving. Whenever Pathi Ji and other dear ones would come from Village 77 RB to see me, I would tell them, "I don't know what is going to happen to me." I was not able to tell them what was going to happen next with Master because it was not in His Will to give out that secret — the news that He would be leaving soon. I would just tell them, "I don't know what has happened to me." Then I thought of leaving that place and going to 77 RB, thinking that maybe by changing the place my mind would get some peace and I would be at ease. So in sadness one evening I left the ashram at 16 PS and I went to 77 RB, twenty-five miles away.

Wherever any beloved of God goes, the people start coming by themselves. So daily from the nearby villages, people started coming and gathering together everyday at one o'clock in the afternoon. Sometimes I would say loving words to them but sometimes I would just weep in front of them. I was not able to tell them what pain I was having.

The Master Leaves

I was sitting at that hut to which I had moved in 77 RB when I heard such news that my heart trembled. That news was, "Now Ajaib is seeing that the dera where Kirpal was dwelling is now empty. Kirpal has left." I learned about Master's departure and that day was one of much suffering and was very painful — I cannot describe the pain that I experienced when I came to know that He had already left the world. It was a very unbearable moment. Even now I remember that day, the most sorrowful day of my life, and the memory of that painful day is still fresh in my mind.

When I came to know that Master Kirpal had left the body, I was sitting at that hut and a police inspector was sitting with me. All thoughts were gone and only this came out of my mouth: "What fault did I have that You have left me? I was Your servant and I did not ask any worldly thing of You. So why did You leave me?" Only this voice was coming from the heart, "Didn't You marry me? Didn't You become my husband? Am I not Your wife? Who is there except You for me in this world? Now You have left me, making me a widow. Don't stab my heart. Again come into this world for me." My condition was like a wife whose husband has died, for the ornament of my heart, Kirpal, was separated from me. If any wife's husband leaves the body, how the wife weeps, carrying the vessels and jewels. One who does not see her beloved anymore, she tears out her hair — the same hair that she once nourished with butter. So many times from within, this sigh was coming out, "My husband has left me and all my ornaments are dead."

If the husband of a wife has all the good qualities in him, if that husband is the owner of all creation, if he loves that wife as nobody else can love her, if he fulfills all the desires of that wife, and then if that husband leaves his wife and goes far away from her, you can imagine her condition. So this was my own story. I was married to Supreme Father Kirpal, but I did not get to enjoy my married life with Him. Whatever few days I was given with Him, I was not satisfied with that, and the pain that He gave me by His separation came very quickly in my life. Even now I feel that pain of separation, exactly as I felt when He left the body.

When the Master leaves the dear ones, that is the greatest suffering. There is no other suffering greater than the suffering one gets when the Master leaves. In the heart of Ajaib the fire of separation from Kirpal was burning. If by mistake we step on a small spark of fire, how much pain we feel. In the same way, so much fire, so much heat, was burning in the heart of Ajaib for his beloved Kirpal.

> *The separation of Guru Kirpal has happened to me.*
> *To whom can I describe this pain in detail?*
>
> *O Lord Kirpal, Your light is divine.*
> *O my Lord — You have gone, leaving me.*
> *The pain of separation has taken my eyes.*
>
> *My marriage decorations had not even faded (before You left me).*
> *My soul suffers the pain in Your separation.*
> *The minaret of my good omen is demolished.*
>
> *Today I have become the orphan of this world.*
> *Only the one of Your Naam is left.*
> *The bee has remained in the flowers of Your Love.*
>
> *You are the resident of Sach Khand and You have come into this world.*
> *Your glance is seen in every single cell.*
> *Because of the body, separation has happened.*
>
> *I have sacrificed my life on You.*
> *I have become mad in Your separation.*
> *I have to cry in Your Love.*
>
> *The arrow of separation from the Lord has pierced my heart.*
> *Kirpal has protected the honor of Ajaib.*
> *He has taken the heart and only the cage is left.*
> — Kirpal Guru Da Vichorda Mainu Pe Gya

Those who have been affected by the pain of separation from Kirpal, they have lost laughter, they have no happiness in this world, and now they have to live with weeping and sorrow. For them this world has no interest and they find no peace, no happiness, in this world. They do not even know when the night has passed and the day has come, because twenty-four hours a day they are in the pain of separation from Master and they are always in His remembrance.

I am not feeling this separation from Kirpal only since that time, since He left physically. Ever since I was born, I always felt this separation from Kirpal, from the gracious Lord Whom I had never seen. Always I had this desire to see the Master, always I had this longing to meet someone who would quench the thirst of my soul. I spent so much time in searching for Him, and when the time came to come in contact with Him, for a while the outer separation was removed and I was united with Him outwardly. But I did not know at that time that it would not last for long. I did not know that the pain of separation would still come, and that I would have to suffer that throughout my life. I did not know that my Master, who had come to me to quench the thirst of my soul, would leave very soon, and that I would have to suffer this pain again. As Farid has said, "It seems my mother gave me birth only that I might suffer the pain of separation from my Master, from the Lord." I also feel the same way, that I was born into this world only to feel the pain of separation from the Master. Before I met Him physically, I suffered from this pain, and since He left physically, I once again have been suffering the same pain.

> *O Writer of Fortunes,*
> *Graciously write on my heart love for the Master.*
>
> *In my hands write the service of the Guru.*
> *Write the sacrifice of my body and mind for the Guru.*
>
> *On my tongue write the name of the Guru.*
> *For my ears, write the voice of the Sound Current.*
>
> *On my forehead write the Light of the Guru.*
> *For my eyes, write the darshan of my Guru.*
>
> *Don't write one thing: separation from the Guru.*
> *It doesn't matter if separation from the whole world is*
>   *written.*
>   — Likhan Valya Tu Hoke

Master Kirpal Singh

Earlier this bhajan, which I wrote in my childhood, was presented, at the end of which I said, "Don't write separation from the Master in my fate, no matter if separation from the whole world is written." This bhajan was written long before I met Master. I prayed to the Fortune Writer, "Don't write this thing in my fate, that I may be separated from the Master; no matter if I have to leave this world." I requested him to write all the things except the pain of separation from the Master. But that never happened; the pain of separation was written in my fate and now also I feel that pain, I am suffering that pain. As long as I remain in the world, in this physical body, I will always feel that pain and it will always remain fresh.

Wandering like Sussi in Remembrance of Kirpal

When Master Kirpal left the body, I left 77 RB, yearning for Him and crying for Him. At that time this soul did not even know where his shoes were, he didn't even know whether he was wearing pants or not, his turban was off and he didn't know anything about his body. I left with only ten rupees with me, and I didn't have any other clothes except those I was wearing. Previously I told about how I had taken some dust on which Master Kirpal had stepped when He first came to visit me at 16 PS and how I had kept that. So when I left I didn't take anything along with me except that dust. I took that sacred dust with me and after He left the body I left my home, yearning and crying for Him. For seven or eight months I was wandering here and there, like a mad person, in that difficult condition.

Just as Sussi was repeating the name of Poono while waiting for him, in the same way, a voice was coming from my heart, and I was also weeping and repeating the name, "Kirpal, Kirpal."

Sussi was a princess. The astrologer of her father, the king, told him, "This girl is going to be a great lover and she will defame you. She is going to be in love with someone you don't like." The king did not want his name defamed, so on the advice of the astrologer, he put Sussi in a box along with the money that would have been her dowry and a locket with his picture, and he put it in the river. The astrologers had thought that they would go and remove that money, but unfortunately for them they weren't able to get that box, and it was found by a washerman. He found the small girl and using that money he raised her, and she was very beautiful.

Years later the king, Sussi's father, came to the same place. When he saw that girl he fell in love with her, and he told the washerman to give the girl to him because he wanted to marry her. The washerman said, "All right, we will ask her, and then we will tell you." When the washerman told Sussi, "That king wants to marry you," Sussi answered, "Father, whatever you tell me to do, I will do it. Wherever you send me, I will go." (In India, whatever the parents say, the children do. Wherever the father wants the girl to go to get married, she will not have any objections.) When Sussi was brought back to the palace by the king, he went to enjoy with her, but he recognized her necklace and the locket that had his picture. He realized that this Sussi was his daughter, and he realized his mistake. To repent for that, he gave a big garden to Sussi and from that time on he treated her like his daughter — because she was his daughter.

Poono was a young man, and he was very beautiful. Once Sussi saw a painting of Poono, and when she saw that portrait of him, she fell in love with him. She had never met him physically, but she was always dreaming of Poono and for twelve years she waited for him to come even though she did not know who or where he was. She did not sleep for twelve years because she was always waiting for Poono to come.

Because heart speaks to heart, on the other side, Poono started having dreams of Sussi and he also fell in love with Sussi. In both their hearts the fire of love was burning. At last, one day, after waiting twelve years, Poono came to Sussi. When Poono came into Sussi's garden, someone went and told her that Poono was here. When the lovers met, Sussi, who had not slept for twelve years, found the lap of her beloved and she fell into a deep sleep, and she slept for a long time.

When Poono's parents came to know that he was mad in the love of one girl, they thought, "He won't come back and he won't do any work." They were afraid they would lose him. So they sent some people to bring Poono back. When they arrived, both lovers were sleeping in deep love. When Poono awoke, they gave him wine and in the intoxication of that wine, Poono was brought back to his home on a camel.

When Sussi awoke the next morning and did not find Poono there, she went mad and started weeping and pulling out her hair. Her father, her mother, everyone came to reason with her, but she said, "Don't try to make me understand, because I am separated from my beloved." She started searching for Poono, following the footsteps of the camel across the desert. The sand was burning and in the burning sand she followed those footsteps. She became very thirsty but she kept repeating, "Poono, Poono," calling to him. She saw that there was an oasis nearby, but she was afraid that if she left the footsteps to go and drink the water, the footsteps would be blown away and she would not be able to follow them. So she said to the footsteps, "I am afraid that if a storm comes, you will cease to exist, and I am afraid that if you no longer exist, I will not be able to continue my search. So give me your promise; if you go away, you will have committed a crime and you will have to pay for that in the court of God. But if I go away from this path that is leading me to my beloved, then I will pay for this in the court of God, because it will mean that my love was not true."

At the oasis there was a shepherd and she went to the shepherd to ask for water. But she was in such bad condition that she didn't look like a woman, she looked like a witch. The shepherd became very afraid and ran away without giving her any water. When Sussi went back she found no footsteps there; because of the blowing wind, all the footsteps were gone. She was stunned – now where should she go? She had lost her path and she started weeping. Repeating the name, "Poono, Poono," she left the body in the pain of separation of her beloved. When the shepherd came back, he saw that Sussi was a woman and he dug a grave and placed her in it.

Meanwhile, when the intoxication of the wine had passed and Poono realized that he had left his beloved back in the garden, he started back on the same camel to meet Sussi. On the way he also came to that oasis. There he saw a fresh grave. When Poono saw this grave he asked the shepherd, "Who has died here? Whose grave is there?" He answered, "I don't know who she was. It was some woman who was repeating the name, 'Poono, Poono.' She was weeping like mad, and she left the body."

When Poono knew it was his beloved Sussi, and that she had left the body for him, he got down from his camel. Because his love was real and he also was in the pain of separation, the grave was torn apart and the earth gave way so that he could join Sussi, his beloved.

Saints and Mahatmas very often tell the stories of Sussi and Poono, Laila and Majnu, to demonstrate Real Love. These lovers' love was not like the love of worldly people; it was chaste, and that is why the Saints speak of their love.

In the same way, I was always weeping for my Poono, for my Kirpal, since I was six years old. For thirty-five years my search for Him was always going on. Just as Poono came by himself to quench the thirst of Sussi, that God Kirpal came to me by Himself, to quench my thirst. But when He left the body, when He left me alone in this world, at that time not even this earth gave way to let me go and dwell within it.

Separated from Kirpal, I Wept

So when Supreme Father Kirpal left the body, this poor Ajaib wept very much in His remembrance, and because of constant weeping one of my eyes became bad. In that constant weeping, one of my eyes was hurt, and later I had to have it operated on. I did not go to anyone's house to eat — you know that the body needs food also — but I didn't go to anyone to ask for it and nobody was there to take care of me. After wandering for some time, I came to a rest house of the Canal Department in the village of Killianwali and stayed there. It was a place where nobody knew me and at that time I wanted to be in a place where I was unknown and nobody would bother me.

If one wants to have an idea of what pain I had at that time, what yearning I had at that time, it is expressed in this bhajan, "Being Separated from Kirpal I Wept." This soul was in a very bad condition, suffering and yearning for the darshan of the Master, at the time this bhajan was written. I knew that He was with me, but still, I realized that the One Who had lifted all the pains from me in this Iron Age, now He had left the physical body. No doubt He was with me always, but still, the physical separation from the Master was so unbearable that I couldn't help myself; I was weeping day and night. At that time I wept so much that it became an important part of my life.

> *Being separated from Kirpal I wept.*
>
> *After being separated from the Beloved I came into this world.*
> *I wandered here and there and was kicked and knocked. No one came to my rescue.*
>
> *Without the Beloved I am writhing in pain.*
> *I am longing for His darshan, as this world has become my enemy.*
>
> *I come and go in this world and suffer a lot.*
> *Separated from the Lord as I am, I repent, as I am lost in the realm of the Negative Power.*
>
> *He resides within me but how do I know?*

*I am mad and do not recognize my Master. Oh! I didn't
  get to talk to Kirpal.*

*Nobody knows me here. This is a foreign land for me.
He sent me here but has not come back to take me.
  I'm neither dead nor alive.*

*O Merciless, You forgot me! I didn't like to be separated
  from You.
Without Kirpal, who else is my supporter?*

*I have forgotten the path. Which way should I come?
I request You to come and take me as it has now become
  very difficult for me to live without You.*

*O Kirpal, shower Grace on me and listen to me.
O Giver of Grace to the miserable ones, listen to me.
  I also am a miserable one crying for Your help.*

*I am a sinner. Embrace me and make me sit in Your boat
  of Naam.
Ajaib has now become of Kirpal.*
  — Mai To Kirpal Se Vicherde Ke Roi Re

When the beloved Master leaves the world, the disciple has nothing with him except the weeping in the separation from the Master. Even if the kingdom of the whole world is offered to him, he will not be attracted by that, and as the hands of the watch always go to the place where they should, in the same way, the heart of the disciple of the Master always goes toward the Master.

At that time there were many people who were reasoning with me, and they were saying, "Once You were telling us it is not a wise thing to weep after anyone leaves you, and now what is happening to You? Why are You weeping so much?" I told them, "I know my Master has not left me, but physically He has put a veil between Him and me, and now I cannot talk to Him with my physical tongue. His heart has become stone; that is why I cannot see Him physically."

At that time I had only one request for Hazur Kirpal: "Just as You were coming before, now also You come into my ashram. I have laid down my life as Your bedding. For the road I have laid down my life so that you may walk on that and I have made a courtyard of my heart for You to come and dwell. You are my God, my Master, my everything." Only this sigh was coming out of me: "Who is there except You for me in this world? Don't stab my heart. Again come into this world for me."

Guru Arjan Dev said, "I am not satisfied even after looking at the physical form of the Master many times." When Guru Nanak left the physical body, Guru Angad Dev, who later guided the sangat, said, "It is better to die before the Beloved One. Curse on the life which is lived after the departure of the Beloved." When His Master left this world, Hazrat Bahu said, "O Bahu, I will always have this pain of separation, and I will die in this pain."

Even today, if Supreme Father Kirpal were to come in His physical form, I am ready to give up everything I have; I would not hesitate in making any sacrifice. No doubt He is with me in the form of Shabd all the time. No doubt He is helping me, taking care of me and giving me everything I need. In my life I have had a lot of opportunity to have the darshan of His physical form, but still I think that it was not enough; I need to do more. That is why if He were to come in His physical form, I would give up everything that I have.

Who Will Throw the Shawl Over My Faults?

When I was weeping like this, someone came to me and said, "You have always said that you should never cry or weep when anyone leaves the body, because just by weeping or crying for someone you cannot bring that person back. You have always said that, but now You Yourself are crying. You are a wise person; why are You crying?"

At that time I was in deep pain, I could not talk properly, but still I told him one story. I told him that once there was a king who decided to go on a tour to some other states, to some other kingdoms. He told his queen that he was going on the tour. When he went on the tour he did not really go on the tour; after some time he just came back, canceling his tour. But his wife, the queen, was in love with another man, and when the king had gone for the tour she had already made arrangements with this man she loved, saying, "The king has now gone on tour and he will not come for some days, so you come and we will enjoy." But when the king came back, at that time the queen and the other man were enjoying and sleeping together. When the king came there, he was surprised to see that there was another man with the queen and he was also surprised because that was the palace. How could another man come into the palace? But when he saw that the other man was with his wife and they were both sleeping naked, he did not get upset. He did not show that he was there and they did not know that the king had come back. The king simply took off his shawl and covered them with it, and he went into the other room.

When both of them woke up, the queen was terrified to see the king's shawl over them. She thought that the king would give her punishment because the king had seen all that they had done. This was the shawl of the king and nobody else would have come and covered them with that shawl except him. So when the queen thought of that she became very afraid. But the king did not mention anything about that to the queen. Even though they met many times after that and lived together for many years the king never mentioned anything about that to the queen.

After some years, when the king's end time came, he called his sons and gave the successorship to the sons and then he told his sons that they should respect their mother and obey her. "Take good care of her; she is a good woman. Do whatever she tells you." Then he transferred some property and things for the expenses of the queen. When the king was saying all these things to the sons, that they should take care of their mother, etc., the queen started weeping and went on weeping very bitterly.

The king asked her, "Why are you weeping now? I have transferred so much property into your name and you will be comfortable when I die. What else do you want, why are you weeping?" She said, "I am not weeping for any wealth. I am crying because now, when you are leaving, who will come and throw the shawl over me? Who will hide my faults?"

I told the dear one that that was why I was weeping. I told him that when the beloved Master was in the physical form, He used to hide my faults. He used to forgive me for my faults. Even now, when He has gone back to Sach Khand, in His Radiant Form He is showering grace on me and He is forgiving me and hiding my faults. But when you have the physical form of the Master in front of you, you can express what is in your heart, you can go and weep at His feet.

Just by having the darshan of the physical form of the Master you can get rid of so many bad sins and bad karmas that you have done, which you cannot do very easily when the Master is not there in His physical form. Those who go within and see the glory of the Master within, who know how the darshan of the Master works, only they know how many sins are cut, how many karmas are paid off, just by having the darshan of the physical form of the Master. That is why they weep in the remembrance of the Master, because they know that now the Master is not going to come back in His physical form and hide their faults. He is not going to come and throw the shawl over their faults.

To Whom Can I Tell the Pains of My Heart?

He mends the broken heart.
Ajaib remembers Beautiful Guru Kirpal.

The breaths of hope are exhausting.
The tears of Your separation are also coming to the end.

May I always go on telling people Your glory.
Dwell within my eyes, O Beautiful One, so that I may behold You constantly.

You are the One who makes our lives.
We won't find another one like You, Who could kill the five dacoits.

The people smile in the happiness.
The world is empty without You; who cares if the world exists?

Give me Your darshan so that my within becomes green.
O Beautiful One, look at us so that our life may become insured.

Teach us how to love.
Make the separated souls reach Sach Khand.

The pains of separation are very bad.
Day and night I weep. I wander like the crazy ones.

I want to tell You about the pains of my heart.

*Who except You would listen to it? In front of Whom can
I open the lock of my heart?*

*We are the erring ones, full of faults.
Showering Your grace, forgive us. We are Your poor
souls.*

*In Your Will come again.
I have demolished all other piles and I have only Your
support.*

*The garden is full of fragrant flowers,
But I have to weep in that happiness as my husband has
left me a widow.*

*Love cannot be measured in a scale.
Without Guru Kirpal, Ajaib is not worth even a penny.*
— Dil Tutde Aabad Kare

I am looking for someone to whom I can tell my pains. I always say that if I can get someone who can understand my pain, I will tell them all about my pains and my sufferings. Those who have not experienced any pain, how can they know my pain?

If there is anyone suffering like me, only he can understand my suffering. That is why, in the separation from beloved Master Kirpal I always say, "If I ever find anyone who is as unhappy as I am, I may tell him about my pains. Those who have not experienced any pain, how can they value the pain? Those who are always happy, how can they know the taste of suffering? The eunuchs, how can they know the taste of enjoyment? The *hafids,* the illiterate ones, how can they know what is really written in the *Koran*? What words can relay the suffering if the Master leaves the body before the disciple? Because this happened to me, that is how I know."

Within me I still have the same amount of pain from the separation from my beloved Kirpal as I had at the time it happened. The pain has not been reduced. I have the pain of love, and this pain is experienced by all lovers.

When Guru Nanak left the body, his sons and family members were very happy that He had left. They thought that now people would come and follow them, that the people would bow down to them, that

they would become the owners of the property that Guru Nanak had left, and that the people who were obeying Guru Nanak would now come and obey them. They were very pleased to get all that name and fame. But Guru Angad, who knew the inner secret of Guru Nanak, was not at all happy. He was very sad, and whatever happened with Him, only He knows or God knows. He has written, "It is better to die before your beloved. Curse on the life lived after the beloved's departure."

When Hazrat Bahu's Master left the body, Hazrat Bahu was also in great pain, and He said only this, "O Bahu, I will always feel the pain of this separation and I will die weeping in this pain."

I always say, "Dear ones, don't ask me about my pains and sufferings because I have become like a madman. Kirpal Singh gave me this separation and He left me unattended with all the wounds. He gave me this pain of separation and He has left me weeping."

Song to Kirpal

What can I say in the praise of my beloved Master? He is the One Who makes us recognize Him. On the earth there is Kirpal, in the water there is Kirpal, in the sky there is Kirpal. Kirpal is the One Who comes; Kirpal is the One Who protects. Everywhere there is Kirpal.

There are many great rishis and munis, but even they could not sing the praises of the Master. Guru Nanak says, "How can we praise the Master? Because Master is the One who is capable of doing everything. He is the Omnipotent One." When I met Beloved Lord Kirpal, the love that He gave me was such that I became the intoxicated one in that love, and I forgot everything. I only remembered Him, because His love was such that I cannot describe it with words. It cannot be talked about, it can only be felt in the soul. That was something that my soul experienced, which my soul felt and I can only say a few words about it, but I cannot truly describe the love that I received from my Beloved Lord Kirpal.

This was the reason, when He went away from my eyes, when He departed from this world, it became very unbearable for me to live in this world. It is not that I am not seeing Him now or that He is not with me. I am seeing Him now also and He is always with me, but he who goes within and he who has manifested the Form of the Master within him, he realizes, he knows what is the value of the physical darshan of the Master. So when He left the body, it became very unbearable for me to live. The love that I got from Him, I can never forget that. Always I keep remembering His love and I always wish that He was in front of me.

The Name of God is a beautiful fragrant tree;
Beloved ones, Master has planted that tree within me.
Daily watering it with the water of Satsang,
Beloved ones, He made it flourish wonderfully.
The tree within me has given the fragrance of Naam;
Beloved ones, it increased and is now bearing fruit.
Long live beautiful Master Kirpal;
Beloved ones, it is He Who has planted this tree.
Through the remembrance of Kirpal, many sinners have been liberated.

Ajaib says, never stop bowing at Kirpal's feet.
O Master of Masters, listen to my plea;
I have only one request, my Beloved.
I will never find another like You,
But You will find thousands like me.
Do not turn me away from Thy door, O Beloved;
Do not look at the account of my faults.
If I had no faults, my Beloved,
Then whom would You have forgiven?
I am Your guilty one at each and every step,
I am full of faults moment after moment.
Beloved Master, forgive me.

I was useless, who paid attention to me?
Then I found Master Kirpal Singh, Who made my body useful.
If I were someone else's child, I would have been bankrupt of devotion,
But Master Kirpal had mercy on me and gave me this immeasurable wealth.
My lips are saturated with His bani and tears fall from my eyes;
In the separation from my Guru I am writhing day and night.

*I sigh, "When will I see Kirpal?" At this thought my
   heart is breaking.
When will that day return when I will have His darshan
   ceaselessly?
If I don't have His darshan tomorrow, my mind won't
   rest on this earth —
Only Master Kirpal can relieve Ajaib of this pain.
To You I offer my prayers.
I am Your lover in heart and soul.
Nanak and the others sing Your praises; I am nobody.*

— Song to Kirpal

* * * * *

*My heart was stuck in the false world; someone came
   and cut the bonds.
Millions of times I thank Him Who united my soul with
   Shabd.*

*My soul wanders in this world. I have got no sympathizer.
In this attached world the whole world is merciless.
Forgetting the Path I had gone astray; He diverted me to
   the Real Path.*

*I, the foolish sinner, murderer got involved in sins.
I forgot the remembrance of the Lord and was buried
   under the sins.
He had pity on me. After coming He cut the chains of the
   Negative Power.*

*I, the ignorant one, do not know anything; I get kicked
   and knocked.
May I meet Beloved Kirpal; I have had this desire for a
   long time.
The soul of Ajaib had forgotten her home; catching hold
   of her, He diverted her toward home.*

— Jhuthi Duniya 'ch Faseya Dil Mera

APPENDIX

The Finding of Ajaib

The following selections provide an account of the finding of Sant Ji by the sangat of Master Kirpal Singh.

First is an excerpt from the book *Support for the Shaken Sangat* by A. S. Oberoi, titled "After Kirpal's Passing." This chapter, based on Mr. Oberoi's extensive conversations with Sant Ji and those close to Him, provides a description of the events of this most difficult time.

Second are excerpts from a letter by Arran Stephens, who served as Master Kirpal Singh's Canadian representative for many years. These excerpts, published in the October 1974 issue of *Sat Sandesh* (the monthly magazine established by Master Kirpal Singh), describe Arran's experience of going to visit Sant Ji immediately following the passing of Master Kirpal Singh in August 1974. This meeting was the first contact of any western disciple with Sant Ji; prior to it His existence was completely unknown to the western sangat.

Third is a letter from Dr. Cristobal Molina, a Colombian disciple who later became Sant Ji's representative for South America.

Fourth is a description by Pathi Ji, a close Indian disciple of Sant Ji, about the events of this time from the perspective of the satsangis in Rajasthan.

The final two pieces are accounts by Russell Perkins. Russell was the editor of *Sat Sandesh* magazine, and group leader at Sant Bani Ashram in New Hampshire; he later became Sant Ji's principal representative for the West. Russell tells of his journey to find Sant Ji in February 1976, through which the presence and whereabouts of Sant Ji became known to the disciples in the West. This is followed by Russell's description of his experiences during Sant Ji's first Initiation of western seekers.

At Kirpal's Passing

from *Support for the Shaken Sangat*

"After Master Kirpal Singh found him and gave him the further way up on the inner path, Sant Ji was made to devote full time to meditation, without caring for anything else, not even to come to Sawan Ashram, so that he could cover the remaining stages of the path and witness the beauty and glory of the Lord; and for this purpose the Guru was gracious enough to assure him that despite His age, health and preoccupations, He would Himself come to see him whenever necessary. Strange indeed is the process of "making" and "perfection" — that on the one hand the Guru wants the disciple to put in his best inside, and on the other, makes him suffer the pangs of separation, so that the process of cleansing and quickening is accelerated. During this period, Hazur Maharaj Ji [Master Kirpal] had gone to meet him numerous times, sometimes in flesh and blood and many more times in His Radiant Form. But who knows what the Master does? Even those who think they are nearest remain unaware; He does what He does, and does not always bother to consult us.

"On hearing the news of the passing away of Hazur Maharaj Ji, Sant Ji was stunned and left for Delhi. Overwhelmed with grief, He had practically lost His wits; and in a mood of utter despondence, He got off the train to Delhi on the way, not knowing why; with the result that He covered the distance in twenty-four hours which should have taken Him twelve hours only. On reaching Sawan Ashram with great difficulty, due to His grief and to the fact that He had never been there before, He met respected Tai Ji, and both wept bitterly, but silently, in the depths of their hearts in the remembrance of the holy Master. In doing so, they recalled incident after incident from the glorious past, and the atmosphere became charged with His radiation and remembrance. While they were deeply engaged in the love and remembrance of the Guru, some responsible and respected persons sitting nearby were engrossed in mundane 'matters of consequence,' and did not care to share in the emotions to establish fellowship. Tai Ji accommodated Sant Ji in a room of the guest house, made Him take tea, almost by force, as He had not taken anything for about thirty-six hours, since hearing the news. Both spent hours instead in tears and shared their heart's grief the best they could.

"Mata Sheila Dhir, who knew Sant Ji very well, and whom he always remembers with affection and respect, came up on hearing of His arrival, and shared the burden with Him. The distinguished editor of Hindi *Sat Sandesh*, who had heard about Sant Ji but had never met Him, also went to Him, and extended love and regards. He told Arran Stephens afterward that He had been greatly impressed by Him, and that he saw His eyes changing into those of Maharaj Ji.

"Next morning, respected Tai Ji, seemingly under great stress, asked Sant Ji to go back to Rajasthan; and arranged to send Him to the railway station earlier than midday, even though the train for Rajasthan departed at ten at night. The gentleman, a nephew of Maharaj Ji, who escorted him to the railway station in his car, under instructions of Tai Ji, told me much later that he had asked Sant Ji, "Sardar Sahib, you came only last evening, and are leaving too soon, without waiting for the funeral assembly to be held!" And He is reported to have told him in reply that He was already in terrible distress, but was further shocked to see that even though the going away of the beloved Master, the Lord of the Universe, was an enormous loss, the responsible people at the Ashram exhibited little grief and sorrow, and were busy in matters of no consequence, without betraying even slightly the gravity of their loss. He told me, when talking of this incident, that even when a child of six months dies, people seemed more grieved than they had looked to Him.

"On the way back, Sant Ji was more sorrowful and afflicted with grief and again got off the direct train at a village station, and walked to the nearby jungle; where, under the severity of His feelings of loss and separation from the beloved Guru, He tore up His clothes and tormented His body. The priest of a local gurdwara, who saw Him in that condition, somehow prevailed upon Him to go with him and take some food. He left the place in a few hours, and arrived at Sri Ganganagar, where the dear ones who had respected and loved Him for many years, took care of Him, made Him change His clothes, realized how deeply He was lost in the memory of His Guru, and arranged to send Him to 77 RB, where He had gone from 16 PS, about one and a half months earlier, on getting indications of His Guru's decision to leave the world.

"While recalling that period, Sant Ji told me that on receiving the indications from inside of Hazur Maharaj Ji's proposed departure, no amount of begging before the Guru helped, with the result that it became difficult for Him to pass days, and in the intensity of inner feeling, He went to 77 RB. There He lived in a tattered hut, with instructions to the dear ones not to disturb Him from meditation, except in the evening when He met them every day for some time, and sang devotional hymns with them. A reporter who had known Him for years, asked Him why He had moved to the hut, and He told him that no one could realize His inner pain, and He had not the orders to speak out. Sant Ji told us that earlier, on receiving inner indications, and later on the way back from Delhi, He had made up His mind to go away to some God-forsaken place, and spend the rest of His life there without showing His face to anyone. But very shortly after His return, the Guru Power which had its own plans sent an initiate of Hazur Maharaj Ji, who managed to reach Him despite serious difficulties. The Inner Power is very potent, and gets done what it wants, whether one wants it or not.

"After meeting Sant Ji, this dear one [Arran Stephens] published an account of Him, which in effect introduced Sant Ji to the worldwide sangat. The author made it clear, however, both that he was not sure whether Sant Ji was the next Master, and that Sant Ji was not interested in that topic, being concerned only with the passing of Lord Kirpal.

"Sant Ji left 77 RB and went by tractor to Gajsinghpur, from where He wandered from place to place in utter grief and pain; after some days Sant Ji unwittingly landed at the same gurdwara where the priest had taken Him from the jungle and prevailed on Him to take food. That priest talked to Him very sweetly, and found to his surprise and joy that He was well versed in the teachings of the *Holy Granth*, and could explain them with great facility. The priest asked Him to stay there for some time and enlighten them on the *Gurbani*. Sant Ji had not made up His mind, but the priest himself cleaned a room for Him, and begged Him with so much love and affection to stay there. Sometime later some more people of the area, including the village leader, supported the request of the priest, and prayed to Him to stay on and spend some time with them.

"As love has great pull, He could not hold out for long, and finally agreed to stay there for some time. Giving the money which was in His possession to the headman of the village, Sant Ji requested him to find and pay some lady who would prepare and serve some simple food, without spices or chilies, for Him daily — if she were willing to recite the *Jap Ji* and think of God Almighty all the time she was preparing His food.

"During His stay there, He spent time in the quiet surroundings under shade trees and would not speak nor talk to anyone unless someone asked Him about the Godway. Gradually, people started pouring in, as word about Him spread in the surrounding area, and He began to give out the teachings of Sant Mat, without getting involved in any manner; and when people offered money to Him, He refused, saying that God had given Him enough.

"The villagers were impressed by Him and His words, which carried conviction especially as they were in accordance with the *Gurbani* to which those people were greatly attached. They wondered who He was and what He was up to, as He accepted no favors nor money nor anything else from anyone. Some thought that He was a secret intelligence officer, and others had their own estimations. One dear one, who was more inquisitive than the others and had some inner urge, asked Him whether He could give him the way on the inner path of Guru Nanak and Kabir; He told him in confidence that He would give him the way, but that he should not speak out to anyone, as He was in no mood for that to happen, nor was the time opportune. He initiated him and that dear one had good inner experience and was convinced of His real greatness and stature in Spirituality.

"After He had spent some months there, some people from His native village and area, who had relatives living in that village, came there, and on recognizing Him told the people of the respect and status which Sant Ji's family enjoyed in their area. About the same time, the government announced in the papers the amount of compensation payable to the people of Sant Ji's native village, whose lands had been acquired by the army authority for setting up a cantonment. As His own land, which He had kept at the pressure of His mother at the time of leaving the huge parental property, had also been acquired, people came to know that the government compensation payable to Sant Ji ran into seven figures. At that very time, the wife of a highly placed officer of the canal department, who had known Sant Ji for years and had tremendous faith in Him, came to that village to meet one of her nieces. Coming to know of a

Saint in that village, she was led to think that it must be Sant Ji, as she did not know where He had disappeared and the details of the personality given to her tallied with His personality.

"She therefore went to see Him, and finding Him there in such surroundings — what seemed to her to be degradation and nothingness — wept bitterly, and calling a jeep, forced Him to go with her to their place. By then, due to constant weeping, shedding tears in the remembrance of His Guru, Sant Ji's eyes were damaged considerably, impairing His vision greatly. Seeing the condition of His eyes, the family arranged for an immediate eye operation, and keeping His health and need for rest in view, shifted Him to a rest house where greater comfort and convenience was available. It was at this place that Mr. Gurdev Singh, known as Pathi Ji, later found Him, after waiting at 77 RB for His return for a long time. Having no news about Sant Ji, Pathi Ji was compelled by his inner self to search for Him, and not come home till He was found.

"Pathi Ji recalled to me the tremendous difficulties he had to face because Sant Ji had left no hint of where He was going. Where to search in the vast land was a big problem, but the Inner Power which impelled him to go, helped him and gave him confidence that his efforts would succeed. Accordingly, when Pathi Ji was led to the place by the Inner Power, Sant Ji expressed much surprise to find him there, and said that He had had a dream a day before, finding that the sangat at 77 RB was building a place for Him and were doing good seva, but were quarreling among themselves at times. This was exactly what had happened sometime before Pathi Ji had set out. Pathi Ji told me that after seeing Him, Sant Ji had told him to go away, as He was absolutely unwilling to go there; but when Pathi Ji told Him that the entire sangat was weeping due to His absence, and was passing a difficult time, and would not bother Him at all if He returned there, Sant Ji relented, agreed to go and told Pathi Ji to go back and that He would come there Himself, indicating the date and approximate time when He would reach them. True to His word, Sant Ji arrived there while the sangat was sitting together waiting anxiously for Him, and He gave a Satsang immediately on arrival."

A Possibility

The following is taken from an article, "The Matter of Succession" by Russell Perkins, published in the October 1974 *Sat Sandesh* magazine.

APPENDIX: THE FINDING OF AJAIB

Prior to Sant Ji's meeting with Arran Stephens, referred to in Mr. Oberoi's account and described further here, Sant Ji was completely unknown in the western world, and indeed unknown in India outside His local area. As Mr. Oberoi notes, while Arran was unsure if Sant Ji had been commissioned to give Naam, it was through this meeting that the satsangis became aware of Sant Ji and His whereabouts.

* * *

"Arran Stephens has sent along a fascinating account of a visit to a disciple of the Master in a remote part of India, about whom he feels there is a *possibility* that he may be commissioned to give Naam . . .

"Arran recounts a conversation between Mr. H. C. Chadda, Editor of the Hindi-Urdu *Sat Sandesh* and author of *Father and Son* (a book in Hindi about our Master and His Master), and himself, in the course of which Mr. Chadda mentioned 'that he had the good fortune to meet [at the time of Master's cremation] one saintly disciple of the Master from Rajasthan who was virtually unknown to the sangat in other parts of India.' . . . 'Then Chadda Sahib told me that when this disciple spoke of the Master, he saw his eyes turn into the eyes of the Master. That was enough for me: I wanted to go and see him for myself. I was scheduled to leave on a flight the following day; I decided to cancel it and go to Rajasthan.'

" 'I left for Rajasthan with Diwan Chand the evening of the next day by train, after extending my plane ticket. I felt Master Himself dragging me there to satisfy my mind, and I was helpless to resist the pull. The area to which we were going, the Ganganagar district in northern Rajasthan, is a hot dusty desert reclaimed and turned green in parts by hard-working Punjabi immigrants and an elaborate canal system. For an unaccustomed Westerner, the heat of the midday sun couldn't be much cooler than an oven. We arrived in Ganganagar after a 13-hour journey on a third class coach and located the local Satsang leader, Dogar Mal Ji, a distinguished elderly disciple who held a high position in the Food Ministry of the Indian Government. He kindly arranged a jeep to take us across the desert to the farming village where Sant Ajaib Singh lived.'

" 'Halfway to village Padampur, the jeep's clutch-plate broke, and we had to wait until a rickety bus came along, which we caught to Padampur where we met my old friend and *gurubhai*, Jagir Singh, who was the Master's group leader in Padampur. Jagir Singh has a beautiful mango orchard and farm called *Kirpal*

Amar Bagh or "The Garden of the Deathless Kirpal," in which our Beloved Master had given Satsang and Initiation on several occasions in the past. It was my privilege to be there with Him in 1967.'

" 'From Kirpal Amar Bagh another jeep was rented, and Dogar Mal, Jagir Singh, Diwan Chand, the driver and myself again set off for our destination. We doubted that the second jeep would be able to take us there, as it kept stalling and overheating. The ingenuity of the driver somehow nursed the battered vehicle along the bullock cart path by using a canful of mud on the side of the engine block to cool the carburetor, and a brick wedged in the other side to prevent the engine block from falling off the unbolted frame.'

" 'Night falls suddenly in India at about six o'clock and all is dark. In spite of the jeep's failing headlights we reached the village where Ajaib Singh was then residing. We were taken through the adobe walled compound and up to the roof where Ajaib Singh was sitting in meditation on a *charpai*, an Indian bed of woven ropes. He welcomed us all very warmly. We all sat down cross-legged and he began speaking in Punjabi. I had several reservations, but as I glanced at him in the dim light of a sputtering kerosene lantern, I caught a brief glimpse of a physical resemblance to both Baba Sawan and Master. As it was dark and I was tired I asked if he would mind answering my questions in the morning, after I had finished meditation, and if he would mind my putting some very blunt questions for the satisfaction of my mind and possibly for the sangat. He said I was most welcome to ask any questions, and that he would do his best to reply. He does not speak English, and he continued in Punjabi. At 11:00 that night we retired from his presence and slept on charpais in an adjoining adobe compound under the stars.'

" 'Meditation was extremely fruitful. Master's presence and peace continued to increase with the passing of hours in sweet remembrance of Kirpal. The atmosphere of purity in this village is astounding. No electricity, no rush, no noise, except the humble sound of cattle lowing and men and women, predominantly Sikhs, going about their tasks . . . I found that there were about 120 people in this village, and that Ajaib Singh holds Satsang daily between 1:00 and 3:00 p.m. About 200 villagers from surrounding areas, who seem to love and revere him, regularly attend.'

"That morning they visit him in his 'tiny adobe room . . . where we all sit on a common level on the floor.'

"Arran then, with some apologies, began questioning him:

"ARRAN: 'In the terminology of Sant Mat, a Sant is only one who has reached Sat Lok and become one with the Sat Purush. You are called Sant Ajaib Singh. Have you reached that attainment which justifies the name or epithet of Sant?'

"A.S.: 'I cannot say what I am, or what has been attained. My heart is deeply pained by the loss of Hazur Maharaj.' At this he began weeping quietly and nobly. 'Yesterday when I was conducting Satsang I could not control my heart and left the Satsang weeping. I decided to leave this place for the jungle. Let the others do with the property what they like; it no longer has any attraction for me. I would have left yesterday, but I have been waiting for you people. Now I understand why Maharaj Ji made me wait.' (No one had informed him of our planned visit; and since there were no phones or electricity in the area, it would have been impossible.)

" 'I asked him about some prominent features in the third and fourth planes, and he refused to answer, saying: "I cannot say just now. I am not allowed to say. My heart is disturbed and I am leaving everything to go to the jungle, where no one will know me and where no one can find me. I am going alone and I am not telling anyone where I am headed for." '

"ARRAN: 'Has Master given you any work to do?'

"A.S.: 'Maharaj Ji has given me the order to give Naam. He has told me, "You are to distribute the riches of Naam. I will stand behind you and will be responsible for all your actions." . . .'

"ARRAN: 'If you can irrefutably prove to me from within that you *are* the Master, then I shall proclaim from the rooftops that the new Master has revealed Himself. But Master will first have to show me within, several times, beyond all doubt, that this is where His Power is. And if this is so, then I shall serve that Power as though it were my own Guru.'

"A.S.: 'I do not want to be a Guru and I do not want to sit on any platform. My heart is suffering the pain of His physical separation. I am leaving for the jungle.' . . .

"Arran says, he understood that this man was not about to reveal anything about his inner practice or attainment. However, he says, he interviewed people who have lived around him for up to twenty years, and they say that 'he has spent his whole life in search and in performing spiritual practices. He is famous throughout Rajasthan for his purity.'

"ARRAN: 'If you have reached this stage, then what about *Kam, Krodh, Loh, Moh, Ahankar* (that is, lust, anger, greed, attachment, egotism). Have they left you?'

"A.S.: 'I have been a *brahmchari* (i.e. strictly chaste) since birth and I have never known Kam (lust or desire). Now I have left everything — all property and wealth and the attachment to it.'

"ARRAN: 'Have you ever dreamed of a woman?'

"A.S.: 'Since birth I have never known Kam, in dream or otherwise. If I had experienced Kam, I would have married, but this never entered the mind. Since childhood my only desire has been for God-knowledge and service of the Saints.'

"And Arran here inserts a biographical note: 'He's known in Rajasthan as a *balbrahmchari*, which means "chaste from birth." His parents were Sikh farmers and since childhood he has been steeped in the Sikh scriptures; he has practiced Surat Shabd Yoga since a Sadhu initiated him into the first two Shabds. He served in the army, fighting on the front lines in Germany during World War II. He is now 50 years old, and speaks only the Punjabi language.'

How Pathi Ji Found Sant Ji

Gurdev Singh is a disciple of Sant Ji from the village 77 RB, better known among the sangat as Pathi Ji as he served as the pathi or chanter, chanting the hymns on which Sant Ji based His Satsangs for many years, including the first several world tours. Pathi Ji's association with Sant Ji was long standing, dating back to the time when Sant Ji was meditating on the Two Words in Rajasthan and he is referred to in the story "The True Renunciation," from Chapter Seven, "In the Bushes of Rajasthan: Cultivating the Two Words" (pp. 213-215)." As described below, after Master Kirpal Singh left the body, Sant Ji left 77 RB in profound grief, without telling anyone His whereabouts or plans. It was Pathi Ji who eventually went to search for Him. The following is a translation of Pathi Ji's account of those events and of the finding of Sant Ji provided by Pathi Ji to the editor of this book in December 1977, and in greater detail in November 1998 to Mr. Oberoi.

* * *

After Sant Ji came back from Sawan Ashram, Delhi, where He had gone upon getting the news of the passing away of Master Kirpal, He looked very sad and serious. He told the people around Him in 77 RB that He had become an orphan and that there was nothing left for Him in life. He said that He would go to a place where nobody knew Him and He knew no one, to pass the time unknown and unrecognized. Soon after His return from Delhi however, as providence would have it, Arran Stephens of Canada, after facing considerable difficulties, reached 77 RB in search of the spiritual successor of Master Kirpal.

After Arran's visit, Sant Ji left 77 RB, saying that He did not know where He would go or where His Guru would take Him to, but no one should come searching for Him. He gave no indication whether He would be back there at all.

Before He had come to know of Master Kirpal's departure from the physical plane, Sant Ji had told the sangat at 77 RB in detail of His plan to construct a small ashram there, where His own simple needs and also those of the visiting dear ones could be met. However before going away, He had told them that the proposed construction plan was no longer active due to the changed situation.

During this time the sangat in 77 RB used to get together daily at 3:00 a.m. for meditation and singing of bhajans. A few days after Sant Ji left, it was decided collectively that in order to keep the remembrance of the Guru fresh and to maintain the activities of Satsang and the contact between the satsangis, construction seva could be started. In this way the ashram conceived by Sant Ji could one day come to exist, and be available to Him for use upon His return. The work went on enthusiastically for quite some time but then with the passage of time it became slack and unnecessary arguments and wrangling began to crop up amongst the sangat. By then about six months had gone by, and the absence of Sant Ji had started telling heavily upon the dear ones.

At that time I developed a strong desire that I should go in search of Sant Ji. Many others were also of the same view. I talked about it with my mother and she inquired, 'Son, where will you go to search for Baba Ji?' and I replied in a very innocent way, 'to the place where He has gone.' Hearing this she remarked, 'Dear son, it is very difficult to know where a Saint has gone or how to reach Him.' However, finally the idea was approved by practically every dear one, and I set out on this hopeful mission. Before I left though, all the dear ones collected at the ashram, meditated for some time and then prayed to Sant Ji collectively, 'O True Lord, we do not know where You are, nor do we know how to find You. But we are eager to have your darshan and we therefore humbly pray that You kindly have pity upon us. Take Pathi Ji to Your feet so that he may tell You our plight, and prevail upon You to agree mercifully to come back to us here.' When my mother asked me when I would be back, I told her that I had no idea, and if I did not come back for six months, she need not worry, as I would be pursuing the search.

"After leaving 77 RB, I went to Sri Ganganagar where Sant Ji had many old associates and friends, who were mostly initiates of Master Sawan, and with whom He used to spend a good deal of time. I went to every dear one and to every corner of the city, but got no clues. From there I moved on to Sangariya, another town where Sant Ji had gone often to give Satsangs, and where He had close association with some high officers of the canal system. As I was making inquiries there, I came across a very handsome and tall Sikh gentleman, and I asked him where was the residence of the Sub-Divisional Officer (SDO) for the canal system. He immediately looked to the first floor of the house he was standing opposite to and called out loudly, "O *Patwaris* [canal revenue officials], guide this person to SDO's residence." Quickly a person came and took me to the desired place. When I knocked at the door, both the SDO and his wife came out. I found that I was familiar with their faces, as they had sometimes attended Sant Ji's Satsang at 77 RB. Upon seeing them, I began weeping and asked them where Sant Ji was. Both of them replied in one voice that they had no idea. Upon my insistence that Baba Ji was definitely with them, the lady said very meekly, "No brother, he is not here. You can even check our house." However, I continued weeping and said, "Sant Ji may not be in your house, but I can see Him in your eyes and you definitely know where He is." It seemed that the lady was more moved by my pleas than her husband and I pleaded with him to help. Finally the man yielded and said that he had orders from Sant Ji not to tell anyone, but was doing so, seeing my helplessness. He told me that Sant Ji was in a canal rest house which was further up in the forest at a distance of about six kilometers from there. I felt heartened, thanked the couple and walked on to the place indicated.

When I reached there, it was already late in the evening, about 9:00 p.m., and I saw a gardener tending the plants, even at that late hour. I inquired from him if there was a sadhu or a saint in the rest

Sant Ji and Pathi Ji

house. In a muted voice the gardener confirmed that a saint was there who comes at 8:00 a.m. and goes back to the residence of the Junior Engineer at about 9:00 p.m., but he has instructions not to talk about it to anyone. I hastened to the residence of the Junior Engineer, where I met both the Junior Engineer and his wife. Still sobbing I asked about Sant Ji, to which they said that Sant Ji was about to come there, but if He came to know that they had revealed His presence then He would be angry with them. I said that they need not worry because as soon as they know Sant Ji is coming, they should tell me and I would hide myself below the wooden bed.

Just as I was uttering these words Sant Ji arrived. He was wearing a green piece of cloth over His eye but had seen me standing and conversing there. Sant Ji's face, mood, and tone became abruptly serious and stern, and He said, "O Pathi, how are you here? How did you come to know that I am here? As you have been able to find me at this place, I will now go to such a god-forsaken place where nobody will ever be able to trace me."

My mood was already down, and I was sobbing and weeping intermittently. Upon encountering Sant Ji's unbelievably strong reaction and hearing His stern words delivered in an exceptionally ringing tone and tenor (never experienced before), I became very scared, even terrified. I could not utter even a word and I stood there stunned. Sant Ji sat in the same position for about an hour, sitting there absolutely non-communicative and non-responding, with eyes mostly closed, showing no sign of relenting. After an hour, the tense contours of His face became abruptly relaxed and He asked me how the sangat and every one in the family at 77 RB was. While narrating the events that had transpired there, I saw that the circumstances at 77 RB made Him very disappointed and depressed. Seeing Sant Ji's unusually hard attitude, I felt that life had gone out of my frame, and I lost any ray of hope. While still weeping and in a mood of despair, I responded to Sant Ji's questions rather casually, if not callously, saying, "I do not know anything."

Hearing my reply, Sant Ji became very soft, like a father to His sobbing son and tried to involve me in talking, so that I might become more responsive and burden free. I resisted initially, but gave way soon enough when Sant Ji said that He had seen in a dream that the sangat had collected at the ashram, and were having heated arguments because of the shortage of volunteers to work. I said, "Sir, for You it is a dream, but I was getting beaten in the process, because one family who had promised to send ten people every day for seva was somehow backing out, and I had to say something forthright." Sant Ji was thus able to pull me out from my desperateness, enabling me to calm down and respond properly. Sant Ji then inquired from me as to what I did and thought before leaving 77 RB on my mission to find Him. I described how the whole sangat had gotten together and after some meditation had prayed collectively to Sant Ji to have mercy upon them, and guide me to His feet. On hearing this Sant Ji said smiling, "Oh, you all meditated and prayed collectively, then how could your plea and petition go without a response? My gracious Guru had to see that your sincere desire is fulfilled, and you are very much here before me." Sant Ji patted me very lovingly and told me not to worry, as He would be back in 77 RB, after a few days, on His own. He told me the exact time and date that He would arrive there. He also asked me to have dinner, sleep there during the night, and said that the next morning the Junior Engineer would escort me to the bus station on his motor-

Sant Ji giving Satsang at 77 RB with Pathi Ji, in 1976

cycle. At that time Sant Ji gave me much love and confidence and made me realize that my mission had succeeded.

"On my part I begged Sant Ji's pardon and forgiveness for causing Him inconvenience and problems by trying to locate Him, despite clear instructions to the contrary. In reply Sant Ji said in a very reflective mood, "We all have our own plans, but little do we know what the Guru has in view. The Guru gets the things done the way He wants. Outwardly you did wrong in coming after me, but with your efforts the fortune of thousands of sincere seekers all the world over has bloomed and they will be able to draw immense spiritual benefit from it. Have I not been telling you emphatically all along that my Guru — Supreme Father Kirpal was and is All-wisdom, All-knowing, and All-powerful, and does everything in His own Will? He needs no suggestions, advice or help, He always makes decisions in the larger interest of those sincere seekers who want Him and not of the world." I am unable to explain how much grace Sant Ji showered on me then, and how happy and satisfied I felt in the core of my heart. I went back to 77 RB as directed by Sant Ji, bringing much hope and satisfaction to the dear ones waiting for Him. Sant Ji also came back at the time and date given by Him, and the sangat celebrated His return with rejoicing and thanksgiving. Thus ended a very difficult period of life for the sangat at 77 RB.

A Man Has Been Born

The following letter, dated July 7, 1975, from Dr. Cristobal Molina of Bucaramanga, Colombia, to his daughter and son-in-law, Silvia and Joe Gelbard who were living at Sant Bani Ashram, Sanbornton, New Hampshire, was published in the July 1976 *Sant Bani Magazine*.

* * *

"My dear children,

"This letter brings you cordial greetings and the most beautiful news. As you already know I have been working real hard since my Initiation, December 12, 1971, and day after day I try to put in more time in my spiritual practices, especially after Master's physical departure.

"On some holidays I have reached up to eleven or twelve hours of meditation and Bhajan and since last June I have been dedicating seven hours daily, five of meditation and two hearing the Sound. Well, this effort has been rewarded enormously by Our Beloved Father, Kirpal, because I have no other merit, if I have any at all, since it is well known that is all due to His love and mercy. All I have done is to try to follow His teachings, staying still so that He may work.

APPENDIX: THE FINDING OF AJAIB

From left: Dr. Cristobal Molina, Sant Ji and Pathi Ji

"Authorized by Him, who asked me to give faithful testimony of what had been revealed to me in meditation and Bhajan, I will tell you some details. I had been feeling that something of great transcendence was about to occur to me, because of some signs and symbols which are not necessary to speak about right now.

"When meditation was about to finish the 25th of June, right in front of me the SS initials which denote *Sat Sandesh* (quite big) appeared to me but this was really fast. I asked Master what it was about, and He answered saying it was the *Sat Sandesh* issue of October 1974, and could not know any further since meditation ended.

"The following day during meditation I asked Master to please make clear everything about the *Sat Sandesh* issue, since I had not found it anywhere at home and maybe had loaned it. He said, 'All has been told in *Sat Sandesh* October 1974. All the Truth.' He added: 'Master Power is already manifested in a human pole, but actually is given to meditation in order to perfect Himself and then enter into action.'

"All the time premonitory signs something really great and about to happen were going on, both during meditation and Bhajan. Beautiful music, the prettiest bell sound, and — as for meditation — everything all right.

"Several days passed by in the sweet remembrance of the Beloved; my life is centered around Him. It is because of Him, that I am in such happy state. With His help I hope the turn will be of 180 degrees.

"And so the 1st of July arrived, the month of SAWAN. I had told Master that I was worried about the confusion that was being formed around His Spiritual Succession; that to the Satsangs which take place in my home, came a group of people who had not received the Holy Initiation, and I feared that some of them would be led astray by offers of all kinds that were arriving, and that if one soul was led astray, I considered it something very painful. Of course, He knows everything, but one is so childlike, and has to say things, and in this way I felt more calm.

"The meditation on the 1st of July was triumphal and Master without me asking Him, said: 'A MAN HAS BEEN BORN — AJAIB SINGH IS THE NEW MASTER.'

"On several occasions Master has authorized me internally and without me asking Him, and on one occasion He said, 'YOU SHOULD GIVE FAITHFUL TESTIMONY OF WHAT HAS BEEN GIVEN TO YOU.' This I am doing now.

"In the Satsang of July 1st, I read 'The True Master and His Mission,' and I ended by informing them that the human pole that was to succeed Kirpal Singh was incarnated, and His name was AJAIB SINGH. It was a surprise for everyone and I saw happy faces. I should say that in our Satsang we only read the teachings of Master Kirpal Singh and we have not read out loud the letters that now circulate, no matter where they come from.

"After Satsang I took home some people that live far away. The last person to be left off told me that the meeting had been very beautiful and that more beautiful still had been the 'proclamation' I had done about Ajaib. This commentary worried me. The word 'proclamation' bothered me, since I had only tried to give some information; I thought that I was not doing anything different than that done in Mr. M—'s Satsang in Bogota with another name. So I went home and practiced Bhajan for half an hour in order to fulfill my usual schedule. About twenty minutes had passed by (here I must take a deep breath so that I may be able to tell you what follows)... there was a short silence in that which I had been listening to, which was a very harmonious, sweet music, and suddenly other music began to reverberate . . . and later the sound was drowned by the ringing of thousands of bells tolling, all kinds of tones: clear, fine, low, high, that shook my poor soul. I understood Master was approving all I had done. One of the bells ended with a golden brooch. A bell with the voice and the deepest sound or tone resounded four or five times. If it had lasted longer my soul would not be here in this poor body. It is impossible to describe this in words. In this world no bell has been cast with that sound, no metal could give such a grave, clear and vibrant sound or else it would break into pieces trying to imitate it. If in the time I have left of life I do not hear this bell again, I could tell you, my children, that it has been worth living what I have lived, suffered what I have suffered, having had the privilege of listening to God's voice in the resonance of this Bell.

"This ending of my Bhajan practice was Beloved Master's mark to what this puppet had done. I do not want to do anything that does not come from Him, and this letter—it is He who writes it because it is His wish.

"Last, I would like to tell you that a chorus has been intonating a song all these days during my Bhajan practice. The tune repeats itself but with music from all parts of the world, say, Chinese, Oriental, American, Latin etc.

"The only thing it says is:

'A MAN HAS BEEN BORN
AJAIB'
'A MAN HAS BEEN BORN
AJAIB'

"Up to here I can tell you. The curtain has fallen and the rest is only for me. If it comes up again, I will write. He will say.

"My children, your father has been looked upon with eyes of great mercy. Merits I have none. I am only trying to follow the Path the Beloved Master has shown me. If I succeed, it is through His Grace. Exert yourselves as much as possible, please, on God's way back; as Master Kirpal would say, I am also making efforts to 'crawl' in meditation and Bhajan.

"Blessings in His Holy Name, your father,
"C. Molina"

Our Friend with a Different Coat On

This talk was given by Russell Perkins in February 1976, after returning from Rajasthan, as the first western disciple to travel to India to see Sant Ji. The talk was published in the July 1976 *Sant Bani Magazine.*

* * *

"My only prayer is that I can do justice to what I have experienced, and the message that I have been given. I see that the trip was the easy part; the hard part is coming up now. I don't know to what extent you know the reason why I went. I had no personal desire to go; in fact, I was terrified of going. But it came very strongly from within that the time had come to go to Rajasthan and find Ajaib Singh. I resisted it like anything; I did not want to go. I was afraid, my mind rebelled — perhaps he's not there. But the call was very clear and there was no evading it.

"So I went. And I was apprehensive and frightened on a hundred different levels. I was frightened of all the various human pressures I was going to be under and I was frightened of being fooled — I was frightened that I would be fooled one way or the other: either that I would think that somebody was a Master that wasn't, or that I would think that they weren't when they were! But now that I'm back I can say with all assurance in the world that Master was with me every inch of the way — not just every step but every inch. He very unerringly put me exactly where I had to be at exactly the right time, with exactly the right people.

"I was grateful that Arran had given me his wife's cousin's name as a translator and to accompany me. He and his wife were in India (they had been living in Canada, his wife is a Westerner) visiting his parents, and Arran cabled them and asked them to give me any help they could. And the first day I went to a hotel when I arrived and I debated whether to look them up first or to go to Sawan Ashram first; and the thought came very clearly, *Go to Sawan Ashram.* So I went to Sawan Ashram and they were there. That was the first sign that things were going right. I spoke with them (Khulwant and Linda Bagga), told them my plan to go to Rajasthan and why, and asked them to go with me; they accepted in a second.

"Two days later I moved into the Bagga household and it was a very loving place; they were so kind and good, it made all the difference in the world. And on Monday morning we left for Rajasthan.

"When I reflect on our trip to Ganganagar and our adventures there, the image that comes to mind is the Princess's thread, in George MacDonald's *The Princess and the Goblin*. I had a hold of a thread like that, and all I knew was to keep hold of it and follow it, no questions asked. Ganganagar, while a big city, is very remote, unmechanized, and unused to Westerners; after many adventures, some of them scary, we did manage, with Master's incredible grace, to locate Dogar Mal, the local group leader, who knew how to find Ajaib Singh. When we found him, he said, 'Well, I took Stephens to see Sant Ajaib Singh; but then Sant Ji told me he didn't want anybody else to see him and not to give his address to anybody.' And he just stopped there. And it just fell flat out into the air. And we were sitting there and my brain was working like anything — what to say to convince him?! — that I was really okay. And Linda was getting nervous and she said, 'Well, does he know that Russell has come all the way from America to see this man?' And there was silence for a while; finally he said, 'Well, I will arrange for the jeep tomorrow.' We were greatly relieved. Mr. Aroda, Dogar Mal's relative, graciously and kindly put us up for the night, and the next morning we started out.

"And just a short while after we left Sri Ganganagar we were in a world so remote that I can't even describe it. We went through roads that weren't roads, and places where there aren't houses for miles and miles, where the only animals you see are camels, where everyone that you meet is a peasant, where there's no electricity — it's hard to explain. At one point the driver asked directions of two men riding on a camel that came along. It was surrealistic, it was so remote. Each village that you go through gets more and more primitive.

"Before we left him, we asked Dogar Mal what he thought of Ajaib Singh; he said, 'In my opinion, he is a Sant, definitely. But he doesn't want to be a Guru — I'll tell you that right now.' I asked him would he be happy to see us; he said, 'Oh yes, he'll be happy to see you.'

"So we drove on and on through the wilderness — I never knew the meaning of that term before — it was another world, as different from Delhi and Dehra Dun as Delhi and Dehra Dun are different from America.

"We finally reached the village of Satatararbi (77 RB) where Ajaib Singh lives, and we came to the house and we went in and —

here is where I really want to convey what happened as carefully as possible. Master uses the phrase, 'revolutionizes the thought pattern of the disciple.' And that is what happened to me during the next five hours.

"We were ushered in — nobody seemed surprised to see us — and Sant Ajaib Singh came out to meet us. And nothing I had heard had prepared me for how much like Master he was going to be. This was the first thing: physically and personality-wise, he's astoundingly like Him. More than I would have dreamed possible. How subjective these things are I'm not in a position to say — somebody may go there and feel that he's not at all like Master — but that was my first impression as he came toward us: of someone who is very much like Master. And he greeted us warmly, and with a total lack of surprise, as though he got visitors from America every day; he was very much on top of everything. We sat down, and he asked me why I had come. And I was looking into his eyes (because I had looked into other people's eyes and I had not got what I wanted), I was looking into Ajaib Singh's eyes and I was realizing that they *were* indeed very much like Master's eyes. So when he asked me why I had come, I said very boldly, "I had Master's orders from within to come to Rajasthan and find you — but I don't know why." And that was conveyed to him and he nodded, he accepted it, and we began talking. And every time he would say something (it would have to be translated of course; he spoke in Punjabi) — he would look at me. And I would be looking at him. And every time he looked at me — and this is the thing that it took me about a minute to realize what was happening and then the flood-gates opened up inside me — every time he looked at me, it was Master looking at me. There was no doubt about it. It was Master doing it. It was like — it was like — he would say something — one thing was happening physically, outer, and yet, on this *other* level, I would look — his eyes would be *dancing just* the way Master's eyes used to dance — at me, just the way Master's eyes used to dance at me! And his smile — the way that his face crinkled up and the way that his smile *happened* — was exactly the way that Master's smile used to happen. And I found myself — I'd look into his ... and this *tremendous* inner joy — that I had never experienced since the last time that I saw Master, began to come up. It just welled up inside me. And I couldn't believe it. I suddenly understood what is meant by 'our Friend with a different coat on.' This is the way it is. And I was just sitting there looking at him and he'd say these things and then he would sit back, and look at me, and smile, and there would be Master! It happened over and over and over again. And it was like, you know he was saying — on the face of it he didn't even know my name — you know, who I was or anything — he was not even terribly interested, maybe, on that level. But on the other level he was saying, 'Yes, here I am, hello, it's so nice to see you again,' that was happening on the *other* level.

"Now I also must say that he is exceedingly *simple* — this is a very simple man, who lives, as you've already gathered, in an environment as simple and uncluttered as probably exists on this planet. He lives in one room in an ashram built by his devotees — we sat in the inner courtyard of it; — the bathroom is a hole in the floor; there are no amenities of any sort; he dresses in simple clothes that are nothing at all, and this is his world.

"Well, in the first place he said he was hiding. He said that many times. He said it with great glee, and I must say that another way in which he is astoundingly like Master is his sense of humor. The same things appeal to him — the same things tickle him, you might say, that used to tickle Master. And the more that I was with him, the more that feeling of love was evoked.

"So he said that he was hiding, and I questioned him quite a bit about various aspects of what his plans were and what he was going to be doing and he said that the time had not yet come, that he was hiding, that the Master Power could not come forth in fullness until the squabbling among the satsangis had died down. The squabbling over property, the hatred for each other that the satsangis have been manifesting, this has to totally stop — or subside at least — before anything can happen. And I'll tell you, he has absolutely no interest in a personal way in being a Guru — none. Nothing appeals to him less. What Dogar Mal said was absolutely right: he has absolutely no interest in being a Guru. And he told me that Tai Ji had telegraphed him last December, to come to Delhi — and the presumption is that she was going check him out and see if he would be given the dais at Sawan Ashram. But he wouldn't go. And he said, 'Who wants to be a guru? What is there in being guru — tell me that? Is it not better to be a disciple?'

"He was really displeased with me, setting him up in opposition to Darshan Singh. He said to me, 'I have respect for Darshan Singh — he's my Master's son. I have respect for Tai Ji, too. Why should I have been dragged into this?' And I saw very clearly that he was not fighting anybody, had no interest in fighting anybody, didn't want anybody to fight for him — this was totally who he was *not*. And that I had been wrong in using him that way. And I apologized.

"And then he did something that Master used to do all the time also: he rebuked me — he taught me — through seemingly making a mistake. In Shirley Tassencourt's account (printed as 'The White Brilliance,' *Sat Sandesh* Nov. 1974) she relates how Master made the ludicrous error of reversing what she had said, saying 'ten and a half hours shopping and one half hour meditation' and everybody was saying, 'No, no, Master' — but Shirley knew that Master was doing that on purpose to show her something. Well, that's also happened to me many times with Master. And Sant Ajaib Singh and I were talking about the various letters that had been circulating amongst the sangat, some of which had been translated into Hindi and he had seen. And he said, 'I was very surprised to read the letter that Russell wrote.' As he said it — he looked at me and smiled and his eyes were dancing and it was Master smiling. And I got a real pang, a sinking feeling in my stomach, like I used to get when Master was getting after me. And I said, 'Why?' And he said, 'Because it had nothing to do with Sant Mat.' And instantly it clicked, you know — I understood that on one level he was confusing my letter to Darshan Singh with someone else's. But while I realized this, at the same time I understood instantly and totally that Master was using this to tell me that I had been wrong to write that letter. I knew with my whole being that my Master was telling me something which I ignored at my soul's peril. And I looked into his face and there was Master there — totally loving, eyes dancing, smiling at me, and yet, he was rebuking me. And I said, "I was wrong." And . . . Master smiled. He accepted it.

"He had many questions to ask about why people were doing this and that; on one level the whole affair that has been going on since Master's death was incomprehensible to him; on another level he understood it totally, and was totally above it. For example, some of the local satsangis in Sri Ganganagar asked him to hold Satsang down there after Master had died. And he agreed; he went down and held it a couple of times. And Mr. Aroda, whose house we stayed at, who was one of the ones who had asked him, told us that he thought they were very beautiful — that he had held Satsang very much the way Master had done and it was uplifting and everybody got benefit. But some people put tremendous pressure on the local satsangis and objections were raised: they said that he was after the guruship. So he wouldn't go down and do it then; he just stayed up in his village. And with all that he had no negative words for anybody.

"After we talked for a long time in the courtyard, we washed up; people had brought water in buckets and poured it over our hands. Then he served us, he fed us — he didn't eat anything, but he sat at a table with us while we ate, in an inner room — and we talked some more. He put on dark glasses at that point. (He has had difficulty with his eyes.) Of course that prevented me from looking into his eyes any more. But he was still beautiful to look at. The three of us agreed that the very least that can be said is, 'he's a very holy man, and I love him.' We agreed that that was the *minimum* that can be said. When we left him, Linda was crying. She had never seen the Master. And he patted her on the head — he said, 'You are my daughter.' So similar to the way Master would do it.

"I realize that hiding business — on one level that was Ajaib Singh talking about hiding away from the world, and on the other level it was the Master talking about the Master Power hiding away from a sangat that didn't really want It. I mean: Who has Him? A few hundred villagers in the Rajasthan desert have the Master all to themselves! Just think of it! Remember when Guru Amar Das was kicked off the platform by the son of the previous Guru — Guru Angad's son? He went off and he went into a house and he bricked up the door and he put a sign, "Whoever breaks down this door is no Sikh of mine." Do you remember that? — he went into meditation full time. And after a while the disciples decided that they had been wrong and they came bombing in and they read the sign and they tore down the wall (because he had said not to go through the door), and begged him to come out. Perhaps something like that has to happen. I didn't feel it; when he explained to me that he was in hiding, and that the time had not come, the Master Power was not yet ready, I felt that he was telling me the simple truth. That it was not in my hands to change that. And I said, 'Well, you know best.' That's the way I felt. He does know best.

"Still, later when we were eating, he said that when Master had told him to give Naam, He had told him not to hide it. And I asked the very obvious question, I said, 'Well, if Master told you not to hide it, why are you hiding?' And when the question was translated, the whole room just broke up, including him. He roared with laughter, the disciples all laughed, everybody laughed. And then he explained that he was in hiding only on a temporary basis, and that the time just hadn't come yet, that's all.

"He spoke very lovingly of Arran. He said that the question that Arran asked him — whether or not he had ever dreamed of a woman — he said that nobody had ever asked him a question like that before in his whole life. He still remembered it! He said he respected that question, and he respected the concern out of which it came. And his last words to me were to give his love to Arran.

"You know, it's so hard to believe in what you feel yourself. You hear what other people have to say and you think, 'How can I be right? How could I possibly know, when so many other people don't know? Why is it that I have this pull in this direction, if this is the truth, and other people don't?' We think like that; we're very insecure. And even when we get glimpses of what's real, well, we tend to ignore them.

"I asked him about privacy — he confirmed that he had indeed told Dogar Mal not to bring anybody else up there, and I said 'Are you unhappy that we have come?' He said *'No!'* — very emphatically. He said, 'I am very happy when anyone who really wants to know the truth comes.' And he said that Arran and I were the only two people from outside the area who had come see him, since Master had left. Even when Tai Ji wanted him she sent him a telegram. Nobody came up. So really it's small wonder that he's hiding. There's nobody wants him! Why should he not hide?

"Anyway, I'll tell you that he's not concerned (and this is the thing I think that I understood and *must* keep hold of — I *must* keep it in my mind) — that he is totally unconcerned in a personal way, with anything. If he never is recognized by a single person as Guru, it wouldn't bother him one bit. He's very happy that way. He doesn't care if anybody believes in him; he's just himself. He's sitting there, this incredibly simple man, in this incredibly remote and primitive village, sitting there doing his meditation. And if nobody knew who he was, it wouldn't make a bit of difference to him. And it doesn't bother him if somebody wants to go to this person or that person, he just doesn't care. And that's the way it's got to be with us, too. This is the Master's attitude, there's no doubt about it.

"I asked him — because he *was* displeased at my setting him up in opposition to Darshan Singh — 'Is it all right if I write an account of this experience also?' He said, 'Yes; write the truth as you see it,

Sant Ajaib Singh, taken by Russell Perkins, at their first meeting

but no propaganda, no publicity, no big splash.' It's a simple matter of bearing witness and leaving it right there. Those who are inclined in this direction, why should they not come this way? And those who are not inclined, why should they come? What *he* wants — and I think nobody will deny that this is what the Master wants — what he wants from us is for us to love one another, to love the Master, and to do what He says. There is no necessity for anyone to believe in him, as an individual, as the Successor. If it happens, it will happen, it just doesn't matter.

"Reflecting on all this on my return, I thought: 'We can only speak from our level. The whole thing is beyond me. Master's dragging me there, the transformation of the almost mythical Ajaib Singh into a very Master-like, very *lovable* human being — suppose I had gone all that distance and it was nothing? What would I have done then?' I thought, 'Well, I would go back home and meditate and follow Master's commandments and not worry about the Successorship.' And the funny part of it is that that's exactly what I have to do anyway. The only difference is that now I know to my satisfaction that the Master Power *is* on earth and that he not only is more like our Master than I could have dreamed possible, but also that he speaks wisdom and truth devoid of self-interest that is food for the soul. And that makes all the difference."

Return to Rajasthan

from *Impact of a Saint*

"Eventually Sant Ji sent word for me to return, as it was time to begin the work of world-wide Initiation. He had initiated seekers from His own area in Rajasthan, but up till now no one else. In response to His request, I did go back in May 1976, this time accompanied by my wife Judith, our son Eric, and several others, including two seekers wanting Initiation. We stayed eleven days with Him, and I agreed to serve Him as His American Representative with all my heart and soul, recognizing that it was Master Kirpal Whom I was serving in fact; and He did initiate the two candidates, authorizing me at the same time to initiate on His behalf elsewhere in the world.

"That Initiation represented the final open door in the long passageway to my Master's Feet. I have told of the various ways in which my Master had shown me that He was indeed wearing this new coat. But up till now this had not been solidly and unmistakably confirmed in my meditations. I had had glimpses within of Sant Ji's beauty and His oneness with Kirpal, but they had been only glimpses; and that had troubled me a little bit, mostly because of the taunts of others. I knew from the inside out that my destiny lay with Sant Ji, and knew that to serve Him was to serve my Master; but there was so much controversy and bitterness in those days and people talked so loudly about never doing a thing without having it confirmed a hundred times over in meditation, that it worried me that my strong experiences on the outer had been backed up by glimpses only on the inner. Nevertheless, I agreed to work for Him and to initiate for Him because I loved Him and because the voice of my Master, which was the voice of my soul, was telling me with every breath to do it. But that first westerner-Initiation changed everything; I received the confirmation that everyone said I ought to have a hundred times over, stronger that I would have presumed to ask for under any circumstances.

"When the meditation sitting that is the central part of the Initiation began and I closed my eyes, two things happened simultaneously: my Simran (that is, the mental repetition of the mantra which is given to each disciple at Initiation) became almost unbearably strong; it was as though my bones and intestines were shouting the Names. I did not feel like I was doing anything; I felt like a trumpet that is being blown through. At the same time I became aware that Baba Sawan Singh, my Master's Master, was standing within in a blaze of brilliant light looking at me with infinite tenderness and compassion. After a few minutes (I have no idea how long, but it was not a very brief period), He turned into my Master, Kirpal Singh. The Light was the same, the expression on the face was the same, only the facial features were different. After some time He changed into Sant Ajaib Singh, Who continued to look at me out of the same Light and with the same tenderness. After a while, Baba Sawan Singh returned, and the cycle repeated itself — again and again and again and again, one Form followed by another, while my Simran was continuing as strong as before — so strong I felt as though I were a bellows and the Names were being pumped out of me. This continued throughout the sitting, but it didn't stop there — for three glorious days and nights, those three beautiful Radiant Forms were with me whenever I closed my eyes, while my Simran continued to be shouted by the soul of my soul.

"From that time I have understood with every ounce of my being that all true Masters are One, that the Master in Ajaib is the same Master that was in Kirpal, and that the road to Rajasthan led directly to my Master's Feet."

Sant Ji on tour in the U.S., May 1977

EPILOGUE

The Mission of Sant Ajaib Singh

Only You know Your nature – no one else can know.
Only he upon whom Your Grace will descend will recognize You.

Age after age You came. First you were called by the name "Kabir."
Liberating the world from rites and rituals, You made them devoted to the spiritual path.
You suffered all the pains and tortures, and told the secret of the Real Home.

Becoming Nanak You liberated the world; (then) You had the name "Angad."
You were called "Amar Dev," "Guru Ramdas Ji," and "Arjan Dev."
Guru Arjan Ji sat on the heated iron and became grateful to the Will.

Har Gobind, Hari Rai, Hari Krishan Ji are the beloved ones.
Satguru Teg Bahadur sacrificed His head for religion.
Guru Gobind Singh graced Ratnagar Rao and gave honor to the honorless ones.

> *Tulsi Sahib, the lover of Naam, liberated Swami Ji.*
> *Swami Ji made Jaimal Singh board the ship of Naam.*
> *Beloved Sawan of Jaimal Singh separated the milk from the water.*
>
> *Beautiful Sawan developed this garden in which He placed a gardener.*
> *His name is "Beloved Kirpal" and He is the protector of the Sangat.*
> *Listen to this request of poor Ajaib: Protect the honor of the honorless ones.*
>
> — Teri Kudart Tu Hi Jane

As Sant Ji writes in the bhajan above, the line of Masters in the modern age began with Kabir. Flowing through the ten Sikh Gurus, it continued with the Masters of recent times. The account in this book covers Sant Ji's search and discipleship and ends as His mission as a Master begins.

After becoming known to the world outside Rajasthan through the events described earlier in this book, Sant Ji spent the next twenty years of His life carrying out the orders of His Master to give Naam to seeking souls. During numerous international tours, He visited North and South America, Europe, Africa and Australia as well as various locations within India. On His tours He would hold programs of meditation and Satsang, and would meet with initiates and seekers for private interviews. In addition, groups of initiates would come to visit Him at His ashram every month, except in the hot summer season, for 10-day programs of meditation. These were first held at Village 77 RB, and then moved, in 1981, to Village 16 PS, where Sant Ji constructed a new ashram at the site of the underground room. In the early 1990's political instability made travel to that part of India impractical for westerners. Eventually Sant Ji oversaw the construction of a retreat center closer to Delhi, to which He came to meet with these visiting groups.

On July 6, 1997, Sant Ji left the body for the last time. However, eleven years earlier He had recorded a tape, to be played after His passing, providing instructions to His disciples. He urged them to maintain love amongst themselves and also advised: "Of course, if you find someone who has meditated like my Master made me meditate, very happily you can take advantage of him."

REFERENCES

The following references identify sources for the material in each story. Unless otherwise noted, the references refer to an issue of *Sant Bani Magazine*, identified by month of publication. Issues that cover two months are identified by the initial month (i.e. July/August 1977 issue is identified as 7/77). Material that was transcribed from a previously unpublished talk is identified either by the date and place of the talk, or the tape from which it was taken. In some of the early groups to India, tapes from the groups did not identify specific dates on which the talks were recorded. The bhajans (hymns) are identified by the Hindi/Punjabi titles and the page number from *Songs of the Masters* (SOTM), 2002 edition.

Dedication; *Mujhe Apna Bana Lo Kirpal*, SOTM p 253, 10/95 p 8

1. Childhood
The Yearning of My Heart; 8/78 p 5, 8/83 p 5
The Stories of the Sikh Gurus; 8/82 p 7, 7/86 pp 17-18, 12/86 p 12, 5/87 p 30, 5/88 p 21, 10/88 p 16, 10/88 p 23, 11/91 p 30, 10/92 p 18, 9/95 pp 29-30, 5/03 p 31
The Prayer of My Childhood; 2/80 p 8
The Example of My Parents; 3/85 p 28, 10/87 pp 3-4, 10/87 p 18, 9/89 pp 10-11, 5/90 p 3, 4/93 pp 29-31, 7/94 pp 18-19, 3/97 p 22, 12/97 pp 29-30
The Attitude of My Mother; 9/89 pp 17-18
Troubled by the Mystery of Death; 12/76 p 26, 6/77 pp 7-8, 8/78 pp 5-6, 2/80 pp 5-6, 1/86 p 7, 11/86 p 32, 9/90 p 23, 8/91 p 3, 1/97 p 7
The Heaps of Sand; 8/81 p 7, 10/87 p 18, 4/90 pp 5-6, 8/91 p 7, 3/95 pp 39-40, 12/97 pp 31-32
O Writer of Fortunes; *Likhan Valya Tu Hoke*, SOTM p 29, 8/81 p 21, 11/86 p 17, 1/87 p 22, 3/92 pp 15-16, 12/97 pp 30-32
My Mother's Brother-in-Faith; 9/85 p 30, 11/94 pp 27-29, 11/98 pp 39-40
Taking Care of the *Guru Granth Sahib;* transcription 7/30/80 Glenwood Springs, Colorado, USA
The Village Sadhu and an Important Lesson; 2/80 p 6, 6/86 pp 5-6, transcription tape 5, Dec. 1977 group, 77RB, Rajasthan, India

The Element of Kindness; 3/91 p 14
Drinking the Water of the Muslims; 2/03 pp 19-21, transcription 1/13/83 Bombay, India
The Question of Food; 5/93 p 21, 8/93 pp 23-24
Performing the Seva; 7/03 p 39
The Sign of the Star and My First Meeting with Baba Bishan Das; 2/80 pp 23-24, 12/85 pp 5-6, 11/91 pp 4-5, 8/93 p 25
Our Domineering Dog; 6/88 p 4, 5/91 pp 4-7, 12/00 p 15, 2/03 pp 7-8, transcriptions tape 2, Oct. 1981 group, 16PS, Rajasthan, India and 6/16/94 Silly-Tillard, France
My Father and the *Jap Ji Sahib;* 1/82 p 7, 2/89 pp 27-28, 9/96 p 15, 7/00 p 7, transcription 12/12/77, 77RB, Rajasthan, India
A Pure Heart; 6/86 p 5, 4/93 pp 25-28
Death Does Not Spare Anyone; transcription 6/16/94 Silly-Tillard, France
The Enticements of My Parents; 8/78 pp 7-8, 2/80 p 9, 8/83 p 5, 11/85 p 5, 1/86 p 7, 2/86 pp 28-29, 1/87 p 19, 7/97 p 31, 6/03 p 22, transcription tape 2, March 1978 group, 77RB, Rajasthan, India
The Question of Marriage; 8/81 p 19, 8/83 p 3, 1/96 p 37, 11/99 p 42
The Merchant from Shergarh; 2/80 p 7
Baba Bishan Das' Blessing; 8/78 p 8, 9/99 p 11

2. The Search Begins

Leaving My Parents' Home; 6/77 p 8, 4/82 p 7, 10/90 p 18
My Promises to My Mother; 8/81 pp 19-20, 5/90 p 6, 1/91 p 24
Giving up My Inheritance; 8/78 p 8, transcription 10/13/76, 77 RB, Rajasthan, India
Early Encounters with Different Mahatmas; 6/77 pp 8-9, 9/77 p 6, 2/80 p 7, 10/82 p 7, 8/83 p 5, 5/84 p 8, 11/84 p 4, 10/86 p 5, 8/87 p 9, 10/90 p 20, 1/96 p 37, 6/97 p 5, 6/98 pp 4-5, 1/99 p 4, 3/03 p 9, transcription 10/13/76, 77RB, Rajasthan, India, *A Brief Life Sketch of Sant Ajaib Singh Ji,* 9/81 pp 3-4
Obtaining the Degree of Gyani; 7/77 pp 27-28, 5/86 p 26, 11/95 pp 27-29, 1/98 p 24, 3/98 p 7, transcriptions tape 4, Dec. 1977 group, 77RB, Rajasthan, India and 6/4/94 Accra, Ghana
Doing the Sevas; transcriptions 10/9/76, 77RB, Rajasthan, India and 10/20/96 Sampla, India
The Udasi Sadhus; 10/82 pp 7-9, 5/90 pp 4-6
Rotinand, the Sadhu with Faith in God; 10/90 pp 23-25
Blowing the Conch; transcription 10/13/92 Ahmedabad, India
Wear and Tear Money; 11/84 pp 3-4
The Angry Muni; transcription 12/30/90, 16PS, Rajasthan, India
O Sadhu, There is Nothing in Hypocrisy; *Pakhan Me Kuch Nahi Sadho,* SOTM p 142, 5/95 pp 7-8, 5/96 pp 43-45
The Practice of Jaldhara; 5/88 p 30, 10/88 pp 24-26, 11/88 p 5, 1/89 p 5, 1/89 p 5, 1/99 p 4, transcription 1/1/91, 16PS, Rajasthan, India

3. Coming to the Feet of Baba Bishan Das

I Ask Baba Bishan Das to Show Me God; 9/83 p 12, 3/85 pp 6-7, 5/93 p 28, 1/98 p 8, 10/98 p 25
Obeying the Instructions of Baba Bishan Das; transcription tape 2, Oct. 1979 group, 77RB, Rajasthan, India
The Spiritual Heritage of Baba Bishan Das; 5/83 p 6, 4/84 p 6, 4/85 p 9, 10/85 p 5, 10/88

pp 24-25, 10/90 p 27, 9/93 pp 27-28, 2/95 pp 7-8, 12/96 p 8, 7/97 p 9, 8/97 p 19, 11/97 pp 23-24, transcriptions tape 5, March 1978 group, 77 RB, Rajasthan, India, 5/23/89 Ribolla, Italy and 6/16/94 Silly-Tillard, France
Baba Amolak Das Gives a Boon to Hira Singh; 4/84 pp 7-8, 11/97 pp 24-25
The Efforts of Baba Bishan Das; 2/83 p 10, 5/86 p 31, 12/87 p 5, 9/93 p 27, transcriptions 10/9/76, 77RB, Rajasthan, India and tape 5, Dec. 1977 group, 77RB, Rajasthan, India
Baba Bishan Das and His Mind; 5/86 pp 31-32, 4/91 p 19
The Religion Does Not Matter; 6/97 pp 6-7
The True Remembrance; 6/81 p 15, 4/82 p 4, 11/84 pp 4-5, 7/98 p 43, 3/03 pp 6-9, transcription 12/30/89, 77RB, Rajasthan, India
Baba Bishan Das Explains the *Guru Granth Sahib;* 7/77 pp 28-31, 5/78 pp 60-64, 6/81 pp 16-17, 10/83 pp 5-6, 6/89 p 30, *Karo Benanti Suno Meri Mita,* SOTM p 168
The Two Pundits; 12/92 pp 8-9
Baba Bishan Das Teaches Me about Criticism; 1/90 p 4
The Story of Sheik Chili; 10/90 pp 28-29
The False Attachment; 3/86 p 7, 3/86 pp 30-31, 7/94 pp 16-18
Baba Bishan Das Gives Me Knowledge of My Past Lives; 6/87 pp 4-5, 6/88 p 4, 1/91 p 24, 4/94 p 32, 3/95 p 32, transcription 6/16/94 Silly-Tillard, France

4. Into the Army

I Volunteer to Join the Army; 2/83 p 11, 3/85 p 28, 7/85 p 8, 3/87 p 19, 9/88 pp 14-15, 11/92 p 26, 10/94 p 9, 7/01 p 46, 3/02 p 32, 8/02 p 14
Baba Bishan Das Explains the Value of the Heavens; 10/95 pp 28-30, 7/00 p 13
The Valuable Lesson of Obedience; 4/77 p 29, 5/83 p 3, 5/90 pp 31-32, 9/93 p 26, 12/00 p 3
Learning to Shoot; 2/82 p 12, 9/83 p 10, 11/85 p 26, 6/89 pp 17-18, 5/90 pp 31-32, 7/99 p 5, transcription 10/12/76, 77 RB, Rajasthan, India
Maintaining a Pure Life; 9/76 pp 7-8, 11/79 p 7, 3/80 pp 27-28, 8/82 p 7, 11/85 p 32, 9/87 p 5, 4/88 p 30, 5/96 p 41, 5/99 pp 5-10, 1/00 pp 27-29, 10/00 pp 26-27, transcription tape 2, March 1978 group, 77RB, Rajasthan, India
Serving the Officers; transcription tape 2, Dec. 1977 group, 77RB, Rajasthan, India
The Man Dancing Dressed as a Woman; 8/78 p 7, 2/80 p 6
Missing the Train; 11/88 pp 21-22
Keeping the Schedule; 5/92 pp 28-35, 6/99 p 26
My Work as a Signal Man; 3/80 pp 31-32, 9/83 p 12, 5/85 pp 30-31, 1/94 p 13, 10/95 p 26, 1/96 p 48, 1/98 p 27, 5/03 p 6
The Religion of the Teacher Doesn't Matter; 10/98 p 10
Doing the Work that the Teacher Gives Us; 7/77 pp 63-64, 8/82 p 8, 1/98 pp 24-25, 11/03 pp 27-28
A Brush with Death; 9/03 pp 26-27
Winning the Race; 11/79 p 7, 3/85 p 29, 4/88 p 30, 3/92 p 29, transcription tape 2, March 1978 group, 77RB, Rajasthan, India
The Wrestlers in the Ring; 10/94 pp 6-8
Regularity in the Devotion; 7/77 p 28, 6/94 p 8
My Experiences in Combat; 9/87 pp 5-6, 4/88 p 30, 10/94 p 9, 3/95 pp 37-39, 9/03 pp 25-28

5. Further Experiences in the Army: Baba Bishan Das Makes the Foundation of My Life

"Hai Ram, Hai Gobind"; *A Brief Life Sketch of Sant Ajaib Singh Ji,* 9/81 pp 4-5

Baba Bishan Das Teaches Me About Sleep; 11/80 pp 21-22, 9/81 pp 43-44, 9/89 p 6

The Diamond Light of Chastity; 9/76 pp 4-7, 2/79 p 11, 12/82 p 8, 12/86 p 13, 4/93 p 27-28

A Great Incident in My Life; transcription tape 5, Dec. 1977 group, 77RB, Rajasthan, India

The Boy with No Self-Control; 3/98 pp 23-27, transcription tape 2, March 1978 group, 77RB, Rajasthan, India

Content in the Will of God; transcription 10/9/76, 77RB, Rajasthan, India

Requesting Leave to See Baba Bishan Das; 1/85 p 7

A Punishment for Not Playing Cards; 12/93 pp 27-28, transcription tape 5, Dec. 1977 group, 77RB, Rajasthan India

The Encounter with the Dacoits; transcription tape 2, March 1978 group, 77RB, Rajasthan, India

The English Magician and the Power of Constant Repetition; 10/76 p 9, 3/80 pp 29-31, 10/82 pp 6-7

The Stolen Guns; 11/85 pp 31-32

My Experiences Sight-seeing in Delhi; transcription tape 4, Jan. 1990 group, 77RB, Rajasthan, India

Death is Predetermined; 9/03 pp 25-28

The Austerity of the Five Fires; 2/80 pp 8-9, 11/82 p 5, 1/96 pp 38-39, 3/03 pp 8-9

My Strict Treatment from Baba Bishan Das; 5/83 p 4, 1/85 p 30, 1/87 p 19, 6/88 pp 13-14, 11/88 pp 6-7, 11/91 p 25, 9/96 p 10, 11/96 pp 12-13, 3/97 pp 29-30, 3/98 pp 4-5, 7/03 p 40, transcription tape 5, March 1978 group, 77RB, Rajasthan, India

6. At the Feet of Baba Sawan Singh

My Fortune Awakens; I Meet Baba Sawan Singh; *Vah Mere Sawan,* SOTM p 21, 12/82 p 9, 10/88 pp 25-27, 12/92 pp 27-28, 3/94 p 21, 1/99 p 4, *Support for the Shaken Sangat,* p 216

I Take Baba Bishan Das to Meet Master Sawan Singh; 2/80 p 24, 12/82 p 9, 12/85 p 10, 10/87 pp 29-30, 6/88 p 4, 10/88 pp 25-27, 12/92 p 28, 3/94 p 21, 4/94 p 32, 11/94 p 7, 1/96 pp 42-43, 8/98 p 32, 8/02 p 12, transcription 3/23/88, 16 PS, Rajasthan, India

The Beauty of Master Sawan Singh; *Lakha Shakala Takiya Akhiya Ne,* SOTM p 22, 1/79 p 11, 5/88 p 28, 7/88 p 7, 12/92 pp 30-31, 6/94 p 19, 7/94 p 10, 11/95 p 4, 1/96 pp 43-44, 9/96 pp 31-32, 4/97 p 13-14, 7/00 p 30, 10/01 p 19, *Aaya Sawan Jhadiya La Gya,* SOTM p 23

Sawan's Love for His Guru, Baba Jaimal Singh; 5/85 p 4, 1/87 p 8, 1/87 p 29, 6/89 pp 29-31, 9/90 p 3, 9/91 pp 7-8, 4/92 pp 4-5, 5/96 p 14, 2/98 p 20, 5/98 p 15, transcription 9/2/95 Brisbane, Australia

The Hard Work of Master Sawan Singh; 12/87 p 21, 7/97 p 11, 5/00 p 12

Master Sawan Singh Explains the *Guru Granth Sahib;* 10/83 p 6, 1/89 pp 3-4, 3/97 pp 22-32, 9/99 p 27

The Humorous Nature of Baba Sawan Singh; 1/91 p 20, 11/95 p 4, 1/96 pp 43-44, 9/96 pp 31-32

The Value of Darshan; 12/76 p 25, 10/84 pp 7-8, 6/85 pp 8-9, 8/85 p 5, 2/91 p 27, 6/95 p 4, 1/98 pp 30-31, 1/00 p 11, *Sawan Kehria Ranga Vich Razi,* SOTM p 15

Sawan Singh and His Critics; 2/77 p 7, 12/79 pp 5-6, 11/82 p 7, 4/83 pp 6-7, 7/83 p 9, 1/86 pp 10-11, 4/92 p 7, 7/97 p 26, 6/99 p 8, 6/02 p 25
Advice on Marriage; 7/84 pp 30-31, 11/86 p 31, 5/94 p 30
On the Vegetarian Diet; 3/85 pp 30-31, 10/96 pp 8-10
The Sevadars Fighting; 8/85 pp 13-14, 2/95 pp 26-28, 11/03 p 7
Guarding the Kings; *Dukha Vali Ghari,* SOTM p 229, 6/80 p 5, 8/81 p 7, 6/82 p 5, 5/89 p 32, 7/89 p 8, 4/97 pp 41-43, 12/01 p 10
Asking for the Forgiveness; 12/82 pp 5-6, 7/92 p 11, 1/98 p 10, 8/99 p 13, 4/02 p 4, transcription 6/11/95 Subachoque, Colombia
Some Dear Ones of Sawan; 11/87 p 5, 1/91 p 27, 10/93 pp 3-4, 11/93 pp 31-32, 8/02 p 12
Bhai Lehna Throws His Bomb; 9/77 pp 2 & 32, 4/78 p 10, 5/84 p 19
Mastana Ji, the Intoxicated One; 10/77 pp 9-13, 2/78 p 8, 7/93 p 6, 1/96 p 43, transcription tapes Oct. 1976 group, 77RB, Rajasthan, India
Mastana Ji Crosses the Border; 10/77 p 10
Mastana Ji Jumps in the Well; 2/98 pp 31-32
Dance, O Mind, Dance in Front of the Satguru; *Nach Re,* SOTM p 10, 10/77 pp 9-10, 1/96 p 43
Master Protects the Souls at the Time of Death; 9/84 pp 4-5, 1/85 pp 10-11, 4/86 pp 29-31
With Baba Sawan Singh at Sirsa; 10/85 pp 29-30, 1/93 pp 42-43
"Let us all go to Sirsa — Let's go, let's go"; *Chelo Ni Saiyo Sirsa,* SOTM p 4, 1/84 p 27, 12/92 pp 29-30, 4/97 p 13, 7/00 pp 28-30, 10/01 pp 19-20
The Beautiful Inner Form of Baba Sawan Singh; *Sawan Sawan Duniya Kehendi,* SOTM p 252, 12/92 pp 28-32, 11/97 pp 4-9, 7/98 p 6, *Sawan Chan Varga,* SOTM p 249
The Partition of 1947; 4/83 p 18, 1/85 pp 5-6 & 9-10, 2/85 pp 3-6, 5/85 p 29, 2/86 pp 6-7, 5/96 p 27, 5/98 p 31, 7/98 p 44, 1/99 p 30, transcription tape 2, March 1978 group, 77RB, Rajasthan, India
Master Takes on the Karmas of the Dear Ones; 1/85 pp 9-10, 2/85 p 3, 12/85 pp 3-5, 4/86 pp 26-28, 12/86 pp 3-5, 9/90 pp 25-27, 1/98 p 9, 6/98 p 48, 7/03 p 18
The Unique Humility of Master Sawan Singh; 10/83 p 8, 11/85 p 9, 8/87 p 5, 11/91 p 25, 4/96 pp 3-13
The Passing of Master Sawan Singh; 1/80 p 4, 2/85 p 5, 5/97 pp 45-47

7. In the Bushes of Rajasthan: Cultivating the Two Words

Baba Bishan Das Leaves the Body; 9/76 p 5, 2/77 p 11, 6/77 p 10, 9/78 p 6, 8/81 p 25, 4/83 pp 21-22, 8/83 p 4, 6/84 p 8, 6/90 p 30, 10/92 pp 14-15, 1/94 p 12, 2/98 p 25, 4/01 p 45, transcription tapes Oct. 1976 group, 77RB, Rajasthan, India
Rajasthan: "the Land of Mahatmas"; 11/79 p 5, 8/83 p 4, 1/87 pp 19-20, 9/94 p 27, 11/94 pp 30-31, 12/97 p 30, 1/99 pp 4-5, transcriptions tape 2, Dec. 1976 group and tape 3, March 1978 group, 77RB, Rajasthan, India
Meditating in the Solitude of Rajasthan; 9/76 p 4, 6/77 p 11, 11/78 pp 6-7, 11/79 p 5, 8/81 p 25, 8/82 pp 5-6, 8/83 pp 3-4, 1/87 p 20, 9/87 p 5, 1/89 p 32, 11/89 p 29, 10/91 p 26, 8/97 p 8, 12/97 p 30, 1/98 p 27, 2/98 p 25, 9/01 pp 16-18, 3/02 p 32, 1/03 pp 8-9, transcriptions 10/12/76 and 10/13/76, 77RB, Rajasthan, India
The Story of Sunder Das and His Madness; 7/77 pp 12-13, 6/80 p 10, 6/87 pp 6-7
Living with Sunder Das; 11/78 p 6, 3/81 p 26, 3/84 p 32, 11/88 pp 22-24, 11/89 p 7, 12/94 p 31, transcription 1/9/79, 77RB, Rajasthan, India

Sunder Das' Experiences with Master Sawan Singh; 5/83 p 9, 5/85 p 28, 5/96 pp 39-40, 7/97 p 28
Intoxicated in the Love of God; 10/87 p 29
Sunder Das and His Astrology; 12/76 p 30
The Injured Dog; 1/77 pp 30-31, 3/91 pp 12-14, 11/91 pp 6-7
Celebrating the Bhandaras of Sawan; *Sohna Sawan Shah Da Bhandara,* SOTM p 24, 10/88 p 27, 1/89 pp 31-32, 12/92 pp 30-31
"Are You a Sadhu or a Swadhu?"; 8/83 pp 4-5, 12/92 p 31, 8/93 p 23, 1/95 pp 25-26
Meditating with the Initiates of Sawan; 1/89 pp 31-32, 10/94 p 22, 1/99 pp 19-20
"Pour This Tea on My Head!"; 5/77 pp 7-8, 11/89 pp 28-29, 10/94 pp 21-23
Mastana Ji, the Emperor of Baggar; 10/77 p 10, 2/78 p 8, 1/79 pp 6-7, 11/86 p 28, 5/88 pp 19-21, 1/96 p 43, transcriptions 10/13/76 and tape 3, March 1978 group, 77RB, Rajasthan, India
Mastana Ji Distributes the Money; 10/77 pp 10-12, 1/79 pp 6-7, 7/86 p 18, 2/87 pp 11-13, 5/88 pp 19-22, 6/98 pp 17-18, transcription 10/13/76, 77RB, Rajasthan, India
Mastana Ji Makes Me Describe the Beauty of Master Sawan Singh; 4/86 p 31, 7/86 p 18, 1/91 p 27
Mastana Ji Tells Me about the One Who Will Come to Initiate Me; 4/86 pp 31-32, 10/86 p 18, 11/86 p 18, 2/87 p 13, 5/88 p 21, 10/88 p 27, 9/98 p 28
Mastana Ji Leaves the Body; 5/77 pp 6-7, 10/77 p 12, 6/98 p 18, transcription 10/13/76, 77RB, Rajasthan, India
Practicing Ayurvedic Medicine; 10/82 pp 11-14, 3/00 pp 47-48
Worldly Thoughts at the Moment of Death; 3/86 p 31, 2/95 p 9, 3/98 p 26
On Abortion: Adopting the Baby Named Gopi; 9/87 pp 6-7, 6/88 pp 11-12, 7/97 p 32
The True Renunciation; 9/90 pp 5-6, 5/94 pp 18-19
The Disease of Anger; 5/77 pp 3-4, 3/93 pp 27-30
The Problem of Caste and Untouchability; 6/84 p 4, 5/86 pp 8-9
Meditating on the Two Words; 11/78 p 7, 4/83 p 22, 5/84 p 4, 3/85 p 5, 5/93 p 28, 7/93 p 7
Hearing the Sound Current; 3/96 pp 13-14, 10/00 pp 24-25, 12/00 p 11
"Do Not Lose Heart, Do Not be Disheartened"; 8/82 p 6, 11/89 pp 29-30, 8/02 p 15
Dharam Chand Asks Me to Become a Guru; 8/83 pp 4-5, 12/92 p 31, 8/93 p 23, 1/95 pp 25-26, transcription 5/29/92 Las Palmas, Mexico
O My Beloved, Do Not Delay!; *Likh Chitthiya Sawan Nu,* SOTM p 251, 9/78 p 6, 1/87 p 20, 11/89 p 31, 9/03 p 24

8. The Meeting with Kirpal

The Story of Harnaam Singh; 1/77 p 7, 7/77 p 28, 12/85 pp 30-31, 10/87 p 30, 5/98 p 6
The Master Sends the Message that He is Coming; *Ajaib Kirpal Nu Yad Karda,* SOTM p 230, 6/77 p 11, 1/87 pp 8-9, 5/88 p 28, 5/89 p 6, 9/90 p 4, 10/90 p 20, 1/92 p 15, 6/92 p 15, 9/93 p 28, 1/94 p 6, 12/95 pp 12-13, 4/97 pp 6-7, 7/97 pp 9-10, 3/99 p 27, 2/00 pp 26-27, transcription 1/13/83 Bombay, India
The Master Arrives; 10/76 p 5, 9/79 pp 6-7, 1/80 p 10, 6/92 pp 15-16, *Support for the Shaken Sangat,* pp 264-265
Master Kirpal Comes Like the Groom, and He Marries Me; *Satguru Sohna Mera,* SOTM p 115, 8/81 p 20, 5/83 p 7, 8/83 p 3, 6/94 p 20, 5/95 pp 5-6, 11/95 pp 29-32, 1/96 pp 37-39, 10/99 p 41, 5/00 p 24
"I Do Not Believe in Any Wahe Guru, I Believe Only in You"; 7/85 p 6, 10/86 p 6, 11/92 p 7

My Mind, My Heart is Empty; 3/84 p 31, 11/85 p 32, 10/92 p 15, 11/92 p 7, 4/94 pp 4-5, 6/94 pp 19-20, 2/95 pp 5-6, 11/95 p 21, 7/97 p 10, 7/98 p 17, 8/00 p 7, transcription 2/2/90, 16 PS, Rajasthan, India

He Asks about My Meditation; 5/85 p 9, 2/89 p 32, 6/97 pp 7-8, 11/98 p 8

I Ask Master about Seeing Him as Swami Ji; 10/82 pp 9-10, 9/93 p 28, transcription 10/13/76, 77RB, Rajasthan, India

Master Kirpal Offers Me His Ashram; 8/83 pp 6-7, 1/86 p 7, 7/86 pp 59-60

Master Stays and Gives Grace to the Sangat; 9/79 pp 6-7, 1/80 p 10, *Support for the Shaken Sangat* p 265

Seeing the Master as Light; 1/90 p 55, 4/93 p 5, 9/93 p 29

A Message for My Soul; 3/97 p 32

Kirpal Tells Those Who Want to See God to Close Their Eyes; 6/77 p 11, 10/77 p 61, 11/82 p 9, 5/83 p 9, 9/93 pp 28-29, 3/94 pp 18-19, 2/99 p 9, 7/99 pp 12-13, 4/01 pp 46-47, transcription 10/30/81, 16PS, Rajasthan, India

"Today is the Auspicious Day and It Has Come with Good Fortune"; *Aj Shub Diharda E*, SOTM p 32, 10/77 pp 61-62, 5/84 p 22, 1/92 p 16, 6/92 pp 26-29, 4/97 pp 4-5, 6/97 pp 3-11, 1/99 p 3, 11/00 p 18, transcriptions tape 7, Dec. 1977 group, 77RB, Rajasthan, India and tape 2, March-April 1989 group, 16 PS, Rajasthan, India. See also: *The Ocean of Love, the Anurag Sagar of Kabir,* pp 141-148 for the story of Dharam Das. *Banda Banke Aaya,* SOTM p 34, *Tumse Tumse Meri Prit Purani,* SOTM p 267, 12/95 p 25, 10/03 p 3

Receiving the Initiation; *Bhave Jan Na Jan* SOTM p 237, 5/77 pp 21-22, 2/80 pp 5-10, 1/87 pp 21-22

9. At the Feet of Kirpal

The Instructions of Master Kirpal; 9/77 pp 8-9, 2/80 p 11, 8/81 pp 25-26, 9/88 pp 17 & 24-25, 9/93 pp 26-27, 2/00 p 28, 12/00 pp 3-4, 4/01 pp 45-46, *A Brief Life Sketch of Sant Ajaib Singh Ji,* 9/81 p 12

The Love Which Master Kirpal Gave Me; 3/78 p 6, 8/81 pp 18-19, 5/85 pp 28-29, 10/89 p 16, 10/92 p 16, 1/96 p 41, 10/99 pp 43-44, transcription 10/3/80, 16 PS, Rajasthan, India

Singing the Bhajans for Master Kirpal; 1/80 p 15, 1/85 pp 8-9, 6/86 p 29, 12/87 pp 18-19, 2/89 pp 12-13, 1/93 p 44, 9/93 p 17, 7/94 pp 29-30, 1/99 p 3, 3/01 p 30, 9/02 p 15, 10/03 p 26, transcription tape 2, March-April 1989 group, 16 PS, Rajasthan India

Like Lord Rama came to Shivri, Lord Kirpal Came to My Home; *Guru Kirpal, Mere Ghar Aana,* SOTM p 248, 3/80 pp 6-8, 7/85 p 32, 4/97 pp 10-11, 11/97 pp 3-4, 3/98 p 4, 3/98 p 32

Controlled by the Love of the Disciple; *Satguru Pyare Mere,* SOTM p 27, 9/90 pp 7-11, 3/92 p 15, 2/98 pp 28-29, 10/99 pp 46-48, *Kirpal Guru Aaja,* SOTM p 36

Master Kirpal's Love for His Master; 5/85 p 7, 6/86 p 29, 1/87 pp 29-30, 9/90 pp 3-4, 1/91 p 32, 12/93 p 13, 12/95 pp 28-29, 3/98 p 16, 5/98 p 14

The Humility of Lord Kirpal; 5/77 p 8, 9/78 p 9, 7/80 pp 8-9, 5/83 pp 6-7, 4/86 p 31, 4/92 p 5, 1/93 p 28, 8/93 pp 26-27, 9/94 pp 7-8, transcription 1/9/79 PM darshan, 77RB, Rajasthan, India

Master Takes Care of This Lowly One; *Teri Soch Kare Kirpal,* SOTM p 124, 1/80 p 5, 2/99 pp 12-13, 3/99 p 4, 11/01 p 27, transcription tape 5, March 1978 group, 77RB, Rajasthan, India

Asking Only for the Darshan; *Dikhade, Dikhade, Dikhade Data Ji,* SOTM p 234, 5/83 p 9, 1/85 p 28, 11/87 pp 6-7, 10/92 p 18, 12/92 p 31, 6/95 pp 5-6, 5/99 p 4

"I Wish I Were Your Mirror;" 7/00 p 30
The Stolen Bus; *Tere Prem Bavari Kita,* SOTM p 96, 4/78 p 13, 2/80 p 9, 8/87 pp 31-32
I Understand Myself as the Guilty One in Front of the Master; *Mere Vich Na Guru Ji Gun Koi,* SOTM p 53, 10/83 pp 8-9, 5/86 p 25, 5/93 pp 28-29
"How Beautiful You Seem to Me"; 4/86 p 31, 3/98 pp 30-32, 1/99 pp 10-11
Tear Up the Paper of the Account of My Sins; *Mera Kagaj Gunah Vala,* SOTM p 70, 7/87 p 9, 11/96 pp 16-19, transcription 5/19/89 Accra, Ghana
Accompanied by the Master; 2/86 pp 5-6, 3/86 p 29, 4/93 pp 5-6, 5/93 pp 30-31, 10/96 p 19, 12/99 pp 30-31
Saving the Dust from Under Master Kirpal's Feet; *Menu Tere Bina Kise Di Na Lor Datiya,* SOTM p 119, 11/85 pp 4-5, 5/92 p 7, 1/93 pp 42-43, 4/94 pp 12-13, 10/94 p 13, 12/97 pp 22-23, 11/01 p 8, transcription 5/19/89 Accra, Ghana
I Ask Master How He Made Me His Wife; *Aaya Satguru Aaya Ni,* SOTM p 133, 4/84 pp 22-23, 12/85 p 27, 12/96 pp 14-15
The Fight with the Mind; 9/83 p 13, 3/85 p 14, 7/85 pp 8-9, 11/85 p 9, 9/88 p 15, 9/93 p 30, 10/94 p 9, 12/94 p 26, 7/97 p 10
The Journey Within; 7/85 p 9, 1/86 p 1, 5/86 pp 26-27, 3/87 pp 31-32, 7/92 p 29, 7/93 pp 12-13, 9/93 pp 26-27, 1/99 pp 3-17, 6/99 pp 12-14, *Tapde Hirde Thare Aake,* SOTM p 41, *Aa Kirpal Guru Mai Sagan,* SOTM p 128
People Call Me Mad; 10/78 p 12, 2/80 pp 11-12, 3/94 p 19
Gracious Sawan Has Caused the Drizzle to Shower; *Sawan Dayalu Ne,* SOTM p 254, 11/92 pp 15-18, 1/93 pp 39-48, 9/93 p 26, 8/97 pp 3-4, 5/00 pp 22-23
One Should Never Love a Foreigner; *Sohna Sohna Mukra,* SOTM p 223, 7/87 p 8, 11/90 pp 19-20, 1/91 pp 24-25, 10/92 pp 16-18

10. Kirpal the Gracious One

Kirpal, the Giver of Grace; *Sab Par Dya Karo Guru Pal,* SOTM p 258, 1/99 pp 22-23, 9/99 p 29
Masters Come for the Sinners; 3/78 p 4, 4/85 p 8, 6/90 pp 14-15, 9/94 pp 9-10
Kirpal Tells Us to Remember the Death; *Bande Naam Guru Da Japle,* SOTM p 64, 1/97 pp 16-17, 4/97 pp 44-45
The Death of My Father; 4/78 pp 5-6, 11/80 p 19, 3/81 p 27, 5/82 pp 5-6, 4/83 p 21, 9/85 p 8, 10/87 pp 3-4, 1/92 p 35
Performing the Rites and Rituals after My Father's Death; 8/97 pp 26-27
Sunder Das Burns His Leg; 6/87 p 7, 10/87 p 29, 12/87 p 25, 11/88 pp 22-23, 1/89 p 32, 7/99 p 13, 3/00 p 28, transcription tape 3, March 1978 group, 77RB Rajasthan, India, *Support for the Shaken Sangat,* pp 306-307
Master Kirpal Shows Sunder Das the Fate of the False Masters; 6/85 p 7, 3/90 p 15, 3/95 p 29, 1/94 p 8, 3/95 p 29, 11/95 pp 10-11, 7/98 p 16, 3/00 p 28, 7/00 p 13, *Support for the Shaken Sangat,* pp 307-308
Sunder Das Leaves the Body; 7/77 p 13, 6/80 pp 10-11, 11/80 p 19, 3/81 pp 26-27, 3/84 pp 12-13 & 32, 12/87 pp 25-26, 8/97 p 10, 4/98 pp 28-29
Jagroop Singh Leaves the Path, But Still Master Kirpal Comes to Liberate Him; *Tusi Araj Suno Kirpal Guru,* SOTM p 93, 2/79 p 11
The Death of My Young Relative; 4/78 pp 6-7, 5/82 p 5, 4/83 pp 19-20
The Dear One Who Listened to Criticism; 6/79 pp 5-10, 11/81 p 8
No Light Due to Lust; 5/94 pp 7-10
People Who Tried to Deceive the Master; 7/93 pp 31-32
Donating in the Spiritual Cause; 8/88 pp 28-31, 1/92 pp 9-11

REFERENCES 439

The Boy Named Gopi; 1/84 pp 27-29, 9/87 pp 6-8
The Elderly Disciple Who Asked to be Excused from Meditation; *Tenu Varo Vari Aakhe,* SOTM p 183, 5/77 pp 19-20, 9/85 pp 28-29, 12/01 p 9, 4/03 p 23
Praise Just the Master; 12/78, pp 6-7, 8/00 p 14, transcription tape 5, March 1978 group, 77RB, Rajasthan, India
The Conferences of Master Kirpal; 3/87 pp 16-18, 4/01 pp 45-46
Master Takes on My Fever; 9/79 p 32, 1/98 p 10, 6/98 pp 26-27, 3/00 p 6, 3/00 pp 45-47, 7/03 p 18
Asking for the Worldly Things from the Master; *Kirpal Guru Ji Satho,* SOTM p 50, 9/77 p 7, 1/91 p 7, 4/91 pp 3-5, 5/91 pp 13-14, 6/91 pp 7-12, 3/98 pp 12-13, 5/98 pp 31-32, 3/00 p 45, 2/02 pp 7-12, 6/03 pp 26-27, transcription tape 3, March 1978 group, 77RB Rajasthan, India
Remaining in the Will of the Master; 4/86 pp 3-4, 7/97 p 30, 4/01 pp 41-44
Master Showers Grace on the Souls; *Tapde Hirde Thare Aake,* SOTM p 41, 12/79 p 9, 1/99 pp 22-22, transcription tape 4, Nov. 1980 group, 77RB, Rajasthan, India

11. Into the Underground Room:
My Soul Mingles with Kirpal

"Are You Awake or Asleep?" *Ab Mohe Nainan Syo Guru Diya,* SOTM p 224, 2/77 p 11, 6/77 p 11, 2/78 p 8, 11/88 pp 6-7, 8/97 p 27, transcription 12/12/77, 77RB, Rajasthan, India
Master Kirpal Gives Me the Duty to Continue His Mission; 9/78 p 4, 1/80 p 8, 4/82 pp 7-8, 4/83 pp 7-8, 7/83 pp 6-7, 5/84 p 6, 7/86 pp 59-69, 11/86 p 29, 12/86 pp 5-6, 10/87 p 4, 11/88 pp 10, 19 & 27, 12/89 pp 4-5, 3/90 p 16, 9/90 pp 23-24, 1/91 p 25, 1/92 pp 17-19, 3/92 pp 19-20, 6/92 pp 3-9, 11/92 p 29, 5/93 pp 5-9, 1/94 pp 7-8, 7/96 p 13, 7/97 pp 27-32, 8/97 p 14, 10/01 pp 15-16, transcription 7/27/89 Bangalore, India
Master Tells Me to Give Initiation, and I Ask Him to Show the Dear Ones His True Form; *Hamare Pyare Satguru Jaisa,* SOTM p 261, 1/86 p 16, 1/87 p 22, 9/88 p 25, 4/91 p 7, 2/95 p 30, 3/95 pp 43-45, 10/02 pp 16-18
"The Fragrance Will Come Out from Your Body"; 8/81 p 27, 10/87 5/88 p 22, pp 4-5, 2/98 p 6, 2/00 p 28, transcription tape 3, Nov. 1980 group, 77RB, Rajasthan, India
Master Tells Me to Leave Kunichuk; 5/83 p 4, 8/83 p 7, 6/84 p 8, 5/86 p 8, 8/88 p 31, 10/92 pp 14-15, 1/94 pp 5-7, 1/96 pp 39-40, 1/97 pp 24-25, 6/97 pp 8-9, 2/00 pp 26-27, transcriptions tape 3, March 1978 group, 77RB, Rajasthan, India and 2/2/90, 16 PS, Rajasthan, India
The Orders to Meditate; 1/87 p 22, 3/87 pp 16-18, 5/87 p 30, 4/90 p 30, 6/90 p 29, 10/90 p 21, 7/91 p 6, 11/92 pp 26-27, 7/93 p 10, 2/95 p 25, 6/98 p 18, transcription tape 3, March 1978 group, 77RB, Rajasthan, India
Meditating at 16 PS; 9/76 p 3, 11/81 pp 16-17, 4/82 pp 5-7, 8/82 p 7, 11/83 p 32, 7/86 p 15, 1/98 p 27, 2/03 p 22, transcriptions 10/12/76, 77RB, Rajasthan, India and tape 5, Dec. 1977 group, 77RB, Rajasthan, India
Opposed by the Negative Power; 3/85 p 14, 7/85 pp 8-9, 9/88 pp 14-15, 9/93 p 30, 10/94 pp 8-9, 2/99 p 10
I Need Only the Grace of Kirpal; 10/83 pp 10-11, 11/87 pp 5-6, 6/98 pp 27-28, *Sohana Shah Kirpal Pyara,* SOTM p 66
My Relatives Offer to Take Me for Electric Shock Treatments; 9/77 pp 7-8, 5/84 pp 22-24, 5/86 p 31, 10/87 pp 31-32, 5/89 p 32, 10/92 p 18, 12/92 p 31, 1/93

pp 45-46, 3/94 pp 19-21, 2/95 p 5, 6/97 pp 8-9, 6/98 pp 25-28, transcriptions 10/27/81, 16 PS, Rajasthan, India and 6/15/94 Silly-Tillard, France
The Dear Ones Meditate with Me at 16 PS; 6/77 p 29, 11/78 pp 5-6
My Soul Mingles with Kirpal; 1/91 pp 30-31, 12/96 pp 28-29, 6/99 pp 12-14, 1/00 p 24, transcription 6/15/94 Silly-Tillard, France
The True Disciple; 5/84 p 22, 4/85 p 8, 6/85 p 3, 2/86 p 32, 7/92 p 27, 12/95 p 25, 7/97 p 10, 2/99 p 11, 2/00 p 10, 10/03 p 3
Master Kirpal Comes to the Underground Room; 12/81 pp 21-22, 11/83 p 15, 10/90 p 22, 10/92 pp 15-16, 4/93 p 29, 8/97 p 13, 3/00 pp 28-29, 8/00 pp 29-30, transcription of interview with Joe Swan October 1982, letter to Joe Swan 6/26/83, *Jot Rab Di Hai Aai,* SOTM p 218

12. Separation from Kirpal

Getting the Hints that Kirpal Was Leaving, I Leave 16 PS; 10/76 p 5, 6/78 p 30, 12/81 pp 20-21
The Master Leaves; 6/78 p 30, 8/78 p 1, 1/80 pp 3-11, 8/81 p 21, 12/81 pp 20-22, 8/83 p 3, 12/91 p 9, 12/97 p 30, transcription tape 3, March 1978 group, 77RB, Rajasthan, India, *Kirpal Guru Da Vichorda Mainu Pe Gya,* SOTM p 225, *Likhan Valya Tu Hoke,* SOTM p 29
Wandering like Sussi in Remembrance of Kirpal; 8/83 p 3, 11/85 pp 4-5, 1/98 pp 21-22, 10/99 p 48, transcription tape 3, March 1978 group, 77RB, Rajasthan, India
Separated from Kirpal, I Wept; *Mai To Kirpal Se Vicherde Ke Roi Re,* SOTM p 38, 8/78 p 6, 1/80 p 5, 8/81 pp 21-24, 5/83 p 9, 10/93 p 5, 12/95 pp 30-31
Who Will Throw the Shawl Over My Faults?; 12/81 p 21, 6/86 pp 29-30
To Whom Can I Tell the Pains of My Heart? *Dil Tutde Aabad Kare,* SOTM p 270, 6/78 p 30, 11/82 pp 11-12, 7/92 pp 31-32, 2/99 pp 7-9
Song to Kirpal; 11/97 p 30-31, *Jhuthi Duniya 'ch Faseya Dil Mera,* SOTM p 185

Appendix: The Finding of Ajaib

At Kirpal's Passing; *Support for the Shaken Sangat,* A. S. Oberoi, pp 287-292
A Possibility; *Sat Sandesh,* 10/74 pp 28-32
How Pathi Ji Found Sant Ji; transcription of interviews with Pathi Ji by the editor in December 1977 and Mr. A. S. Oberoi in November 1998
A Man Has Been Born; *Sant Bani Magazine,* 7/76 pp 28-31
Our Friend with a Different Coat On; *Sant Bani Magazine,* 7/76 pp 13-19
Return to Rajasthan, *The Impact of a Saint,* Russell Perkins, pp 168-170

Epilogue: The Mission of Sant Ajaib Singh

Teri Kudart Tu Hi Jane, SOTM p 113, 7/97 pp 18-21

* * *

GLOSSARY

Akalis: Orthodox sect of Sikhs.

Akhand Panth: A ceremony where the entire *Guru Granth Sahib*, the Sikh holy scripture consisting of over 4,000 hymns, is recited non-stop.

Amardas: (1479-1574) Third Guru of the Sikhs.

Anaami: The Nameless, the Absolute Formless God; the Essence before it comes into expression or existence. The final spiritual stage.

Anna: An Indian coin, equal to 1/16 of a rupee; no longer in use.

Arjan: (1563-1606) Fifth Guru of the Sikhs; compiled the *Guru Granth Sahib*.

Ashram: Spiritual or retreat center.

Astral: Subtle region, the plane of creation above the physical universe.

Ayurveda: School of traditional Indian medicine.

Baba: Reverential prefix added to the name of old or holy men.

Banis: Verses or songs of the Saints.

Bhai: Literally "brother"; also used to designate a priest of the Sikh temples.

Bhajan: Spiritual verses or hymns generally meant to be sung. Also refers to the meditation practice of listening to the Sound Current.

Bhandara: Literally "religious feast"; the celebration of a spiritual event such as a Saint's birthday.

Bhanwar Gupha: Fourth inner spiritual plane.

Brahm: Second inner spiritual plane, on top of the physical and astral planes; also known as the causal plane or *Trikuti*.

Brahma Gyani: Literally "knower of *Brahm*."

Chakras: Plexuses or centers of subtle energy in the body.

Chapati: Indian flat bread.

Dacoit: Thief, professional criminal.

Darshan: Gracious glance from a spiritual figure.

Dera: Colony, sometimes used as another term for ashram or retreat center.

Dev: Lord, also a suffix added to names of spiritual figures.

Dhun: Sound, another name for the inner Sound Current or *Shabd*.

Farid: (1181-1265) A Sufi Master from an area now in Pakistan.

Fakir: Muslim term for a renunciate or Saint.

Gaggan: Eye Center.

Ghee: Clarified butter.

Gobind Singh: (1660-1708) Tenth and final Guru of the Sikh religion.

Gunas: The three attributes or qualities of life: *Satva* (purity or truth), *Rajas* (action) and *Tamas* (inertia or sloth).

Gurbani: The writings of the Sikh Gurus.

Gurdwara: A Sikh temple or shrine.

Gurmat Siddhant: An extensive spiritual scripture published by Baba Sawan Singh.

Guru Granth Sahib: The Sikh scriptures compiled by Guru Arjan Dev. Includes the hymns of Nanak, Angad, Amar Das, Ram Das, Arjan, Teg

Bahadur, Gobind Singh, Kabir, Sheikh Farid, Ravidas, Namdev, Ramanand, and many other Saints, both Hindu and Muslim.

Gurubhai: brother-in-faith.

Gurumukh: Literally "mouthpiece of the Guru"; a highly advanced or perfect disciple.

Gyani: Literally "knowledgeable one"; indicates one with inner spiritual knowledge. Also used for one who has completed a course of study of the Sikh scriptures.

Jaimal Singh: (1838-1903) Master of Baba Sawan Singh.

Jap Ji Sahib: Composed by Guru Nanak, it appears as the opening portion of the *Guru Granth Sahib*.

Jholi: The front part of the loose shirts worn in India, which the devotees hold out as a means of accepting *parshad*. "Filling the jholi" thus becomes a term for giving grace.

Ji: Suffix added to personal names as a mark of love and respect.

Jiva: Embodied or individual soul.

Jot Niranjan: Owner of the astral plane, the first inner plane.

Kabir: (1440-1518) A great Indian Saint and contemporary of Guru Nanak. The modern age of Sant Mat in which the practice of the inner sound current is openly taught began with Kabir. See also *The Ocean of Love: The Anurag Sagar of Kabir* for additional material on this profound spiritual figure.

Kal: The entity who is ruler of the three perishable worlds (physical, astral and causal) and responsible for their maintenance. Kal, also known as *Dharam Rai* (the Lord of Judgment) or the Lord of Death, is responsible for keeping the souls trapped within the perishable worlds, in contrast to the Positive Power, manifested in the Saints and responsible for liberating the souls.

Kali Yuga: The Age of Time or the Iron Age. The present cycle of time wherein moral and spiritual living are overshadowed by evil. The compensating factor is that true Spirituality is offered more freely to those who will accept it than in any other time cycle.

Kam: Sexual desire.

Karma: The law of action and reaction which governs the fate or destiny of each person. Used as a term for a given action, which creates karma, or for fate, the result of existing karma. See also *Life and Death* by Kirpal Singh for an in-depth explanation.

Lakhs, 84: Refers to the cycle of incarnations through 84 hundred thousand species.

Langar: Free community kitchen sponsored by a religious group.

Maha Sunn: Region of intense darkness, void of any matter or light, lying between the third inner plane, *Par Brahm,* and the fourth inner plane, *Bhanwar Gupha.* In Par Brahm the soul gains the radiance of twelve outer suns, but still she needs the light of the Satguru to pass through this region of darkness.

Maharaj: Literally "great king"; used as a term of greatness or respect.

Mahatma: Literally "great soul"; used to designate a holy person.

Maya: Illusion, the feminine aspect of Kal, separates the soul from God.

Muni: Refers to a holy man, a sage, a devotee; also a religious sect in which the followers take a vow of silence.

Naam: The Creative Power of God; His original expression, the essence of the whole manifested Universe and of each individual. Also called Word, *Shabd, Kalma,* etc. See also *Naam or Word* by Kirpal Singh for a detailed explanation of this key spiritual term.

Nanak: (1469-1539) First Guru of the Sikhs, honored by them as the founder of the Sikh religion. A younger contemporary of Kabir, He had close associations with Kabir and continued His mission, ignoring religious and caste differences and teaching the practice of the inner Sound Current.

Negative Power: Another term for Kal.

Ojas: Power arising from sexual continence.

Pal: Affectionate nickname for Kirpal Singh.

Palanquin: A sedan chair.

Par Brahm: The third inner spiritual plane.

Param Sant: Saint of very high order, having access to the highest spiritual realms.

Parmarth: Spiritual way of life, spiritual work or effort.

Parshad: Food blessed by a Saint, given as a way of bestowing grace.

Pathan: Brave tribal people of the Northwestern Frontier Province, now in West Pakistan.

Pathi: The person who sings or chants the verses that serve as a basis for the Master's spiritual discourses.

Planes Of Creation: The different regions of creation or universes containing varying mixtures of physical and spiritual elements. The five inner planes corresponding to the "Five Words" include astral (*Sahansdal Kanwal*), causal (*Brahm*) supracausal (*Par Brahm*), *Bhanwar Gupha* and purely spiritual (*Sach Khand*).

Pundit: Hindu scholar or priest learned in the *Vedas*.

Puranas: Ancient Hindu scriptures.

Radha Swami: Lord of the Soul, a term coined in the time of Swami Ji Maharaj to mean absolute God.

Radiant Form: Inner astral form of the Master.

Rishi: In Hinduism, an inspired poet or sage. Usually refers to saints of ancient times to whom the *Vedas* were revealed.

Rupee: Indian currency.

Sach Khand: The region of Truth, the fifth inner plane and the first purely spiritual one. Seat of the Supreme Lord or *Sat Purush*, not subject to decay or dissolution, it is the goal that Saints set for Their disciples as it is not until this stage is attained that true liberation is achieved.

Sadhu: Popularly used in India to mean a wandering monk; literally "a disciplined soul." Also used in Sant Mat to indicate one who has attained the third inner plane.

Sahansdal Kanwal: Headquarters of the astral plane, site of thousand-petaled lotus full of lights. Also used as a term for the astral plane, the first inner plane.

Sahib: Literally "The Lord"; the Supreme Being. Frequently used as a suffix added to names of Saints as a mark of respect.

Samadhi: Absorption in God. Deep meditation, a state of concentration in which all consciousness of the outer world is transcended.

Sangat: The spiritual congregation.

Sant Mat: The Path of the Masters. The essence of all religions, it is attached to none and consists of the practice of *Surat Shabd Yoga*.

Sat Lok: "Region of Truth"; used to denote the purely spiritual regions of *Sach Khand* and above.

Sat Naam: Literally "True Name"; used as a term for *Naam* and also for *Sat Lok*.

Sat Purush: The True Lord.

Satguru: Literally "True Guru"; a perfect Master, a fully realized soul who has been commissioned by God to teach the inner path to seekers after Truth.

Satsang: A discourse given by a Saint or Master on the subject of Spirituality. Also refers to the congregation where seekers gather to hear the teachings of the Saints.

Satsangi: A term used to refer to a disciple of a True Master, or any sincere seeker after Truth, literally "one who attends Satsang."

Seva: Selfless service in a spiritual cause.

Sevadar: One who does seva or service for the Master.

Shabd: Another term for *Naam* or the inner Sound Current vibrating in all creation. Also used as a term for spiritual hymns. Alternate spellings include: **Shabda** and **Shabad**.

Simran: Constant remembrance. Also refers to the mental repetition of a mantra or of God's names; a spiritual practice given by Saints to still the mind and clear it of the repetitive thoughts of worldly impressions.

Sound Current: Another term for *Naam* or *Shabd*, the audible life stream. Listening to the inner Sound Current is one of the meditation practices given at Initiation by a Perfect Master.

Sufi: Muslim mystic. The most advanced Sufis were perfect Masters.

Sunn: Void region.

Surat: Literally "attention"; expression of the soul; *Surat Shabd Yoga* is the union of the attention with the *Shabd* or Word.

Swami Ji: (1818-1878) Shiv Dayal Singh of Agra, the Guru of Baba Jaimal Singh.

Teg Bahadur: (1621-1675) Ninth Guru of the Sikhs.

Tilak: a mark on the forehead, used in certain religious traditions.

Trikuti: A term for the second inner plane, the causal plane.

Udasis: An order of Hindu monks.

Vedas: The ancient sacred books of Hinduism; includes the *Upanishads*.

Word: Another term for *Naam* or *Shabd*. "In the Beginning was the Word, and the Word was with God and the Word was God." John 1:1.

Words – Five Words and **Two Words:** The Five Words refers, on the outer level, to the mantra given by the Masters at Initiation. They focus the soul's attention during meditation, and function as passwords to the five planes. In the soul's upward ascent it hears and merges with the inner Words (Sounds or Shabds) which emanate from Sach Khand. The Two Words refers to the first two words given at Initiation and provide passage through the first two planes, but not beyond.

Yajna: Sacrifice; a religious deed.

Yama: An angel of death; Lord Yama is the Lord of Death or *Dharam Rai*.

FOR FURTHER READING

Books by Ajaib Singh

Streams in the Desert*: Discourses & Conversations 1976-1980* by Ajaib Singh. A selection of Satsang and darshan talks given by Sant Ji to His western disciples that include many interesting comments about His days as a seeker and answer important questions about meditation and man-making.

In the Palace of Love*: The Asa di Vars of Guru Nanak.* Translation and commentary by Sant Ajaib Singh on this hymn in which Guru Nanak has touched on almost every subject and talked about every possible thing. Sant Ji said, "In the end you will realize how much grace Guru Nanak showered and in what a good way He has explained everything, which will be helpful to us."

The Jewel of Happiness*: The Sukhmani of Guru Arjan.* Translation and commentary by Sant Ajaib Singh on one of the five basic Sikh scriptures; an integral component of the *Granth Sahib*. Written in the sixteenth century, it receives here a definitive modern explanation.

The Two Ways*: The Gauri Vars of Guru Ramdas.* Translation and commentary by Sant Ajaib Singh on this hymn which compares the characteristics of the *gurumukh* (one through whom the Guru speaks) and the *manmukh* (one through whom the mind speaks).

Books Mentioned in this Book

The Impact of a Saint by Russell Perkins. The story of Russell's association with his guru, Kirpal Singh, and following His physical death in 1974 of the sweet and wonderful way in which the author was dragged to meeting with Kirpal Singh's successor, Ajaib Singh.

Naam or Word by Kirpal Singh. A poetic, carefully drawn study of the expression of God, *Naam,* Word or *Logos;* the aspect of God that at once creates and sustains the Universe and also, because it is the essence of each individual, serves as the most natural and effective means of reaching Him. Many quotations from Hindu, Buddhist, Islamic and Christian sacred writings demonstrate the universality of the concept.

The Ocean of Love: *The Anurag Sagar of Kabir.* An epic poem in which Kabir describes to his disciple, Dharam Das, the creation of the universe and Kal; how Kal deceives the souls; and Kabir's four incarnations to liberate the souls. Translated by Raaj Kumar Bagga, and edited with introduction and notes by Russell Perkins, under the direction of Sant Ajaib Singh.

Songs of the Masters. Bhajans (devotional songs) by Kabir Sahib, Guru Nanak, Guru Angad, Guru Arjan, Sant Kirpal Singh, Mastana Ji, Brahmanand, Baba Somanath, and many, many bhajans by Sant Ajaib Singh.

Support for the Shaken Sangat: *Personal Recollections of Three Great Masters* by A. S. Oberoi. Brief biographies and personal reminiscences of three contemporary Saints with whom the author was closely associated: Baba Sawan Singh, Master Kirpal Singh, and Sant Ajaib Singh.

The Way of the Saints: Sant Mat by Kirpal Singh. A collection of Master Kirpal's short writings from 1949 to 1974. Contains biographies of Kirpal Singh and Baba Sawan Singh.

For these and other books about the spiritual path practiced and taught by Sant Ajaib Singh, please contact:

Sant Bani Ashram Publications
30 Ashram Road
Sanbornton, NH 03269 USA

By email: SBAOffice@aol.com

About the Editor

Michael F. Mayo-Smith, came to the feet of Sant Kirpal Singh in 1971 and was initiated by Him. He was a follower of Sant Ajaib Singh Ji throughout His mission, and he attended many meditation programs with Sant Ji both in India and during Sant Ji's tours to North and South America. These included trips to both 77 RB and 16 PS ashrams, where he had the opportunity to visit Sant Ji's underground meditation room several times.

He lives in New Hampshire with his wife and two children, and works as a primary care physician and medical administrator for the U.S. Department of Veterans Affairs.